ELECTRONIC COMMERCE AND INTERNATIONAL TAXATION

Electronic Commerce and International Taxation

by
Richard L. Doernberg
K.H. Gyr Professor of International Legal Studies
Emory University School of Law
Atlanta, Georgia, U.S.A.

Luc Hinnekens
Professor, University of Antwerp
Partner, Baker & McKenzie
Brussels, Belgium

Prepared under the auspices of the International Fiscal Association

The Hague • London • Boston

Published by Kluwer Law International,
P.O. Box 85889, 2508 CN The Hague, The Netherlands.

Sold and distributed in the U.S.A. and Canada
by Kluwer Law International,
675 Massachusetts Avenue, Cambridge, MA 02139, U.S.A.

In all other countries, sold and distributed
by Kluwer Law International,
P.O. Box 85889, 2508 CN The Hague, The Netherlands.

Library of Congress Cataloging-in-Publication Data

Doernberg, Richard L.
    Electronic commerce and international taxation / by Richard L.
Doernberg, Luc Hinnekens
        p. cm.
    "Prepared under the auspices of the International Fiscal
Association."
    ISBN 9041110534
    1. Taxation--Law and legislation. 2. Electronic commerce--Law and
legislation. 3. Internet (Computer network) I. Hinnekens, Luc.
II. International Fiscal Association. III. Title.
    K4460.4.D64 1999
    341.4'844'0285--dc21   98-49975
                                                              CIP

ISBN 9041110534

Kluwer Law International incorporates the publishing programs of
Graham & Trotman Ltd, Kluwer Law and Taxation Publishers,
and Martinus Nijhoff Publishers.

TABLE OF CONTENTS

Foreword

*by David R. Tillinghast, Chairman of IFA's
Permanent Scientific Committee*

For many years, the International Fiscal Association has been a unique contributor to the study and solution of international tax problems through the high-level presentations made at its annual Congresses and through the annual publication of the *Cahiers de Droit Fiscal International.* In 1996 the Permanent Scientific Committee of IFA decided to expand the scope of the Association's work by sponsoring independent research studies of international tax issues of timely interest.

No topic has generated more controversy in recent years and months than the question of how the advent of the Internet and other means of conducting commerce electronically will impact on existing international tax rules, both those found in domestic law and those found in tax treaties. While electronic commerce is still in its relative infancy, it promises to alter dramatically not only the application of particular international tax rules but also, potentially at least, the division of revenues between source and residence countries. Several governments and inter-governmental organizations including both the Organization for Economic Cooperation and Development and the European Community have focussed on the resulting problems and possible responses that might be appropriate. The Permanent Scientific Committee of IFA felt that the Association, as the foremost non-governmental organization in the international fiscal field, could make a unique contribution by sponsoring a study of electronic commerce conducted by two eminent Rapporteurs with the support of experienced Consultants and input from the National Branches of the Association.

The present volume is the product of that decision. All of us at IFA wish to express our gratitude and admiration for the scholarship, insight and dedication which Richard Doernberg and Luc Hinnekens contributed to this effort. The task was difficult and huge, but they did it with distinction. We wish also to thank the Consultants who worked with the Rapporteurs, Emilio Romano of Mexico, Prof. Yoshihiro Masui of Japan and Prof. H.A. Kogels of the Netherlands, Professor Jean Pierre Le Gall of France, who prepared the most excellent *Précis* which accompanies the Rapporteurs' paper, and the many members of the National Branches of IFA who submitted both written and oral comments on the subject.

This study does not represent the views of the International Fiscal Association. IFA has not prepared it or approved it. It has sponsored it as an independent study. The paper presents the views of the Rapporteurs, and the *Précis* summarizes views of individual IFA branches to the extent that these are not reflected in the Rapporteurs' text.

IFA looks forward to sponsoring additional research projects of this kind, which will be published in a similar way.

Electronic Commerce
and International Taxation

Richard L. Doernberg and Luc Hinnekens

1

Introduction*

A discussion of the internet often starts out with a proclamation that the internet is the most important development in communications since. . . . The blank may be filled in with any manner of impressive comparisons. Following the far-reaching claim is a dizzying display of large numbers and upward sloping graphs showing the meteoric rise of internet use.[1] For ex-

---

*The Rapporteurs wish to express their thanks for the helpful guidance and suggestions of David Tillinghast, Professor Kees van Raad and Professor Howard Abrams, as well as the contributions of Emilio Romano, Professor Yoshihiro Masui and Professor H. A. Kogels who have served as Consultants for this report. Many others have also made valuable contributions, including Jeffrey Owens and Jacques Sasseville of the Organization for Economic Cooperation and Development. The authors also wish to express their thanks to Kyrie Thorpe and David Voss for their research assistance.

The Rapporteurs received helpful comments from IFA branches in the following countries: Argentina, Colombia, Germany, Ireland, Israel, Italy, Japan, Korea, Malaysia, Mexico, Republic of China, South Africa, Sweden, Switzerland, United Kingdom, and the U.S.A.. The contents of these comments have influenced all aspects of this Report and have been incorporated. Specific references are made where appropriate.

[1]Owens, *The Tax Man Cometh to Cyberspace,* Tax Notes Int'l 1833 (2 June 1997).

A number of OECD studies have focused on electronic commerce including: OECD, Dismantling the Barriers to Global Electronic Commerce, http://www.oecd.org/dsti/iccp/e-comm/dismantl.htm (1997); OECD, Electronic Commerce: Opportunities and Challenges for Government (The "Sacher Report"), http://www.oecd.org.dsti/pubs/sacher.htm (1997); OECD, Electronic Commerce: The Challenges to Tax Authorities and Taxpayers, Discussion Paper for the OECD Conference, Turku Finland, 19-21 November 1997.

More information regarding international taxation of electronic commerce may be found in the following: Lejeune, Vanham, Verlinden and Verbeken, *Does Cyber-Com-*

1

ample, fewer than 40 million people around the world were connected to the internet during 1996. By the end of 1997, more than 100 million people were using the internet.[2] Traffic on the internet has been doubling every 100 days.[3] This increased use is reflected in the growth of internet commercial

---

merce Necessitate A Revision of International Tax Concepts? (Part 1), 38 EUROPEAN TAXATION 2 (1998); Lejeune, Vanham, Verlinden and Verbeken, *Does Cyber-Commerce Necessitate A Revision of International Tax Concepts? (Part 2)*, 38 EUROPEAN TAXATION 50 (1998); PRICE WATERHOUSE, CAUGHT IN THE WEB: THE TAX AND LEGAL IMPLICATIONS OF ELECTRONIC COMMERCE (1998); Benjamin and Nathanson, *Conducting Business Using the Internet: Gauging the Threat of Foreign Taxation*, J. INT'L TAX. 29 (March 1988); Sanderson, Merrill and Dunahoo, *Consumption Tax Treatment of Electronic Commerce: Issues and Policy Recommendations*, TAX NOTES INT'L 1083 (6 April 1998); McLure, *Taxation of Electronic Commerce: Economic Objectives, Technological Constraints, and Tax Law* (forthcoming); Pinkernell, *Writer Criticizes Treasury Paper on Global Electronic Commerce*, available in LEXIS/NEXIS, 97 TNT 84-40 (1 May 1997); Hinnekens, *The Challenges of Applying VAT and Income Tax Territoriality Concepts and Rules to International Electronic Commerce*, 26 Intertax 52 (1998) and *New Age International Taxation in the Digital Economy of the Global Society*, 25 INTERTAX 116 (1997); Powers, et al., *International Tax Issues in Cyberspace: Taxation of Cross-border Electronic Commerce*, 25 INTERTAX 120 (1997); Nugent, *Implications of State Tax Practices for United States Tax Policy on Electronic Commerce — MCI Telecommunications Corp.*, International Fiscal Association (27 Feb. 1997); Mall, Leow & Murata, *Taxation of Cross-Border Internet Transactions in Australia, Japan and Singapore*, available in LEXIS/NEXIS, 97 TNI 36-2 (24 Feb. 1997); Owens, *Tax Reform for the 21st Century*, available in LEXIS/NEXIS, 97 TNI 32-27 (18 Feb. 1997); Cigler & Stinnett, *Treasury Seeks Cybertax Answers with Electronic Commerce Discussion Paper*, 8 J. INT'L TAX. 56 (1997); Horner & Owens, *Tax and the Web: New Technology, Old Problems*, IBFD Bulletin 516 (Nov./Dec. 1996); Hamilton, *US to Focus on Substance Rather Than Form in Taxing Electronic Commerce, Treasury Official Says*, available in LEXIS/NEXIS, 96 TNI 221-7 (14 Nov. 1996); Donmoyer, *Tax Principles Must Adapt to Wired Economy, Richardson Says*, available in LEXIS/NEXIS, 96 TNI 185-9 (23 Sept. 1996); Lodin, King & McLure, *Visions of the Tax Systems of the XXI Century*, Jubilee Symposium (1-6 Sept. 1996); Zukowski, *Tax Benefits for Internet Export Sales*, available in LEXIS/NEXIS, 96 TNI 156-11 (12 Aug. 1996); Glicklich, Goldberg & Levine, *Internet Sales Pose International Tax Challenges*, J. TAX. 325 (June 1996); Muscovitch, *Taxation of Internet Commerce*, http://www2.magmacom.com/~dbell/tax.htm; Weizman, *Danish Ministry Rules on Scope of Offshore Activities as a Permanent Establishment*, available in LEXIS/NEXIS, 94 TNI 30-9 (14 Feb. 1994).

[2] U.S. Department of Commerce, *The Emerging Digital Economy*, Introduction, http://www.ecommerce.gov (1998).

[3] *Id.*

transactions. For example, Cisco Systems, a producer of computer hardware, booked just over $100 million in internet sales in 1996. By the end of 1997, internet sales were running at a $3.2 billion annual rate.[4]

People often compare the growth of the internet to the historic growth of other technologies, sometimes to suggest that the internet is just the latest technological advance and may not signal a revolutionary advance.[5] But there are differences between the birth of the internet and technologies that preceded it. For example, electricity was first harnessed in 1831, but it was not until 1882 that the first power station was built, and it was another 50 years before electricity powered 80 percent of the factories and households across the United States. Radio was in existence 38 years before 50 million people used it; TV took 13 years to reach the same benchmark. It was 16 years before 50 million people used a personal computer. Once the internet was made available to the general public, it took only 4 years for 50 million people to go on-line.

Electronic commerce is an important part of the growth of the internet. The term "electronic commerce" refers to a wide array of commercial activities carried out through the use of computers, including on-line trading of goods and services, electronic funds transfers, on-line trading of financial instruments, electronic data exchanges between companies and electronic data exchanges within a company. To provide figures documenting the growth of electronic commerce is to state the obvious, often with speculative and/or outdated mind-numbing statistics. Electronic commerce is here; it is growing; and it poses new questions for all aspects of society.[6]

---

[4]*Id.*

[5]The figures in this paragraph are contained in U.S. Department of Commerce, *The Emerging Digital Economy,* Introduction and Chapter 1, http://www.ecommerce.gov (1998).

[6]From the birth of the internet in 1986, there are now more than 16 million hosts (*i.e.,* domains with an Internet Protocol address). The growth is not evenly distributed. Some countries like Canada, the United States and many northern European countries have more than 20 hosts per 1,000 inhabitants, while many southern and Eastern European countries, Mexico, and Japan average less than 10 hosts per 1,000 inhabitants. Owens, *The Tax Man Cometh to Cyberspace,* TAX NOTES INT'L 1833 (2 June 1997). It is estimated that while less than 1% of business is conducted over the internet today, that figure will grow to 5% by the year 2000. Interactive Services Association, *White Paper: Logging onto Cyberspace Tax Policy,* STATE TAX NOTES 209 (January 1997).

This report is concerned with the implications of the growth of electronic commerce for domestic and international tax systems. It explores the concern of some tax authorities that current tax principles and rules may not be equipped to deal with challenges posed by doing business in what is sometimes referred to as "cyberspace," a hazy realm without boundaries inhabited by servers, daemons and webmasters. While the technological changes over the last 25 years have affected all aspects of human life, the focus of this report is on the conduct of electronic commerce over the internet. Even that focus covers a wide array of activities. The discussion and observations will focus on basic rules and policy choices, rather than making specific recommendations.

While electronic commerce is here and is growing, it is also in its very early years and currently represents a small percentage of total world commerce. That is not to say that it is premature to discuss the implications of electronic commerce for taxing systems. The dialogue has begun and should proceed in a reasoned manner with taxing rules reflecting the technological realities of the market. In *A Framework for Global Electronic Commerce*, the United States offers its view of some general principles that govern electronic commerce:

> It should neither distort nor hinder commerce. No tax system should discriminate among types of commerce, nor should it create incentives that will change the nature or location of transactions.
> The system should be simple and transparent. It should be capable of capturing the overwhelming majority of appropriate revenues, be easy to implement, and minimize burdensome record keeping and costs for all parties.[7]

Similar unassailable principles were set forth in the Bonn Declaration, a product of participating ministers from the European Union, the European Free Trade Association member states, central and eastern European nations and Cyprus,[8] which expressed the sentiments as follows:

---

[7]White House, *White House Release on Global Information Infrastructure*, available in LEXIS/NEXIS, 97 TNI 128-23 (3 July 1997).

[8]Hamilton, *World Enters 'Second Wave' of Work on Electronic Commerce*, available in LEXIS/NEXIS, 97 TNI 140-26 (22 July 1997).

Tax on information distributed electronically should be technology neutral i.e. not be discriminated in comparison with the tax on similar data distributed by other means.

* * * *

Further study is needed, allowing companies and individuals to trade throughout Europe in the most cost-effective way possible. High administrative burdens and complicated registration systems must be limited to an absolute minimum.[9]

It is not surprising that there is consensus on these general principles, but it becomes quickly apparent that how these principles are reflected in domestic and international tax systems will spawn a spectrum of approaches. For example, the United States articulates the view that: "The system should be able to accommodate tax systems used by the United States and our international partners today."[10] The US *Framework* urges that "no new taxes should be imposed on internet commerce." The Bonn conference articulated a different approach: "The technological advances, which the world is experiencing by the phenomenon of electronic commerce, are not compatible with the existing tax rules. Conservative application will lead to nonsensical attempts of taxation. . . ."[11]

It is not the purpose of this report to take sides in a debate that inevitably will involve geopolitical factors as well as scientific factors. Rather the report approaches the subject by looking at existing tax principles, how they might apply to hypothetical transactions involving electronic commerce and what alternative approaches might be available.[12] The basic principles that govern the income and value added taxes are addressed in

---

[9]European Ministerial Conference, *Bonn Industrial Declaration on Electronic Commerce,* available in LEXIS/NEXIS, 97 TNI 141-21 (23 July 1997). *See, also,* European Ministerial Conference, *Bonn Theme Paper, Section 6, on Electronic Commerce,* available in LEXIS/NEXIS, 97 TNI 141-22 (23 July 1997); European Ministerial Conference, *Bonn Ministerial Declaration on Electronic Commerce,* available in LEXIS/NEXIS, 97 TNT 140-37 (22 July 1997).

[10]White House, *supra* note 7, at ¶23.

[11]European Ministerial Conference, *Bonn Industrial Declaration on Electronic Commerce,* available in LEXIS/NEXIS, 97 TNI 141-21 (23 July 1997).

[12]For an overview of the problems presented by electronic commerce to existing international tax principles, *see* Tillinghast, *The Impact on the Taxation of International Transactions,* Tax Notes Int'l 524 (November/December 1996). *See also* Horner and

section 2.[13] Section 3 provides an overview of the technological changes that have brought about electronic commerce and a brief explanation of how and what happens when electronic commerce is conducted. Section 3 also addresses how businesses are using the new technology in the conduct of their everyday activities. The application of existing tax principles to electronic commerce is considered in section 4. Taking an open-ended hypothetical as a starting point, this section explores the questions and problems raised by applying tax rules that evolved before the dawn of electronic commerce to transactions that were unimaginable at that time. Finally, section 5 makes some general observations and suggests a variety of approaches to international tax problems resulting from electronic commerce. No specific course of action is advocated. Wherever appropriate, this section points out the benefits and problems associated with the different approaches.

Commentators have identified several characteristics of the internet that have an impact on tax policy.[14] The internet offers a global communications system that is inexpensive and is growing increasingly secure. Both of these factors are important to the business community. The low start-up costs and huge potential markets that can be accessed are attractive not only to large companies but also to small companies which may not have otherwise conceived of engaging in cross-border transactions. Part of the cost savings associated with the internet may come from the reduction in the

---

Owens, *Tax and the Web: New Technology, Old Problems,* TAX NOTES INT'L 516 (November/December 1996).

[13]This paper does not look at customs issues which also may have to be reevaluated in light of technological changes. In *A Framework for Global Electronic Commerce,* available in LEXIS/NEXIS, 97 TNI 128-23 (3 July 1997) (hereinafter sometimes referred to as "Framework"), the United States stated that it would advocate in the World Trade Organization and other appropriate international forums that the internet would be a tariff-free environment when used to deliver products and services. While the Bonn Conference agreed that there is a future role for the WTO and other organizations to coordinate a uniform system of international tax, the Conference included the harmonization of excise taxes as one of the areas to be explored. There was no suggestion that the internet be a tax-free zone. Because of budget considerations, South Korea has more explicitly rejected for the time being any move to make the internet a free-trade zone. Hamilton, *supra* note 8.

[14]*See e.g.,* Owens, *The Tax Man Cometh to Cyberspace,* TAX NOTES INT'L 1833, 1835-36 (2 June 1997).

need for intermediaries in the business process. Distributors, sales representatives, brokers, etc. may in many cases no longer be needed in some business activities.[15] For example, downloadable software may eliminate the need for retail establishments; downloadable airline tickets may eliminate the need for ticket agents. As methods of encryption and other security measures become more sophisticated, businesses and their customers will more freely trust the on-line ordering of goods and services and payment mechanisms.[16]

While the marquee aspects of electronic commerce involve retail transactions, currently it is the "back office" aspects of commerce that make the most use of the new technology. Businesses dealing with other businesses have transferred data electronically for years.[17] Within a business, the client-server architecture has been used successfully before the internet explosion. Now the internet and intranets[18] promise to integrate business functions (*e.g.*, design and production) involving participants who may be scattered all over the world. It is expected that the synergies created by joint-production within and among companies will produce efficiencies that will translate into more responsive production of goods and services at lower prices.

Perhaps the most significant characteristic of the internet that is relevant for electronic commerce and international tax policy purposes is the total irrelevance of geographical considerations. The internet is a borderless technology. Servers can easily be located anywhere and their location is generally unknown and unimportant in a business transaction. Moreover, there is essentially little central control over the internet. In its current form, it is a triumph of private sector capitalism. These features which make electronic commerce attractive to businesses and consumers may make electronic commerce worrisome for tax authorities who have difficulty identifying transactions and tracing where transactions take place.

---

[15]In many cases these intermediaries may replaced by other intermediaries such as web page designers, internet security experts, marketers of web pages, etc.

[16]These issues are discussed in more detail in section 3.

[17]The OECD estimates that at least two-thirds of business internet transactions fall into this category. Owens, *The Tax Man Cometh to Cyberspace,* TAX NOTES INT'L 1833, 1836 (2 June 1997).

[18]An "intranet" is a network using the same TCP/IP protocols as the internet but is private (*e.g.*, within a single business or among specified businesses). *See infra* section 3.7.2.

These general characteristics of electronic commerce carried out over the internet are producing a wide variety of economic activities — too wide to easily encapsulate. However, at the retail level the activities include: the sale (or lease) of goods; the provision of services (*e.g.*, banking, health care, technical advice); the sale or licensing of computer software, the downloading of entertainment (*e.g.*, movies, books, CD's); the provision of on-line information (*e.g.*, LEXIS/NEXIS database); the provision of advertising; gambling; and round-the-clock global trading in all manner of financial instruments.[19]

Some of the most difficult issues that electronic commerce has thrust into the tax debate involve administration and enforcement of tax rules. For example, questions surrounding how to determine when a taxable event has occurred, audit trails, exchange of information, and tax collection are clearly of great importance in designing or implementing a tax system.[20] While these issues are referred to where appropriate, this report does not contain a detailed discussion of these procedural considerations. Instead, the report analyzes some of the substantive issues. A primary substantive issue is jurisdiction to tax.[21] Do longstanding tax concepts such as permanent establishment retain sufficient vitality to govern commerce today? A second significant substantive issue is the characterization of income. The rise of electronic commerce has blurred distinctions between different types of income (*e.g.*, royalties vs. sales income vs. income from services). To the extent that different tax consequences attend different classifications of income, the classification issue takes on new urgency. These substantive issues permeate both income tax and VAT systems.

In evaluating the application of current international tax principles to new problems presented by electronic commerce, this report looks at national and international law and organizations. The national law analysis is not undertaken in any comprehensive manner. Rather, representative national law is discussed at applicable points. The current OECD model treaty

---

[19]Owens, *The Tax Man Cometh to Cyberspace,* Tax Notes Int'l 1833, 1837 (2 June 1997).

[20]*See e.g.,* Discussion Report of the Australian Tax Office Electronic Commerce Project, *Tax and the Internet* (August 1997).

[21]The term "jurisdiction" is used broadly here to include substantive tax issues that relate to the mode of taxation such as allocation of income, taxation of controlled foreign corporations and determining appropriate rates of taxation.

is used to illustrate treaty considerations. Where appropriate, reference is also made to developments in the European Community (EC) and in other international organizations.

Electronic commerce is revolutionizing all aspects of commercial and noncommercial life. The use of the internet and other means of communication and dissemination of information has different implications for different industries and sectors of the economy. For example, the banking and the financial products industries face industry-specific issues that may be different from issues faced by the software industry or traditional mercantile industries. By necessity, this report does not focus on the detailed operation of individual industries but looks at the more general issues that cut across all industries. Conversely, while the digital revolution affects all aspects of life and not just electronic commerce, this report will specifically focus on electronic commerce.[22] Issues such as privacy or the rise of new forms of electronic crime are not addressed, even though these issues may well have implications for the development of national and international tax policy.

---

[22]Not everyone sees the development of electronic commerce as a "revolution." "In the view of some commentators the establishment of the Silk Road presented legal challenges in much the same way as the Internet does, because both of these trade routes transcended national boundaries, and created the need to adapt laws to reflect the international transportation of goods." German IFA Branch (Portner), *Comments on Electronic Commerce Report* (5 May 1998) (on file with the authors).

2

The Traditional International Tax Rules

2.1. DIRECT (INCOME) TAXATION: JURISDICTION TO TAX AND THE EXERCISE THEREOF

2.1.1. Jurisdictional nexus

Jurisdiction to tax the income of an individual or an entity may be primarily based on the personal status of that person, such as residence, domicile or citizenship where individuals are concerned, or incorporation or effective management, with regard to corporations. This type of jurisdiction is referred to as "domiciliary jurisdiction."[23] It typically includes the right to tax the worldwide income of the person involved. In addition, a state may base its jurisdiction to tax on the source of the income being situate within the territory of that state ("source jurisdiction"). The latter type of jurisdiction is typically restricted to the income that arises from sources within that state.

Since source jurisdiction is considered to take precedence over domiciliary jurisdiction, domiciliary states which tax worldwide income will usually take reasonable action to remove the double taxation that results from the concurring tax claims on income arising outside the domicilary state of the person receiving the income (section 2.1.4). Before examining

---

[23]This term is derived from AMERICAN LAW INSTITUTE, FEDERAL INCOME TAX PROJECT — INTERNATIONAL ASPECTS OF UNITED STATES INCOME TAXATION 6 (1987) (General Reporter: David R. Tillinghast).

in section 2.1.5 the various forms of double taxation relief domiciliary states may apply, attention will be paid first to the notions underlying the two types of jurisdiction to tax: residence, domicile, and nationality of individuals, incorporation and effective management of corporations (section 2.1.2) and source in respect of both individuals and corporations (section 2.1.3).

2.1.2. Domiciliary jurisdiction

2.1.2.1. Citizenship

The United States is one of the few countries in the world that assumes the right to tax the worldwide income of individuals on the basis of the individual's (US) citizenship. Quite a number of countries, however, employ citizenship for limited purposes: they impose worldwide income tax liability on their diplomatic and consular officers,[24] to avoid a scenario where these persons are not subjected to taxation anywhere in the world in respect of their earned income.

2.1.2.2. Domicile and residence

Virtually all countries in the world employ residence or domicile of individuals as a basis for their tax liability in respect of worldwide income. The concept of residence as applied for tax purposes varies considerably among states. It usually refers, however, to the personal connection an individual has with a particular territory. In some countries this connection is based on the individual circumstances of the case, in other countries on an arithmetical test regarding the number of days the taxpayer has spent in the given territory. In the United Kingdom and some of the Commonwealth countries not a single concept but three concepts of residence are used to determine the scope of the UK's tax jurisdiction with regard to an individual's worldwide income: residence (referring to where one mainly lives in a given taxable year), ordinary residence (where one usually lives) and domicile (which is in the country with which one has the strongest connections).

---

[24]Some countries (*e.g.,* the Netherlands) even on all their civil servants.

Domicile is a concept applied particularly in Anglo-Saxon countries. Whereas citizenship can be said to refer to the political ties between an individual and a state, and residence reflects an individual's factual ties with a particular territory, a person's domicile is where he has his permanent home to which he always intends to return.

2.1.2.3. Incorporation

While this criterion is commonly referred to as "incorporation," — referring to the state under whose law a company is created — more accurately it should be described as "corporate status," (*i.e.,* referring to the country from which the corporation derives its status as a corporation). Under international company law a corporation may be recognized as an entity legally distinct from its incorporators either because of its incorporation under the law of a given state (incorporation doctrine) or because a company has its administrative seat in a given state (administrative seat or "siège réel" doctrine). The following example may illustrate the difference: a company incorporated under German law (an "administrative seat" country) but with its administrative seat in the Netherlands (an "incorporation" country) simply does not exist: to be a Dutch compnay it needs to be incorporated under Dutch law whereas to be a German company it needs its administrative seat located in Germany. Whether a country is an "incorporation" country or an "administrative seat" country is not only important for the existence of a corporation but also determines which country's law controls the internal relations of the company (legal rules on, *inter alia,* the scope of authority of the board of directors, of the general meeting of shareholders, etc.).

Not surprisingly, many countries that apply the incorporation doctrine for recognizing a corporation as a legal entity for company law purposes, also employ incorporation as the basis to subject a company to worldwide tax liability (the United Kingdom being an exception until 1988[25]). However, many countries that use the "administrative seat" system for determining whether a company exists as an entity legally separate from its incorporators, nevertheless employ incorporation as a criterion for tax jurisdiction in respect of worldwide income, either exclusively or in addition to to effective management.

---

[25]Until 1988 the United Kingdom employed "central management and control" of the company as the sole test for UK worldwide tax liability of corporations.

2.1.2.4. *Effective management*

If incorporation of a company can be compared to citizenship of individuals, in many countries the corporate equivalent of an individual's residence is the place where a company is managed. "Place of management" is, however, not a single concept. Under Anglo-Saxon tax law the notion of "central management and control" as developed by the courts refers to highest level of management as provided by the board of directors. In other countries, where the criterion often refers to "effective" or "real" management, lower levels of management may also be taken into account in determining where a company resides.

2.1.3. Source jurisdiction

2.1.3.1. *In general*

Source jurisdiction in taxation is generally claimed with respect to items of income that have a reasonable nexus with the territory of the state concerned. These are economic activities and capital interests that are substantively connected with that state. Typical examples include real property income and income from economic activities carried on through a commercial or industrial establishment or through agency. With regard to income from intangible property the taxing right of the source state (*i.e.*, the state where such capital is (deemed) to be located), if any, is generally considered to be restricted to a low-rate gross-basis (withholding) tax.

The historical basis for the the factors used in determining source jurisdiction is found in the "Report on Double Taxation" that four economists wrote in 1923 at the request of the League of Nations.[26] After examining various alternatives for a basic touchstone of tax jurisdiction (political allegiance or nationality, residence, domicile or permanent residence, and location of wealth or origin), they concluded that in the end the

---

[26]*Report on Double Taxation* submitted to the Financial Committee by Professors Bruins, Einaudi, Seligman and Sir Josiah Stamp, Geneva 5 April 1923, published by the Economic and Financial Commission of the League of Nations (doc. E.F.S.73.F.19), reprinted in Vol. IV of the LEGISLATIVE HISTORY OF UNITED STATES TAX CONVENTIONS, prepared by the staff of the Joint Committee on the Internal Revenue Taxation (US Government Printing Office, 1962; hereinafter referred to as "LHUSTC," at 4003-4056.

basic choice is between domicile and origin. Both factors were viewed as expressions of the still broader principle of economic allegiance. In their report the economists distinguished four aspects of this economic allegiance: origin, situs, enforceability or legal status, and domicile. Next, they examined the preponderant of these aspects of economic allegiance in the following six categories of sources of income:

1. Land and houses;
2. Business enterprises of an immovable character (with distinctions for: (a) mines, oil wells, etc., (b) industrial establishments, and (c) commercial establishments);
3. Movables with a fixed location, dependent: (a) on the land (equipment and cattle) or (b) on an individual (money, household items, libraries);
4. Movables ordinarily not capable of a fixed location (ships);
5. Securities and loans: (a) mortgage loans, (b) shares, (c) corporate bonds, (d) government bonds, and (e) commercial loans;
6. Professional income.

After some discussion and a narrowing of the choices within economic allegiance to origin and domicile, they found that the categories 1, 2, 3(a), 4 and 5(a) (the latter only for purposes of property taxation) have a stronger allegiance with origin, whereas the categories 3(b), 5(a) (for income taxation), 5(b) through (e), and 6 have a stronger tie with domicile. Consequently, they advocated that (the income from) all intangible wealth be assigned predominantly or wholly to the domicile or residence state whereas all "corporeal" wealth, comprising immovables and tangible movables, be assigned to the state of origin. On the basis of the work of these findings the League of Nations developed from the late 1920's through the mid-1940's a series of model conventions which were to a considerable extent based on the findings of this committee.

2.1.3.2.   Source rule for business income

In its 1927 Report the Committee of Technical Experts on Double Taxation and Tax Evasion drafted provisions according to which business income should be taxed in the countries where the entrepreneurs possess permanent establishments.[27] If there were such establishments in both countries, each of them was entitled to tax the portion of the income that is produced in that country. Similar rules were included in the later models developed by the Fiscal Committee of the League of Nations.[28]

The meaning of the term "permanent establishment" has remained largely unchanged. In recent decades, however, the term has been extended in the domestic law of some countries and occasionally in tax treaties as well, *e.g.*, by deeming any business activities carried on during a minimum period of time to have been carried on through a permanent establishment. There is nothing sacred about the term "permanent establishment" and nothing wrong with this development. The term "permanent establishment" is merely a term of art denoting the threshold that business activities in the source country must have reached in order to entitle that country to tax the pertinent income. It is not unreasonable for this threshold to be adjusted to changes in the nature of business and in the way business is carried on.

2.1.3.3. *Source rule for capital income*

In the 1927 draft convention, interest income (Article 3) and dividends (Article 4) were assigned to the source country of the income.[29] The 1927 draft did not contain any rule on royalties. The same is true of the 1928 draft, but that draft provided for an "other income" article (Article 9), which assigned royalty income to the residence state of the recipient of the income.[30] The 1931 draft for a multilateral convention expressly provided that income from patent rights are to be taxed exclusively by the residence

---

[27]Article 5 of the Draft Convention for the Prevention of Double Taxation, Report "Double Taxation and Tax Evasion" presented by the Committee of Technical Experts on Double Taxation and Tax Evasion (Geneva, April 1927; doc. C.216.M.1927.II), reprinted in LHUSTC at 4111-4150, at 4124-4125.

[28]See Article 5 of the draft of 1928 (LHUSTC at 4162). Article 4 of draft A for a multilateral convention of 1931 (LHUSTC at 4237), the (entire) draft of a special convention on allocation of business income of 1933 (LHUSTC at 4243-4247) and the revised text thereof of 1935 (LHUSTC at 4253-4255), and Article IV of the Mexico (1943) and London (1946) drafts (LHUSTC at 4378-4405).

[29]LHUSTC at 4124.

[30]LHUSTC at 4162.

country of the recipient,[31] albeit that if it constitutes business income and is derived from a permanent establishment in the other country, that other country may tax it. The 1943 Mexico Model and the 1946 London Model took opposite views on the right to tax "royalties . . . as a consideration for the right to use a patent . . . or other analogous right."[32] Under the Mexico Model, the taxing right was assigned exclusively to the source country, whereas the London Model attributed the taxing right exclusively to the residence country of the recipient.

2.1.4.   Double taxation and causes thereof

Most countries exercise both their jurisdiction to tax residents on worldwide income and their jurisdiction to tax nonresidents in respect of local source income. As a result, a resident of one state who receives income from a source in another country will often be subject in respect of that income to double taxation (concurrent application of residence-based and source-based taxation). Other causes of double taxation include divergent characterization of facts for tax purposes and divergent personal attribution of income.

2.1.4.1.   *Overlapping jurisdictional bases*

When one country imposes tax on the basis of domiciliary jurisdiction and another country taxes on the basis of source jurisdiction, the same income will be taxed twice. In such accumulation of tax claims, it is generally accepted practice that the claim of the source country is given priority and that the domiciliary country provides relief from the otherwise arising double taxation. For providing such relief most commonly either the exemption method or the tax credit method is employed. The domiciliary country may exempt the income derived from the source country either by leaving it outside consideration altogether ("income exemption") or, if the applicable tax rate structure is progressive, by taking the source country income into account only for purposes of determining the rate applicable to the domestic part of the income and/or if the income derived from the foreign

---

[31]Article 9, LHUSTC at 4238.
[32]Article X(2) of each Model (LHUSTC at 4384-4385).

country is negative, by reducing the amount of taxable (domestic) income with the foreign loss (and a corresponding reduction of any future positive exempt foreign income). Alternatively, the domiciliary country may grant a credit for the tax imposed by the foreign source country. These two methods are usually applied both under tax treaties and, in the absence of a treaty, under domestic double taxtion relief rules.

In addition to a concurrent application of source-based and residence-based taxation, double taxation may also arise if two (or more) countries claim to be the domiciliary country of a given corporation or individual. This may easily happen where one country employs citizenship (in case of individuals) or a company's corporate status as the basis for exercising domicilairy jurisdiction whereas the other country looks at the effective residence of the individual or company as apparent from the facts (place where family lives or where the taxpayer's personal life is centered [individuals] or where company is effectively managed). But even when two states apply exactly the same criterion for exercising domiciliary jurisdiction, e.g., regular residence in respect of individuals and place of effective management in respect of companies, the taxpayer may have more than one place where he resides or where a company's management is exercised.

In addition to dual residence, dual source may occur and result in double taxation. For example, suppose that a bank's foreign branch office receives interest from a debtor in a third country. Both the third country and the country where the branch office is located will typically consider themselves as the source country of the interest income and subject it to tax.

2.1.4.2. *Divergence in tax characterization of the facts*

As a consequence of the dissimilarities among tax systems and of the legal systems of which they form a part, facts that arise in a transborder situation may be characterized divergently in the tax jurisdictions involved. For example, a transaction that is treated as a sale by the transferor's country may be treated as a lease by the transferee's state of residence. Where the latter country may have no taxing right in respect of income a nonresident derives from a sale to a resident person, lease payments by a resident to a nonresident person may give rise to source country tax liability for the latter person. In numerous instances such divergences in classification may arise, sometimes resulting in no taxation in either of the two countries involved while at other times leading to double taxation.

2.1.4.3. Divergence in personal attribution of the income

Tax treaties typically do not deal with the issue to whom the Contacting States tax a given item of income is. Such issues may arise at the personal level where the investment income of one spouse may be taxed to the other spouse, or at the company level where one country taxes the income to a given company whereas the other country views the company as a transparent entity and taxes the income to the company's participators.

2.1.5. Relief of double taxation provided through tax treaties

In the preceding section three causes of double taxation were discussed: overlapping application of jurisdictional bases (residence/source, residence/residence, and source/source); divergent characterization for tax purposes of facts; and divergent attribution of income. A tax treaty concluded between two countries whose tax rules overlap, will not solve double taxation in all these instances. Tax treaties are typically restricted to cases of overlapping exercise of taxing jurisdiction (and, within that restriction, do not generally deal with the dual exercise of source jurisdiction) and of divergent personal attribution of income by the contracting states. They only deal with cases of divergent tax classification of facts to a limited extent.

2.1.5.1. Classification and assignment of income

The regular way through which tax treaties solve instances of overlapping jurisdictional claims of the domiciliary state of the taxpayer and the source state of the income is distribution of the authority to tax among the two states. With respect to some items of income, such as income from immovable property and private pension payments, the authority is unconditionally vested in either the source state (income from immovable property) or the residence state (pensions payments). In other instances, the source state is granted a taxing right only if the taxpayer's nexus with that state is sufficiently strong in the given case, *e.g.,* in case of business income when the business is carried on through a permanent establishment in the source state, or in case of employment income by exercising employment activities in the source state during a period of at least 183 days.

As the restriction of the source country's taxing right (and, correspondingly, of the obligation of the residence state to provide double taxation relief) varies with the category of income, it is important that the two countries give the same interpretation to the terms used in the distributive treaty rules, such as "enterprise" and "royalty." Unfortunately, treaties do not provide definitions of all the core terms employed and leave the interpretation of such terms typically to the domestic law of the two countries involved, leaving much room for divergencies in interpretation and double taxation that is not relieved.

2.1.5.2. Resolution of overlapping claims of domiciliary jurisdiction

Occasionally, two countries may claim to be the residence country of the taxpayer. As a consequence, in the exercise of domiciliary jurisdiction they will tax the worldwide income of the taxpayer. Tax treaties effectively deal with such cases by attributing the status of residence country to only one of the states involved and restricting the other country's taxation to that of a source country ("tie-breaker rule"). In this way, the dual taxation of a taxpayer's worldwide income (concurrence of residence-based taxation and residence-based taxation) is transformed into concurrence of residence-based taxation and source-based taxation, *i.e.,* the regular case that tax treaties deal with (*see supra* section 2.1.4.1). Unfortunately, when negotiating treaties, countries are not always able to agree on a tie-breaker rule, with the result that in cases of dual residence double taxation may remain unrelieved.

2.1.5.3. Uniform classification of facts

As indicated in section 2.1.5.1, under tax systems of different countries a given type of income may be classified divergently. For example, the price paid for standard computer software may be considered a royalty under the law of some countries whereas other countries treat it as sale proceeds. As royalties may be taxed in the source country differently from trading income, and the relief offered in the residence country in respect of royalties may diverge from the treatment of sale proceeds, the importance of identical definition of such terms is evident.

2.2.   VAT AND SALES TAX

A general sales or turnover tax is applied to the sale of all commodities and services. As such it is distinguished from an excise tax imposed upon the sale of particular commodities or services. A general sales, or turnover tax, by its comprehensive nature, tends to be more neutral than excise taxation. The general sales or turnover tax thus applies in principle to the supply of goods and services, irrespective of their distribution through traditional or electronic channels, and irrespective of the physical or digital form of the goods. Alternatively, electronic commerce can be carved out from the base of the general sales tax and become subject to a special excise tax. For instance, the United States imposes an excise tax on communication services. This type of carve-out and excise taxation of information technology, communications services and electronic goods tends to result in a less neutral system of taxation, unless special characteristics make it difficult to apply the general sales tax.

In a multiple-stage tax model, a sales or turnover tax is imposed at all stages in production and distribution. Alternatively, it may be applied only once in the production and distribution channels (single-stage taxation). It may thus be applied to the sale by the manufacturer to the wholesaler or to the retail sale. The Value Added Tax (VAT) is described as a hybrid of those two forms as it combines characteristics of each: it involves multiple application of the tax rate, but produces the same overall burden as a single-stage tax because the sum of the value added at the various production and distribution stages is equal to the retail selling price.[33] From an economic viewpoint, turnover and VAT types of taxation are all consumption-based. They are an indirect tax on the consumption of economic wealth. A VAT

---

[33]DUE, SALES TAXATION 5 (1959).

system is applied in most OECD Member countries.[34] A common VAT system is in place in all 15 Member States of the EC.

Consumption-based taxation is an increasingly important source of national revenues. It represents, on the average, 30% of the total of OECD Member States' tax revenue.[35] In its 1988 report on Taxing Consumption, the OECD Committee gave favorable consideration to a partial shifting of personal income taxation to general consumption taxation. The European Commission, in its 1996 Verona Memorandum, suggested that if substantial tax reductions are needed to alleviate overcharged income from labor, they can better be financed out of VAT in view of its more steady tax base. In its 1996 (Monti) Report on Taxation in the European Union, the Commission referred to 1980–1994 statistics confirming that the European average of the implicit tax rate (consumption tax revenues divided by tax base) rose from 13.1% to 13.8%. Examining tax structure and the distribution of tax burdens in selected EC Member States, a recent study for the Commission pointed to consumption taxes as the single most important source of EC average tax revenue. Out of a total of 41.2% (tax revenue-to-GDP ratio), 12.9% was from consumption taxes.[36] The sales and use taxes, applied by 45 US states, yield 34% of total state tax revenues.

Some commentators are optimistic about the prospects of consumption-based taxation, especially when it is compared with the fiscal degradation of income taxation.[37] One explanation for finding that VAT and sales taxes are a more steady and dependable source of tax revenue than income taxes is that the consumption base is less vulnerable to international tax flight. However, McLure cautions that "the tax is likely to be applied to a di-

---

[34]Canada imposes a goods and services tax. In the United States, most of the individual states impose a sales and use tax.

[35]In addition to producing a considerable and steady tax revenues, VAT or other general sales taxation also supports the effective income taxation of profits made on the taxable supplies of goods and services.

[36]Social security contributions, 11.9%; personal income tax, 10.9%; corporate income tax, 3%; property tax, 1.9%. De Kam D.A. et al., *Who pays the taxes? The distribution of effective tax burdens in four EU countries,* EC Tax Review 183 (1996).

[37]For example, Charles McLure expects "a shift from income-based taxation to consumption-based taxation. In any event, the value added tax will continue to be — or become, where it is not — the revenue workhorse throughout the world." McLure, *Tax Policies for the 21st Century,* IFA Congress Seminar Series, Vol. 21d, 1996, Kluwer Law International.

minishing share of consumption, because of the 'dematerialization of pro-duction and consumption.'" The European Commission also cautions that the VAT-base is vulnerable to mobility and may become more vulnerable in the future: "VAT is threatened in particular by the growing number of in-ternational services which use new technologies to locate taxable trans-actions outside the territorial scope of the common VAT-system. Telecommunications are the most frequently quoted examples." (Verona Memorandum 1996).

While the VAT legislation of EC Member States is harmonized by EC Directives, outside the Community context no international bilateral or multilateral agreements were concluded dealing with the coordination of or administrative cooperation on VAT, sales taxes, double taxation, tax avoidance or distortions of conditions of competition.[38] However, the 1988 Multilateral Council of Europe/OECD Convention of Mutual Assistance in tax Matters also applies to VAT and consumption taxes in the countries which ratified it. The OECD subgroup of the Special Session on Consump-tion taxes examined the issues of VAT and GST (Goods and Services Tax) controls and international mutual assistance. The OECD Committee on Fiscal Affairs reports that work is proceeding to introduce a system of in-ternational cooperation between OECD Member countries in the field of indirect taxes.[39]

While many countries implement a VAT or comparable tax, the Euro-pean Community VAT serves as the focus of the discussion that follows.

---

[38]A single provision of the World Administrative Telegraph and Telephone Con-ference — WTTC ("Melbourne Convention") — of 9 December 1988, signed by the Members of the International Telecommunication Union (including EC Member States), deals with taxes on settlements of charges between public postal and telecom-munications operators. It is discussed in section 4. The Swedish IFA Branch comments on this Electronic Commerce Report point out that the prohibition to restrict the free movement of labor, goods, services and capital and the right of establishment and the non-discrimination clause according to the EEA Agreement may have implications for consumption taxes. Still other international trade agreements such as WTO have impli-cations for consumption taxes in situations of trade outside the EC as well as between EC and non-Member countries. Swedish IFA Branch, *Comments on Electronic Com-merce Report* (1998) (on file with the authors).
[39]OECD, ELECTRONIC COMMERCE: THE CHALLENGES TO TAX AUTHORITIES AND TAXPAYERS, Discussion Paper for the OECD Conference, para. 141, Turku Finland, 19-21 November 1997.

2.2.1. General nature of Community VAT

The Community VAT-system is described in the First Directive (1967) as follows:

> The principle of the common system of Value Added Tax involves the application to goods and services of a general tax on consumption exactly proportional to the price of the goods and services, whatever the number of transactions which take place in the production and distribution process before the stage at which tax is charged. On each transaction, Value Added Tax, calculated on the price of the goods or services at the rate applicable to such goods or services, shall be chargeable after deduction of the amount of Value Added Tax borne directly by the various cost components. The common system of Value Added Tax shall be applied up to and including the retail trade tax.

The VAT is thus intended as a general tax on final consumption. However, unlike a sales tax levied at the stage of the retail sale, it is technically and directly levied on each of the transactions involved in the production and distribution of goods and services. It is measured by the value added by those transactions to the business process. The tax is shifted to the final consumer by a system allowing its recovery between businesses, or taxable persons (*see infra* section 2.2.4.1). To this effect, a taxable person deducts from the VAT chargeable with respect to its supplies, output VAT, the VAT paid on its purchases of goods and services used for its VAT-able activities, input VAT. This is the "VAT credit" or "invoice" method. Where no output VAT is chargeable, because the taxable person is based in another Member State or without the EC, the VAT incurred by such taxable person, on the input, is in principle also recoverable.

Being exactly proportional to the price makes VAT neutral both with respect to the length of the production and distribution chain (internally) and with respect to the relative tax burdens on domestic and imported goods in the market place (externally). Because it is proportional to the price and it is measured by the contribution of value added, it is also neutral as to the method of commerce (electronic versus traditional). According to the preamble to the First Directive, the EC chose the VAT-system, instead of the cumulative, multiple-stage sales tax system applied by most

Member States until 1969, mainly because the VAT-system does not distort conditions of competition or hinder the free movement of goods and services. It is important to note for purposes of electronic commerce taxation that the neutrality envisaged by the description of the VAT system in the First Directive must exist at the level of the consumer and is not primarily directed at providing EU businesses with a level playing field for competition.

The VAT system sometimes must rely on the reverse charge and self-assessment method for applying and accounting for VAT. Where a person outside the country supplies relevant services to a person in the country in connection with the recipient's business, the recipient is treated as though the recipient supplied and received the service. He thus accounts for output VAT based on the value of the service received and at the same time recovers this VAT as input VAT if it relates to a taxable supplier. This obligation of the local person to account for reverse charge VAT addresses the problem of tax avoidance or evasion on the part of the foreign supplier and of the competitive advantage of lower VAT rates applicable to suppliers established in certain Member States. This method will turn out to be important as an alternative for dealing with certain transactions of electronic commerce (*see infra* section 2.2.7.3).

2.2.2.   VAT harmonization legislation

The authors of the Rome Treaty (1957), having dealt with import duties, also saw the need for the harmonization of Member States' legislation concerning turnover taxes. To this effect, the EC Council adopted harmonization measures to the extent necessary to ensure the establishment and functioning of the internal market (Article 99). The latter concept is defined as an area without internal frontiers in which the free movement of, *inter alia,* goods and services is ensured (Article 7a).

Except for a single "regulation" (concerning administrative co-operation), all VAT- harmonization provisions under Article 99 were adopted in the legal form of "Directives." The First and Second Council Directives, of 11 April 1967, required Member States to replace their turnover tax system with a common VAT system by 1 January 1970. Mostly because a portion of Member States' VAT revenue was to become a main EC resource, further harmonization of the common VAT system and, in particular, the basis of assessment was required and imposed by the Sixth Directive (1977)[40].

The many subsequent VAT Directives, and the detailed nature of several provisions, limit the discretion left to Member States in implementing the common system. The provisions defining "taxable person," "taxable event," "taxable amount," "place of supply of goods and services" and "exemptions" are sufficiently detailed so as to limit the discretion of the Member States. However, several other aspects of Member States' VAT laws are not harmonized, others are optionally regulated (the word "may" appears more than 70 times in the Sixth Directive) and others are uneven implementations of the applicable Directives. In its 1996/97 Opinion Statement to the European Commission, the Confédération Fiscale Européenne advocates a rewriting of the Directives as a VAT Community Code (in the form of regulations) and recommends a new approach to assure the uniform interpretation and application of rules throughout the Community.

2.2.3. Systems of cross border trade taxation

The VAT is levied on cross border trade at the rate and conditions of the Member State of destination. This "destination taxation principle" implies that exports are relieved from VAT in the country of origin and that imports are subject to the VAT in the country of destination. However, there are exceptions to this general rule as well as official plans to replace it by a definitive system of origin-based taxation.

2.2.3.1. Original system (Sixth Directive)

Because Community VAT is essentially a consumption tax and because it is reasonable to assume that the goods and services are consumed at the place of their destination, the tax is levied in principle at the rate of the Member State of destination. The revenues generated by it, in cross border trade situations, should also accrue to the country of destination. Initially, the VAT collection mechanism operated at the border. The system

---

[40]Council Directive of 13 June 1977 on the harmonization of the laws of the Member States relating to turnover taxes — common system of Value Added Tax: uniform basis of assessment (77/388).

worked in the following manner: exports were exempt from VAT and imports were taxed at the border of the importing Member State.

2.2.3.2.   Transitional (1993) system

In its 1985 White ("Cockfield") Paper, the Commission found intra-Community fiscal borders to be incompatible with the single market concept. It initially proposed to replace the existing system of taxation (the destination principle) with one in which goods would be taxed in their country of origin (origin principle). The sale from one Member State to another would no longer be a (an export- and import-) taxable event. A central clearing system would redistribute VAT revenue between Member States according to the destination pattern of the flows of supplies between them (as can be expected from a final consumer tax). Concrete proposals were worked out, in document COM (87) 320 of August 1987, as part of the talismanic year and program, "Europe 1992."

The far-reaching proposal to completely dismantle internal fiscal borders was not retained by the Council. Its "1993 changes" to the Sixth Directive maintain the destination system (taxation at the rate and conditions prevailing in the country of destination), but abolish collection and controls at the fiscal borders. They were replaced with administrative controls at the enterprise level and are based on taxpayer identification, administrative records of the enterprises ("parties responsible for providing statistical information") and the automated exchange of information between tax authorities of Member States. In order to establish interconnection among the 15 tax administrations, the Member States which supply goods to other Member States list data on an electronic database and the Member States receiving goods are given on-line access to the database (VIES-Value Added Tax Information Exchange System).

2.2.3.3.   Towards a definitive system (1999?)

The 1993 system is known as the "transitional system"; it will probably be replaced by a "definitive system for the taxation of trade between Member States based in principle on taxation of origin of the goods or services supplied" (Article 35a of Sixth Directive). However, as no replacement decision was reached by the Council by 31 December 1996, the transitional

27

arrangements of 1993 continue to apply until the Council decides on the definitive system.

The definitive system should be effective, simple, modern and neutral, treating intra-Community transactions in much the same manner as domestic transactions, in accordance with the concept of an internal market. To this effect the following options are open:

- moving to a federal Community VAT;
- moving to a general final consumption tax;
- moving to a system based on origin principle coupled with a clearing system;
- continuation of the present VAT system subject to appropriate modifications.

A federal type of Community VAT, applied in a uniform fashion, would suit the internal market concept. Its revenue would be shared by the Community with Member States being responsible for compensating for the loss of VAT revenues, much in the same manner as German VAT is shared by the German federation and the Länder. The Directorate-General for Research of the European Parliament considered this option in its document, *Options for a definitive VAT system* (1995). By eliminating the competitive disadvantage and administrative burden caused by divergent tax rules, it would respond to some of the problems caused by electronic commerce. However, it is, from a political viewpoint, not realistic to expect that individual Member States will easily agree to the loss of fiscal sovereignty resulting from harmonization.

The model of a general sales tax was examined in 1960-1962, by the so-called subgroup B, as a possible harmonization model. It was turned down mainly because an adequate system of central registration of tax liable businesses, the intra-administrative assistance needed for its controls and collection and a system of financial compensation via central clearance were simply not available at that time. Prospects became better with the emergence of new information and communication technologies as tools of cross border VAT administration.

The growing interest in a VAT-formula which moves effective taxation to the final consumption stage is evidenced by recent proposals.[41] The first

---

[41]Outside the Community, the Swedish IFA branch mentions the Norwegian NTO-Model Suspension Regime. VAT on transactions between businesses with a certi-

proposal was made by Lord Cockfield in his report, *A VAT Suspension Regime* (1995). VAT on transactions between businesses with an authorized VAT number would be suspended up to and including the wholesale stage. Cockfield brings his proposal within the scope of the provision of Article 27 of the Sixth Directive: the Council may authorize Member States to introduce special measures for derogation from the provisions of that Directive in order to simplify the procedure for charging taxes and to prevent certain types of tax evasion or avoidance as long as such measures do not affect (except to a negligible extent) the amount of tax due at final consumption.

In 1996, the Dutch Commission for the study of Community VAT and cross border movements of goods within the EC, prepared a report containing proposals to simplify VAT along similar lines.[42] VAT would be applied at zero-rate to supplies of goods and services between taxable persons. The system thus avoids the complication of VAT remissions and refunds at each stage of production and distribution. Unlike the origin-based tax model, it also avoids the need of tax clearance or relocation of tax revenues according to destination. The zero-rate system does raise the concern that its controls and collection might be less reliable. However, the Commission points out that administrative controls in such a system are better than those in a system of suspension or shifting of VAT accounting to the businesses receiving the goods. It also believes that the availability of new information and communication technologies should offer adequate controls regarding central VAT registration and identification of taxable persons, tracing supplies and collaboration between administrations. The Commission suggests that, if need be, the application of this system might initially be limited to authorized traders.

The issue of services raises the question of where they should be taxed. Should they be taxed in their country of origin, where the supplier is established, or rather in the country where they are used and/or where their recipient is established? Should different principles govern the taxation of services supplied respectively within the EC and across EC borders? In a sit-

---

fied VAT number would be suspended up to and including the retail stage. The proposal was based on an extensive study and was never implemented. The main concerns were related to the control mechanisms and the high amounts to be paid by the weakest partner in the value-added chain, the retail outlet. Swedish IFA Branch Comments, *Comments on Electronic Commerce Report* (1998) (on file with the authors).

[42]Rapport van de Commissie ter bestudering van de BTW-heffing ten aanzien van grensoverschrijdende goederenbewegingen binnen de EU, Geschriften van de Vereniging voor Belastingwetenschap No. 202, Kluwer, 1996, 15 and 86-88.

uation of trade across EC borders, the Dutch Commission proposes the application of WTO principles of taxation to services (in the country of destination or consumption). The Community VAT would thus not be levied if the recipient of the service is established outside the EC, unless their effective use takes place in a Member State. Likewise, it would not be levied if the customer is established in the EC and the services are effectively used outside the EC.

In an intra-Community situation the rule is different. It should approximate the tax treatment of the supply of services to customers in the domestic market on the basis of taxation in the country of the supplier's business establishment, or where the service is supplied. In that situation, it is questionable whether it is appropriate to provide further special rules for determining the place of supply to provide taxing authority in the country of use, depending on the nature of the service and the recipient. Where the recipient in Member State B is a business, another question is whether it makes sense to maintain the system of shifting VAT accounting to the recipient, thereby creating the unnecessary complications of proof, of tax status of the recipient, of risk of non-payment of tax, etc.

The Turnover Tax Commission, established by the German Bundesministerium (Kommission Umsatzbesteuerung in Europa nach dem Ursprungslandprinzip ab 1997), proposed, in April 1994, a "Leistungsortmodell," based on taxing goods in the country of origin, coupled with a system of bilateral settlement of intra-Community VAT. It would replace the present system (of taxation according to destination of goods based on zero-rating of intra-Community supplies, of taxation of intra-Community acquisitions in Member States where goods arrive and of distance sales arrangements). Taxation of services would follow the "Sitzortmodell," based on taxation in the place of establishment where the supplier sells to private consumers, and on taxation in the place of establishment of the person receiving services, if it is a business. This model is subject to the risk (from the point of view of tax authorities) that enterprises may want to move their businesses to the consumers in the Member State with the lowest tax rate. This risk is particularly acute when commerce follows electronic channels.

The European Commission proposes to generally modernize essential provisions of the existing system. This would include the definition of taxable transactions (supply of goods and of services) and taxable persons (including the definition of economic activity and the direct link between the supply and the consideration), the determination of the taxable amount, standardizing rates, including the list of supplies which may be subject to reduced VAT rates, a review of exemptions (which should be maintained or abolished, but in any event harmonized) and a re-examination of the rules concerning the right to deduct.

On 22 July 1996, the European Commission embarked on an ambitious program involving a complete overhaul of the common VAT system by 1999.[43] According to the Commission, the new system should achieve the following objectives: equality of treatment between domestic and intra-Community transactions, maintenance of the level of tax receipts, legal certainty, effective controls, simplicity and uniform application.

To achieve those objectives, the common system requires a single place of taxation for operators in the EC. This concept of single place of taxation in the proposed common system probably means that the operator will charge VAT in that single place without regard to where the goods and services are otherwise supplied. For example, a UK retail chain with branches in Ireland will charge the UK rate of VAT on sales made in the Irish branches where the single place of taxation is the United Kingdom.[44] EC operators would register only once, irrespective of the number of Member States in which they operate. The system would be based on the principle of taxation in the country of origin, *i.e.,* the place where goods and services are situated at the time of sale by a business. As taxation and deduction would be brought within the purview of a single administration, the Commission would strengthen its monitoring capability. As transactions would be taxed in the country of origin, the complex rules determining the place where a transaction takes place (where goods and services are deemed consumed) would be simplified.[45] For an EC-based trader doing business throughout the Community, it would no longer be necessary to divide up the turnover among 15 Member States, as taxation would only take place in the Member State where the business is established. The new common system would thus avoid the unnecessary costs of administering transactions carried out in other Member States.[46]

---

[43] European Commission, *A Common System of VAT. A Programme for the Single Market,* Com (96) 328 final, 22 July 1996.

[44] Irish IFA Branch, *Comments on Electronic Commerce Report* (1 May 1998) (on file with the authors).

[45] The Commission counts no less than 25 different rules and concepts in the current system.

[46] The European Commission estimates that these costs are 5 or 6 times more than the costs would be for similar transactions in the companies' home countries.

The single place of taxation concept has problems from an administrative viewpoint because the place of consumption may be some distance from the place of taxation. Perhaps this can be overcome by mutual assistance and proper administration with the application of minimum standards throughout the EC and with the help of the electronic tools. Looking at today's situation, it appears that the level of confidence and trust between Member States may need improvement. There is also much debate regarding where the place of taxation should be and whether or not VAT grouping (already operated in some Member States but strongly resisted in others) will apply.[47]

However, the proposed system requires a number of changes which may not be accepted by the Council:

- Further harmonization, particularly of the rates, is necessary if the tax is to remain neutral with respect to the conditions of competition between firms. The Commission has stated its preference for a single standard rate, but does not exclude the possibility that an approximation within a band of two percentage points might prove sufficient. However, even a band of two percentage points is likely to become a stumbling block for the single place of taxation concept. It is difficult to see how an approximation within such a band could be sufficient if retailers selling the same product and located on the same street are charging different rates. This pressure would not be adequately dealt with by the application of the fixed establishment of supplier concept and may challenge the whole concept of single place of taxation. Even the application of the same VAT rate, say 15%, in both countries may still not be neutral as it would permit re-allocation to Ireland of revenues of the goods sold in Ireland (consumption state) but recorded as UK revenues.
- Uniformity of application should be ensured by the VAT Committee that would be transformed from an advisory into a regulatory committee. A proposal for a council Directive to change the legal status of the VAT Committee has already been presented by the Commission (Brussels, 28 June 1997 — Com (97) 325 fin).
- Re-allocation of displaced VAT revenues between Member States is necessary so as to guarantee maintenance of the current level of rev-

---

[47] *Id.*

enues. The Commission proposes to do so on the basis of consumption statistics rather than on data from the tax declarations of taxable persons, as the application of the latter system would not achieve the proposed radical simplification.

2.2.4. Individual VAT rules and concepts

2.2.4.1. Scope of VAT-able transactions

Article 2 of the Sixth Directive defines the scope of VAT to include: the supply of goods and services within the territory of the country by a taxable person, the intra-Community acquisition of goods within the territory of the country by a taxable person or a non-taxable legal person, and the importation of goods. Under Article 4(1), "taxable person" shall mean any person who independently carries out, in any place, any economic activity defined to include all activities of producers and traders. "Supply of services," under Article 6(1), "shall mean any transaction which does not constitute a supply of goods within the meaning of Article 5." It expressly includes the supply of intangible goods. Under Article 5(1), "Supply of goods shall mean the transfer of the right to dispose of tangible property as owner." "Importation," under Article 7(1), means the entry into the Community of goods from a third country, irrespective of whether they are imported by a private individual or by an enterprise.

Since 1 January 1993, the system of taxation of "imports of goods" from other Member States has been replaced by "intra-Community acquisitions of goods." The system of "exports of goods" to another Member State has been replaced by that of "intra-Community supplies." The new system is still based on the principle of taxation according to destination, but the formalities take place at the destination point rather than the border. The following conditions must be fulfilled in an intra-community acquisition of goods: the goods must be exchanged between taxable persons, dispatched or transported to the acquirer by, or on behalf of, one of the taxable persons, from one Member State to a Member State other than that from which the goods are dispatched or transported. Intra-Community supplies are exempt, in the Member State of the enterprise which sells them, and are taxable in the Member State where the goods arrive. The taxable person thus reports the output VAT on his VAT return and deducts the input VAT on the same return, if he has the right. Member States thus fully preserve their fiscal sovereignty: the Member State of arrival ensures that the goods acquired are subject to taxation; the Member State of the seller, or of origin, does not have to ensure that the goods are effectively taxed as an acquisition, which is a condition for their exemption as intra-Community supply.

Goods purchased (origin-based VAT included) by a private individual, outside of his Member State, are free of VAT in the private individual's Member State. However, purchases from mail order companies, including all (franco domicile) sales in which the vendor is responsible for shipments, are taxable in the country to which they are sent, if the dispatch is on behalf of a supplier whose total sales in that country exceed a threshold value (35,000 or 100,000 ECU, depending on Member State). This is the "distance selling exception" to the system of origin-taxation applicable to private consumers effecting their purchases in another EC-jurisdiction.

2.2.4.2. Place of taxable transactions

2.2.4.2.1. Supply of goods

The place of import of goods is the Member State where the goods are when they enter the Community (Article 7(2)). The following general rules in Article 8 apply to determine where goods are supplied:

- For goods dispatched or transported: the place where the taxable transaction is effected is where the goods are at the time dispatch or transport begins.
- For goods not dispatched or transported: the place where the goods are when supply takes place.

Article 28(b) provides the following exceptions to the general rules:

- For intra-Community acquisitions of goods it is the place where the goods are at the time dispatch or transport to the person acquiring them terminates. Under Article 28(b)(A), the place is deemed to be within the Member State issuing the VAT identification number of the acquirer.

- If, in the framework of an intra-Community sale, goods are dispatched or transported by, or on behalf of, the supplier and the purchaser is a non-taxable private person, or other person who is not liable for VAT in the Member State of arrival, the place of supply is the place where the transport to such customer ends. (Article 28(b)(B)(1)).

- However, if the total value of the distance sales of goods dispatched to that same Member State is less than the aforementioned threshold value, the VAT is due in the originating Member State. (Article 28(b)(B)(2)). The concern justifying this exception is that, given the divergence of rates, private persons would, via mail order, teleshopping or otherwise from their home state, buy from such distance selling businesses in the Member State with the lowest rate.

2.2.4.2.2. Supply of services (Article 9)

Unlike the supply of physical goods in international trade, the cross border supply of services cannot be controlled at the border. VAT application to "imported" services cannot, therefore, be dependent on border controls. The taxable place of supply of services is not defined according to the application of some general criterion of territoriality or nexus. Its rules are detailed and complex. The place of taxable supply is different for different categories of services and also takes into account the (taxable or non-taxable) status of the customer, the country of establishment (within or without the Community) and the supplier's country of establishment.

1. The general and residual rule refers to the place where the supplier has established his business or has a fixed establishment from which the service is supplied or, in the absence of such a place of business or fixed establishment, the place where he has a permanent address or usually resides.
2. However:
    a) the place of the supply of services connected with immovable property shall be the place where the property is situated;

b) the place where transport services are supplied shall be the place where transport takes place, taking distances covered into account;

c) the place of the supply of services relating to cultural, artistic, sporting, scientific, educational, entertainment or similar activities shall be the place where those services are carried out;

e) the place where the following services are supplied when performed for customers established outside the Community or for taxable persons established in the Community (but not in the same country as the supplier), shall be the place where the customer has established his business or has a fixed establishment to which the service is supplied or, in the absence of such a place, the place where he has a permanent address or usually resides:

- transfers and assignments of copyrights, patents, licenses, trade marks and similar rights;
- advertising services;
- services of consultants, engineers, consulting bureaus, lawyers, accountants and other similar services as well as data processing and the supply of information;
- obligations to refrain from pursuing or exercising, in whole or in part, a business activity (a non-competition agreement) or a right referred to in (e);
- banking, financial and insurance transactions, including reinsurance;
- supply of staff;
- services of agents who act in the name and for the account of another, when they procure for their principal the services referred to in (e);
- renting movable, tangible property with the exception of all forms of transport;
- telecommunications services (added to the list in accordance with the 1997 derogations).

3. To avoid double taxation, non-taxation or competitive disadvantage, Member States may, with regard to the supply of services referred to in 2(e), consider:

a) the place where services are supplied which, under that Article, would be situated within the territory of the country, as being situated outside the Community where the effective use and enjoyment of the services take place outside the Community (Article 9(3)(a));

b) the place where the services are supplied which, under that Article, would be situated outside the Community, as being situated within the territory of the country where the effective use and enjoyment of the services take place within the country. (Article 9(3)(b)). In order to avoid non-business users going to VAT-free sources outside the EU, a non-EU supplier may be required to VAT register and charge EU VAT to the customer.

The place of services rules thus provide, generally speaking, for two kinds of criteria:

- The place of establishment (of the supplier or of the customer, depending on the type of service), the fixed establishment (from or to the place where the service is supplied) or, in the absence of such a place of business or fixed establishment, a permanent address or usual residence.
- The place of performance or effective use and enjoyment (irrespective of the place of establishment of the supplier or of the recipient). The expression "effective use and enjoyment of services" is not defined and its terminology in the different language versions is rather sloppy. The notion, when applied to services falling under Article 9(2)(e), raises several problems of interpretation. Mainly for that reason, it was retained as a secondary test to determine the taxable place of supply of a service which, otherwise, would be taxed twice or avoid taxation altogether.

Those rules give rise to three problems of interpretation and practical application relating respectively to:

(i)   the categorization of the services

For instance, do management services fall under the categories in Article 9(2)(e) ("consulting and other similar services" deemed to be supplied in the Member State of the establishment of their customer) or, alternatively, do they fall under the general rules of Article 9(1) (referring to the supplier's establishment or his fixed establishment from where the services are supplied)?[48] For purposes of determining the place of supply of electronic services, their characterization as services, under Article 9(2)(e) or under the residual category of Article 9(1), will be a crucial issue. Those definitional uncertainties create the risk of divergent applications (taxation in country of the customer's establishment or in that of the supplier) and hence to situations of double taxation or non-taxation.

(ii) the specific criterion of territoriality

The "permanent address or usual residence" means the place shown as such in the identity document which the Member State, in whose territory the supply takes place, recognizes as valid. The expression "fixed establishment" is not defined in the Sixth Directive. The proposed Nineteenth Directive would clarify that an establishment need not carry out chargeable transactions. The European Court of Justice, in the *Berkholz* case,[49] required the permanent presence of technical and human resources for performing the services. The place where the supplier has established a business is "a primary point inasmuch as regard is to be had to another establishment from which the services are supplied only if the reference to the place where the supplier has established his business does not lead to a[n] irrational result for tax purposes or creates a conflict with another Member State." This case has been interpreted as expressing, on the part of the Court, a systematic subordination of the criterion of a secondary establishment. This is not necessarily so according to Farmer and Lyal:

> The Court's words, however, must be read in the light of the circumstances of the case, in which a taxable person sought to escape the Community's tax jurisdiction by creating national establishments outside Community territory. It is submitted that, in a genuine case in which a supplier or customer has several business establishments, all capable of performing services, the most appropriate method of determining the place of supply for purposes of Arti-

---

[48]The Irish IFA branch suggests that the challenge to the term "management services" is not so much trying to identify into which category it falls but rather trying to identify the exact nature of the management services themselves. It is a term which is in common use and can mean almost anything. Irish IFA Branch, Comments on *Electronic Commerce Report* (1 May 1998) (on file with the authors).

[49]ECJ, case 168/84 (1985) ECR 2251, *Berkholz* (discussed in section 4.3.4.4.1).

cle 9(1) or 9(2)(e) would be to identify the establishment of the supplier whose resources were primarily used for supplying the service or the establishment of the customer which made primary use of the service.[50]

(iii)   the practical application, controls and enforcement of compliance of those rules

It is difficult to employ effectively the VAT system to the supply of digitized goods or intellectual services covered by Article 9(2)(e) supplied by non-EC based suppliers to private customers using and enjoying them within the territory of one or more Member States, applying Article 9(3)(b) of the Sixth Directive.

2.2.5.   Rates and exemptions

2.2.5.1.   Rates

The rate is fixed by each Member State. It may not be less than 15%.
    Table of standard VAT in Member States (1 June 1998):

Austria	20
Belgium	21
Denmark	25
Finland	22
France	20.6
Germany	16
Greece	18
Ireland	21
Italy	20
Luxembourg	15

[50]FARMER & LYAL, EC TAX LAW 160 (1994).

Netherlands	17.5
Portugal	17
Spain	16
Sweden	25
UK	17.5

The reduced rates apply only to the goods and services specified in Annex H of the Sixth Directive. They include books, newspapers and periodicals (other than material wholly or substantially devoted to advertising matter), the services of writers and composers, admissions to shows, reception of broadcasting services, etc. Non-taxed items may apply, in some Member States, to basic foodstuffs, medicines, etc.

The risk that divergent national rates cause competitive disadvantages within the internal market has been addressed by the Commission. It plans to propose a standard rate, with the allowable deviation of two percentage points mentioned above.

2.2.5.2. *Exemptions*

Two types of exemptions are distinguished: those without and those with credit for input tax. Member States are only allowed to exempt supplies listed in the Sixth Directive. Exemptions for certain activities in the public interest include the supply of services by the public postal offices, other than passenger transport and telecommunications services. Other exemptions are technical and include insurance and finance services. They do not give rise to a right to deduct input VAT.

An exemption from VAT and customs applies to the import by private individuals of small packages with value below a stipulated threshold. It is mentioned because of proposals to increase the threshold in an effort to facilitate international movements of small order goods and and to facilitate the development of electronic commerce by reducing costs and creating timesaving benefits. Member States may also exempt ("zero-rate") certain supplies with a right to deduct input VAT. They include, mainly, the supply of goods dispatched or transported to a destination outside the Community by, or on behalf of, the vendor (exports), international transports and like transactions. Intra-Community supplies are also exempt from VAT, with a right to deduct input VAT, in the Member State where the goods are dispatched to another taxable person in another Member State.

2.2.6. Deduction and refund

A taxable person claiming a deduction must be in possession of an invoice containing the required VAT information. With the proper invoice, the tax paid on goods or services previously supplied by another taxable person can be deducted. The other taxable person must also be liable for tax within the territory of the country in question. A taxable person is also allowed to deduct the tax paid in respect to imports and the tax due with respect to intra-Community acquisitions, if they are used for the purposes of his taxable transactions.

The conditions and procedures of VAT refunds to taxable persons established in other Member States, and to persons established outside the EC, are dealt with by the Eighth and Thirteenth Directives respectively. In practice, refund claims may entail extra compliance costs and cash flow burdens. They also work against the overseas suppliers of EC-based business customers. If goods and services are used by a taxable person both for transactions where VAT is deductible and for transactions where VAT is not deductible, only the portion attributable to the deductible transactions can be refunded. These taxable persons are referred to as "mixed" taxable persons.

In this system, VAT on incoming invoices is not a real cost for taxable persons who can claim a deduction for the input tax on the goods and services which they use for business purposes. It is a real cost for private consumers and for legal persons who are non-taxable persons (banks, etc.) or those who do not use them for business purposes and who are unable to claim the deduction. Those persons and mixed taxable persons will, therefore, want to actively seek opportunities to avoid the tax normally due on the supplies to them.

2.2.7. VAT accounting and administration

2.2.7.1. Person liable to pay the tax

The taxable person carrying out a taxable supply of goods or services is, in principle, liable for the tax due on that transaction. In some situations, the customer, or any person including VAT on an invoice, or the person effecting a taxable intra-Community acquisition may be liable for the tax.

2.2.7.2. Identification and designation of tax representative

Within a Member State, every taxable person supplying goods or services with the right of deduction must, in principle, be identified for VAT purposes and issued an individual identification number. Where the taxable supply is made by a taxable person established without the Member State of supply, Member States may designate a tax representative that will be liable for payment of the tax. The appointment of a tax representative is not required in all Member States. The rules governing tax representatives differ throughout the Member States.

2.2.7.3. Reverse charge

When services covered by Article 9(2)(e) (*e.g.,* advertising, consulting, data processing, information services, software license, etc.) are carried out by a taxable person established without the Member State of supply, the taxable person to whom those services are supplied becomes liable for VAT in his Member State. Services under Article 9(2)(e) are, therefore, sometimes described as "reverse charge services." Under this particular mechanism, the EC-based business customer of those services becomes responsible, in lieu of the non-EC based supplier, for accounting and payment of the tax, as if the business customer had self-supplied the good. The input tax is available as a deduction if the recipient is a taxable person. The idea is to ensure the application of tax in the country of the recipient even if it is an exempt business which purchased the services from a third country supplier not accountable for VAT.

2.2.7.4. Administrative obligations

Administrative obligations mainly involve taxable persons and concern, in particular, the keeping of accounting records, the issuance of invoices containing the required information, the submission of periodical VAT returns and declarations for statistical purposes and the payment of the net amount due.

2.2.8. Overview of VAT applications to international transactions

In the following applications of current VAT rules to concrete cases of international trade, R Corp. is a resident of country R and the supplier of a good or service to a customer who is either a business (S Corp.) or a private person established in country S. R and S may be EC Member States or third countries. The overview is general and focuses on direct and indirect electronic commerce as well as on telecommunications services.

1. If R Corp. is established in third country R and supplies a good to S Corp. established in EC Member State S, the good is subject to customs duty and VAT upon importation into the Community. As S Corp. is a taxable person, using the imported good for a business purposes, it may fully credit the input VAT against its output VAT.
2. If, in (1), S Corp. is a non-taxable person, *e.g.*, a bank or insurance company using the imported good for its exempt bank or insurance business, the input VAT is not recoverable and becomes a cost to S Corp. In practice it may be difficult for a bank or insurance company to find an alternative source to avoid or reduce this cost.
3. If, in (2), S customer is a private person, the VAT paid at the border, on the imported good, is a cost to him, creating an incentive of tax avoidance or evasion.
4. If, in (1), R Corp. is established in Member State R and effects an intra-Community supply to S Corp. in Member State S, the supply of the good is exempt for R Corp. and the intra-Community acquisition is taxable to S Corp. at S's VAT rate. The VAT payment and formalities do not take place at the border, but at the premises of S Corp. The latter reports the purchase on its return and deducts the input VAT from the output VAT (assuming S Corp. has the right to deduct).
5. If, in (4), S customer is a private person, the sale of the good by R Corp. is taxable in R at R's VAT rate, not S's.
6. However, if in (5), R Corp. is a company (*e.g.,* a mail order company) selling and dispatching the good to a private purchaser in country S, where R Corp's total sales exceed the applicable distance selling threshold, the sale becomes taxable in S where R Corp. becomes a registered trader.

7. Suppose the transaction involves the supply of a service — instead of a good — by R Corp. to S customer. Generally, under Article 9(1), the service is taxable in R if R Corp. is established in a Member State. It does not give rise to VAT liability if R Corp. is established without the Community, even if its is established in Member State S. In applying Article 9(1), we have assumed services which do not qualify for the rules of Article 9(2)(e) and the anti-avoidance measure of Article 9(3)(b) (see examples (9) and (11)).

8. However, if in (7), the service is provided from a fixed establishment which R Corp. (a country R corporation) maintains in Member State X, its fee is taxable in X.

9. Suppose, in (7), that the services are intellectual or telecommunications services in the sense of Article 9(2)(e). The place of taxable supply is that of the customer's business establishment, if the customer is established outside the Community or is a taxable person established in another Member State. In the latter situation, S Corp. will apply the VAT of S under reverse charge procedure.

10. If, in (9), the intellectual services are supplied to the fixed establishment which S Corp. maintains in third Member State X, VAT is due in X, under Article 9(1).

11. If, in (9), intellectual or telecommunications services are provided by R Corp. to customers in non-Member State S, no VAT liability arises under Article 9(2)(e), except that VAT liability may arise under the alternative rule of Article 9(3)(b), in Member State S, if the services are used or enjoyed in S. If those services are also used and exploited in the territories of Member States X and Z, R Corp. may also owe VAT in those states. Thus a business receiving telecommunications charges from outside the EU applies the reverse charge. To avoid non-business users going to VAT free sources outside the EU, the non-EU supplier may have to register or designate a fiscal representative in each of the Member States (S, X and Z), if such designation is a requirement in those Member States.

12. If, in (9), intellectual services are supplied by R Corp. to S Corp., both being established in a member country, but are used and enjoyed outside the Community, Member State S may under Article 9(3)(a) opt for nontaxation. Under Article 9(3) EU VAT does not apply to supplies made outside the EU.

3

Technological Changes
and Electronic Commerce

3.1. BACKGROUND

The term "electronic commerce" refers to the use of computer networks to facilitate transactions involving the production, distribution, sale, and delivery of goods and services in the marketplace. While many people associate electronic commerce with the buying and selling of information, goods, and services over computer networks, the components of electronic commerce are more robust. Not only can electronic commerce embrace the streamlining of the relationship between consumer and business, it also embraces more efficient business processes within a firm and inter-firm.

Applications of electronic commerce are many and varied. They include the paperless exchange of business information from business computer to business computer using electronic data interchange (EDI) technology, electronic mail (email), electronic bulletin boards and conferencing software, electronic funds transfers, and many other technologies. In addition, the term "electronic commerce" includes an on-line approach to conducting business with customers including advertising, marketing, order entry and processing, payment, and customer support.

Electronic commerce will not replace more traditional modes of commerce. However, electronic commerce will not be insignificant either. The growth of electronic commerce has been exponential. In ten years, 16 million hosts have been established on the internet.[51] As new methods of con-

---

[51]A host is a computer with an Internet Protocol address and domain name (*e.g.*, tax.law.emory.edu). Owens, *The Tax Man Cometh to Cyberspace*, TAX NOTES INT'L 1833, 1834 (2 June 1997).

ducting business replace or supplement existing methods, it is useful to re-examine existing tax rules to see if those rules can apply both from a theoretical and an administrative point of view to the new ways in which income is generated. In order to analyze existing tax rules in a thoughtful and thorough manner, it is necessary to have some understanding of the technology that makes electronic commerce possible. Without an understanding of the factual underpinnings of an income producing transaction, tax authorities cannot design an international tax system that is grounded in concept and is practical in implementation.

What follows is a summary presentation of the technological development and features that have made the current applications of electronic commerce possible and future improvements likely. The goal of this presentation is to indicate what is actually occurring when, for example, a purchaser in Canada makes an on-line purchase from a Japanese company or when companies in Brazil, Germany, and India design on-line a piece of manufacturing equipment which can be assembled automatically at a plant in Turkey. Some of the background is general in scope, but most of what is covered is directed at explaining (1) the business of providing the technology that makes electronic commerce possible, as well as; (2) the use of that technology in the business world at large.

3.2.   DESCRIPTION OF THE INTERNET, INFORMATION SUPERHIGHWAY AND WORLD WIDE WEB

The information superhighway generally refers to the interconnected series of networks that provides the infrastructure for transporting information throughout the world. The development and construction of the information superhighway is a global phenomenon that is being undertaken by thousands of entrepreneurs, sometimes acting independently and sometimes in cooperation with others in order to establish standards. There is no centralized authority in charge of this massive undertaking, although governments also play an important role.

Is the information superhighway the same as the internet and the world wide web (WWW or web)? The internet (**inter**connected **net**works) is a term that refers to thousands of interconnected logical networks linking millions of computers worldwide. The internet refers to the logical connections between computers and not to the physical connections (*e.g.*, phone lines, cable, radio transmissions). These interconnected computers include stand-alone computers and computers connected to the internet through various networks including local area networks (LAN's), metropolitan area networks (MAN's) and wide area networks (WAN's).

The term "world wide web" is sometimes used interchangeably with the term "internet." More accurately, the WWW is a navigation tool for locating and accessing information presented in graphic form available on the hard drives and other storage facilities of computers known as web servers on the internet. The WWW allows access to information in a multimedia format featuring color, graphics, audio, and video. Users can access the web through web browser software, such as Microsoft's Internet Explorer or Netscape Communication's Communicator, and can travel from site to site easily by using a pointing device (*e.g.*, a mouse) to click on a word or picture on one site that takes the user to another site.

The information superhighway is best thought of as an evolving superset that includes the internet along with the physical telecommunications networks, cable TV, mobile, and cellular networks. Essentially, it describes a high-capacity (broadband), electronic highway that is capable of simultaneously supporting a very large number of electronic commerce applications that permit interactive connectivity between users. Historically, the communications infrastructure has not provided integrated voice, data, and video services. For example, a business user requiring voice, data, and video conferencing might have to use three separate networks. The information superhighway holds out the possibility of using multimedia capabilities seamlessly operating in the background. Although the internet has not yet fully evolved into the information superhighway, the term "internet" will be used in this paper as a synonym for information superhighway.

3.3. DIGITIZATION

It is easy to associate the technological revolution with computers, robots, cell phones, and other physical artifacts. But underlying these technological products is a more fundamental change — a change in the way information is communicated. If information could not be digitized, the internet could not exist. The ways in which the digitization of information will affect the economy are still unfolding. However, a basic understanding of the digitization sea change is necessary in order to consider whether current trans-border tax rules and norms continue to be viable.

Historically, commerce has been conducted based on a variety of physical exchanges. Businesses plan business strategies through face-to-face meetings. Information may be conveyed within a business through a report. Goods and services may be delivered to customers or purchased from suppliers in face-to-face transactions. Bills of lading or other contracts may be exchanged. Customers typically may receive an invoice for any goods or services performed. Payment may be made with a check or cash.

These transactions all involve physical events or changes. The techno-logical revolution is about the global movement of bits which are colorless, sizeless, and weightless.[52] A bit is the most basic form of information — "as a state of being: on or off, true or false, up or down, in or out, black or white."[53] The global movement of bits, while a revolution, does not render obsolete physical events or changes. Goods will still be manufactured and delivered, services will still be offered, meetings will still take place, but the way in which these physical events occur may be substantially altered by the use of bits in the digitization of information.

The digitization of information is the process of converting informa-tion into a sequence of numbers. The converted information may be im-ages, speech, music, diagrams, or the written word. Once converted, the information can be sent at the speed of light throughout the world where a recipient can convert the information back into its original format or oth-erwise manipulate it. To understand the benefits of digital information, consider the following problem.[54] Suppose you have a room that you want to illuminate with as much as 250 watts of electric lighting. If a 250 watt bulb were wired to a rotating dimmer, the dimmer could be turned to pro-duce the desired level of lighting. But this system has drawbacks. Suppose that you adjust the dimmer lower for an intimate dinner. If the dimmer is unmarked, you can only guess what the wattage is. Even if the dimmer dis-plays different wattage levels, it would be difficult to reproduce exactly the same level of lighting.[55] If you wanted to communicate to a friend the exact

---

[52]NEGROPONTE, BEING DIGITAL 14 (1995).

[53]*Id.*

[54]This discussion comes with a few modifications from GATES, THE ROAD AHEAD 23-26 (1995).

[55]Indeed, even the line on the dimmer has a thickness that would defeat precision.

level of lighting, you could only do so approximately (*e.g.*, "turn the dimmer 1/5 of the way"). Errors might be magnified as the information is retransmitted from one friend to another. This is an example of "analog" information. The dimmer provides an analogy to the bulb's lighting level.

Now consider a different way of describing the lighting in the room. Suppose that instead of a single 250 watt bulb, you use eight bulbs in a row — the first of which on the right is 1 watt with each other bulb doubling the wattage of the bulb to its right.[56] Each bulb is connected to its own on-off switch. By turning switches on or off, any desired level of lighting can be achieved from 0 watts (all switches off) to 255 watts (all switches on).[57] For example, if you desired 23 watts, you would turn on the 16 watt, the 4 watt, the 2 watt and the 1 watt bulbs. With this method of lighting, it is possible to duplicate precisely the level of lighting from one occasion to the next. Moreover, the exact level of lighting can be transmitted to another with precision so that the recipient of the information can accurately duplicate the sender's lighting level. Assume that an "on" light switch is recorded as 1; an "off" switch is recorded as 0. Under this system, 167 watts of lighting would be represented by:

$$10100111$$

Eight bits of information (sometimes referred to as a "byte") with each bit representing an "on" or "off" state can be transmitted, providing perfect information. Reducing the information concerning the level of lighting to a digital form underlies the technological revolution but is only part of the story. It is the ability to translate data into binary numerical form (*i.e.*, bits) combined with the ability to handle very large numbers of bits that account for the revolutionary changes we observe in all aspects of the economy.

If we had the single, variable intensity light and wanted to record a particular intensity for later use, we could use the row of eight bulbs to "digitize" the state of the analog bulb. First, we would set the intensity of the analog bulb to the desired intensity. Second, we would set the row of eight bulbs so that they approximated the variable intensity bulb. For example, it might be the case that a setting of 115 watts on the row of bulbs is a little

---

[56]The bulbs would be: 128, 64, 32, 16, 8, 4, 2, 1 watt bulbs.

[57]More accurately, any level of lighting can be achieved at 1-watt intervals. It would not be possible to have, say, 56½ watts of lighting.

brighter than the analog setting we want to digitize but a setting of 114 watts is a little less bright. We would pick either 115 or 114 (say, 115) as our digitized value and record that for later use. Then, when we wanted to recreate the initial variable intensity, we would use the row of bulbs and set them to 115 watts. While we would never recreate the exact initial intensity (unless it happened to be an exact integral wattage value), we could indefinitely recreate the initial intensity with no more than a 1 watt error created when the analog bulb was first digitized.

As this example demonstrates, digitization of real-world information such as light or sound involves a trade-off. The initial digitization (sometimes called "digital mastering"), because it is limited to a finite combination of states, can never fully record the infinite variability of voices and visions. But once digitized, the information can be transmitted and recreated without introduction of further error. Thus, digitization introduces a small but discrete initial error in exchange for the capability of faithful reproduction. And the more accurately we can digitize the initial information, the smaller the error introduced by the mastering. For example, if we use a row of 9 bulbs rather than 8 (with the new bulb offering an intensity of exactly ½ watt), we can cut the mastering error from a maximum of 1 watt to a maximum of ½ watt. Similarly, if we use 10 or 11 or even 100 progressively smaller bulbs, we can limit the mastering error further and further.

Similarly, sound waves are also analog information. A vinyl record is an analog representation of sound vibrations with grooves cut to different depths and densities to capture different tones. Like other analog devices for storing information, a record is susceptible to imperfections like dust, fingerprints, scratches, improper revolution speed, and deterioration of the grooves. Cassette tapes, while an improvement over vinyl records, suffer from similar quality threats. Copying analog recordings further degrades the quality.

In contrast, a compact disk stores music as a series of binary numbers, represented by a microscopic pit on the surface of the disk which can be read by a reflected laser beam. Because a sound wave is continuous and a digital representation is discontinuous (*i.e.*, either a 0 or 1), it is necessary to sample the sound wave frequently in order to produce a continuous sound. The frequency with which a sound wave is sampled corresponds to the number of fixed intensity bulbs used to represent an analog, variable intensity one. On an audio CD, the sound is sampled more than 40 thousand times per second.[58]

Images can also be digitized. Imagine a grid placed over an image. In each cell, the color, intensity and hue can be represented by a series of bits. If a very fine grid is used (*i.e.*, like a high level of sampling for digitized audio), the ability to produce a continuous, sharp image from the digital information is enhanced. To reduce an image to a digital representation takes a lot of bits. The ability to transmit all those bits along with bit representation of sound and text places a great demand on the computing power and storage space of computers and on the information superhighway that connects them. However, there have been tremendous advances both in the development of more powerful computers and in networking that have made multimedia transmission a reality that will profoundly affect how commerce is conducted.

The light bulb example above illustrates how nonnumeric information (*i.e.*, lighting intensity) can be represented in digital form. But the most significant use of digital representation is the conversion of text into binary form. By convention, an uppercase "A" is represented by the number 65, an uppercase "B" by the number 66, and so on. A lowercase "a" is represented by the number 97, a lowercase "b" by the number 98, and so on. A computer would translate this numerical representation into binary format. For example, an uppercase A becomes 01000001. A space break is represented by the number 32, or 00100000. The sentence: "Order by credit card" would be represented as follows:

```
01001111   01110010   01100100   01100101   01110010   00100000
01100010   01111001   00100000   01100011   01110010   01100101
01100100   01101001   01110100   00100000   01100011   01100001
01110010   01100100
```

One important distinction between digitizing analog information such as sounds and images and representation of textual information in binary form is that no error is introduced when text is converted into binary digits because *text is already digitized;* that is, because alphabets (including punctuation) consist of a finite number of symbols, these symbols can be

---

[58]NEGROPONTE, *supra* note 52, at 14.

represented in binary form without loss of information, assuming only that we use a sufficient number of bits to represent each alphabetic symbol. Representing each symbol as a specific combination of 16 bits is sufficient to fully distinguish every alphabetic symbol used by all major languages on the earth.

Advances in data compression have speeded up transmission. Data compression is based, in part, on an area of mathematics known as information theory. Information can be defined as the reduction of uncertainty.[59] Accordingly, if you know that today is 14 October and someone tells you that it is 14 October, you have not received any information. Similarly, if you know that it is before 18 October and that is sufficient for your needs, being told that it is 14 October does not provide any information. These principles are useful for compressing data. For example, in English if a "q" is transmitted, sending a "u" as the next letter is redundant.[60] Similarly, there is much redundant information in the thirty frames that comprise 1 second of video.[61] The information can be compressed from about 27 million to about 1 million bits, still producing video that is enjoyable to watch. Even with improving compression techniques, the ability to transmit information is a function of the internet infrastructure.

3.4. DEVELOPMENT OF THE PHYSICAL NETWORK INFRASTRUCTURE

The physical network infrastructure refers to the physical components that allow computers to transmit information to each other. The physical network infrastructure alone does not provide the ability of computers to communicate with each other. It is the logical network infrastructure that makes such communication possible. The components of the logical network infrastructure are considered after the examination of the physical network infrastructure.[62]

---

[59]GATES, *supra* note 54, at 30.

[60]In the English language, the letter "q" is always followed by "u." WEBSTER's NEW WORLD DICTIONARY 1159 (2nd ed. 1984).

[61]GATES, *supra* note 54, at 30.

[62]The physical and logical network infrastructure categories overlap to some degree.

Three major components form the physical network infrastructure that makes the information superhighway possible: network access equipment; local on-ramps, and telecommunications networks.[63] The term "network access equipment" refers to the end user's terminal equipment that enables access to the information superhighway.[64] While such equipment can be characterized in different ways, essentially it consists of some type of terminal and equipment needed to establish a connection with the network. For specialized uses, the terminal might be integrated into some common piece of business equipment. For example, a cash register can include an internet connection used exclusively for verifying credit information. More general use of the internet often requires a personal computer.[65] In order for any terminal, whether a simple dedicated cash register or more complex computer, to connect to the information superhighway, the user must have access to a connection device. Many computers connect to the internet though a modem which connects the phone line to the computer. Cable modems perform the same function for cable TV systems. A modem may not be necessary where a computer is linked to the internet through a high-speed digital phone line, sometimes known as a T1 line. Local area networks within a business are often connected to the internet in this fashion.

The metaphor of the information superhighway has supplied some useful images for understanding how the pieces fit together. The connection between an end user and the physical backbone of the information superhighway is sometimes referred to as the "last mile" or "local on-ramp." Current local on-ramp alternatives include copper wire, fiber, coaxial cable, and radio-based wireless.

Copper wire (sometimes known as "unshielded twisted pair," or "utp") provides the medium for connecting most households to the internet. It is

---

[63]KALAKOTA & WHINSTON, FRONTIERS OF ELECTRONIC COMMERCE 50 (1996).

[64]This component is known as customer premises equipment (CPE).

[65]Recently, vendors have begun to offer less expensive, stripped-down computers known as network computers that can be connected to the internet but have no storage capability. Instead, storage of data would be centralized on some other computer. Applications would be downloaded and used as needed.

A developing method of accessing the internet is through a cable converter box, sometimes known as a set-top box. These boxes enable users to make phone calls, access the internet and receive digitally-compressed cable channels. The more sophisticated set-top boxes will permit interactive services such as banking and shopping.

considered a low bandwidth medium because it cannot carry large numbers of bits at the same time.[66] Telephone calls are analog transmissions through copper wire.[67] Computers which produce digital information can be connected to copper telephone wires through a modem (*i.e.*, a **MO**dulator/**DEM**odulator) which changes digital signals coming out of a computer into analog tones for the journey through the wires and can reverse the transformation, turning incoming analog signals from the copper wire into digital information that the computer can process.[68] Copper wire can also carry digital transmission. For example, a technology known as integrated services digital network, or ISDN, permits the transfer of voice and data at faster speeds than analog modems. Additional calling capacity is achieved by adding special electronic components to the ends of the telephone line linking the user to the central office. At ISDN speeds, text and still pictures can be transmitted rapidly. Routine video conferencing could operate using ISDN, although the quality would only be marginally acceptable, producing some visible jerkiness. Another technology, asymmetrical digital subscriber line (ADSL) allows telephone companies to increase the carrying capacity of copper wires even more, enabling better video and audio delivery over phone lines.

Some users may prefer a faster, dedicated copper phone line as an on-ramp, sometimes referred to as 56K service because of the transmission speed. For a still faster connection, some businesses or LAN's install digital T1 lines which essentially bundle together many 56K lines to produce an on-ramp with the capacity for rapid multimedia transmission. Finally, a T3 line offers high-speed connectivity for some very large, far-flung businesses which run private lines from point-to-point. More often T3 circuits can be found as part of the backbone rather than as on-ramp connections.

---

[66]Bandwidth is a measure of the number of bits that can be moved through a circuit in a second. On the information superhighway, there is more room on the equivalent of an eight-lane national highway (*e.g.*, a T3 line) than on a single-lane local road (*e.g.*, copper wire). Cables with limited bandwidth, generally used for text or voice transmissions, are called narrow-band circuits. Those with a high bandwidth, that allow multiple video and audio signals, offer broadband capacity.

[67]Telephone transmissions are sometimes referred to as plain old telephone service, or POTS.

[68]Actually, once the computer's digital transmission is changed by the modem to an analog transmission for the journey to the phone company's switching station, the signal is converted back to digital until it reaches the recipient's local switching station where it is converted to analog for the final journey to the recipient's residence or office.

Fiber optic technology is a substitute for copper wire, transmitting information via pulses of light conducted through glass fibers. One can think of the capacity of fiber as almost infinite. A fiber the size of a human hair could deliver every issue of the Wall Street Journal ever published in less than 1 second.[69] Moreover, the supply of glass fiber is plentiful since it is essentially made from sand. Fiber optics has been used to interconnect the global physical infrastructure. Gradually, telephone companies are replacing copper wire with fiber, although fiber is still more expensive to manufacture and work with than copper.

Coaxial cable is a special type of copper wire in which conductors are arranged to resist interference from external electrical signals. Cable companies have used coaxial cable to wire homes and offices for cable television. Most cable today carries analog signals with limited bandwidth, but cable modems make it possible for coaxial cable to carry digital signals, thereby providing more bandwidth than ISDN technology. Wireless direct broadcast satellite (DBS) offers availability of cable access to the internet in areas where it is too expensive to build a wired cable system. DBS technology sends scrambled signals to a central location where it is processed and distributed throughout the coverage area. The signals are received by special satellite dishes which are connected to the cable set-top box.

The wireless industry covers a variety of technologies that include radio-based systems. Radio-based systems might be further subdivided into land-based and satellite-based systems. Land-based systems — which include cellular communications — send and receive data using low power transmitters and receivers.[70] In a cellular system, the coverage area is broken into overlapping cells which contain a grid of transmitters and receivers (transceivers). A signal from the sender is handled by the nearest cell which passes the signal along normal telephone lines where possible. If a cellular device moves from one cell to another, the signal is handed off from one transceiver to another. Cellular packet data systems enable the wireless transfer of data with acceptable error-handling capabilities. A satellite wireless system might be thought of in the same manner as a land-based system but with a really long transceiver. For example, an oil company may have sites scattered all over the world. Each site may have a very small aperture terminal (VSAT) — a small satellite dish — which can send and receive signals to a hub which contains a larger, more powerful dish that can commu-

---

[69]NEGROPONTE, *supra* note 52, at 23.

[70]KALAKOTA & WHINSTON, *supra* note 63, at 733.

nicate with a satellite. Data and voice communications can be sent and received from the VSAT through the hub to the satellite down to another hub and to the recipient's VSAT.

Once a user (or users through a LAN) have established an on-ramp to the internet, the information transmitted over the on-ramp must be able to travel on the internet until it reaches its destination — another user. The telephone companies provide the most important physical piece of infrastructure — the coaxial and fiber cable that spans much of the globe. Interexchange carriers (IXC's) use submarine fiber cable to connect continents. A series of Transatlantic Telecommunications (TAT) cables link Europe and North America. A series of trans-Pacific cables (TPC) also cross the Pacific Ocean. Cables also cross the Indian Ocean and regional cables link the Pacific Rim countries with each other as well as linking North and South America, Europe and Africa, Europe and the Middle East, the countries of Latin America, and the islands of the Caribbean.[71]

Satellite networks have grown in importance over the past two decades. Approximately 150 satellites in geosynchronous orbit provide broadcast video and overseas telephone links. These satellites are in an orbit 22,300 miles above the equator rotating with the earth so that they appear stationary.[72] Satellites function in the same manner as an earth-based microwave relay station. A satellite receives signals on a particular frequency, amplifies them, and retransmits them on another frequency. The length of the satellite link makes these satellites unsatisfactory for interactive use such as video conferencing.[73] A number of low earth orbit satellites circling the earth overcome some of the problems by requiring less power and shortening the transmission time. In the 1980's, a new satellite technology was developed which uses a narrow beam to focus the transmitted en-

---

[71]HUDSON, GLOBAL CONNECTIONS: INTERNATIONAL TELECOMMUNICATIONS INFRASTRUCTURE AND POLICY 377 (1997). The world's longest submarine fiber cable stretches from Southeast Asia across the Indian Ocean and the Mediterranean to southern France.

[72]KALAKOTA & WHINSTON, *supra* note 63, at 78.

[73]Assume that the round-trip from a satellite is 45,000 miles and that radio waves travel at the speed of light. The delay from one ground station to another is approximately ¼ of a second. If there is another ¼ second delay for acknowledgment, the total ½ second delay would cause transmission problems. KALAKOTA & WHINSTON, *supra* note 63, at 738.

ergy on a small geographic area. These satellites are known as very small aperture terminal satellites (VSAT's) which are able to offer point-to-point services rather than a wide beam.[74] Large corporations can use a VSAT network to link far-flung business locations. VSAT technology promises to expand internet access throughout the world because of easy deployment at relatively low cost.

Intelsat remains the primary satellite service provider for most nations of the world. Intelsat is an international consortium of countries that owns and operates approximately 20 satellites in the Atlantic, Pacific, and Indian Oceans, providing voice, data, and television services to its more than 180 user countries and territories.[75] Intelsat provides a variety of services including television transmission. Intelsat Business Service provides voice, data, and video connectivity generally to large multinational corporations.[76] Other major satellite organizations include Immarsat, which provides satellite communications for the international maritime industry. Arabsat provides communications services to a consortium of Arab countries. Eastern Europe and Russian territories are served by satellites owned by a consortium of countries called Intersputnik. In the Pacific Rim, the Palapa satellites provide services for Indonesia, Malaysia, Singapore, Thailand, and the Philippines. Eutelsat, a cooperative of European nations, has several satellites.

Competition among satellite companies promises to lower the costs and improve the availability of satellite connections. For example, Pan American Satellite was the first US company authorized to provide international satellite services separate from Intelsat. Many of the new competitors seek to provide communications for mobile users. Teledesic, a system sponsored by Microsoft and McCaw, envisions a system of more than 800 satellites that will provide a terrestrial network so people anywhere on earth can transmit and receive data and video.[77]

---

[74]Typically, a user of VSAT technology would equip outlying nodes with small satellite dishes (VSAT's) which would send signals to a hub which would then transmit and receive from a satellite. KALAKOTA & WHINSTON, *supra* note 63, at 738.

[75]HUDSON, *supra* note 71, at 358.

[76]*Id.* at 363.

[77]HUDSON, *supra* note 71, at 386.

3.5. LOGICAL NETWORK INFRASTRUCTURE

The physical infrastructure (*e.g.,* computers, modems, telephone lines, satellites) provides the pavement for the information superhighway. But in order for information to move down the highway, there is a need for a logical infrastructure. The logical infrastructure can be thought of as the laws that govern the movement of traffic down the network highways. Each network forming part of the internet must be set up to provide laws concerning the upkeep of the system (*i.e.,* proper voltage levels and establishing signal paths), the types of vehicles allowed (*i.e.,* how information is transported), what can go in those vehicles (*i.e.,* how information is packaged), how the vehicles enter and leave the various highways, where those vehicles are headed (*i.e.,* destination addresses), how they will get there (*i.e.,* routing), how to maintain an even flow of traffic (*i.e.,* load-leveling), what happens in case of an accident along the way (*i.e.,* error control) and the means of notifying the sender that the vehicle containing the information has arrived safely. Moreover, networks comprising the internet need to communicate with each other in an understandable manner.

Born in the mid-1960's, the internet was developed to connect a US Defense Department network called the ARPAnet and various radio and satellite networks. The ARPAnet itself was an experimental network designed to support military research — specifically, research on how to build a network that could withstand partial outages (*e.g.,* a bomb attack) and still operate. The ARPAnet linked universities and high-tech defense department contractors. In the mid-1980's, the National Science Foundation created a handful of supercomputer centers to help researchers. Out of this effort the NSFNET was designed to provide connectivity for a wide variety of research and educational uses. The NSFNET was a backbone, connecting together a group of regional networks. By 1991, the US government decided to stop funding ARPAnet and NSFNET. Various commercial entities took over responsibility for running the internet, connecting to the NSFNET backbone through the Commercial Internet eXchange (CIX) association. In 1995, the NSFNET backbone was decommissioned, paving the way for a new internet architecture.[78]

---

[78]International research networks have been in existence since the mid-1970's when sites in the United Kingdom and Norway connected to SATNET, and thereby to ARPAnet. In the 1980's, CSNET and BITNET both had European gateways and other

The new architecture includes several priority network access points (NAP's) connected by very high bandwidth (*i.e.,* capable of carrying high volumes of information).[79] These NAP's are the "official" locations in the United States where service providers can interconnect. But there are a host of other locations both within the United States and throughout the world where a variety of commercial, international, and federal networks can connect with each other through "peering agreements." For example, in the United Kingdom, the London Internet Exchange (LINX) performs that function. The European backbone (EBONE) maintains hubs on the European continent, and there are distributed global information exchanges (D-GIXes) located in Stockholm and Paris.[80]

A peering agreement, which may be bilateral or multilateral, is a reciprocal agreement by an internet service provider to carry the traffic of another internet service provider on its backbone. For example, a customer who has chosen ISP1 as its internet service provider can connect with a vendor, R Corp., which has chosen ISP2 as its internet service provider because ISP1 and ISP2 have entered into a peering agreement either directly or through one or more intermediaries to hand off data traffic to each other. It is the central interconnect points throughout the world where data is handed off from one service provider to another that form the backbone of the internet. Because most of the national private backbones interconnect at multiple points, a temporary breakdown on one part of the information highway will not disable most data flow. Instead, data can be rerouted along some alternate path, much as an individual flying from Los Angeles to Boston might transfer planes in Chicago, Cincinnati, or Dallas. Should a single airport close, most air traffic can be rerouted via some alternative airport.

As the internet has moved from an academic and government run enterprise to a commercially dominated enterprise, ISP's have emerged to offer commercial access to the internet and to provide resources for both

---

gateways throughout the world. Network projects sprung up in many countries, including DFN in Germany, UNINET in Norway, SDN in Korea, and JUNET in Japan. The focus of the discussion that follows is the development of the internet architecture in the United States. However, comparable developments are taking place throughout the world.

[79]The NAP's are located in San Francisco (operated by Pacific Bell), Chicago (operated by Ameritech), Pennsauken, New Jersey (operated by Sprint), and Washington, DC (operated by Metropolitan Fiber Systems).

[80]DOWD, GETTING CONNECTED: THE INTERNET AT 56K AND Up 3 (1996).

companies and individuals. ISP's may be grouped in three basic categories: (1) backbone providers; (2) regional providers; and (3) local providers. The large telecommunications and cable companies which are backbone providers offer a perfect illustration of the blurring of the physical network infrastructure concept and the logical infrastructure concept. These companies provide the wires (sometimes called "pipes") that allow the physical connection among network users, but they also provide the logical infrastructure that makes it possible for customers to transmit and receive information on that physical network. Virtually all the US telecommunication companies and many international telecommunication companies are involved in developing and maintaining the internet infrastructure. Cable companies and the commercial on-line services like CompuServe, Prodigy, and America Online also compete as ISP's.[81]

Competing with the telecommunication, cable, and on-line companies are some established national independent companies that are essentially nationwide internet wholesalers and retailers. They lease high speed telephone lines from telecommunication companies and establish points-of-presence (POP's) for access nationwide. They resell these services generally to regional and local ISP's but also to end-users as well. For large businesses, these national providers offer a wide area network with many POP's. Rather than leasing dedicated phone lines from every business location to every other business location, a large business can lease one line from each location to the nearest POP.

Regional networks can provide the link between local organizations and the backbone providers. While a regional network operates within a limited geographic area, data sent over a regional network can still reach any computer anywhere in the world that is connected to the internet. This can occur because the regional network has purchased the services offered by a backbone provider (*i.e.*, by interconnecting with one or more backbone providers at one or more central locations) so that information can flow from the regional network to the backbone provider and then from the backbone provider perhaps to another regional carrier across the world that is the internet service provider for the intended recipient.

---

[81]Sometimes companies that provide internet access without many enhanced services (*e.g.*, a newspaper or magazine database) are referred to as internet service providers, while companies (*e.g.*, America Online) that provide access plus enhanced services are referred to as online service providers (OSP's). The line between the two categories is difficult to draw.

To illustrate how regional providers fit into the network infrastructure, suppose that a regional provider, RegNet, wanted to create a network in New York, Washington, DC, and Atlanta.[82] RegNet would lease data lines from one or more long-distance exchange carriers.[83] RegNet might pay the long-distance carriers to manage the physical network (leaving RegNet to worry about the routing of information) or might purchase and manage the data communications equipment itself. Once RegNet has established its regional network so that information can flow seamlessly from New York through Washington DC to Atlanta, RegNet will have to link to the internet at one of the exchange points. For example, RegNet might tie into the backbone through the Washington DC NAP or through other providers that are connected to that or any other NAP. Finally, RegNet would set up points-of-presence (POP's) in New York, Washington DC, and Atlanta where customers could link to a router that RegNet maintains at each POP.

Local ISP's provide internet access usually within a city or limited geographical area. A local ISP subleases circuits from national or regional ISP's, adding their own support and applications services.[84] Generally, local internet service providers operate an equipment room in a single area code, lease connections to a backbone provider, and offer dial-up connections and leased connections to customers and businesses in their area. They tend to focus on customer service, configuration, and training.

3.6.   INTERNET OPERATION

While telephone lines, cable lines, and wireless connections make it possible to link any computer user to any other user, in order for information to be transmitted and received there is a need for a set of agreed rules — protocols — that govern the flow of information. These protocols address issues from how the physical connections carry the electronic impulses to how the information is packaged and delivered to how the information will be displayed and used. They operate in the background, standardizing the transmission and receipt of information. Consider a hypothetical transmission over the internet. Suppose C, a customer in California is sending an

---

[82]Dowd, *supra* note 80, at 26-28.

[83]As an alternative, RegNet could lease a "private virtual circuit" network — essentially bandwidth on a line that is shared with others.

[84]Services provided might include email and newsgroup access, disk storage space, bulletin board access, and library access.

email message to B, a business in Sweden. The message is directed by software instructions from C's computer across the on-ramp (*e.g.*, a telephone line) into a local network which might serve 1,000 users. The message travels in pieces called "packets," each packet containing B's address. Each packet travels through a type of a series of computers called routers dedicated to determining the best path for each packet. Different packets may travel along different paths as the packets move from a local network to a regional network to the US backbone to the European backbone to a European regional network and ultimately to B's computer. Once the packets all arrive, they are reassembled in the correct order for display on B's computer screen. If any packets did not arrive or were corrupted along the way, there is a protocol that provides acknowledgment of receipt and error control so that C's computer can resend the faulty packet. By breaking information into packets, and having routers along the internet handle traffic control, the internet architecture maximizes the chances of information reaching the intended recipient even if part of the internet is unavailable. This built-in redundancy makes the internet a stable infrastructure.

3.6.1. Protocols

Protocol stacks are computer software that handle data transmissions between computers, allowing computers to communicate. The term "stack" refers to layers of protocols from the highest layers, dealing with protocols for specific programs (*e.g.*, email) to middle layers dealing with transportation issues to the bottom layers dealing with physical network access. Two protocol stacks that are in wide use today are TCP/IP[85] and ISO/OSI.[86] The TCP/IP standards have gained greater acceptance throughout the world.[87] Also, many ISP's enable users to send and receive OSI traffic or any other non-OSI traffic as well as TCP/IP traffic.[88]

---

[85]Transfer Control Protocol/ Internet Protocol.

[86]The Open System Interconnection (OSI) protocol stack is a product of the International Standards Organization (ISO), a group of government and private standards organizations, formed in 1946 to promote uniform international network standards. DOWD, *supra* note 80, at 71.

[87]TCP/IP really refers to a family of protocols — an internet protocol suite KALAKOTA & WHINSTON, *supra* note 63, at 633.

[88]For example, Novell Netware which uses IPX protocol can connect to TCP/IP networks.

3.6.1.1. High layer protocols

In the example above, the highest level protocol (*e.g.*, RFC 822) is for the email application itself so that when B receives C's email, B's email program will be able to decipher who is the sender, who is the receiver and what is the body of the message. Moving down the stack, the Transfer Control Protocol (TCP) is responsible for making sure that the email message gets through to the recipient, keeping track of what is sent, and retransmitting if necessary.[89] If a message is too large for one datagram (*i.e.*, an envelope with the destination address and the message text), TCP will break up the message into several datagrams and verify that all arrive correctly. If TCP is like an envelope, Internet Protocol (IP) is like the mailroom.[90] IP addresses data packets received from the transport layer (*e.g.*, TCP) and consults with a router to determine where the mail will be sent next.[91] Actually, the entire route is not known when the mail is first sent. At each router along the way, the next portion of the journey is determined.

---

[89]TCP is a connection-oriented transport protocol that establishes and maintains a connection between the sending and requesting computers until a receipt acknowledgment is received. In contrast, User Datagram Protocol (UDP) is a connectionless transport protocol that does not guarantee delivery of any packet. UDP is suitable for video conferencing where retransmission delays would be awkward.

[90]KALAKOTA & WHINSTON, *supra* note 63, at 637. Two popular forms of IP are Point-to-Point Protocol (PPP) and Serial Line Interface Protocol (SLIP) which allow a user to become a fully functional host of the internet able to use graphical display programs such as Netscape Communication's Communicator or Microsoft Internet Explorer. These graphical programs could not run if a user connected to the internet directly as a "dumb" terminal using a terminal emulation program.

Variations of IP can handle different types transmissions. For example, combinations of audio and video (*e.g.*, video conferencing) are handled by IP multicast. IP multicast uses User Datagram Protocol (UDP), a connectionless protocol, rather than TCP because the reliability and flow control features of TCP are not suitable for broadcasting (*e.g.*, if an audio packet is lost, a retransmission delay would be not be acceptable in an interactive conference).

[91]Every computer linked to the internet has a unique IP address which is assigned by the Internet Network Information Center (InterNIC). Addresses are in the form: 170.140.36.102, with the digits on the left determining the network's address and the digits on the right defining a particular machine's address on the network. Because IP addresses are difficult for people to remember (computers have no problems with them), the Domain Name Service (DNS) is a system that maps the numerical addresses to names. For example, the address above is mapped to: tax.law.emory.edu.

3.6.1.2. Low layer protocols

Lower level protocols which handle the physical connections essentially decide what vehicles (*i.e.*, frames or cells) will deliver the mail and prepare the road surface for those vehicles.[92] The higher level protocols, like TCP/IP, are independent of the lower level protocols. In determining the nature of the vehicles that deliver the mail over a network, two different switching techniques are used — circuit switching and packet switching. Circuit switching, which is used for voice communications, requires that there is a dedicated link between the sender and the receiver for continuous transmission of information. In a packet switching network, datagrams are split into packets (*i.e.*, envelopes), each with its own destination address, traveling along its own independent and temporary route. Packet switching can be divided into slow packet switching and fast packet switching. For example, X.25 is a slow packet switching protocol that is widely used and is reliable, but operates at low speeds. Fast packet switching, which offers greater transmission speeds, is either frame relay or cell relay.[93] Frame relay networks provide variable-sized packets while cell-switched networks provide fixed-sized packets (*i.e.*, cells). The simplicity of the standardized fixed cells lends itself to very high-speed networking. Along a network, data may move in different vehicles. For example, in a local network, the data packets may be transported by the X.25 protocol which at a router hands the packets to Asynchronous Transfer Mode (ATM) which stuffs the packets into cells until they reach the recipient's local network router which empties the cells and sends the data to the recipient using a frame relay technology.

Asynchronous Transfer Mode (ATM)[94] is a cell relay which can handle data, voice, and video.[95] This flexibility combined with the fact that ATM

---

[92]KALAKOTA & WHINSTON, *supra* note 63, at 699-700.

[93]The advantage of fast packet switching over traditional circuit switching is that in circuit switching, each call is assigned a fixed bandwidth irrespective of use. For example, there is no transmission down a dedicated line when there is a pause in the conversation. In fast packet switching, bandwidth is dynamic, expanding or contracting based on the transmission needs. Also, fast packet switching means that the routing will be set up dynamically rather than fixed permanently.

[94]This should not be confused with the ATM that stands for automated teller machine. Another popular cell relay protocol is Switched Mutimegabit Data Service (SMDS).

[95]ATM is connection-oriented as opposed to Ethernet and Token Ring which are connectionless networks. The advantage of a connection-oriented network is that for

cells can be transported over any type of physical connection (*e.g.*, copper, coaxial cable, or fiber optic networks)[96] has led ATM to develop into a standard for many local and wide area networks throughout the world. ATM also provides plenty of bandwidth. For example, MCI will use ATM switching technology running over SONET[97] transport technology in providing very high speed backbone services (vBNS) to the NSF backbone. SONET and its European counterpart SDH[98] are a set of standards that govern transport over fiber, providing massive bandwidth and the flexibility to add (or drop) additional channels on the fiber, thereby easily accommodating new users.

3.6.2. Routers and switches

Routers and switches are really special purpose computers that send each packet of information on its way to its intended destination.[99] Each packet that is sent may travel a different route to its destination. The router directs each packet based on information contained in the header of the packet and the routing tables maintained by the computer. Routers operate based on information provided by the high level internet protocol. Routers function well but as traffic and the number of users expand, routers can begin to operate slowly. A switch also routes traffic, but at a lower layer proto-

---

real-time applications, such as video conferencing, a user has a dedicated connection that is not affected by heavy usage on the network. The advantage of a connectionless network is that a user only receives as much bandwidth as is necessary, subject to the needs of others, thereby maximizing available bandwidth to others. ATM actually offers the advantages of both through two different service levels: available bit rate (ABR) and constant bit rate (CBR). A user might specify ABR for sending text files while using ABR for video conferencing.

[96]Protocols, like Ethernet or Token Ring, are used on many LAN's to manage transmission over coaxial cable or copper wire. Fiber Distributed Data Interface (FDDI) is a standard designed for use with optical fiber.

[97]Synchronous Optical NETwork.

[98]Synchronous Digital Hierarchy. The specifications underlying SONET and SDH were adopted by the CCITT (International Telegraph and Telephone Consultative Committee) in 1989. SONET used by American telephone companies is not identical to SDH used by European telephone companies.

[99]*See* Mitchell, *Routing and Switching: Building Scalable Internets — Expanding networking horizons,* http://www.casc.com/products/whitepapers/building.html.

col. This allows a switch to operate more efficiently than a router.[100] The use of switches gives a network manager more control over the quality of service.[101] Switches and routers work together with switches interconnecting the routers in a way that is more productive.

3.6.3. Client/server architecture

Historically, computing developed on a mainframe-based model where "dumb" terminals (*i.e.,* computers that could not store or manipulate data) were attached to a large, central computer. Users at the terminals did all their computing on the mainframe. This architecture is costly and too slow to handle audio and video.[102] The file server model links individual computers to a storage server, where most of the computing is done on the client computer, and the server is used largely for long-term storage of data. The more modern client/server architecture combines elements of the mainframe model and the file server model by more evenly dividing computing between the client and the server computers. Typically, the client computer would interact with the server through a request-reply sequence. A server can be any computer from a simple PC to a mainframe. It handles client applications, storage and security, and provides scalability (*i.e.,* the ability to add more clients). For example, a web server is a computer that is running web server software that allows client computers with web browser software the ability to interact with the server by passing data back and forth. An email server does the same thing for email. A computer can be both an email and web server or function as a server for a host of other applications. In the context of electronic commerce, a server might handle thousands of simultaneous users, manage the transactions of those users (*e.g.,* information requests, order processing, billing), and deliver informa-

---

[100]A router operating at the IP level protocol, typically processes a 40 byte header. A switch which operates at a lower protocol level processes a two or five byte header. The result is better performance.

[101]A router delivers a connectionless network service where each packet is sent through the network independently. A switch provides a connection-oriented network service. Rather than determining the path of each packet independently, a switch establishes a path between the endpoints of a connection — a virtual connection. The switch can determine the allowable speed and priority of data that flows through the virtual connection.

[102]KALAKOTA & WHINSTON, *supra* note 63, at 13.

tion to clients. In a multimedia context, the data might include text, video, and sound.

A business could locate a server anywhere. It need not be located where the business is managed. For example, a Canadian company could locate its web server in Bermuda. Using telephone, other cable and/or a wireless connection, it would be possible for the Canadian company to have full access to the server's storage capacity. Files could be uploaded from Canada to Bermuda and downloaded from Bermuda to Canada. The server in Bermuda, if it were linked to the internet, could be accessed by client computers throughout the world.[103]

A client computer typically has storage capability that will enable the user to download information from the server and manipulate it using a client application. For example, an email program allows a user to download email from the server to be displayed in a manner dictated by the client's email client. A client's web browser such as Netscape Communication's Communicator or Microsoft's Internet Explorer allows the user to download information from a server to be stored or printed or manipulated in some way (*e.g.*, downloaded data to be entered onto a spreadsheet). Of course, client applications enable two way transfers. An email client allows composition of email which can be sent through an email server to a recipient linked to the internet.

3.6.4. Internet applications

3.6.4.1. In general

While the physical infrastructure and the logical infrastructure make the internet possible, it is internet applications that make the internet worthwhile for electronic commerce. Internet applications might be divided into the following general categories: communications; information databases; information processing services; and resource-sharing services.[104] Probably the most important communications tool is electronic mail (email). The ability to send a message almost anywhere in the world in

---

[103]While the administrator of the server would have easy access to all data on the server, through security protections, clients throughout the world would be given more limited access.

[104]KALAKOTA & WHINSTON, *supra* note 63, at 125.

a matter of seconds is an easily understandable metaphor for the entire internet. It is also possible to send email to a fax machine or faxes to an email account. If an individual wants to communicate with a group, the internet makes group conferencing available through bulletin boards where a user can post a message that a group can see or through interactive audio or video conferencing. The internet offers a wide array of databases, containing textual material (*e.g.,* articles, newspapers, magazines, reports), computer software (*e.g.,* freeware, shareware, and software for purchase), and multimedia materials (*e.g.,* video and audio). The internet offers an increasing number of information processing services, such as statistical analyses and simulation tools. The use of the Java programming language (discussed below) may permit users to make use of word processing, spreadsheet, and database functions on-line as needed, rather than storing such programs on a local hard drive. Finally, connection through a network allows multiple users to share access to printers, fax machines, modems, and other equipment or services that might be underutilized.

3.6.4.2. World wide web

The world wide web (WWW or web) is an all-encompassing moniker that makes the network infrastructure come alive in a user-friendly way. Conceived in 1989,[105] the web was proposed to be a simple system that would allow the dissemination of documents among users. Architecturally, the web consists of users who run a client web browser (*e.g.,* Netscape Communication's Communicator, Microsoft Internet Explorer) and servers which manage information retrieval and other transactions and which provide secure messaging. Through the web, users can access millions of documents and files throughout the world. To make the web useful, there are a variety of "search engines"[106] that can provide a listing of the requested information. The user simply enters one or more keywords and the search engine provides a listing of all the web sites (*i.e.,* servers) that correspond to the requested information.

---

[105]Tim Berners-Lee of the European Laboratory for Particle Physics (known as CERN, an R&D group of European physics researchers) proposed the web project to facilitate research collaboration.

[106]Among the popular search engines are Alta Vista, Excite, Infoseek, Lycos, and Yahoo.

HyperText Transfer Protocol (HTTP) is a request/response application protocol that runs over TCP. HTTP regulates the transfer of information in any form between servers and clients. Assume that a computer is hooked into the internet. When a computer user starts up a computer program called a browser, such as Netscape Communication's Communicator or Microsoft Internet Explorer, the only activity is the opening of an HTTP client application (*i.e.*, the browser). Once the browser is open, if a user enters an internet address[107] (or clicks on a hyperlink[108]), a four-part process begins: connection, request, response, and disconnection. In the connection stage, the client reads the requested address and tries to establish contact with the server. Once that connection is established, the client makes a request of the server by sending a message in a specified form. Common types of requests include "Get" and "Post." In a typical Get request, the client browser essentially demands of the server: "send me the document at the requested address so I can display its contents to the user."[109] A Post command tells the server to accept enclosed information and add it to information available on the server, such as the server's database.[110] The posted information might include information necessary to complete a transaction such as a purchase order, billing information, or specifications. Once the browser has established a connection and has transmitted its request to the server, it waits for a response. The server sends the response, such as a document, or a confirmation if a Post command was sent. If the client's browser receives a document in response to its request, the response contains information that tells the browser whether and how to display the document or whether the document should be saved to the client's hard drive. Once the response has been sent, the server disconnects from the client.[111]

---

[107]The address begins "http://". This address is referred to as a uniform resource locator, or URL. Each document available on the web has a discrete URL.

[108]A hyperlink is an address embedded in a document that, when clicked on with a pointing device, takes the user to another document at the new address.

[109]The "Get" request can be conditioned by dates, ranges, or matches.

[110]The data enclosed in the "Post" command might be passed to a database on the server (or on another server) through a Common Gateway Interface (CGI) script, or it might be added to a document to be viewed by other users.

[111]If the user executes a Stop sequence on the browser or initiates a new hyperlink, the client initiates the disconnect sequence. Newer versions of HTTP can maintain a connection so that multiple files can be downloaded. HTTP is a "stateless" protocol,

HyperText Markup Language (HTML) is the programming language that enables the creation of electronic documents. Text can be entered along with specified codes that indicate titles, headings, graphics, formatting (*e.g.*, bold, italics), and hyperlinks. Hyperlinks are addresses that can be embedded in an HTML document so that when a user clicks on a hyperlink (usually indicated by a highlighted word or graphic in the document being read), the user's browser sends a request for the document at the embedded address. In this way, a user can go seamlessly from document to document. With the growth of multimedia, hypertext documents will allow new kinds of interaction. For example, a customer ordering merchandise over the internet who has a question or a complaint might be able to click on the customer representative icon and receive in response a video clip answering frequently asked questions (FAQ) or perhaps demonstrating installation or repair of the merchandise. Alternatively, the documents might offer the customer the opportunity to have a videoconference with a service representative located anywhere in the world.

HTML enables the creation of forms, which are useful for electronic commerce. The use of forms permits an enterprise conducting business on a server to collect information entered by a user and to act on that information. For example, forms are used by sellers of goods or services to collect information from purchasers such as shipping or credit card information. Or a form might be used to gather information concerning customer preferences so that the server can provide personalized information about available products and services that meet the customer's needs. The generation of forms makes the web interactive.

For a program on the server to respond to the information requested on the form, the program may follow the Common Gateway Interface (CGI) specification, which coordinates the communication of data entered by the user to be passed to the web server and then to a program running on the server (*e.g.*, a database lookup program).[112] A CGI script (*i.e.*, program) handles the movement of data between the web server and the application and can return the program's response to the user's web browser. When any HTML form is filled out, the browser can forward the user's in-

---

running only long enough to complete the operation, rather than keeping the connection open.

[112]The database could be located on another server rather than on the web server — even a server in another country.

formation to the server using the HTTP transport protocol. The server then passes the data on the form to the CGI script which processes the information and returns an answer in the form of a document that the server can pass back to the client browser using the HTTP protocol. The return document may be personalized information or, for example, if the form contained the appropriate credit card information, the return document may be a document confirming the purchase transaction.

Java applets and ActiveX components are application programs that can be downloaded from a server and then used within a browser to perform a particular task. For example, a user need not have a spreadsheet program or a word processing program on a local hard drive. Instead, the user can click on a hyperlink displayed by the user's browser, causing the spreadsheet or word processor program to be downloaded into the client computer's memory where it can be run by the user. Java applets or ActiveX components can offer multimedia, interactive programs that can, for example, guide a user through an interactive product demonstration.

A variation of this interactive programming capability is the inclusion of a script (*i.e.,* a program) embedded in an HTML page that appears on a user's browser.[113] This script can interact with a user's input to produce an interactive result without having to transmit an HTML form to the server or having to download an applet or ActiveX component. For example, suppose an HTML document on a user's browser asks for a credit card number along with other information. The embedded script in the HTML document can automatically validate that the card number was entered correctly without having to transmit the entire form to the server to be checked.

3.6.4.3. Other internet tools

Aside from the web, there are a host of other tools that permit a user's access to information available on a server. For example, Gopher is an information organization method (*i.e.,* a protocol) that facilitates the search for information on servers that run Gopher server software. Another useful tool for downloading files from distant servers is File Transfer Protocol (FTP), available from servers running FTP server software. Publicly-available files can be accessed anonymously with FTP; private files can be ac-

---

[113]Two such scripting programs are JavaScript offered by Netscape Communication's Communicator and VBScript offered by Microsoft Internet Explorer.

cessed only if the server permits access to the requester. One of the virtues of the HTTP protocol used by the world wide web is that it is a superset of FTP so that any web server is also an FTP server. To locate available files by name on the internet, a tool called Archie can provide a list of servers with the file requested.

3.6.5. Emerging internet tools

There are a variety of new tools — some already in existence — that promise to make the internet easier to use. For example, speech recognition and generation technology will enable users to speak to computers and be spoken to by computers rather than, or in addition to, typing in requests or clicking a pointing device on an icon. Computers will also be able to provide more realistic virtual reality interfaces. A virtual reality interface provides a visualization tool that allows a user to feel as if the user is part of the images being shown. Consumers would be able to wander through a three-dimensional virtual shopping mall, browsing in shops and trying out virtual merchandise. The use of a virtual reality helmet with sound and goggles can create the sensation of "being there." Moreover, tactile sensors in virtual reality body suits may provide the sensations of touch, smell, and taste, as well as sight and sound.

3.7. ELECTRONIC COMMERCE

Broadly speaking, the term "electronic commerce" refers to the modern business use of computers that fulfills the need of firms, customers and management to provide more efficient delivery of goods and services. The breadth of electronic commerce encompasses activities such as exchanging business information within a business or between businesses, electronic funds transfers (EFT) and using the web to communicate with customers and potential customers. The discussion below highlights three important aspects of electronic commerce. First, what are the different ways in which electronic commerce can be implemented in business. Second, if commerce is to be conducted electronically, what payment systems will make such commerce possible. Finally, unless businesses and consumers are satisfied that business transactions are secure and that information disclosed on the web can be kept confidential, use of the web would be limited. Some of the security concerns and solutions are presented.

3.7.1. Implementation

3.7.1.1. *Customer-to-business electronic commerce*

This category refers to marketplace transactions where customers learn about products and services through on-line advertising, buy them using electronic cash, and receive post-purchase support through on-line services. Depending on the nature of goods purchased, delivery may be through the internet (*e.g.,* downloading computer software or movies) or by means of conventional delivery methods. In the discussion that follows, a sampling of transactions between businesses and customers are considered.

3.7.1.1.1. Shopping

Electronic malls are developing that will enable a customer to enter on-line stores and browse around using virtual reality technology. This will be the next step beyond television home shopping and catalog shopping. Consumer shopping consists of the pre-purchase information phase where sellers provide information (*i.e.,* advertising) about available products or services, their uses, and their prices. In addition, potential consumers may seek product or service reviews from independent sources and may do some comparison shopping. Once the shopper has gathered the necessary information, the transaction enters the purchase phase. If the search for information is rewarding, the potential customer will negotiate the terms of the purchase such as price, delivery date, method of delivery, and terms of payment. Then an order is placed, payment is made, and the product or services is delivered. Finally, the transaction enters the post-purchase phase where customer service must be provided to answer questions, deal with problems, and handle returns if necessary.

Consider just one example of an on-line business.[114] Cendant Corporation, a $5.3 billion consumer goods and services company offers over a million products and services over the internet, including cars, electronics, books, appliances, gifts, computer hardware and software and flowers. For an annual membership fee of less than $100, Cendant facilitated the sale of more than $1.2 billion worth of products and services in 1997. The company plans to offer a product selection which will cover 95 percent of the products a typical household would buy before the year 2000.

3.7.1.1.1.1. Pre-purchase information

The delivery of pre-purchase information to customers may be provided by the enterprise itself or by independent third parties. Information provided by the enterprise can be characterized as active information and passive information. Active information which is intrusive might consist of broadcasting messages to a group of people who are engaged in some other activity. For example, television advertising fits this model. On the internet, messages might be broadcast on USENET newsgroups[115] to which people subscribe. For example, if the subject of a newsgroup is automobile racing, that newsgroup might be a natural forum for advertisements concerning automobile parts or services. Another means of broadcasting an advertising message is to purchase advertising space on another document that a user may be accessing. For example, if a user is accessing a newspaper on-line, multimedia advertisements along the border of the document may, through a hyperlink, allow a user to click on the advertisement, enabling the presentation of additional information about the advertiser or its products. Perhaps, the most intrusive means of reaching purchasers is one-on-one advertising through mass electronic mailings, sometimes referred to as junk email. At low nominal cost to the advertiser, an email message can be

---

[114]U.S. Department of Commerce, *The Emerging Digital Economy*, Chapter 4, http://www.ecommerce.gov (1998).

[115]A newsgroup is essentially a bulletin board of posted notices by members of the newsgroup who join together to post and receive information concerning a specified theme. It is self-selected, usually with no membership fee. Members regularly may join and leave such groups. The messages posted are sent from a user's client computer to the server where they are posted.

sent to millions of potential customers almost instantaneously. As there is with more traditional forms of mass mailings, there is some consumer resistance to this form of advertising.

There are more passive forms of advertising opportunities available that require the potential consumer to initiate its receipt. For example, enterprises can prepare a home page on the web that through a multimedia presentation may describe the company and its products. Such a home page may be hyperlinked to other pages offering more detailed or personalized information for an interested shopper. An enterprise might through its home page provide an on-line catalog, providing different levels of information that can be controlled by the shopper.

In addition to these methods of advertising by enterprises themselves, internet organizational tools enable independent third parties to offer product and service reviews and comparisons with competing products. Software programs that can be given instructions and then conduct a search over the web are sometimes referred to as robots, wanderers, or spiders. There are also electronic yellow pages organized by product or services listings which can offer all types of information about enterprises including financial information, recent news clippings, and product and services information.

3.7.1.1.1.2. Purchase

While there may be variations in the way purchases take place, a typical purchase may include the following. There may be an interactive negotiation of the terms of purchase, depending on the nature of the purchase. If the negotiation is successful or if the item is not subject to negotiation and the customer accepts the offered terms, the customer may authorize payment to the vendor on-line using an encrypted message containing the customer's digital signature. Upon almost instantaneous receipt, the vendor might forward the information to a billing service for verification of the signature and the means of payment. The payment may be through a conventional credit or debit card or perhaps using electronic cash. Once the vendor receives a "green light" from the billing service, the vendor arranges for delivery of the goods, either by traditional means or by sending the customer an electronic key that enables the customer to download the information (*e.g.*, computer software, a film, a digital book). Upon receiving the goods, the buyer signs and delivers a receipt to the vendor.[116] The vendor transmits the receipt to its billing service that completes the payment process. For example, the billing service may make sure that the funds are transferred from the customer's bank to the vendor's bank.

3.7.1.1.1.3. Post-purchase activities

Post-purchase interaction with customers may include questions on how to use the item purchased, handling contractual disputes and, if necessary, handling refunds. Interactive instructions on-line and the use of bulletin boards to allow customers to interact with each other and with support personnel can address many customer questions and problems that may arise. In addition, a vendor's web page may include a hyperlink that enables video conferencing software to connect the user to a support personnel.

3.7.1.1.2. Entertainment

The internet lends itself to the entertainment industry. For example, a user who wants to watch a movie will be able to browse through an on-line entertainment guide that lists movies, music videos, recorded television shows, etc. After choosing a movie, the user can click on a button, fill out the on-line payment form that appears on the browser, submit the form to the server which, after validating the payment, downloads the movie to a TV set-top box with appropriate copy-protection to makes sure the movie is not reproduced. In this manner, the user can watch the movie on demand. In a similar fashion, users can download interactive games, music videos, or most any other form of entertainment.

It is estimated that nearly 90 percent of internet users go on-line to get news and information.[117] More than 2,700 newsapers have on-line businesses, more than 800 TV stations across the United States have internet

---

[116]The customer may send the receipt directly online or if a shipping agent delivered the goods, the shipping agent may transmit the receipt electronically.

[117]U.S. Department of Commerce, *The Emerging Digital Economy,* Chapter 4, http://www.ecommerce.gov (1998).

sites. There are live broadcasts of sporting events, music and other entertainment events. Music can also be downloaded from CD Jukebox and other internet sites. It is estimated that advertising and other fees for on-line content may exceed $8 billion by 2002.[118]

3.7.1.1.3. Travel

Not only do vacationers and business travelers plan trips on the internet, but in increasing numbers they book their travel electronically as well. In 1996, internet users booked $276 million of travel in this manner; in 1997, on-line travel purchases reached over $800 million.[119] Airlines have lower marketing costs when they process a ticket sale on-line rather than through a travel agent or reservation center. For example, it is estimated that it costs $1 if a customer books an electronic ticket but $8 to purchase the same ticket through a computer reservation system.. Not only do airlines lower costs by on-line transactions, they also generate additional revenues by offering special "cyberfares" or by auctioning tickets on-line, thereby generating incremental dollars in selected markets where traditional distribution has resulted in unused capacity.

3.7.1.1.4. Health care

Suppose that T is on vacation in a foreign country when she is involved in an accident. After stabilizing her, the doctors swipe her health care identification card through a card reader which provides access to her medical records and provides contact information for her home country physicians. Establishing an internet connection to her home country physicians, her attending doctor and permanent physician can view, manipulate, and analyze three-dimensional images of the patient's internal organs allowing them to agree upon the most appropriate treatment.[120]

---

[118]*Id.*

[119]*Id.*

[120]Tapscott, The Digital Economy: Promise and Peril in the Age of Networked Intelligence 125-127 (1996).

3.7.1.1.5. Personal finance and home banking

While direct deposit, on-line bill payment, and telephone transfers are not yet widespread, these technologies will become an increasingly important part of consumer financing and banking management. Basic home banking services include checking and saving account statements available on-line, 24-hour banking through automated teller machines outside the home and through smart cards within the home, funds transfer, and bill payments. Intermediate banking services might include functions such as household budgeting, tax return preparation, and updating stock portfolios. Advanced banking services might include stock and other investment vehicle trading and brokerage services and currency trading.

It is expected that the insurance industry will also use the internet for selling policies and providing customer service over the internet, producing savings of more than 50 percent over the lifetime of the customer.[121] Insurance premiums generated over the internet are expected to grow from approximately $39 million in 1997 to more than $1 billion by 2001.

3.7.1.2. *Business-to-business electronic commerce*

The ways in which the communications revolution will affect commerce is not limited to retail operations. The amount of business-to-business commerce over the internet dwarfs the current level of consumer electronic commerce.[122] Indeed, just one company — General Electric — runs a web site which does $1 billion worth of business a year, which itself exceeds all consumer electronic commerce.[123] By 2000, GE intends to purchase all of its non-production and maintenance, repair and operations materials, estimated to be $5 billion, over the internet.[124] The site permits GE's purchasers to specify to whom they want bid requests to go, and what sort of information is required. GE's software then manages the bids as they

---

[121]U.S. Department of Commerce, *The Emerging Digital Economy,* Chapter 4, http://www.ecommerce.gov (1998).

[122]*Id.*

[123]*Id.*

[124]U.S. Department of Commerce, *The Emerging Digital Economy,* Chapter 3, http://www.ecommerce.gov (1998).

come back. The length of the bidding process has been cut from 21 days to 10, and costs have been lowered by 5–20%.[125] Part of the savings has occurred because GE can now extend bid requests to foreign as well as domestic suppliers.[126]

The growth in business-to-business electronic commerce arises as a result of lower purchasing costs, reductions in inventories, lower cycle times, more efficient customer service, lower marketing and sales costs, and new sales opportunities.[127]

Business-to-business electronic data interchange (EDI) is already an important part of the commercial infrastructure and will continue to grow in importance.[128] EDI can be defined as "the electronic transfer, from computer to computer of commercial and administrative data using an agreed standard to structure an EDI message."[129] It is estimated that 95% of the Fortune 1,000 companies use EDI.[130] Businesses may already trade more than $150 billion in goods and services, typically saving between 5 and 10 percent in procurement costs.[131] EDI allows businesses to handle a mountain of paperwork such as purchase orders, invoices, confirmation notices, and shipping receipts, thereby cutting down on transaction costs and increasing efficiency. Much of this documentation is now in electronic form. Before the advent of EDI, this documentation depended on postal systems, restricting communications with trading partners to working hours — indeed, only those working hours that overlap between the time zones involved. EDI can function all hours of the day or night.

---

[125]*Id.*

[126]*Id.*

[127]For a good discussion of these changes, *see* U.S. Department of Commerce, *The Emerging Digital Economy,* Chaper 4, http://www.ecommerce.gov (1998).

[128]EDI was developed in the 1960's. KALAKOTA & WHINSTON, *supra* note 63, at 334. For a discussion of the savings offered by EDI, *see* U.S. Department of Commerce, *The Emerging Digital Economy,* Chapter 3, http://www.ecommerce.gov (1998).

[129]Article 2.1 of the European Model EDI agreement. Other definitions abound. For example, the UN/EDIFACT Training Guide defines EDI as "the interchange of standard formatted data between computer application systems of trading partners with minimal manual intervention."

[130]Anderson, *Survey of Electronic Commerce: Big, boring, booming — Business-to-business e-commerce is a revolution in a ball valve,* THE ECONOMIST (10 May 1997).

[131]U.S. Department of Commerce, *The Emerging Digital Economy,* Chapter 3, http://www.ecommerce.gov (1998).

As a technical matter, EDI is a standard which enables data in a specified form to be exchanged between software applications on different computers that are working together to process a business transaction. EDI specifies the format for the information transferred, but the underlying transport is handled by email or some point-to-point connection.[132] When a user sends a document, the sender's EDI translation software converts the document from a proprietary (*i.e.*, firm-specific) format to a standard format. When the recipient receives the document, EDI software on the recipient's computer automatically changes the standard format into a proprietary format so the recipient can manipulate the data in whatever way is necessary.

A sample EDI transaction might be as follows.[133] A buyer's computer sends a purchase order to a seller's computer which sends a confirmation to the buyer's computer. The seller's computer sends a booking request to a transport company which sends a booking confirmation to the seller's computer. The seller's computer notifies the buyer's computer of the shipping notice. The transport company's computer sends a status report to the seller's computer. The buyer's computer sends a receipt advice to the seller's

---

[132]EDI architecture has four layers: the application layer, the standards translation layer, the transport layer, and the physical layer. The application layer describes the business application that underlies the need for EDI. For example, for a procurement application, the underlying application will request price quotes, purchase orders, acknowledgments, and invoices. Typically, the application is firm-specific — customized for the firm using the application. The information at the application level must be converted by the EDI standard layer from a company-specific form to a more universal form so that it can be read by trading partners. There are two competing universal EDI standards: the X.12 standard developed by the American National Standards Institute (ANSI), and EDIFACT developed by United Nations Economic Commission for Europe (UN/ECE), Working Party for the Facilitation of International Trade Procedures. The sending and the receiving computer must use the same format for EDI document exchange. ANSI X.12 transactions include: Vendor Registration (Form 838); Request for Quotation (Form 840); Response to Request for Quotation (Form 843); Purchase Order (Form 850); Purchase Order Acknowledgment (Form 855). KALAKOTA & WHINSTON, *supra* note 63, at 371. ANSI and EDIFACT are working towards compatibility.

The EDI transport layer is concerned with how the standard document will be transmitted to the recipient. Email is being used more and more for such transport. Finally, the physical layer is concerned with the physical transmission over the phone lines.

[133]KALAKOTA & WHINSTON, *supra* note 63, at 339

computer which sends an invoice to the buyer's computer. The buyer's computer sends payment to the seller's computer. These interactions are made through EDI forms and most are generated automatically.

3.7.1.2.1.   Sample EDI applications

3.7.1.2.1.1.   International trade

International trade can generate a lot of paperwork because of the number of participants involved in even simple transactions.[134] Often international trade is structured around freight forwarders which can act as middlemen between shippers and customers. Freight forwarders, which often do not own aircraft or ships, can locate and book space for cargo shipments and can arrange for customs brokers to prepare import customs documentation upon arrival to the final destination. Shippers, airlines, forwarders and customs that are connected by EDI facilitate the transmittal of commercial documentation that helps improve delivery efficiency. For EDI to develop its full potential as a facilitator of electronic commerce, it is vital that EDI invoicing be accepted not just intra-country but also inter-country. Within the European Community, there is still not an acceptance of EDI invoicing in all countries.[135]

3.7.1.2.1.2.   Financial EDI

The use of EDI in financial transactions enables the transmission of payments and remittance information among payer, payee, and their banks. The use of EDI in this context can eliminate the need to issue, mail, and collect checks through the banking system. For payment of suppliers of goods or providers of services, businesses typically use automated clearing houses (ACH's). ACH transfers are used to process high volumes of relatively small

---

[134]It is estimated that at least twelve parties are involved in the simplest international trade transaction. KALAKOTA & WHINSTON, *supra* note 63, at 343.

[135]United Kingdom IFA Branch, *Comments on Electronic Commerce Report* (8 April 1998) (on file with the authors).

payments for settlement within a few days.[136] An ACH typically provides services such as direct payroll deposits and repetitive bill payments.[137] A typical transaction may be as follows. A purchasing corporation might transmit remittance information to its bank to pay a supplier. The bank creates an ACH credit transfer instruction, including the specified payment date, and attaches the appropriate electronic remittance data. The bank then transmits the payment instruction with the remittance data to an ACH operator. After receiving the payment instructions, the ACH operator extracts some of the accounting information and transmits the payment instructions and the remittance data to the seller's bank which transmits a payment advice and the remittance data to the seller-payee.[138]

3.7.1.2.1.3.   Health care and insurance EDI

EDI is an important mainstay in the health care industry as medical providers, patients, and payers (*e.g.,* insurance companies) process claims through electronic networks. For example, using EDI software service providers prepare the necessary forms and submit claims to a value-added network service provider,[139] which edits, sorts, and distributes properly formatted forms to the appropriate payor organizations (*e.g.,* insurance companies). The payor organization's computers can transmit transactions to third-party organizations for additional review, prior to payment. The payor's computers can also generate acceptance/rejection reports, requests for additional information, and interim reports concerning claims status.

---

[136]Electronic Funds Transfers (EFT) offers almost instantaneous transfers between banks.

[137]Examples of an ACH include CHIPS (Clearing House Interbank Payments System) which processes a volume of international dollar transfers. SWIFT (Society for Worldwide Interbank Financial Telecommunications), initiated in Brussels in the 1970's, provides standard EDI formats for funds-transfer instructions.

[138]Sometimes the payment information travels through banks as indicated, while the remittance information travels through a separate network.

[139]A value-added network (VAN) is a communications network that typically facilitates the exchange of EDI messages among partners, providing value-enhancing services such as collection and sorting of information.

As EDI standards develop for the health industry, even greater claims processing efficiencies are achievable.[140]

3.7.1.2.1.4. Manufacturing/retail EDI

In the manufacturing process, EDI has made just-in-time manufacturing a reality. No longer do businesses need to stock thousands of spare parts. Instead, industry needs can be generated with a minimum of notice so that a factory can deliver needed parts to the plant just in time for production. For example, a truck-assembly plant need not maintain a tire-and-rim inventory. Instead one of its tire suppliers receives the plant's manufacturing schedule and its tire-and-rim requirements by EDI. This information was transmitted to a production plant where the required tire assemblies were shipped to the truck-assembly plant eight hours ahead of when needed.[141] Just-in-time manufacturing improves the cash flow of businesses who now can pay for parts and raw materials that will be put to use or sold rather than inventoried.

Similar changes are taking place in retail businesses. Quick response systems enable automatic ordering from suppliers, often beginning with point-of-sale (POS) scanning which results in smaller, more frequent deliveries. For example, Wal-Mart implemented a system in the 1980's where each point-of sale terminal at the register was linked to distribution centers and the headquarters in Arkansas. The system enabled Wal-Mart to reduce inventory costs to 1/4 of its previous level.[142] Individual Wal-Mart stores are able to order merchandise directly from both domestic and overseas suppliers. Restocking time has been cut from an industry average of six weeks to a little more than one day.[143]

Manufacturers, wholesalers and retailers are cooperating to issue standards for better forecasting and restocking known as Collaborative Planning Forecasting Replenishment (CPFR).[144] With CPFR, a retailer and

---

[140]KALAKOTA & WHINSTON, *supra* note 63, at 357-359.

[141]Richards, *The Business Plan,* THE WALL STREET JOURNAL R10 (18 Nov. 1996).

[142]KALAKOTA & WHINSTON, *supra* note 63, at 37.

[143]*Manufacturing and the NII,* http://iitf.doc.gov (1996).

[144]U.S. Department of Commerce, *The Emerging Digital Economy,* Chapter 3, http://www.ecommerce.gov (1998).

supplier post their forecasts for a list of products. Software then compares the forecasts and flags any differences so they can be addressed by planners. It is estimated that CPFR could yield inventory reductions of between $250 and $350 billion across the economy which will lead to savings in materials handling warehousing and general administrative costs.

3.7.1.2.2.   EDI implementation

In order to use EDI, trading partners must agree on which EDI standard to use — ANSI X.12 or UN/EDIFACT, although the two standards are converging. Essentially, EDI messages share a common structure. A single transaction set consists of a business document such as a purchase order. This transaction set is subdivided into data segments which are logical groups of data, such as invoice terms or shipping information. Data elements are individual fields, such as purchase order number or unit price.

3.7.1.2.2.1.   EDI software

EDI software has four layers: business application; internal format conversion; EDI translator; and EDI envelope for document messaging. The business application software generates a document (*e.g.,* an invoice) with all the appropriate information. The applications software sends the invoice to an EDI translator which automatically reformats the invoice into the agreed-upon EDI standard. Translators map the data elements in the business application to the agreed-upon EDI standard. For example, the information on a purchase order must be mapped onto data fields as specified by the EDI standard. The communications layer actually establishes the connection with the other party, usually in one of three ways: direct modem-to-modem connection; limited third-party value-added network; or full-service third-party value-added network. In a direct-dial system, the sender has direct access to the partner's modem through a dial-up or direct connection. Limited VAN's are regional or international communications services that provide basic technical services, such as protocol conversion and data error detection and correction. Full third-party VAN's provide more than mere communications as explained in more detail below. Full-service VAN's may provide electronic mailboxes, security features, and document tracking. The fourth layer of EDI software is an EDI envelope for message transport. A special envelope can differentiate EDI from regular mail.

3.7.1.2.2.2. Value-Added Networks (VAN's)

A VAN is a network that adds value to the data being communicated. The value-added is in the form of services that might include holding EDI messages in electronic mailboxes, supporting protocols that allow interfacing with other VAN's,[145] and providing security. To illustrate, company A may put an EDI message for its trading partner, company B, in the VAN mailbox at a time of its own choosing. The VAN picks up the message and delivers it to company B's mailbox to be picked up by company B at its convenience.[146] Many VAN's are repositioning themselves to provide internet operation, although many companies may not yet trust the internet's security or reliability. Of course, the internet can be used for the direct exchange of EDI messages without relying on a VAN.

3.7.1.3. *Intra-business electronic commerce*

It is not surprising that computer networking has impacted all phases of intra-business operation as it has impacted dealings between businesses or between businesses and customers. Virtually all phases of a business operation, including accounting and finance, management, R & D, marketing and advertising, sales, customer service, engineering, production, logistics, and distribution are affected by networking. For example, Colgate-Palmolive is now using software[147] that can organize and interconnect most tasks of a business, including entering orders, tracking product shipments,

---

[145]*E.g.,* converting ANSI X.12 to EDIFACT.

[146]VAN service providers include AT&T, British Telecom, Cable & Wireless, GEIS, Saturn, and Infonet.

[147]The R/3 software was introduced by SAP AG, a Germany company. Among other companies using the software are: International Business Machines Corp., Chevron Corp., Compaq Computer Corp., and Microsoft Corp.

scheduling production, and updating sales forecasts and balance sheets.[148] When a Colgate-Palmolive technician at a fragrance plant uses ingredients to produce a fragrance, Colgate's computer system adjusts electronic information from inventory figures to shipping schedules to show that ingredients have left the shelf. Managers at soap factories hundreds of miles away can pore through computer data to show that shipment is a step closer to arrival. Estimates are that the new system has cut the time to deliver a customer's order by 40% and working capital has been cut 25%. This is an example of what is sometimes referred to as "just-in-time" manufacturing. It has been estimated that inventory storage might often account for 6% to 30% of sales.[149] Electronic commerce applications seek to reduce these costs by as much as 90%.

In the early 1980's, the automotive industry took a car from concept to mass production in four to six years.[150] Sharing information electronically has allowed designers, engineers, suppliers, manufacturing and assembly personnel to work as a team through computer-aided design (CAD) and computer-aided engineering (CAE) to reduce the automotive cycle to 30 months. Now automotive companies are striving to shorten the cycle to 24 months by setting up teams in different parts of the world and linking them electronically. For example, engineers in Detroit can pass a problem to engineers on their team in India who can respond to their Detroit counterparts by the next business day.

"Data warehousing" and "data mining" are terms that describe the sharing of database information between different departments of a company.[151] Data warehousing systems hold all of a company's data and contain software that can sort and analyze the data (the mining function). For example, Bank of America's data warehouse holds data from 30 disparate corporate mainframes. The data is accessible to 1,500 different users that make 2,800 queries on the system every day.

---

[148]The discussion that follows is taken from Brownlee, *Overhaul*, THE WALL STREET JOURNAL X.12 (18 Nov. 1996).

[149]KALAKOTA & WHINSTON, *supra* note 63, at 35.

[150]U.S. Department of Commerce, *The Emerging Digital Economy*, Chapter 3, http://www.ecommerce.gov (1998).

[151]The discussion that follows is taken from Gomes, *Let's Share*, THE WALL STREET JOURNAL R23 (18 Nov. 1996).

3.7.1.3.1.   Telecommuting

The importance of central offices has diminished for some businesses with the growing improvement of communications networking. Fax machines, telephones, and email all provide communications opportunities. The ability to access shared databases, combined with improving technology that allows supervisors to evaluate the quantity of work done, has made telecommuting possible for all levels of workers. A worker's office is becoming synonymous with the worker's whereabouts.

3.7.1.3.2.   Video conferencing

Video conferencing is possible today but will become more widespread as shared standards are adopted and bandwidth is increased. The quality of video conferencing is largely dependent on the capacity of the transmission lines. It is possible to send both voice and video over ordinary phone lines[152] relatively inexpensively, but such analog phone service provides very poor video quality because the limited speed of an analog phone line is not sufficient to carry the data-heavy video. The result can be grainy, jerky images. In addition the audio and the video cannot be closely synchronized. However, the development of integrated services digital network (ISDN) technology permits much faster transmission over ordinary phone lines which permits acceptable video quality, although not television or movie quality. On faster phone lines, the video conferencing quality would be better still. Point-to-point video conferencing over ISDN lines is possible without any special arrangements (*e.g.*, setting up a special time for the video conferencing) with the phone company. Typically, video conferencing software will allow "whiteboard" capabilities that allow video conferencing participants the ability to jointly edit documents that can be displayed on the participants' monitors.

In addition to point-to-point video conferencing, the internet provides the ability of one-to-many or many-to-many video conferencing. The Multicast Backbone (MBONE) was created in 1992. It is a virtual network

---

[152]Sometimes referred to as plain-old telephone service or POTS.

that shares the same physical network as the internet, but uses a network of special routers that support special protocols needed for video conferencing (IP Multicast). MBONE software makes video conferencing possible over the MBONE network.[153]

3.7.1.3.3.   Virtual corporation

The virtual corporation concept is centered on the idea that advanced communications and networking make it possible for a corporation to contract out most support functions while retaining core functions.[154] In this way, the corporation may virtually disappear, yet carry on significant entrepreneurial activity. For example, when Oy Nokia, a Finnish entity widely known for its cellular phones, wanted to introduce its computer monitors into the United States in 1992, it hired an outside engineer to market, sell, and distribute the products.[155] Along with two independent companies, a marketing and sales firm, and a customer-service and technical support firm, the outside engineer handled all aspects, other than manufacturing, of the computer monitor business in the United States. The ability to communicate easily and constantly permits Nokia to avoid the bureaucratic layers of some larger competitors. Of course, it has always been possible for firms to contract out work while maintaining core functions, but improving communications make it easier to coordinate the outside efforts with the core efforts. The nominal corporation can stay lean while extending its influence through outside relationships.

Virtual corporations may increase their reliance on virtual offices.[156] Virtual office companies rent out space in central city locations. Customers get telephone service, voicemail, and fax. A team of receptionists provides 24-hour service, answering the phone in the lessee's name. The lessee can hire rooms or workspaces. Video conferencing equipment and studios are

---

[153]Another popular video conferencing application is CU-See-Me which provides inexpensive video conferencing but the quality of the transmissions may make the product unsuitable for some business purposes.

[154]DAVIDOW AND MALONE, THE VIRTUAL CORPORATION (1992)

[155]The discussion that follows is taken from King, *The Company We Don't Keep*, THE WALL STREET JOURNAL R22 (18 Nov. 1996).

[156]Strassel, *European Technology: Virtues of Virtual Offices Are Praised by Companies*, WALL STREET J. INTERACTIVE EDITION (19 December 1996).

available for hire. These serviced offices are being used by small companies and by large multinationals such as American Express, Warner Brothers, and Electricity de France, as well.

3.7.2. Intranets

Essentially, an intranet is a private network using the same TCP/IP protocol that is used on the public internet. But where the internet is open to everyone, an intranet is a closed network,[157] only available to specified users who are permitted to logon to the server only if the users are authorized by the network server. For example, a company with offices scattered throughout the world might link those offices through an intranet to facilitate the dissemination of memos, marketing information, training manuals, confidential financial information, etc. An intranet can be connected to the internet so that computers on the intranet have access to resources on the internet but those who logon to the internet would not be able to logon to the intranet unless authorized to do so.

3.7.3. Software agents

3.7.3.1. *Characteristics and properties*

Most computer software is passive — a user initiates an action and the software reacts. For example, the user instructs software to download a file or compute a spreadsheet column. Emerging software is capable of performing tasks based on a general set of standards issued by the user proactively. The software acts as an agent of the user.[158] In the workplace, human agents might be divided into office-bound workers and mobile field

---

[157]An intranet is sometimes referred to as a local area network — LAN — or if spread over a wider area, a wide area network — WAN. Traditional LANs offered by Novell, IBM and others used proprietary protocols that limited hardware and software choices and lacked scalability that would enable an extended network. Using the standardized TCP/IP protocol, an intranet possesses scalability and the flexibility to use a wide variety of hardware and software.

[158]Computer programmers working on artificial intelligence (AI) coined the term "software agent" in the early 1960's to describe programs that act on behalf of people. KALAKOTA & WHINSTON, *supra* note 63, at 598.

89

agents.[159] Software agents can also be divided into static agents that reside on a principal's computer and mobile software agents that can travel to a remote location. An example of a static agent would be a mail agent that operates in the background, processing mail arrivals. In contrast, a mobile agent can be sent over the internet to a remote location where it can then carry out its tasks. For instance, a user might send a mobile software agent to a financial service to monitor the fluctuations of a particular stock, instructing the agent to sell if the stock reaches a specified price. The agent might attach itself to the server for an extended period of time before executing the sale. Similarly, an agent might travel to an on-line travel agency to search for the least expensive round-trip fare to a selected destination. After purchasing the ticket, the agent returns to the user's computer, entering the flight information in the user's scheduling software. The ability of software agents to conclude contracts binding the user (*i.e.*, the principal) may have implications under international tax law.

An intelligent software agent has a variety of capabilities. It can carry out user-defined tasks autonomously once the conditions for carrying out the tasks are set forth by the user. Those tasks can be executed immediately or at a later time when the user may not be present. An intelligent agent may have the ability to learn and incorporate the user's preferences over time in its execution of the assigned tasks. For example, an intelligent chess program may learn from its losses and not repeat losing moves when the same situation arises in the future. An agent may learn from observation, user feedback (*e.g.*, never perform that act again) or from training (*e.g.*, user provides the agent a list of hypothetical situations and the action to be taken). Not only can an intelligent agent learn, it can cooperate with users and other agents. For example, a seller's agent may be able to work with a buyer's agent to negotiate a contract of purchase. An intelligent agent can reason (*i.e.*, choose among different strategies) if provided with rules for handling information received.

Software agents might be grouped into three categories: event monitors; work-flow assistants; and data gathering and retrieval agents.[160] An event monitor is an agent which watches an environment and offers a user in that environment help or instruction. Within a company, an event mon-

---

[159]*Id.* at 596.

[160]KALAKOTA & WHINSTON, *supra* note 63, at 621.

itor might enable central management to monitor point-of-sale activities to determine whether a network is functioning smoothly. Unlike event monitors, work-flow assistants can often act without direct instructions from a user. A work-flow assistant that had decision-making capabilities might be authorized to conclude and digitally sign a contract if certain parameters are met or to track and report the status of a shipment or to provide sophisticated customer service advice.

3.7.3.2. *Technology*

A software agent is a program that typically includes the following embedded features.[161] It contains the owner's name, billing information, and electronic addresses. In some cases, agents will be charged for services performed by billing the owner. The duration of the agent will be programmed. Some agents exist for a short time and are rendered inactive after a task is complete. Others might have a longer duration. The agent's goals and measures of success (*e.g.,* within the next day, find a supplier that does not charge more than $150 per unit) must be made clear. An agent will also have topic information attributes which provide information such as boundaries of the agent's task and what resources might be called on. This information may allow a server to decide whether or not to service the agent. Finally, the agent may provide background information, indicating what data the agent understands or what languages it can understand.[162]

Traditional agents operate from the client by sending a request to a server for information and then waiting for a response.[163] In order to perform its task, the agent must be in connection with the server constantly or establish connection periodically. This is inefficient, particularly where the information on the server is being updated regularly. Remote programming offers a more efficient agency model. Instead of keeping a connection open or logging in periodically, an agent can be uploaded to a server where it resides while completing its tasks. The principal can disconnect from the

---

[161]*Id.* at 604-605.

[162]Agent software is often written in Telescript, or Safe-Tcl, programming languages intended for created software agents.

[163]The technology behind this model is synchronous communication-oriented remote procedure call (RPC).

server and complete other tasks. When the agent has completed the assigned tasks, it can dial-up the principal, deposit information on the principal's computer, and notify the principal that the tasks are completed.

Mobile software agents are a lot like computer viruses. Both are software programs that migrate to a remote computer and execute. However, software agents operate by invitation only and must present correct credentials before access to a remote computer is permitted. There are two sides of the security issue with respect to mobile software agents. The principal must be confident that an agent will not run amuck. For example, if the agent is directed to purchase a commodity when the price hits $30, the principal may not want a purchase to be made every time the price hits $30, which may be quite often if the commodity fluctuates in price. Controls can be built in that limit the resources that an agent can commit or limit the time frame. From the remote host's perspective, there are also security issues. Like a human agent that is going to seek access to confidential data, a mobile software agent must present to the server credentials that verify the identity of the principal, proof that the agent has not been tampered with after it was sent by the principal and proof as to the scope of the agent's authority.

3.7.4. Payment systems

The success and future of electronic commerce is interwoven with the development of electronic payment systems. If payment mechanisms cause a bottleneck in the electronic commerce environment, then many of the advantages of networked commerce will be negated. Traditional payment methods such as checks or bank drafts can take days to process and can disrupt the mercantile process. Moreover, the delay along with the processing costs make traditional payment methods unsuitable for micropayments — payments for small amounts of information made available by a vendor (*e.g.*, a report or an answer to a question).

Before electronic payments are widely accepted, several issues must be addressed. A user making an electronic payment expects privacy — particularly with respect to electronic cash payments. Along with privacy, security is a major user-concern. In a secure payment system, the sender must be identified and the message authenticated. Identification is the process of verifying that the sender of a message (*e.g.*, a digital payment) is who it is stated to be in the message. At an automated teller machine (ATM), the use of a personal identification number performs the function of identifying the ATM card user as the rightful user. If a person signs a check, the handwriting serves to identify that the signer is who he/she claims to be. Authentication is the process of verifying that the sender of a message and that the message itself has not been changed. Digital signatures can perform the authentication function as explained below. In order to ensure security, both parties must be sure that the other party cannot disavow a transaction. Nonrepudiation is the quality that prevents anyone from denying that they sent data or received data when they, in fact, did. Issues concerning standards for electronic payments and the design of user-friendly payment interfaces also have to be worked out.

What follows is an introduction to four different types of electronic payments: electronic cash; smart cards; electronic checks; and credit cards. The security measures that make electronic payments possible (as well as other sensitive transmissions) are discussed after the different forms of electronic payment are considered.

Electronic cash (e-cash) systems differ in implementation, but any electronic cash system must have the following properties: monetary value, interoperability, storability and retrievability, and security.[164] Monetary value is present if the electronic cash is backed by hard currency, a bank-certified cashier's check, or bank-authorized credit. To be interoperable, electronic cash must be exchangeable for goods, services, paper cash, other electronic cash, lines of credit, or any purpose for which money is used. Interoperability depends on acceptance of electronic cash by an international clearinghouse because parties to most transactions will not be using the same bank. The ability to store and retrieve enables customers to use electronic cash from home, the office or while traveling. For example, electronic cash might be stored on a computer or in an electronic wallet. Finally, electronic cash should not be easy to alter or copy while being stored or exchanged. Procedures must also be in place to verify that electronic cash is spent only once. Otherwise there may be multiple claimants for the underlying cash. The security features that affect electronic cash also affect other data transmissions (*e.g.*, contracts, confidential memoranda). They will be discussed below.

---

[164]Okamoto & Ohta, *Universal Electronic Cash*, PROCEEDINGS OF CRYPTO '91 (1991); KALAKOTA & WHINSTON, *supra* note 63, at 301.

The use of electronic cash in an electronic commerce transaction might work as follows. A customer would obtain cash from an on-line bank. To do this, a customer will have set up an account with the bank. When a customer wants to withdraw electronic cash, the customer's computer software generates a secure, digitally-signed software withdrawal note which is transmitted to the bank. The bank debits the customer's account, digitally signs the note and transmits the digitally-signed note to the customer. The bank's signature commits the bank to back the note with hard currency. Both the customer and the merchant can verify that the bank's signature is authentic. It is possible to withdraw electronic cash in a manner that allows anonymous spending. That is, neither the bank nor anyone else need know how the money was spent or who spent it. Electronic cash can offer the same anonymity as paper cash.

Once the customer receives the bank's transmission, the electronic cash is stored on the customer's computer. The customer can then spend the electronic cash at any on-line store that accepts that electronic cash, without having to open a store account or reveal credit card information. Upon receipt of the ordered goods or services (or proof of shipment), a customer can transmit the bank-signed note to the merchant. Once the merchant has verified the bank's signature, the electronic cash can be stored on the merchant's computer and later deposited into the electronic clearinghouse.[165] Eventually, the cash that was debited from the customer's account is credited to the merchant's account and the bank's database is updated to show that the note was spent. This updating is necessary to prevent double spending.

The use of electronic cash internationally is still in the very early stages. Eventually, if a customer in one country wants to use electronic cash to purchase goods or services in another country, the customer will be able to have the bank debit his/her account in one currency, receive and spend the electronic cash, and the merchant in another country will be able to convert the electronic cash into a deposit in the local currency. Presumably, the risk of currency fluctuation can be placed on the customer or the merchant, depending on the transaction. For example, if the customer withdraws $100 of electronic cash, the bank could be instructed to immediately

---

[165]Depending on the size of the transaction, the merchant may want to verify that the e-cash has not already been spent by checking with a third party (*e.g.,* the purchaser's bank) that tracks the serial numbers on the e-cash note.

convert the debited $100 to yen which would be credited to the Japanese merchant's account upon presentation of the electronic cash. Alternatively, the transaction could be structured so that the Japanese merchant receives the yen-equivalent of the debited $100 at the time of presentation.

Smart cards are credit and debit cards that contain wafer thin microprocessors capable of storing more information than the traditional magnetic stripe. Smart cards have been widely used in countries such as France, Germany, Denmark, and Japan to pay for public phone calls and transportation. While there are a variety of smart cards, debit smart cards, referred to as electronic purses, electronic wallets, etc. will play a significant role in on-line transactions. The smart card can be loaded with money at an ATM machine, through a special, inexpensive telephone, in a smart-card reader attached to a personal computer, or in an electronic wallet that has dial-up capabilities. As money is spent from the smart card, the user can see the remaining balance on a balance-reading device. When the smart card is empty, it can be refilled with more money. If a customer wants to make an on-line purchase, the customer can put the smart card in the card reader attached to the customer's computer and send the purchase price to the merchant's computer.

Unlike electronic cash and smart debit cards which are real-time payment methods, electronic checks serve as a credit-based payment system. A customer establishes a bank account which enables him/her to write electronic checks that can be sent using email or by some other transport mechanism when a customer purchases goods or services on-line. On receiving the check, the merchant presents it to a third-party accounting server that verifies the digital signature. The accounting server then forwards the check through the banking system in much the same way as a paper check. The electronic check will bear a digital signature.

Traditional credit cards also enable internet purchases. On-line credit card payments might take three forms: unencrypted; encrypted; and third-party verification.[166] Providing an unencrypted credit card number over the internet raises security issues. Programs that scan internet traffic for credit card numbers can easily intercept the transmission of a credit card number. Also, a vendor is unable to authenticate that the person using the credit card is the owner. With encryption, the customer gains a level of security and can send the merchant a digital signature that allows authentica-

---

[166]KALAKOTA & WHINSTON, *supra* note 63, at 317.

tion of the user. Upon receipt, the vendor can verify the information with the customer's bank which can authorize the transaction. Third-party verification may offer a means of lowering transaction costs that would make microtransactions[167] feasible.[168] Much of the process can be automated. Essentially, the customer clicks on a payment icon on the web page displaying the goods or a description of the services to be purchased. Clicking on the icon sends purchase information to a third-party server and directs the customer's browser to the third-party server which authenticates the user by asking for an account number and other identification information. The payment server redirects the customer's browser back to the product page while providing the merchant's computer with proof of payment. The merchant's computer then completes the transaction, arranging for shipment or downloading.

3.7.5. Security issues

If the information superhighway is to be widely used for commercial transactions, security must be established. A security threat is a circumstance, condition, or event with the potential to cause economic hardship to data or network resources in the form of destruction, disclosure, modification of data, denial of service, and/or fraud, waste, and abuse.[169] Security issues can be broken down into two categories: client/server security and transaction security. Client/server security is necessary to make sure that only valid users or software programs have access to information resources such as databases. Transaction security ensures the privacy and confidentiality of the transmission as it travels the information superhighway.

Client/server security is an important concern for commercial enterprises. While access to the internet may facilitate business operations in ways not previously possible, that access also raises the risk of security breaches. Unauthorized persons (*i.e.*, hackers) can break into a server and destroy or alter data. They also can deny service to others by overloading

---

[167]These are very small transactions, such as downloading a file for $.25 or renting a video for $1.00.

[168]Companies like First Virtual (http://www.fv.com) and Open Market (http://www.openmarket.com) are already providing third-party payment services on the internet.

[169]KALAKOTA & WHINSTON, *supra* note 63, at 177.

the server with requests for data that cause the server to stop functioning (*i.e.,* the server crashes). There are a variety of methods used to reduce security threats. Backing up data regularly does not prevent security breaches but does limit the damage if a security breach occurs. Use of ordinary passwords or biometric passwords (*e.g.,* fingerprints, voice recognition) offer some security protection but can be unwieldy, expensive and still be subject to compromise. Software programs offer protection against malicious code (*e.g.,* computer viruses), but these programs do not prevent unauthorized entry into a computer system. Moreover, these programs must be updated regularly to keep up with ever new and sophisticated malicious code.

In addition to these security measures, a company can set up a firewall (*i.e.,* a software barrier) between the outside world (*i.e.,* the internet) and the company network. A firewall is software running on a computer that sits between the corporate network and the internet. The software allows insiders to have complete access to the outside world but grants outside access selectively based on factors such as login name, password, or IP address. Thus, a firewall acts as a filter.[170]

In order for electronic commerce to become a significant mechanism, participants must be assured that transmissions are secure. If electronic cash is to become widespread, users will demand that transactions be private. Privacy concerns not only apply to payment techniques but also to other communications over any public network. Encryption is the process of disguising the substance of a communication whether that communication is a contract, a letter containing personal information, a digital payment, etc. For example, if a user stops at an automated teller machine to withdraw cash, the user's personal identification number (PIN) as well as the withdrawal amount must be transmitted to the user's home bank. To

---

[170]In practice, firewalls range from simple logging systems to hardened firewall hosts. A logging system simply records all network traffic flowing through the firewall. It does not prevent unauthorized entry. An IP packet screening router filters incoming data packets, denying packets based on specified screening rules. A proxy application gateway is a special server on a firewall machine. A proxy is a program that knows how to get through a firewall. It carries requests from a user's browser and the response from a remote server through a firewall. A proxy can limit client and/or server access to specified hosts and otherwise regulate access through the firewall. Finally, a hardened firewall host is a machine that requires both inside and outside users to connect to secure applications on the firewall machine before connecting further. These firewalls are intended to prevent unauthorized logins from remote computers.

make sure that no one can alter the message or obtain the user's PIN number even if the message is intercepted while being transmitted to the bank, the automated teller machine encrypts the message using a "key." A "key" is a set of rules for changing characters. Applying the key changes a user's plaintext into cyphertext which is transmitted to the user's home bank. There, the cyphertext is decrypted back into plain text, the information is processed, and the appropriate response is sent back to the local automated teller machine.

Private key encryption is a system where both the sender and the recipient of a communication share a key which must be kept private. The sender can encrypt the message with the key and the recipient can decrypt the message with the same key. The difficulty with private key encryption is that the key must be distributed to the recipient or recipients while still remaining private. This provides the opportunity for security to be compromised. In the business context, it probably is not practical for vendors and customers to use private key encryption since the vendor would need separate keys for each customer and would have to get the key to a customer in a secure manner.

In a public key system, a mathematical process generates two mathematically related keys for each individual. A message encrypted with one key can be decrypted with the other key. Depending on the use to which the encryption is to be put, either key can be the encrypting or decrypting key. If a customer wishes to send an order to a supplier that can only be read by the supplier, the order will be encrypted by the customer with the *supplier's* public key. Once that is accomplished, the order is fully secure because it can be decrypted only with the supplier's private key, a key only the supplier has. If the supplier then wishes to send an acknowledgment back to the customer, the supplier might encrypt that acknowledgment with its own private key. This acknowledgment can then be decrypted by the customer with the supplier's public key, thereby establishing that the acknowledgment truly came from the supplier. If the acknowledgment must both authenticate the supplier's identity and be secure from prying eyes, it will be doubly encrypted, first with the supplier's private key (to authenticate) and second with the customer's public key (to make the content of acknowledgment available only to the customer). For example, suppose that A wants to send a communication to B. The communication might be a contract, or a digital payment, or a confidential business memo. A would use B's public key to encrypt the communication. B would then use B's private key to convert the cyphertext into plaintext. The major advantage of a public key system over a private key system is that the public key can and will be made public without compromising the security. A communication that is encrypted with the recipient's public key can be decrypted only with the recipient's private key. Accordingly, a business could publish its public key on the internet or in other directories (like a phone book).

If a message is encrypted with the recipient's public key, the message is secure (*i.e.*, can only be read by the recipient), but the recipient has no way of verifying that the sender is who the sender claims to be. Anyone with access to the recipient's public key could be the sender. Encrypting a message with one's own *private* key does not make the encrypted message secure (because it can be decrypted by anyone willing to look-up the sender's pubic key) but does provide proof that the message in fact was sent by the nominal sender. Using one's private key in this way is called a "digital signature." A digital signature can authenticate the communication which is crucial if commerce is to be widely conducted on the internet. Digital signatures also can guarantee that contract terms are not altered or that digital money cannot be forged.

Suppose that A is sending a contract to B using email. First, A uses a "hash" one-way function to create a message digest. A hash function is a computation that takes variable size input (such as a contract) and returns a fixed size output (*e.g.*, a 128-bit number) called a message digest which appears at the end of the communication. A one-way function is a computation that is significantly easier to perform than to undo. For example, breaking an egg can be thought of as a one-way function. The 128-bit message digest cannot be turned back into the message text. The message digest can be thought of as a fingerprint of the message. No two messages will have the same message digest. Even a small change in the message text, such as an extra space, would result in a significantly different message digest. Once the message digest is created, A encrypts both the original message and the message digest with A's private key. When B receives the communication, B decrypts the message and the message digest with A's public key. Then B hashes the decrypted message digest using the same hash function that A used. B compares the message digest produced with the message digest obtained by decrypting A's digital signature. If the two message digests match, the message has not been altered; if the message digests do not match, the message was altered.

While a comparison of message digests allows the recipient to be sure that the message was sent without alteration, it might be possible for someone to impersonate the sender, using the impersonator's private/public keys but claiming that they belong to the impersonated sender. That is, suppose an imposter publishes a public key in some directory of public keys, falsely representing that it is the public key for the CEO of R Corp. Until this fraud is uncovered and exposed, the imposter will be able to send messages that can be "authenticated" as coming from the CEO of R Corp. because public key authentication does not actually authenticate the identity of the sender but merely proves that the sender owns the private key that is paired to some specific public key. Accordingly, for public key encryption to fully authenticate a message, the public key must be verified as belonging to its true owner. In order to prevent such impersonation, a recipient might demand a digital certificate from a trusted third party. A digital certificate is a document which attests to the identity and the public key of the person who digitally signed the message.[171]

Consider a hypothetical transaction where a purchaser, P, wants to send a vendor, V, digital money in exchange for goods and services purchased over the internet.[172] Using a software program, P's computer generates a very large random number. This random number and a withdrawal request is then encrypted by P using the bank's public key. This first encryption ensures that only the recipient bank can determine the amount of money that P wishes to withdraw. The output of this first encryption is then encrypted a second time, but this time using *P's* private key. This second encryption allows the bank to verify that the withdrawal in fact is made by P. This doubly encrypted message is then transmitted from P to P's bank, where the message is first decrypted using P's public key (to verify P's identity) and then decrypted using the bank's private key (to reveal the value of the withdrawal).[173] The bank also records the random number generated by P for use as a tracking number.

The bank then encrypts the random number initially generated by P as well as a dollar amount signifying a withdrawal using its private key. This

---

[171]In some cases, there may be a need for certification hierarchies. That is, the certifying authority may need to have its public key certified by a higher certification authority.

[172]Chaum, *Achieving Electronic Privacy*, SCIENTIFIC AMERICAN 96 (Aug. 1992), reprinted at http://www.digicash.com/publish/sciam.html.

[173]The electronic cash withdrawn from the bank can be stored on P's hard drive or on a "smart card." P might insert the card in a card reader attached to P's computer and transmit the payment to V in this manner. Such a card could be used for everyday payments (*e.g.*, for a pay phone).

message can be verified as a valid withdrawal authorization by anyone willing to look up the bank's public key. When P spends this electronic cash by transferring it to V, V can present the message to the bank for payment. The bank will use its public key to verify that the withdrawal authorization is legitimate and it will cross off the random number from its tracking list, thus ensuring that if a duplicate of the message is presented, payment will not be made a second time.

This electronic cash transaction is secure but not private: the bank's list of tracking numbers allows it to determine how P spent the money. To fully substitute for cash, an electronic cash system must provide a secure method of withdrawal and payment in such a way that no particular withdrawal can be linked to any particular payment. This can be accomplished using a *double-blind* method of public key encryption.

A double-blind transaction would go as follows. Once again P's software generates a large random number that will be used as a tracking number by the bank, but this time that random number is multiplied by another large number (called the blinding factor). This product is then transmitted to the bank by P along with a withdrawal request — doubly encrypted as before, first with the bank's public key and a second time with P's private key.

Once again the bank decrypts the transmission, records the withdrawal, and retransmits the request encrypted with its private key. As before, this retransmitted message is used as the electronic cash and can be accepted by V because the bank's digital signature can be verified. However, before spending the money, P divides out the blinding factor, leaving only P's initial random number in the encrypted message.[174] Thus, when the electronic cash is presented for payment the bank can verify its own digital signature and record the newly-revealed random number.[175] Double pay-

---

[174]In essence, P has put a withdrawal request with a serial number known only to P inside an envelope with the amount to be withdrawn stated on the envelope itself. After withdrawing the cash from P's account, the bank embosses the envelope and message within with its digital signature which also specifies the amount of the withdrawal. P then discards the envelope and uses the request within as the electronic cash. When the request is presented for payment by V, the bank recognizes and honors its embossed signature, even though the bank has never before seen the actual request and cannot determine who originally sent the request.

[175]The crucial element in this double-blind technique is that P can divide out the blinding factor while leaving the bank's digital signature intact. Because of the particu-

ment is avoided because any duplicate of the electronic cash will contain the same random number which the bank can determine has already cleared. From the bank's perspective the tracking number is created when the electronic cash is first presented for payment, so there is no way to associate the tracking number with the prior withdrawal by P.[176]

---

lar mathematical algorithm used to implement public key encryption, decryption, and division *commute* — that is, verifying the bank's digital signature and dividing out the blinding factor — can be done in either order without affecting the resulting message.

[176]More information regarding the internet and its infrastructure, world wide web, digital cash, and electronic commerce (and how it works) may be found in the following: Abrams & Doernberg, *How Electronic Commerce Works,* Tax Notes Int'l 1573 (12 May 1997); Temple, *Electronic Commerce Using Ecash,* Visual Developer 93 (Feb/Mar 1997); *The Internet,* Wall Street Journal Reports R1 (9 Dec. 1996); Lynch & Lundquist, Digital Money: The New Era of Internet Commerce (1996); Udell, *Your Business Needs the Web,* 21 Byte 68 (1996); Gleick, *Dead as a Dollar,* The New York Times Magazine 26 (16 June 1996); Blake & Tiedrich, *The National Information Infrastructure Initiative and the Emergence of the Electronic Superhighway,* http:\\www.law.indiana.edu/fclj/v46/no3/blake.html#1A; Coopers & Lybrand, Global Telecoms Tax Profiles (1997).

4

Applying Current International Tax Rules to Electronic Commerce

This section considers the application of existing international tax norms outlined in section 2 to income arising from electronic commerce described in section 3. In applying existing international tax norms, this section first analyzes income tax issues, focusing on source-based issues and residence-based issues. Then, the application of VAT principles to electronic commerce is explored. The discussion of source-based taxation focuses on the characterization and assignment issues raised by electronic commerce with respect to business profits, income from services and royalties. While these source-based issues are important, the spread of electronic commerce also raises important issues concerning existing residence principles. For example, determining the place of effective management may be complicated by the fact that a management team can make joint decisions while geographically separated. To some extent, this is not a new development, but it has become more feasible as a result of recent technological changes. Finally, an issue that bridges both source-based and residence-based taxation is the treatment of controlled foreign corporations. The ability to avoid both residence and source-based taxation through the use of tax havens will increase through the use of technology in electronic commerce. This section considers some of the implications under existing controlled foreign corporation legislation.

The discussion of the intersection of electronic commerce and income tax principles focuses primarily on the implications for content providers — those who use the internet to sell goods and services. There is also some discussion of the implications for internet service providers —

those who provide telecommunications services and internet access. The VAT discussion that follows the income tax analysis highlights the particular difficulties of applying the VAT to telecommunications companies, including internet service providers, as well as the application of VAT principles to nonresidents selling goods and services over the internet. While the United States does not currently employ a VAT, the individual US states have extensive sales and use tax systems. The issues involved in applying these systems to transactions involving electronic commerce are analogous to those involved in applying a VAT. Some of the US state problems are briefly discussed below.

4.1. GENERAL PRINCIPLES

4.1.1. Blurring of geographical categories

Even before the advent of electronic commerce, it was not always easy to determine where income arose. Countries might differ over whether the presence of a facility, the location of customers, the passage of title or a number of other factors determine where income arises. Over the years, and with the help of the OECD Model Convention, some of the rough edges concerning source rules have been smoothed out. But with the growth of the internet, income is being generated in new ways that raise difficult source issues. For example, if a nonresident company generates income through a sale arising out of a web page that is accessed in another country, what is the source of the sales income?

While geographical issues have always posed problems for developing international tax norms, many of the issues are marginal and not part of mainstream commerce. For example, catalog companies have existed as part of the world of commerce for many years. But it probably is not good tax policy to design tax rules around marginal situations. Consequently, most countries that provide a customer base for catalog sales do not attempt to collect any income tax generated by such sales, even though a nonresident company may produce substantial income, even in the absence of a permanent establishment. However, the technological changes that give rise to electronic commerce have the potential to make marginal behavior mainstream. Companies that had not historically operated as catalog or mail order companies now through a presence on the internet can generate substantial sales. When the marginal becomes mainstream, that pattern of commerce can no longer be ignored.

4.1.2. Blurring of income categories

Traditionally, countries have developed different taxing rules for different types of income. For example, the rules for determining the territorial right to tax income from services may be different from the rules for determining the territorial right to tax royalties. Similarly the rules for determining the territorial authority to tax income from sales may be different from the rules for exercising territorial taxing authority over royalties. Such distinctions, difficult to make in the best of times, become even more problematical in light of electronic commerce. For example, a consumer might pay for the right to download computer software from a software vendor's server. Whether the payment for the software is considered to be a royalty for licensing the use of the software, a rental payment for leasing the electronic equivalent of tangible property, a payment for the performance of services embodied in the software, or the cost of purchasing an asset may be difficult to discern and may hinge on precisely what rights the consumer acquires.

4.2. INCOME TAX

In general, a country exercises jurisdiction for legal purposes based on either *nationality* or *territoriality*. A territorial connection justifies the exercise of taxing jurisdiction because a taxpayer can be expected to share the costs of running a country which makes possible the production of income, its maintenance and investment, and its use through consumption. The principle of territoriality applies with respect to *persons* and *objects* (*i.e.*, income). Territorial jurisdiction over a *person* (*i.e.*, residence) is analytically similar to jurisdiction based on *nationality* and will be discussed below.[177]

Even if a person is not a citizen or resident of a country, that country

---

[177]In both cases it is the connection of the person to a country that justifies taxing jurisdiction. In the case of nationality, that connection is a legal one (*e.g.*, citizenship or incorporation). In the case of territorial jurisdiction over a person, the connection is factual (*e.g.*, whether that person is actually resident in a particular country).

may assert territorial tax jurisdiction over income deriving from within its territory. This is sometimes referred to as "source" jurisdiction because the source of the income is within a country. For example, a country may impose a tax on business profits of a nonresident earned within that country. Investment income, including dividends, interest, royalties, and rent, may also be subject to tax in the country in which such income arises.[178]

4.2.1. Application of traditional source rules to electronic commerce

Whether the growth of electronic commerce will render traditional source-based taxation unusable as a taxing norm is open to question. Source-based taxation principles have been developed in an era when commerce was typically conducted through a "bricks and mortar" presence in a country. The rise of electronic commerce throws open source-based principles to re-examination. This section considers the application of existing tax principles to various types of electronic commerce income. Although no one example can capture the range of tax issues raised by electronic commerce, an electronic commerce hypothetical will serve as a reference point for the discussion that follows.

---

[178]The taxation of income based on *territorial* jurisdiction generally takes one of two forms. A country typically asserts full jurisdiction over business profits generated within that country by a nonresident (and in the case of the United States a noncitizen), taxing those profits in the same manner as if they were earned by a resident of that country. Expenses associated with generating such income are normally deductible. Non-business, investment income, such as dividends, interest, royalties, and rent, typically is subject to limited jurisdiction. Often such income is taxed by a country in which a payer resides on a gross basis (*i.e.,* no deductions permitted) at rates ranging from 0 to 30%. The lower rates that often apply to such income when compared with business profits reflect, in part, the fact that the territorial connection for a fullblown business within a jurisdiction is often more significant than the territorial connection for an investment where the only connection for the investor in that jurisdiction may be that payer's residence. However, it should also be noted that a low tax rate on gross income may in fact result in a high tax rate on net income. Suppose country A imposes a 30% tax on $100 of royalty income earned by a resident of country B from a license with a country A licensee. If the country B resident incurs $60 of expenses to produce the $100 of gross income, the effective tax rate in country A is 75% (*i.e.,* a $30 tax on $40 of net income).

4.2.1.1. Electronic commerce hypothetical

Suppose a country R resident (R Corp.) is a retailer selling a wide variety of goods and/or services. R Corp. is contemplating entering the market for country S customers. R Corp. plans to have no offices, warehouses, factories, or other facilities in country S. No employees of R Corp. will work in country S. However, residents of country S will be able to purchase goods from R Corp. by logging on to R Corp.'s web site on the internet. In order to establish an internet presence, R Corp. arranges with an internet service provider (RISP Corp.) to establish a connection to the internet. R Corp. might maintain its own web server which is connected to RISP Corp., lease space on RISP Corp.'s server, or lease space on a third-party's server that is connected to the internet. R Corp. might maintain the web server in country S, in country R, or in some third country with low tax rates.

R Corp. is contemplating several different ways of providing internet access for country S customers. Of course, once R Corp. has set up a server with an IP address, R Corp. customers may choose an internet service provider which enables access to all IP addresses on the internet. Having gained access, the customers are free to select R Corp.'s internet address (*e.g.*, http://www.rcorp.com), thereby accessing R Corp.'s web site. Alternatively (or additionally), R Corp. may make arrangements with an on-line service provider that provides internet access to customers in country S to prominently feature the R Corp. cybermall to users who log on to the on-line provider. The on-line service provider may either arrange for its own local telephone numbers in country S directly from the telecommunications companies or sublease local access numbers from third-party vendors.[179]

Once a customer has logged on to the internet, the customer can browse R Corp.'s cybermall. Upon selection of the products to be purchased, a customer can click on a payment icon that either transfers electronic cash from the customer to R Corp. or provides the necessary credit (or debit) card information to consummate the sale. When payment is complete, R Corp. permits the downloading of any products or services

---

[179]R Corp. may also directly lease lines from the country S telecommunications company and establish a local access number that will enable customers to make a local call that directly connects to the R Corp. server, rather than accessing it through the internet.

that are downloadable. For example, computer software, films, books, and other data might be downloaded. Similarly, if the payment is for services, a videoconference might be established between the customer and R Corp.'s service personnel. If the items ordered are not downloadable, R Corp. makes shipping arrangements, and the customer may download the payment receipt and the shipping information. R Corp. generates substantial revenues from country S customers in this manner.

Many of the customers in country S connect to the internet through ZISP Corp., an internet service provider that is a resident of country Z. In country S, ZISP Corp. has established a point-of-presence ("POP") network. A typical POP along that network may consist of a leased room with modems and switching/routing equipment. Typically, there is no need for any employees to be present. Problems with software can generally be addressed from a remote location. In the event of a problem requiring service personnel, ZISP Corp. may send one of its employees or hire an independent country S technician.

A customer can access the internet by dialing a local phone number (using a wired or wireless connection) or using a direct connection (*e.g.,* a T1 line[180] or a cable modem). The initial connection is provided by the customer's telecommunications provider and paid for by the customer. This initial connection is essentially an "I want to get on the internet" message. Once this initial connection is made, ZISP Corp. uses telecommunication services perhaps purchased from a long distance carrier to send the message to ZISP Corp.'s hub which generally consists of high-speed data transmission equipment. Alternatively, ZISP Corp. may maintain a dedicated line that it has leased from a telecommunications company between the POP and its hub. The customer's message is then routed through the telecommunications system to ZISP Corp.'s main operations center. At the main operations center, a customer's identification and password are authenticated.[181] ZISP Corp. then sends to the customer a "you are connected" message back through its hub, assigning an internet protocol address. The customer then might send a "show me R Corp.'s web page" message through the POP through the hub to a central connection point (*e.g.,* a Network Access Point (NAP)) for access to the internet. A NAP is operated by

---

[180]In some parts of the world the terminology may be an E-1 line.

[181]Authentication may not be necessary if the customer is using a direct connection.

a transmission carrier as an electronic interchange where electronic traffic is routed to its final destination.

This electronic commerce hypothetical focuses on the tax implications arising out of the activities of two taxpayers — R Corp., which uses the internet to distribute its content (*e.g.*, goods or services accessed through its web page) to potential customers, and ZISP Corp., which provides internet service to customers, allowing them to access the content that companies like R Corp. make available.[182] In the discussion that follows, the primary focus is on the income generated by R Corp. However, the tax implications of ZISP Corp.'s activities in country S are also considered.[183]

4.2.1.2. Business profits

4.2.1.2.1. Problems presented

4.2.1.2.1.1. Where is income generated

R Corp. is generating income from country S customers — income made possible perhaps by the political, economic and social environment of country S, but R Corp. may have very little or no physical presence in country S. If S is to assert the authority to tax R Corp. on the income generated in country S, what is the basis for exercising such taxing jurisdiction? Possible bases for exercising jurisdiction might include: (a) the location of the customer base; (b) where the purchase contract is concluded; (c) the transmission of bits from the R Corp. server to a customer's browser in response to a customer's request; (d) the use of the phone lines and telecommunications infrastructure; (e) the presence of R Corp.'s internet service provider (RISP Corp.); (f) the activities of agents at the telecommunications company or RISP Corp.

---

[182]The electronic commerce hypothetical also raises tax issues with respect to other taxpayers, such as the telecommunications companies, banks, and software companies (providing for secure digital cash transactions). The tax issues involving these taxpayers are not explored in detail.

[183]For an analyses of similar hypotheticals, *see Taxation of Internet Trading*, 25 Tax Planning Int'l Rev. 1 (Feb. 1998) (analysis of internet trading under the laws of United Kingdom, Ireland, Italy, Germany, Spain, the Netherlands and Switzerland) Teo, *Taxation of the Internet: An Australian Perspective*, 1 Tax Planning Int'l: Asia-Pacific Focus 13 (Feb. 1998).

Traditionally, in order for country S to assert taxing authority, it would be necessary for R Corp. to have a physical presence in country S (*e.g.*, an office, retail outlet) and for the income to be connected to that physical presence (*i.e.*, attributable to that physical presence). In the absence of a physical presence, country S might assert taxing authority on the basis of the activities of agents operating in that country on behalf of R Corp. Under these principles, the location of the customer base would normally be irrelevant for establishing authority to impose an income tax. If the only presence of R Corp. in country S were the presence of customers, under generally shared international income taxing principles country S would not have authority to tax R Corp. on its income generated by those customer purchases.[184] Similarly, no physical presence is established merely by the fact that the contracts are concluded in country S. Furthermore, it may be difficult to determine where a contract is concluded in an on-line digital transaction, and the place of contract in any event may be subject to easy manipulation. The transmission of bits (*e.g.*, sending an electronic image of an HTML page from the server in country R to the customer's client computer in country S) is not normally the type of physical presence sufficient to trigger taxing jurisdiction in country S; bits are no more than electrical impulses. If the bits themselves do not provide sufficient physical presence, perhaps the phone lines and telecommunications infrastructure provide the nexus that would allow country S to tax income from R Corp.'s activities. If S were to base taxing authority on the use of the telecommunications infrastructure, it would be virtually impossible for R Corp. to transact any business in country S without triggering country S taxation. Even if R Corp. operated through the mail rather than through the telephone, use of the roads and the postal infrastructure would presumably subject R Corp. to tax if use of the telecommunications infrastructure would.

If the use of the general telecommunications infrastructure does not provide country S with taxing authority, perhaps any specific arrangements by R Corp. to procure a local access number would provide the necessary nexus.[185] To base taxing authority in country S on whether R Corp. leases a

---

[184]The imposition of a consumption tax (*e.g.*, a VAT) might be determined based on where customers are located.

[185]We understand that Germany, for example, has taken the position that a local telephone number can constitute a permanent establishment although there is no reported case to that effect.

local access number would create a curious set of distinctions. If R Corp. made no arrangements for local access numbers in country S, but customers using their own internet service providers shopped through R Corp.'s web page anyway, presumably R Corp. would not be taxable in country S in the absence of a physical presence.

Suppose that R Corp. made arrangements in country R with RISP Corp. to connect R Corp. to the internet and to lease space on the RISP Corp. server in country R for R Corp.'s web page. Suppose further that RISP Corp. also provides internet access for customers in country S.[186] Should RISP Corp.'s physical presence in country S constitute sufficient physical presence for R Corp. to be subject to tax in country S in the absence of any other physical connections? It would not make sense to saddle R Corp. with potential tax liability in country S solely because one of the enterprises it does business with also has a physical presence in country S. Certainly, R Corp. would not be subject to tax liability in country S if, for example, it purchased an IBM computer, solely because IBM Corp. does business and has a physical presence in country S. However, the analysis might be different if R Corp. purposefully availed itself of RISP Corp.'s presence in country S. For example, if RISP Corp. maintains a server in country S that provides advertising for R Corp., country S might have a stronger claim. Even then, advertising, without more, may not provide sufficient taxing authority under general international tax principles.[187] But if RISP Corp. maintains a server in country S and R Corp. maintains its web site on that server, R Corp. will have a sufficient presence in country S to justify an exercise of its taxing authority if country S would have taxed R Corp. had it maintained its own server in country S.

Even if none of the arrangements in the discussion above provides a sufficient physical nexus with country S based on traditional international tax norms, perhaps the activities of agents in country S might bring R Corp. within country S's taxing authority. It is true that R Corp. does not have employees in country S, nor has R Corp. hired agents who regularly conclude contracts binding R Corp. But would R Corp.'s relationships with the telecommunications company or internet service providers render R Corp. subject to the taxing authority because of the activities of employees of those companies in establishing and maintaining internet service?

---

[186]RISP Corp. might have routers, servers and other equipment in country S.
[187]*See e.g.*, OECD Model, 1997, Art. 5(4).

There is an interesting agency issue that will arise out of electronic commerce and is beyond the current contemplation of existing legal principles. Historically, agents have been individuals or firms, which are collections of individuals, who act on behalf of their principals. It is now possible for R Corp. to operate a software agent that can make decisions and conclude contracts with a digital signature in the name of its principal. Like a human agent or a collection of human agents in a firm, a software agent can be given a set of parameters within which it can make decisions without contacting its principal. To the extent that the software agent operates in country R on R Corp.'s server, no agency issues are raised concerning country S's taxing authority. But suppose that R Corp.'s software agent functions on a customer's computer in country S (*i.e.*, the agent software is downloaded by the customer). The agent might be able to help the customer search for merchandise, answer any questions about the use of the merchandise, negotiate any appropriate discounts, conclude a purchase order, process the payment details and arrange for shipping. If these activities done on a regular basis by a human agent in the United States are sufficient to permit the United States to exercise taxing authority over R Corp., perhaps the same result is required in the case of a software agent.

So far the discussion has focused on whether R Corp. might be subject to tax in country S by virtue of its physical contact or through the activities in country S of an agent. Aside from R Corp.'s tax liability in country S as a content provider, questions arise concerning the tax liability in country S of the internet service providers — ZISP Corp. and RISP Corp. Conceptually, it may be easier to determine that ZISP Corp., as opposed to R Corp., should be subject to country S's taxing authority. For R Corp., internet access is a means for delivering what R Corp. produces. For ZISP Corp., local internet access is what ZISP Corp. produces. ZISP Corp. is conducting its business in those countries where local internet access is made available. However, more difficult problems are posed if ZISP Corp. provides service to state S customers in a situation where no land-based equipment is used (*e.g.*, using low atltitude satellites). In this situation, there may be no physical presence in state S to justify state S taxation of ZISP Corp. RISP Corp. should not be subject to tax in country S if its only connection with country S is that it allows persons outside of country S, such as R Corp., to post home pages and other data on the internet which then can be accessed worldwide, including in country S.

4.2.1.2.1.2. What costs are attributable to includible income

To determine accurately the tax base that may be subject to a country's tax jurisdiction, it is necessary to determine both the income produced within the jurisdiction and the deductible expenses incurred in producing that income. Just as electronic commerce raises difficult questions concerning where income is produced, electronic commerce raises a similar problem with respect to where expenses are incurred. For example, suppose that R Corp. earns business income in country S. That income may be a result of joint production that took place when R Corp. employees in countries M, N, O, P, and Q used the internet to design goods that were sold, to compile a database, to plan a marketing strategy, etc. The costs of computer hardware and software, the cost of labor, and costs of overhead must be allocated to the income produced. The problem of allocating costs is not a new problem arising out of the growth of electronic commerce. However, the internet and intranets[188] make it easier than ever for joint production within a firm across transnational boundaries, making cost allocation a central issue.

4.2.1.2.1.3. Enforcement concerns

Assuming for the moment that country S is able to assert taxing authority over some or all of the income generated in country S, does country S have a means of enforcing its authority? Normally, when a nonresident has a physical presence in another country, the taxing authorities of that country: (a) are aware of that presence (*e.g.*, there is a store or factory); and (b) can enforce any failure to pay the taxes owed by encumbering or seizing assets within the taxing authority's jurisdiction. These enforcement issues are explored in a recent discussion report of the Australian Tax Office.[189]

In the example above, R Corp. may not have a meaningful presence in country S. Indeed, country S may not be aware that R Corp. is doing busi-

---

[188]An intranet is a private network within an organization (*e.g.*, a business) that is not connected to the internet. It operates as a mini-internet within that organization. *See supra* section 3.7.2.

[189]*See* Discussion Report of the Australian Tax Office Electronic Commerce Project, *Tax and the Internet* ¶¶ 8.1.1.–8.9.3 (August 1997).

ness in country S. There is no practical way for taxing authorities of country S to be aware of every company worldwide that maintains a web site accessible by residents of country S. Moreover, the taxing authorities of country S have no way of ascertaining how much business R Corp. is doing in country S. This problem is enhanced by the ability of country S consumers to use anonymous electronic cash to pay for their purchases from R Corp.

If R Corp. is subject to the taxing authority of country S but does not pay the taxes due, the country S taxing authorities may have no practical way of seizing R Corp.'s assets to satisfy the tax obligation. If goods are purchased from R Corp. over the internet and those goods are delivered to customers in country S by conventional transport, country S authorities may be able to seize goods that are shipped. This would not be possible for intangibles or services that are provided over the internet itself. Technologically, it may be possible for the country S taxing authorities to program the main routers (*i.e.,* network access points) that connect the country S backbone to other countries to blackout R Corp.'s web site so that country S residents could not access the R Corp. server.[190] However, R Corp. could circumvent any blackout attempt by changing the address of its server or through other techniques. In some cases the threat of disrupted service in country S might provide a sufficient disincentive to compel R Corp. to comply with country S's tax laws. In other cases it would not.

There are additional enforcement problems arising out of new payment methods. In commercial transactions today, cash businesses pose special enforcement problems because there is no external record of a company's income (*e.g.,* no canceled check or credit card statement). However, commercial payments often are made by check or by credit card, creating a paper record of the transaction. For large transactions (*e.g.,* buying a car), the use of cash is unusual in developed economies. In part, the physical logistics of transporting large amounts of cash limit its use. However, electronic cash offers the opportunity for completely anonymous transactions in large denominations. A consumer can download electronic tokens from an on-line bank, use those tokens to consummate a transaction and leave no paper (or electronic) trail whatsoever. Consequently, even if country S asserts taxing authority over the income earned by R Corp. and even if

---

[190]In some countries, like the United States, these main routers are privately owned, thereby requiring legislation or judicial intervention in order to compel the owners to make changes in the routing tables.

114

the country S taxing authorities can enforce that authority in some manner, country S may have no reliable means of determining the extent that R Corp.'s income is generated from country S customers. Attempts to control the use of electronic cash through bank regulation may prove unsuccessful because customers in country S will easily be able to use banks or other financial companies beyond the jurisdiction of country S.

Enforcement of a tax obligation imposed on ZISP Corp. by country S may not be as difficult as enforcement of R Corp.'s tax obligations because ZISP Corp. has some assets in country S (*e.g.*, routers) that can be seized in the event of nonpayment. Also, country S may be able to prevent ZISP Corp. from doing business in country S by regulating the ability of ZISP Corp. to contract with local telecommunications companies.

In the discussion that follows, the application of current tax rules to new methods of producing income are analyzed. First, there is a non-comprehensive consideration of national law. Then, treaty issues are considered in the context of the OECD Model income tax treaty.

4.2.1.2.2. National law

This section will examine the treatment of the participants in the electronic commerce hypothetical under existing national laws. It is not, of course, feasible to discuss the law of every country. The discussion will focus on the law of the United States, as an example of a country which asserts jurisdiction to tax nonresidents even in the absence of a permanent establishment, but will also discuss issues arising under the laws of other selected countries.

If a nonresident conducts a US trade or business, the income effectively connected with the conduct of the trade or business is taxed in the same manner as business income of a US resident.[191] The international tax provisions of the Internal Revenue Code provide little guidance as to what constitutes a US trade or business.[192] However, the threshold for business

---

[191] IRC §§ 871(b) (individuals) and 882 (corporations).

[192] *See* IRC § 864(b). Certainly, passive investment activity does not rise to the level of a trade or business. For example, a nonresident individual or foreign corporation merely collecting interest or dividends from a US payer is not engaged in a trade or business in the United States. The gross interest or dividend income (with no deductions permitted) normally would be subject to tax at a 30% (or lower treaty) rate. IRC §§

activities in the United States to constitute a US trade or business is low. The sale of inventory on a regular basis in the United States constitutes a US trade or business.[193] The IRS has taken the position that a foreign taxpayer present in the United States to demonstrate its product and solicit orders was engaged in a trade or business in the United States even in the absence of a US office.[194]

In some instances, it is clear that a taxpayer is engaged in a trade or business, but it is not clear whether the trade or business is in the United States.[195] A case involving an earlier technology — radio transmission —

871(a) or 881. Similarly, a foreign investor collecting rental income on US property from a tenant under a net lease (*i.e.,* where the tenant is responsible for maintenance, taxes, and insurance) is not considered engaged in a trade or business and would normally be subject to the 30% tax on the rental income without deduction of mortgage interest and other expenses.

[193]*See, e.g., Hanfield v. Commissioner,* 23 TC 633 (1955).

[194]Rev. Rul. 56–165, 1956–1 C.B. 849.

[195]In *United States v. Balanovski,* 236 F.2d 298 (2d Cir. 1956), a taxpayer came to the United States to purchase trucks and other equipment. The trucks and equipment purchased were then sold to the Argentine government. Upon receiving bids from American suppliers, the taxpayer would submit the bids at a markup to the Argentine government. If the government approved the price, the taxpayer would purchase the equipment with funds that were wired to him in the United States by the Argentine government. The taxpayer operated out of a hotel room in the United States with the help of a secretary. The level of the taxpayer's activities including the solicitation of orders, the inspection of merchandise, and the purchase and sale of the merchandise convinced the court that the taxpayer was engaged in a trade or business and that the trade or business was conducted in the United States rather than in Argentina. Accordingly, the taxpayer was taxed on income arising from the sales to the Argentine government.

At the other end of the spectrum, the activities in *Commissioner v. Spermacet Whaling & Shipping Co.,* 281 F.2d 646 (1960), were held not to constitute a US trade or business. There the taxpayer was hired to organize, equip and manage a whaling expedition. The main ship was reconditioned and equipped in Norway; the contracts for reconditioning all took place in Norway. All members of the crew were Norwegian and were employed pursuant to contracts negotiated in Norway. The whaling expedition itself took place in international waters. The taxpayer did not have an office in the United States, nor was it qualified to do business in any state in the United States. Spermacet had no US employees and one US officer. Its operations were managed from an office in Norway. The contacts with the United States were as follows: fuel oil purchases in the United States were arranged by the taxpayer although the fuel oil was delivered off the western coast of South America; the sperm oil produced as a result of the whaling expedition was delivered in New York to a US purchaser; the taxpayer maintained a US bank account; and the board of directors of Spermacet held meetings in the United States on

presents some issues that are similar to those raised by internet technology. In *Piedras Negras Broadcasting Co. v. Commissioner,*[196] a foreign corporation (*i.e.,* the taxpayer) with no office or place of business in the United States broadcasted programs from Mexico intended for US listeners. Advertisers compensated the taxpayer for broadcasting the advertisers' messages to the US listeners. The advertising contracts were executed in Mexico. In some cases, the advertisers forwarded their fees directly to the taxpayer's Mexican office, but in most cases the advertising fees were sent to a US post office address where representatives of the taxpayer opened the mail, depositing some of the proceeds in a US bank.[197]

The court's reasoning mixed together the concepts of being engaged in a US trade or business and whether the income was from US sources. The court first analyzed the taxpayer's physical presence in the United States, determining that the collection of advertising proceeds within the United States did not determine the source of the income or constitute the conduct of business. Nor did the fact that the taxpayer entered into some contracts with advertisers where fees were based on sales of the advertised products render the taxpayer a joint venturer conducting business in the United States. The court dismissed the use of a room in a Texas hotel for purposes of sorting mail as constituting an office for the conduct of a trade or business. The court noted that there was no rent paid for the room and no furniture or desk was owned or maintained by the taxpayer. The court determined that the sorting of mail and collection of income were "incidental" to the conduct of business. *A fortiori,* the maintenance of a post office box did not render the taxpayer engaged in a US trade or business, although the court did not specifically consider this point. Finally, the court

---

four occasions. In addition, the activities of Smidas, the party that hired Spermacet, included the chartering of the vessels and the delivery of the oil in New York to the purchaser with title passing in New York. Smidas was incorporated in the United States. Unwilling to attribute Smidas' activities to Spermacet, the court found that Spermacet's connections to the United States did not rise to the level of a trade or business. The fact that the fruits of Spermacet's services were transported to the United States on vessels that were chartered by a US corporation was not a sufficient nexus to justify US taxation.

[196]BTA 297 (1941), *aff'd* 127 F.2d. 260 (5th Cir. 1942).

[197]Some of the advertising contracts were based on a percentage of the advertiser's sales. In those cases, the customers sent payment to the US post office address where representatives of the taxpayer and of the advertisers divided the payments in accordance with the contracts.

decided that depositing money in the United States did not constitute the conduct of a trade or business in the United States.

Having examined the physical nature of the taxpayer's US operations, the court then considered whether broadcasting to US listeners constituted income from US sources. All of the broadcasting equipment was located in Mexico, and the advertising contracts were executed in Mexico. Relying on a series of state tax law decisions, the court determined that "broadcasting through the ether"[198] did not constitute "doing business." In so deciding, the court noted that shipping goods into a state was not doing business therein, nor was sale by solicitation, transportation of merchandise into a state and collection therefor, nor distributing a magazine by a foreign corporation. The court concluded by quoting from *McCulloch v. Maryland:*[199]

> All subjects over which the sovereign power of a state extends, are objects of taxation; but those over which it does not extend, are, upon the soundest principles, exempt from taxation. This proposition may almost be pronounced self-evident.

Because the subject matter of the tax (*i.e.*, the broadcasting facilities) was in Mexico, and the United States offered no protection to such activities or property, the income generated was not considered to be from sources in the United States.

Activities conducted in the United States by a nonresident alien or a foreign corporation through an agent pose the most difficult questions concerning what constitutes a US trade or business. If the activities of an agent are "considerable, continuous, and regular," the principal may be deemed to have a US trade or business.[200] Historically, the definition of an agency relationship focuses on: (a) the power of the agent to bind the principal as to third parties; (b) the existence of a fiduciary relationship between principal and agent; and (c) the right of the principal to control the conduct of the agent with respect to the assigned tasks.[201] The conduct of even

---

[198]*Piedras Negras,* 43 BTA at 311.

[199]17 US 316, 429 (1819).

[200]*Lewenhaupt v. Commissioner,* 20 TC 151 (1953).

[201]*See e.g., Esmond Mills v. Commissioner,* 132 F.2d 753, 755 (1st Cir. 1943); *European Naval Stores Company, S.A. v. Commissioner,* 11 TC 127, 134-135 (1948); *Griffin v. US,* 588 F.2d 521, 527 (1st Cir. 1979). *See also* Restatement (Second) of Agency, §§ 12-14 (1957).

considerable activities on behalf of another is not sufficient in and of itself to constitute an agency.[202]

If a nonresident alien or foreign corporation is engaged in a trade or business in the United States, the taxpayer is taxable at rates generally applicable to US residents (or citizens) on income that is "effectively connected" with the conduct of the US trade or business. If a taxpayer is engaged in a trade or business in the United States, generally, all sales, services, or manufacturing income from US sources is effectively connected income.[203] For example, suppose that a foreign corporation is engaged in a trade or business in the United States of selling electronic equipment through its US branch. Any income generated by the US branch is clearly effectively connected income. In addition, some, or all, of the income generated from the sale of equipment (or any other inventory in the United States) by the foreign home office without any involvement of the US branch may be effectively connected income if title to the inventory passes in the United States.[204]

---

[202]In *Amalgamated Dental Co. v. Commissioner,* 6 TC 1009 (1946), the taxpayer had no office or place of business, no employees, factory or officers in the United States. For many years it had purchased dental supplies in New York from Dental Supply and resold them in Europe. Because of exchange and shipping restrictions arising out of World War II, the taxpayer could no longer import the equipment. Instead, the New York company shipped the equipment directly to the taxpayer's customers, collected the retail price, and remitted the difference between the retail price and the wholesale price to the taxpayer. No stated charge was made for the services. The court held that the taxpayer was not engaged in a US trade or business because the relationship between the taxpayer and Dental Supply was one of vendee/vendor, not principal/agent.

[203]IRC § 864(c)(3). Income that would normally be US source investment income is effectively connected income if either: (1) the income is derived from assets used in the conduct of the US trade or business; or (2) the activities of the trade or business are a material factor in the realization of the income. IRC § 864(c)(2). For example, the "assetuse" test is satisfied if a taxpayer receives interest from an account receivable arising in the trade or business. The "businessactivities" test determines if dividends derived by dealers in securities or royalties derived from a patent licensing business or service fees derived from a servicing business are considered effectively connected income. Reg. § 1.864–4(c)(3).

[204]Reg. § 1.864–4(b). Not only income from US sources but also some foreign source income is treated as effectively connected with the conduct of a US trade or business. Generally, income from foreign sources is not treated as effectively connected income and is therefore not taxable in the United States. IRC § 864(c)(4)(A). However,

In general, only US source income will be effectively connected with the conduct of a US trade or business.[205] Gain from the sale of purchased inventory is sourced where the sale takes place — generally the place where title passes.[206] For example, gain from the sale of inventory purchased in France and sold in the United States is US source income while gain from the sale of inventory purchased in the United States and sold in France is foreign source income. The title passage rule for purchased inventory allows taxpayers great latitude, but there are limits. If a transaction is structured with the primary purpose of tax avoidance, the title passage rule may not apply. Instead the location of: negotiations; execution of the agreement; the property itself; and the payment may be relevant in determining source.[207] If a nonresident maintains an office or other fixed place of business in the United States, income from the sale of inventory (and other personal property) attributable to such place of business is sourced in the United States regardless of where title passes.[208]

The title-passage rule does not apply to inventory (or other personal property) that is not purchased by a taxpayer but instead is produced by the taxpayer. For example, suppose a foreign corporation has a Spanish factory that manufactures thermostats which are shipped to a US office and then sold in the United States. Income from the sale of such property is allocated for source purposes between the country of production and the country of sale.[209] Once the income has been sourced under IRC § 863(b), taxation in the United States depends on whether the income is effectively connected

---

there are exceptions for certain income from foreign sources that is "attributable to" a US "office or fixed place of business." The foreign source income that is swept into the US taxing net is generally the type of income the source of which could be easily manipulated to avoid US taxation. For example, rents or royalties from intangible property located or used outside the United States which are derived in the active conduct of a US trade or business is effectively connected income. IRC § 864(c)(4)(B)(i). Thus, if a foreign corporation licenses Mexican patents or trademarks through its US office, income generated by the licensing of those intangibles to Mexican licensees may be effectively connected income if the income is attributable to the US office.

[205]*But see* IRC § 864(c)(4).

[206]IRC §§ 865(b) and 861(a)(6).

[207]Reg. § 1.861–7(c).

[208]IRC § 865(e)(2)(A). However, if the inventory is sold for use outside the United States and a foreign fixed place of business materially participates in the sale, any gain on the sale is treated as foreign source income. IRC § 865(e)(2)(B).

[209]IRC §§ 865(b) and 863(b)(2).

income.[210] In the example above, the foreign source portion of the gain attributable to the production is not subject to US taxation. The US source sales portion of the gain is taxable as effectively connected income.[211]

The source rule for services is straightforward: compensation for services performed in the United States is US source income subject to a *de minimis* exception. Typically, a nonresident alien performing services in the United States is deemed to be engaged in a trade or business in the United States, and the compensation is treated as effectively connected income which is subject to US taxation. However to the extent that compensation is paid for services performed outside the United States, generally the compensation is not subject to US taxation.[212] If a corporation receives payments for personal services performed by an employee or other agent, the corporation's compensation is sourced in the place where the employee or agent performs the services.[213]

If the taxpayer in *Piedras Negras* was not engaged in a trade or business in the United States by virtue of broadcasting radio waves into the United States in a commercial venture, it is likely that R Corp. would not be con-

---

[210]IRC §§ 864(c)(3) or (4).

[211]IRC § 882. The Regulations specify a 3-step process for sourcing income from manufactured inventory. First, gross income is allocated to the sales activity and the production activity under one of the specified methods. Second, the gross income allocated to the sales activity and the production activity is then sourced. The sales activity gross income is sourced based on the title passage rule. IRC § 861(a)(6). The production activity gross income is sourced according to the relative domestic and foreign production assets. Third, expenses are allocated in accordance with Regulations. Reg. § 1.863-3.

In lieu of the 50-50 method, a taxpayer can elect to use the independent factory price (IFP) method if an IFP can be fairly established. In the example above, suppose that the foreign corporation regularly sold the inventory to independent distributors that resold the thermostats in the United States. In the example above, suppose that the cost of goods sold for each thermostat was $10 and the gross proceeds from sales to US purchasers was $100. Under the 50/50 method, $45 of profit would be treated as foreign source and $45 would be treated as US source on each sale. However, if the foreign corporation could establish that independent distributors bought the same inventory for $60 per thermostat, then $50 of the gain would be allocated to the production activity (and treated as foreign source because the production assets are located in Spain) and $40 of the gross income from each thermostat would be treated as sales income and sourced in the United States if title passes there.

[212]*See* Reg. § 1.861-4(b).

[213]*See, e.g., Bank of America v. United States,* 680 F.2d 142 (Cl. Ct. 1982).

sidered to be engaged in a trade or business in the United States by virtue of the same broadcasting through the internet in the absence of a physical presence in the United States. This is not an uncommon view. For example, Israel does not tax nonresidents who generate income from the transmission of information to Israeli customers by means of cable or wireless communication.[214]

Of course, the distinction between broadcasting over the airwaves and broadcasting over a wired telecommunications network may conceivably call for different tax rules. To the extent that the United States provides a communications infrastructure (*e.g.,* phone lines, telecommunications offices) that contributes to the production of R Corp.'s income, perhaps the United States' stake in the production of income justifies its taxing authority in a way that does not exist in the case of wireless broadcasting. But such a conclusion would mean that virtually all nonresidents who make use of the US telephone, postal, or transportation infrastructure would be considered to engage in a US trade or business — a result that is at odds with the tax court's decision in *Piedras Negras* (payment by mail) and would represent an expansion of existing US taxing authority. For example, all foreign catalog companies mailing catalogs into the United States might be subject to US tax on income from US purchasers. Moreover, basing authority to tax on whether R Corp. uses wired communications (taxable) or wireless communications (not taxable) suggests a distinction on which differences in tax treatment should not be based. To the extent that the US telecommunications infrastructure contributes to R Corp.'s income, the income of the US telecommunications companies will be fully subject to US taxation.

If the use of the telecommunications infrastructure does not render R Corp. engaged in a US trade or business where US customers make their own arrangements with internet service providers to access the internet, is a different result mandated where R Corp. itself makes arrangements for a local access number? Perhaps the establishment of a local number or a toll-free "800" number through which transactions take place leads to the conclusion that R Corp. is engaged in a trade or business in the United States. However, there is no support under US law for such a conclusion. Indeed, in *Piedras Negras,* the fact that the taxpayer had a US postal address was not

---

[214]Israel IFA Branch, *Comments on Electronic Commerce Report* (9 April 1998) (on file with the authors), citing Income Tax Ordianance, § 75.

consequential. Nor should there be a different result if R Corp. made arrangements with a third-party to sublease local telephone lines.

The location of the server used by R Corp. to make its web page available to customers might be relevant to the resolution of the trade or business issue. In the hypothetical, the server is located in country R so that the United States as country S could not claim taxing authority on the basis of server location. Moreover if server location were instrumental in determining taxing authority, no factor would be more subject to manipulation. A server, or more accurately a computer running server software, can be located virtually anywhere — in country R, the United States, or in almost any other country that has electricity and a telecommunications link. R Corp. can access the server software remotely with ease.[215] There is no particular advantage for R Corp. to locate the server in the United States. For all intents and purposes, the location of R Corp.'s server is irrelevant and invisible to customers in the United States.

All that being said, if R Corp. were to locate the server in the United States, there is a stronger argument that R Corp. may be conducting its trade or business in the United States. Of course, R Corp. could locate its server in the United States in many ways. It could house an R Corp. computer in an R Corp. office in the United States. Alternatively, R Corp. could lease disk space from a US lessor. For example, a US internet service provider might lease disk space for R Corp.'s web pages, and provide local access numbers or toll-free "800" numbers. In both these scenarios, R Corp.'s level of business activity in the United States is more significant than mere use of the telecommunications infrastructure. In Revenue Ruling 56-165,[216] the IRS ruled that regular and active solicitation in the United States was sufficient to constitute a US trade or business under the then-existing Swiss treaty. This broad ruling may not have been justified under US law but was made more palatable by the fact that the logging equipment that was sold in the United States was brought into the United States for demonstration purposes and to generate orders. So in addition to active solicitation, there was also a physical presence in the United States. Active solicitation through the internet combined with a physical presence either

---

[215]There is no technological barrier to locating a server on a satellite orbiting the earth.

[216]1956-1 CB 849.

through ownership of a US-located computer or through a leasing arrangement might establish R Corp. as engaged in a US trade or business.

Returning to the electronic commerce hypothetical set forth in section 4.2.1.1, if R Corp.'s server is located outside country S (*i.e.*, the United States), it may be difficult to conclude that R Corp. is engaged in a trade or business in the United States through its own activities, particularly in light of *Piedras Negras*.[217] However, a nonresident might still be considered to be engaged in a US trade or business through the activities of an agent. While R Corp. may lease local access numbers or authorize one or more US shipping companies to deliver ordered merchandise, these relationships are not agency relationships. No person in country S has been hired to represent R Corp., much less to habitually conclude contracts that bind R Corp. The mere fact that the telephone company is conducting a US trade or business is not imputed to all foreign companies that use telecommunications services.

For the sake of analysis, assume that R Corp. is deemed to be engaged in a trade or business in the United States. In order for the United States to exercise taxing authority, income produced by R Corp. must be effectively connected with the conduct of a US trade or business.[218] Income produced by R Corp. is effectively connected income if it is from sources within the United States.[219] In the case of inventory, if title passes in the United States, the income will be US source income subject to US taxation. But suppose that R Corp. arranges for title to the inventory to pass outside the United States — an arrangement easy to make. Even under these circumstances, the income may be treated as US source income if the income is attributable to a US office.[220] However, it seems unlikely that R Corp. has or would be deemed to have a US office. Consequently, even if R Corp. were found to be engaged in a trade or business in the United States, it appears likely that

---

[217]*But see* Rev. Rul. 56-165, 1956-1 CB 849 (regular and active solicitation constituted a US trade or business). The authority of *Piedras Negras* was reaffirmed in the Treasury's discussion paper on internet taxes. Department of the Treasury Office of Tax Policy, *Selected Tax Policy Implications of Global Electronic Commerce,* Discussion Paper Issued Nov. 21, 1996, 1996 DTR 226 d35 (22 November 1996) (hereinafter sometimes referred to as "US Treasury Report").

[218]IRC §§ 882 and 864(c).

[219]IRC § 864(c)(3).

[220]IRC § 865(e).

R Corp. might not have income that was effectively connected with the conduct of that US trade or business, thereby depriving the United States of taxing authority.

As for the internet service provider, it seems likely that ZISP Corp. (*i.e.,* a customer's internet service provider) is conducting a trade or business in the United States. It also actively provides various web services to its country S customers, including the provision of internet access. It does so through the presence of routers and other transmission equipment which it maintains at various points-of presence (POP's). The activities of ZISP Corp. in country S are "considerable, continuous, and regular."[221] ZISP Corp.'s activities in country S are not incidental to its business; those activities are ZISP Corp.'s business.[222]

The Internal Revenue Code provides a special source rule for income from international communications. Code section 863(e)(2) defines international communications income as "all income derived from the transmission of communications or data from the United States to any foreign country (or possession of the United States) or from any foreign country (or possession of the United States) to the United States." Such income may stem from the use of undersea cables and communications satellites. For purposes of the rule, income is not considered "international" if the originating and terminating points are both in the United States or both in foreign locations, even if the communication is routed through a space satellite at any location in the interim.[223] Instead, to qualify for Code section 863(e) treatment, the income must be generated from communications between a point in the United States and a point in a foreign location.

Code section 863(e) dictates different results depending on whether or not a taxpayer with international communications income is a "United

---

[221]*Inez de Amodio v. Commissioner,* 34 TC 894 (1960), *aff'd* 299 F.2d 623 (3d Cir. 1962).

[222]The treatment of ZISP Corp. would seem to be similar under Japanese tax law. The threshold issue is if the POP constitutes a permanent establishment. There is little help under Japanese Law to resolve this issue. If ZISP Corp. does not maintain its own equipment in state S, it is unlikely that a relationship with an independent telecommunications company would render ZISP Corp. taxable.

[223]Income arising from communication between two points in the United States is US source income. Income arising from communications between two points in foreign locations is foreign source income.

States person." Income of non-United States persons is deemed to be entirely foreign source income.[224] However, an exception applies if the taxpayer has an office or fixed place of business in the United States. In that case, the international communications income attributable to that office or fixed place of business is held to be US source income.[225]

Assuming that ZISP Corp. is engaged in a US trade or business, if its income is deemed to be international communications income, the United States would not have taxing authority if the income were not attributable to a US fixed place of business.[226] All of the income would instead be considered foreign. The presence of routers and other equipment should not constitute a fixed place of business. However, if some sort of office location is maintained where the routers/equipment are kept and especially, where employees work, it is likely that ZISP Corp. would have a fixed place of business and part of the income would be taxable by the United States (the amount attributable to that fixed place of business).

It is not clear, though, that income earned by ZISP Corp. constitutes international communications income. Whether it qualifies depends on the nature of ZISP Corp.'s business. Income generated from providing telecommunications services to ZISP Corp's clients — those services usually considered "enhanced" such as email, newsgroups, etc. — should qualify under the definition as international communications income since data is actually being transmitted by ZISP Corp. However, where ZISP Corp. derives income from simply offering a logical network to its clients for their own use, and does not engage in transmitting any data or communications itself,

---

[224]For United States persons, 50% of the income is treated as having come from a US source and the other 50% is treated as having derived from foreign sources.

[225]Since IRC § 863(e) is a very specific rule, if the activity giving rise to the income is such that it is subject to a more general source rule in addition to the international communications income rule, it appears the latter is applied. For example, if an international communication is sent via cables across the ocean floor or via space satellite, both IRC §§ 863(e) and 863(d) appear applicable. However, IRC § 863(d)(2)(B)(ii) indicates that IRC § 863(e) should control by excluding activities giving rise to international communications income from its definition of space/ocean activity. In a similar manner, IRC § 863(e) also governs where international communications income and rental income coexist.

[226]As foreign source income, the income would not be effectively connected income under IRC § 864(c)(4).

it is highly questionable whether such income would be classified as international communications income.

The US approach is typical of the approach taken by many developed countries that do not tax solely on the basis of territorial connection but require some threshold presence (*e.g.*, a "trade or business"). Of course, how this concept is implemented varies from country to country. In Canada, a nonresident is liable for Canadian income tax on income from carrying on business in Canada.[227] Whether a person is carrying on business in Canada depends on a variety of circumstances including: the place of contract; the place of payment; the place where purchases are made; the place of production; location of inventory, etc. The place where contracts are made is the most important factor. Because the tax issues involving electronic commerce are not clearly resolved, Revenue Canada has been urged to examine the definition of "carrying on business" under the Income Tax Act in light of the role of servers and other features of electronic commerce.[228]

The Japanese Corporation Tax Law does not have a requirement comparable to the US "trade or business" requirement.[229] Instead, R Corp. is taxable in state S only if R Corp. has a permanent establishment in state S.[230] Because R Corp. does not have a branch or factory in state S, the taxability of R Corp.'s business profits earned in state S may hinge on whether R Corp. satisfies the "other fixed place of business" requirement of Article 141. Japanese law, like US law, focuses on physical manifestations in order to find a fixed place of business.[231] Accordingly, it is unlikely that a customer base, transmission of bits, or use of the telecommunications infrastructure would be sufficient to constitute a permanent establishment under Japanese domestic law. The presence of a server in Japan makes the issue more

---

[227]Canadian Income Tax Act §3(2).

[228]Report to the Minister of National Revenue from the Minister's Advisory Committee on Electronic Commerce, *Electronic Commerce and Canada's Tax Administration,* http://www.rc.gc.ca/ecomm (April 1998).

[229]This discussion of Japanese law derives from information supplied by Professor Yoshihiro Masui of the University of Tokyo and from Japanese IFA Branch, *Comments on Electronic Commerce Report* (1 May 1998) (on file with the authors).

[230]Corporation Tax Law, Art. 141.

[231]Corporation Tax Basic Circular, 20-2-1 states that "a room of a hotel which is a center of domestic business of the foreign corporation, a display room, and other similar cases are included."

difficult to resolve, but many Japanese commentators have questioned whether it is good policy to base taxing authority on the presence of a server.

Even assuming that R Corp. does have a permanent establishment within Japan, business profits of R Corp. are subject to Japanese taxing authority only to the extent that they are sourced in Japan.[232] Income from business conducted in Japan is domestic source income. If R Corp. is deemed to be engaged in business both within and outside Japan, inventories transferred within Japan are taxable in Japan if R Corp. purchases the inventories abroad without increasing the value of the inventories by manufacturing.[233] It is not clear whether R Corp. transfers its inventories inside Japan. The applicable provision focuses on: 1) the location of the inventories in Japan immediately prior to their delivery; 2) where the contract is concluded; and 3) important aspects of the securing of orders and the negotiations to enter contracts having been conducted in Japan.[234] It is possible for R Corp. to arrange for these factors to occur outside of Japan.

Some countries take a more territorial approach to taxation, focusing on the source of income rather than whether there is a permanent establishment.[235] For example, The Brazilian Income Tax Regulation contains a general provision for the imposition of a withholding tax at the source on all payments made by a person located in Brazil to any person domiciled outside of Brazil.[236] Currently, the rate is 15%.[237] As electronic commerce spreads, will customers residing in Brazil be required to withhold on payments made to R Corp. on the sale of goods and/or services consummated

---

[232]Corporation Tax Law, Art. 138(1).

[233]Corporation Tax Law Enforcement Order, Art. 176(1).

[234]Corporation Tax Law Enforcement Order, Art. 176.

[235]For example, Colombian legislation does not include the permanent establishment concept. *See* Colombia IFA Branch, *Comments on Electronic Commerce Report* (16 April 1998) (on file with the authors).

[236]Income Tax Regulation, Decree 1.041, 11 January, art. 745. If the payment paid to a domiciliary located outside of Brazil is allocated to a permanent establishment within Brazil, the permanent establishment is taxed in Brazil under the provisions governing the Brazilian corporate income tax. *See generally* Pasqualin, *The Taxation of Income Derived from the Supply of Technology,* 82a Cahiers de Droit Fiscal International [Studies on International Fiscal Law] 260 (1997).

[237]Law 9.249, 26 December 1995, art. 28.

over the internet? Where the goods or services are delivered electronically, how will taxation at the source be administered?

Under Argentine tax principles,[238] the following general principles may apply to income generated by electronic commerce. Income obtained by nonresidents from the sale of goods to Argentine purchasers is not subject to Argentine tax.[239] Services performed within the Argentine territory are taxable. Technical, financial or similar advisory services rendered by nonresidents from abroad are taxable. Income obtained by nonresidents under contracts providing for the transfer or assignment of the right to use copyrightyed property or rights is taxable. In general, the place of execution of a contract or the domicile of parties to a contract is irrelevant for tax purposes. In the electronic commerce context, access to an on-line database maintained in country R by R Corp. by a customer in Argentina would not be deemed to involve taxable advisory services. If software is transferred, the treatment of the income in Argentina depends on the characteristics of the software. Income from the sale of generally available software would be treated as income from the sale of goods. Income from tailor-made software where the client has ownership rights should be treated in the same manner. But if the client is restricted, the income will be subject to an Argentine withholding tax.

In some cases, withholding obligations on the part of customers can extend to payments to nonresidents who perform services outside the country where the customers reside. For example, in Argentina, nonresidents are required to pay income tax on fees received for any technical advisory services rendered from abroad which are deemed to be sourced in Argentina.[240] In *SA Nestlé de Productos Alimenticios*,[241] payments made by a company to foreign firms for architectural drawings, buildings, and new fa-

---

[238]Argentina IFA Branch, *Comments on Electronic Commerce Report* (8 April 1998) (on file with the authors). The imposition of a withholding tax in Malaysia follows the treatment in Argentina. Malaysia IFA Branch, *Comments on Electronic Commerce Report* (10 April 1998) (on file with the authors).

[239]Similar results follow under Colombian law. Colombian IFA Branch, *Comments on Electronic Commerce Report* (16 April 1998) (on file with the authors).

[240]*See generally* Kaplan, *The Taxation of Income Derived from the Supply of Technology*, 82a CAHIERS DE DROIT FISCAL INTERNATIONAL [STUDIES ON INTERNATIONAL FISCAL LAW] 166 (1997).

[241]National Supreme Court of Justice (Feb. 15, 1979).

cilities, and for the analysis of product samples for quality control purposes all rendered abroad were subject to withholding tax. Historically, telephone records may have provided an audit trail for services of this type. But now it is possible for an Argentine purchaser to order goods or services over the internet by making a local telephone call to an internet service provider. The local phone number would provide no help to tax authorities trying to enforce their tax laws.

Not all the Latin American countries take a territorial approach to international taxation. Mexico, for example, more closely follows OECD principles. In accordance with the Mexican *Income Tax Law*[242] ("MITL") R Corp. is not subject to tax on business profits in Mexico if R Corp. maintains no physical presence in Mexico and sells goods which are shipped from R Corp.'s home office in country R through a server located outside Mexico. The MITL subjects foreign residents to tax in Mexico when they have a permanent establishment or fixed base[243] and only for income that is attributed to the permanent establishment or fixed base[244]. The MITL requires a place of business in the Mexican territory in which business activities are carried out but does not call for such place to be a "fixed" place of business. All tax treaties entered into by Mexico contain the requirement of a fixed presence in order to constitute a permanent establishment. R Corp. has no physical presence in Mexico; therefore, no tax will apply.

If the server is located in Mexico and is leased from an internet service provider or some third party, R Corp. will still not be subject to tax in Mexico as long as such internet provider or third party is a real independent en-

---

[242]*Ley del Impuesto sobre la Renta,* in effect since 1 January 1981.

[243]Article 1 of the MITL. Foreign residents are also subject to tax on any income derived from Mexican territory that, in accordance with Title V of the law, is considered to be of Mexican source (*i.e.,* royalties and interest income).

[244]Article 4 of the MITL contains a "force of attraction" provision that also attributes to the permanent establishment any income from the alienation in the territory of any product or property by the head office or any foreign branch of the taxpayer as well as any income obtained by its head office or any of its foreign establishments when the Mexican permanent establishment borne any expense related to such income. Tax treaties entered by Mexico usually narrow this "force of attraction" to the sale of goods by the head office or any other establishment of the taxpayer that are similar to the goods sold by the permanent establishment. If the taxpayer can prove to the tax authorities that such sale was not made by the permanent establishment for sound business reasons no force of attraction will apply in the context of the tax treaty.

terprise that carries out its activities in the ordinary course of business.[245] If such internet provider or third party is deemed to be a dependent agent (*i.e.*, an independent agent that does not carry out its activities in the ordinary course of business) and such dependent agent has the authority to conclude contracts on behalf of R Corp., then R Corp. will be deemed to have a permanent establishment in Mexico through such dependent agent even if R Corp. has no physical presence in Mexico. No permanent establishment will be deemed to exist if the activities carried out in Mexico by R Corp. or its dependent agents are considered preparatory or auxiliary.[246]

Mexico has several tax treaties in effect with its major trading partners and has used the OECD Model Convention as the basis for its negotiations. Therefore, the MITL provisions will be subject to any tax treaty provision in effect between country R and Mexico. It is safe to say that the "treaty law" descriptions already incorporated in this paper will apply to such cases as Mexico has mostly followed the OECD guidelines with respect to these issues. In addition, there is no case law in Mexico, therefore, court decisions have a significantly different meaning than, for example, those from in the United States. Due to the limited resources devoted by the Mexican authorities to deal with permanent establishment issues there is also little guidance outside the law on how the authorities and courts will interpret the law in complex situations.

In case the "goods" are downloaded directly from the server there will be no income tax consequence in Mexico. Nevertheless, value added tax will

---

[245]In accordance with Article 2 of the MITL, such an internet service provider or third party will not be considered to be an independent agent acting in the ordinary course of business if it:

a) has inventories of goods and makes deliveries on behalf of R Corp.;

b) assumes risks on behalf of R Corp.;

c) acts in accordance with detailed instructions or is subject to a strict control from R Corp.;

d) conducts activities that economically correspond to R Corp.;

e) receives a fixed remuneration notwithstanding the activities performed, or

f) carries on its activities with prices that are not arms length.

[246]If R Corp. has any facilities in Mexico exclusively for warehousing or exhibiting its products, for purchasing goods in the territory or providing information, as well as if R Corp. warehouses its goods in a customs free warehouse even if they are later imported and delivered within the territory, no permanent establishment is deemed to exist. (MITL Article 3o.).

be due and payable for such transactions. The Mexican *Value Added Tax Law* ("MVAT")[247] subjects to tax the introduction into the territory of goods, the purchase of intangible assets from abroad by Mexican residents, the use in Mexico of such intangibles, as well as the use in Mexico of tangible goods even if delivery occurred outside the Mexican territory. Any know-how, technical assistance or other services performed by foreign residents in the Mexican territory are also subject to tax.[248]

If in the example R Corp. provides services such as the access to a database that is maintained in its server, the income tax outcome will be the same as above, however the database will be deemed to be used or exploited in Mexican territory, therefore value added tax will be due. Clearly, Mexican tax authorities will have great difficulty verifying compliance of such tax.

If ZISP Corp. maintains servers, routers and other equipment in Mexico (in the offices of an independent telephone company), even if it has no employees or offices in the country, although questionable, there is a case for Mexican authorities to claim that ZISP Corp. has a place in which commercial activities are carried out and consequently be subject to tax on the profits attributable to such permanent establishment. In addition, because ZISP Corp. owns such assets located in Mexico and paid VAT upon entry of such assets into the country, it will not be able to credit such tax as any other Mexican taxpayer would, unless it files tax returns as a fixed establishment. Also, the tax authorities will have physical assets that could permit seizure in case of non-compliance.

---

[247]*Ley del Impuesto al Valor Agregado,* in effect since 1 January 1979. This law establishes a federal value added tax that applies to most sales of goods, provision of services and import of goods. The general tax rate is currently 15% and there are some exemptions and zero-rated transactions (*i.e.,* the purchase of basic food products and the export of goods and services).

[248]Article 24 of the MVAT. Article 26 describes when the tax is due and how it must be paid on any import of goods or services:

a) when the asset is introduced into Mexican territory and a customs entry document is filed, the VAT tax must be paid together with the customs duties, if any, owed; and

b) in all other cases, the importer of the good or service must pay the tax by filing a tax return. In these cases, the tax becomes due whenever the service begins to be exploited in Mexico, partial or full payment is made, the payment becomes due or an invoice is issued.

Provided ZISP Corp. maintains no equipment at all in Mexico but makes arrangements with a Mexican telecommunications company to install local telephone numbers through which Mexican customers can call to log on to the internet, ISP will not be subject to tax liability in Mexico.

4.2.1.2.3.   Treaty law

4.2.1.2.3.1.   Permanent establishment

Even if a country's domestic tax law permits it to tax income in the electronic commerce hypothetical above, in many cases a bilateral tax treaty may impose a higher threshold before a country can tax business profits from the activities of a nonresident in that country. Conversely, if the activities of the nonresident do not give rise to domestic tax liability, a country may not be able to impose an income tax even if an existing treaty would permit the imposition of a tax.[249] In a typical bilateral treaty, a Contracting State is authorized to tax only those business profits that are attributable to a permanent establishment in the Contracting State.[250] There are two types of permanent establishment that are relevant to a discussion of the electronic commerce hypothetical — a physical permanent establishment and an agency permanent establishment.

4.2.1.2.3.1.1.   Fixed place of business

A physical permanent establishment is a "fixed place of business" through which the business of an enterprise is wholly or partly carried on.[251] Source state taxation of business profits of an enterprise of the state of residence is appropriate only if the business activities of the enterprise in the source state are centralized in some manner. Consequently, isolated business transactions in the source state should not trigger taxation of business profits. The "place of business" requirement embodies the centraliza-

---

[249]*See e.g.,* US Model, 1996, Art. 1(2). However, in some countries, treaty obligations can create tax liability not provided by domestic law. *See e.g.,* Art. 4-bis of the Code Général des Impôts (France).

[250]OECD Model, 1997, Art. 7.

[251] OECD Model, 1997, Art. 5.

tion concept. A place of business includes any premises, facility, or installation for carrying on business, whether or not it is used exclusively for that purpose.[252] It is not necessary that the premises, facility, or installation be owned or rented by the enterprise; it is sufficient that it be at the disposal of the enterprise. For example, the OECD Commentary states that an area in a customs depot (*e.g.,* for the storage of dutiable goods) may constitute a place of business.[253]

Though ordinarily associated with immovable property, within the context of the Model, a "place of business" may include tangible assets used in carrying on the business. For example, machinery or equipment may, in given circumstances, constitute a place of business of an enterprise.[254] However, no special facilities are required. As the OECD Commentary indicates, an empty room in which the enterprise conducts business could qualify as a permanent establishment.[255]

The "fixed" requirement contains both a spatial component and a temporal component. To satisfy the spatial component, the place of business must have a definite spatial location. However, it need not be an attached structure.[256] The OECD Commentary states that for a place of business to be fixed, there must be a "link between the place of business and a specific geographical point."[257] In addition to the spatial component, the notion of a "fixed" place of business implies temporal duration. The OECD Commentary states that the "fixed" requirement connotes permanence; a place of business of a purely temporary nature is not "fixed."[258] On the other hand, however, it is not necessary for the place of business to exist for a set period of time to satisfy the temporal component. If the place of business was not originally established for temporary purposes but, in fact, only existed for a short period of time (*e.g.,* due to the nature of the business activity or premature termination), the OECD Commentary states that the place of business nevertheless will be deemed "fixed."[259] Moreover, the subjective purpose for establishing the place of business alone is not control-

[252]OECD Commentary, 1997, Art. 5, para. 4.
[253]*Id.*
[254]OECD Commentary, 1997, Art. 5, para.2.
[255]OECD Commentary, 1997, Art. 5, para. 4.
[256]OECD Commentary, 1997, Art. 5, para. 6.
[257]OECD Commentary, 1997, Art. 5, para. 5.
[258]OECD Commentary, 1997, Art. 5, para. 6.
[259]*Id.*

ling. Even if established for a temporary purpose, a place of business may become fixed if it continues for a period that cannot be considered merely temporary.

To constitute a permanent establishment, the business of the enterprise must be "carried on" through a fixed place of business. Both the terms "fixed" and "carried on" imply that the place of business must serve the enterprise with a certain degree of permanence rather than merely temporarily. Whether a place of business meets the test of permanence depends on all facts and circumstances surrounding each individual case. The enterprise's business must be carried on "through" the fixed place of business (*i.e.*, the fixed place of business itself is not produced, traded, rented out, or processed by the enterprise). Thus, leasing real property located in the source state does not of itself make such property a permanent establishment of the lessor.[260] The type of business the enterprise carries on through the fixed place of business is irrelevant. In particular, the enterprise need not carry on the same type of business through the fixed place of business as it carries on in its head office.

Nevertheless, the business carried on through the fixed place of business must be an "activity." The OECD Commentary states that even the letting or leasing of facilities, equipment, and real property can render a place of business through which the letting etc. is effected a permanent establishment. Consequently, facilities which are exclusively used for property administration are permanent establishments. A permanent establishment will also be deemed to exist where a taxpayer has a place of business in the source state which is used solely for letting or leasing movable and real property. Likewise, letting or leasing intangible property, such as patents, to third parties through a fixed place of business can generate a permanent establishment.[261]

The activity carried on through a facility must be business activity; and the fixed place of business must have features characteristic of a place of "business." For example, living quarters of employees are not normally permanent establishments (*i.e.*, unless business activities of the enterprise are conducted there). The activity need not necessarily be performed by a human being. Vending machines and other automated devices could con-

---

[260]*See e.g., de Amodio v. Commissioner,* 34 TC 894, 908-9, *aff'd,* 299 F.2d 623 (3d Cir. 1962).

[261]OECD Commentary, 1997, Art. 5, para. 8.

stitute permanent establishments if the enterprise engages in business beyond the mere installation of such machines.[262] Even fully automated pumping stations and similar facilities should be considered permanent establishments.

Consider the application of these principles to the electronic commerce hypothetical set forth in section 4.2.1.1. First, assume that R Corp. maintains a server in country S. If R Corp. maintains and operates the server in country S, the server may constitute a permanent establishment, particularly if R Corp. through its employees or other agents "operates and maintains [the server] for its own account."[263] It may not even be necessary for employees or agents to be present for country S to conclude that R Corp. has a permanent establishment in country S. However, if the server functioned "solely for the purposes of storage, display, or delivery of goods or merchandise,"[264] it would not be considered a permanent establishment. If the server merely provides advertising for R Corp., the advertising should be considered auxiliary and preparatory in nature — not enough by itself to constitute a permanent establishment. For example, R Corp. might operate a web server in country S. The web server might merely act as a clearinghouse that receives a request issued by a customer's browser for specified data that is situated on a data server located outside of country S, say in country R, and fills that request by securing the information from the country R computer and forwarding it to the customer. In this type of transaction, much of the computer processing occurs in country R where the data server is located (*e.g.,* the processing of an order form for the product to be purchased). The country S web server merely acts as an intermediary so that customers do not directly access R Corp.'s data server.

However, if the country S web server maintained by R Corp. not only provides advertising and other information concerning R Corp.'s products but also carries advertising for other companies for which R Corp. receives a fee from the companies running the advertisements, then the server may possibly constitute a permanent establishment. The advertising it carries for others (and for which R Corp. is compensated) does not fall within the "preparatory and auxiliary" concept embodied in Article 5(4) of the OECD

---

[262]OECD Commentary, 1997, Art. 5, para. 10.

[263]*Id.*

[264]OECD Model, 1997, Art. 5(4).

Model.[265] Rather, R Corp. is engaged in a business of running the advertisements of others through a server that is situated in country S. If that server satisfies the requirements of Article 5(1) of the OECD Model, then it will be a permanent establishment even though R Corp. is not selling its own products through the server.

Even assuming that the server does not carry the advertisements of others, if the server offers more than "storage, display, or delivery of goods or merchandise" (*e.g.,* sales help, contracting, payment processing, delivery arrangements, database researching with respect to R Corp.'s business), the "warehouse exception" would not apply. Under these circumstances, a server situated in country S may perhaps constitute a permanent establishment. It should be noted that whether R Corp. leases space on a third-party's server in country S from which R Corp. runs its web site or uses a server that is owned by R Corp. should not matter in determining if R Corp. has a permanent establishment in country S.[266] It is the functions performed on the server that may result in the server constituting a permanent establishment, and whether the server is at the "disposal" of R Corp.[267] It is also noteworthy that R Corp. might conceivably have a permanent establishment in country S without its knowledge. For example, R Corp. may have entered into an agreement with its internet service provider, RISP Corp., to establish a web site on RISP Corp.'s server. Unbeknownst to R Corp., that web site might be established on a server maintained by RISP Corp. in country S.[268]

---

[265]OECD Commentary, 1997, Art. 5, para. 28.

[266]OECD Commentary, 1997, Art. 5, para. 23: "It is immaterial whether the premises, facilities or installations are owned or rented by or are otherwise at the disposal of the enterprise."

[267]OECD Commentary, 1997, Art. 5, para. 4. There may be a thin line between a situation where R Corp. has space on a third-party server at its "disposal" and a situation where R Corp.'s web site is located on a third-party server but where it is not at the "disposal" of R Corp. That is, R Corp. does not have the ability or authority to make modifications or cause modifications to be made in the web site. In this situation, R Corp. pays a third-party to set up a web site, but control over the web site resides with the third-party rather than R Corp. In such a situation, the web site may not constitute a permanent establishment of R Corp.

[268]Presumably, R Corp. could specify in its contractual arrangement with RISP Corp. that the server cannot be established in country S if that were important.

If R Corp. conducts its business through a server in country S that takes and processes orders, country S might determine that the server constitutes a permanent establishment.[269] But in order to do so, country S would have to determine that R Corp.'s place of business (*i.e.*, the server) is a "fixed" place of business. Even if the server itself is maintained in one location,[270] R Corp.'s data that is stored on the server's hard drive may be stored in a different location on the hard drive every time it is saved. This fact raises the issue whether the storage of data in different locations on the same hard drive means that R Corp.'s presence in country S is not "fixed."

Case law suggests that the "fixed" requirement is met where R Corp.'s presence is in a delimited area (*i.e.*, the hard drive of a server). For example, in the *Market Vendor* case,[271] the court found a permanent establishment where a vendor sold his goods from different stands within a single marketplace. Similarly, German and Norwegian competent authorities reached agreement that Norwegian truck owners engaged in cleaning up storm-damaged German forests had a permanent establishment in Germany even though they parked their trucks at different locations within the forested area where the clean-up took place.[272] The forests themselves were a sufficiently delimited area. Norwegian and Swedish competent authorities reached a similar result where a Swedish company operated an offshore hotel platform in the Norwegian sector of the North Sea.[273] The floating platform was moved around within the Ekofisk field, an integrated field of permanent oil installations. The movement within the delimited area was not sufficient to prevent the platform from constituting a permanent establishment.[274]

As if it were prescient of the internet development, the OECD included in its Commentary a paragraph which finds a permanent establish-

---

[269]*See e.g.,* Discussion Report of the Australian Tax Office Electronic Commerce Project, *Tax and the Internet* 7.2.15 (August 1997).

[270]If it mattered for tax purposes, the server could be easily moved around or the web site could easily be moved from server to server.

[271]Finanzgericht Münster in EFG 1966, at 501 (Germany).

[272]Skaar, Permanent Establishment: Erosion of a Tax Treaty Principle 134-35 (1991). The same rationale was used in a 1990 agreement involving an almost identical fact pattern.

[273]*Id.* at 138-39.

[274]*See also* IRS Ltr. Rul. 8526005 (Dutch drilling contractor had a US PE where drilling vessel moved around within a limited area over a 2-year period).

ment where automatic gaming and vending machines and the likes are set up by a foreign enterprise and also operate for its account.[275] Some tax administrations may rely on this to find a permanent establishment under national and treaty tax law when a foreign company engages in electronic commerce over its host server.

The Austrian Administration, referring to this paragraph, thus finds a permanent establishment when a British enterprise sells information services via its web site on its own web server in Austria or on a web server maintained in Austria by an Austrian internet service provider from which the British enterprise leases space.[276] The Austrian administration finds no permanent establishment if the web server is maintained in another country. The Austrian interpretation is far-reaching, but does not reach so far that it hedges against the possibility that a multinational enterprise will avoid its application by locating its web server in a tax haven country and use that server for its sales over the internet to customers in Austria.

In the electronic commerce hypothetical set forth in section 4.2.1.1, suppose that instead of using a server in country S, R Corp. sells its products into country S through a server that is located either in country R or in a third country. Technologically, the location of a server is largely insignificant.[277] Does R Corp. have a permanent establishment in country S by virtue of the computers of its country S customers? Certainly where the computers are purchased or leased by the country S customers without any involvement of R Corp., the customers' computers cannot constitute a permanent establishment of R Corp. But consider the fact that the customers' computers will run client software, such as a web browser,[278] that will enable those computers to download HTML files or display their contents from R Corp.'s remote server. Does the presence of the HTML files, the display or downloading of which is initiated by the customers, create a permanent establishment in country S? It would stretch language beyond all meaning to suggest that the momentary display of an HTML file on a mon-

---

[275]OECD Commentary, 1997, Art. 5, para. 10.

[276]Britische Informationsangebote über BTX order internet, Steuer und Wirtschaft International, 1996, 462.

[277]The software can be controlled from a remote location. However, hardware problems or upgrades would require an on-site presence.

[278]Typically, the client software will be acquired by the customer without any involvement on the part of R Corp. However, in some cases, R Corp. might provide proprietary software that enables a customer to easily contact R Corp.'s remote server.

itor constitutes a "fixed" place of business. The HTML page may also be temporarily cached (*i.e.,* stored) on the customer's hard drive, but once the customer's computer disconnects from the internet, the temporary file on the hard drive is erased, unless the customer chooses to save the file.[279] In no sense can the file be considered a "fixed" place of business of R Corp.

Next consider whether the use of the telecommunications infrastructure might be considered a permanent establishment of R Corp. The phone lines, telephone switching equipment, and telecommunications offices all make possible R Corp.'s internet transmissions. If mere use of the telecommunications (or postal) infrastructure of a company were to constitute a permanent establishment of all nonresidents transacting business over the phone lines (or through the mails), the permanent establishment concept would have virtually no meaning. This realization has been treated as self-evident by most taxing authorities which have never argued that such use constituted a permanent establishment. The Danish Ministry of Taxation ruled that a resident of Sweden who transported electricity through a cable over the Danish continental shelf to a transformer station in Sweden did not have a permanent establishment in Denmark where the taxpayer's only connection with Denmark was the cable. *A fortiori,* where R Corp. is not in the telecommunications business, its use of the telecommunications infrastructure solely to carry electrical impulses does not constitute a permanent establishment. A similar result was reached in a 1978 German Bundesfinanzhof decision in which the court ruled that the transportation of oil through a pipeline does not constitute a permanent establishment.[280] The Austrian ruling discussed above reasoned that no permanent establishment would exist if the British enterprise used the network of the Austrian Post Office — a public independent facility — for the advertisement of its products to potential Austrian customers.[281]

---

[279]The user of a browser may have a choice about saving viewed HTML pages on the user's hard drive even after disconnection but that choice lies with the user and is not necessary in order to access the remote server.

[280]BStBl 1978 II 111, 112.

[281]If the telecommunication or postal infrastructure (phone lines, switches, office, etc.) of a telecommunications company were to constitute a permanent establishment, such expansive reach would result in the taxation of all enterprises selling goods and services over telephone lines of that country. It would make the entire permanent establishment concept meaningless as a territorial basis and restraint.

However, the Second Chamber of the German Supreme Tax Court (BFH) ruled that a Dutch corporation that supplied oil and oil products through underground pipelines in Germany constituted a German permanent establishment for purposes of the German Net Worth Tax Act.[282] German oil companies maintained delivery stations that supplied the companies with oil. The necessary oil pressure for transportation of the oil was supplied in the Netherlands. The Dutch company had no employees in Germany. All maintenance and repair of the pipelines in Germany was done by independent contractors. The court reasoned:

> [t]he pipeline in dispute is the way the [Dutch corporation], whose business is the transport of oil, conducts its business; indeed, it is the most important part of the [Dutch corporation's] business.[283]

The Court reasoned that it was irrelevant that the Dutch taxpayer operated the pipeline through a remote control system without any employees present in Germany. Fully automated equipment could constitute a permanent establishment. The *German Pipeline Case* may bolster the view that a server can constitute a permanent establishment. This position was previously articulated by the Court in an earlier case which noted that it is "not seriously doubtful" that a German pumping station, even though controlled from abroad, constitutes a permanent establishment.[284] It is the dominion and control of equipment, not its ownership, that can lead to a permanent establishment.[285]

This German decision does not truly speak to the issue of whether R Corp. has a permanent establishment in country S because of its use of the country S telecommunications infrastructure. Rather, the Court's decision by analogy may apply to telecommunications companies or internet ser-

---

[282]Decision of 30 October 1996, II R 12/92, *Betriebs-Berater* 1997. The Second Chamber of the BHF decides tax cases not involving the income tax.

[283]Hey, *German Court Rules Remote-Controlled Pipeline Constitutes a PE,* Tax Notes Int'l 651, 652 (24 Feb. 1997).

[284]Decision of 12 October 1977, Docket No. I R 226/75, Federal Tax Bulletin 1978 II, p. 111. *See* Hey, *supra* note 283, at 652.

[285]BFH of 11 October 1989, Federal Tax Bulletin 1990 II, 166; BFH of 3 February 1993, Federal Tax Bulletin 1993 II, 462.

vices providers (*e.g.*, ZISP Corp.) that maintain any equipment (*e.g.*, a satellite dish, a computer, switching equipment) in the host country. ZISP Corp. has present in country S various routers and other equipment that are stationed in offices of the country S telecommunications company. This equipment, which is used by ZISP Corp. to conduct its own trade or business, may very well constitute a permanent establishment in country S.[286] The fact that this equipment is perhaps used in space not owned by ZISP Corp. (*e.g.*, ZISP Corp. may place its equipment in a telephone company office) is not relevant.[287] It is also not relevant that for other persons the internet access equipment that is maintained by ZISP Corp. in country S is in essence a facility for the purpose of "display or delivery of goods or merchandise."[288] While that may be true for other persons, like R Corp., for ZISP Corp. the equipment maintained in country S enables ZISP Corp. to carry out its own business.[289]

If the "pipes" that carry bits do not constitute a permanent establishment for R Corp. in country S, does the presence of local access numbers (*i.e.*, nodes) constitute a fixed place that is "at the disposal" of R Corp.?[290] First, consider the situation where R Corp. makes no arrangements in country S for customer access. That is, the customers in country S make their own arrangements for internet access through internet service providers. Certainly in this situation, R Corp. cannot be considered to have a permanent establishment any more than if R Corp. were a mail order business sending catalogs to the private postal addresses of customers in state S. But suppose that R Corp. makes its own arrangements with internet service providers to provide a local access number that directly connects to R Corp.'s remote server or perhaps the local access number connects to the internet and the internet service provider advertises R Corp.'s web site. Do these voluntary actions by R Corp. to acquire a local presence in country S amount to a permanent establishment in that country? We know of no decisions or rulings that have directly addressed this issue. The decisions that indirectly bear on this issue do not provide much guidance. In *Piedras Ne-*

---

[286]OECD Commentary, 1997, Art. 5, para. 10.

[287]OECD Commentary, 1997, Art. 5, para. 4.

[288]OECD Model, 1997, Art. 5(4)(a).

[289]OECD Commentary, 1997, Art. 5, para. 24, 26.

[290]OECD Commentary, 1997, Art. 5, para. 5 (third sentence).

gras Broadcasting,[291] the court found that a local post office address for a nonresident broadcaster did not amount even to the conduct of a trade or business in the United States — a lower threshold than the permanent establishment standard. However, in *Consolidated Premium Iron Ores,*[292] the court noted the absence of a "telephone listing" as one of the factors leading to its determination that the taxpayer did not have a permanent establishment in the United States.[293]

Certainly, the mere fact that R Corp. has chosen RISP Corp. as its internet service provider does not mean that R Corp. has a permanent establishment in country S, even if RISP Corp. has a permanent establishment in country S. That is, suppose that RISP Corp., which is hired by R Corp. to connect it to the internet, also has a physical presence in country S in the form of various computers, routers, and switching equipment. This presence is used to connect residents of country S to the internet. Assume that R Corp. makes no direct use of any of the equipment in country S. RISP Corp.'s physical presence in country S should not be imputed to R Corp. any more than if R Corp. happens to purchase products produced by a company that happens to have a physical presence in country S.

Assuming *arguendo* that none of the internet factors discussed above would cause R Corp. to have a permanent establishment in country S, would the fact that R Corp. arranges for shipment of purchased merchandise from country R to country S be sufficient to constitute a permanent es-

---

[291]*Piedras Negras Broadcasting Co. v. Commissioner,* 43 BTA 297 (1941), *aff'd,* 127 F.2d 260 (5th Cir. 1942).

[292]*Commissioner v. Consolidated Premium Iron Ores,* 28 TC 127, 151 (1957), *aff'd* 265 F.2d 320 (6th Cir. 1959). In that case, a Canadian corporation (Consolidated) had a mailing address at the office of a US corporation (Otis) whose officers and stockholders owned most of the stock of Consolidated. The chief purpose of this arrangement was to finance the extraction of iron ore owned by an unrelated corporation (Steep Rock) and to sell the ore through Consolidated to US iron ore customers. To that end, Consolidated arranged for financing in exchange for stock of Steep Rock and negotiated a long-term requirements contract for the largest US iron ore purchaser to purchase virtually all of Steep Rock's production. The Service tried to tax the sales agency fees earned by Consolidated, but the Tax Court determined that Consolidated had no permanent establishment in the United States.

[293]*Cf. Wisconsin Department of Revenue v. William Wrigley, Jr., Co.,* 505 US 214, 219 (1992).

tablishment? Generally not, so long as R Corp. does not have a fixed place of business in country S. A finding of no permanent establishment is easy if R Corp. contracts with an outside company to have its goods delivered. However, R Corp. may also deliver the goods itself without causing it to have a permanent establishment in country S, since mere delivery of goods at a terminal (i.e., the purchaser's address) does not usually require a right to use a place of business in country S.[294] Only if R Corp. sets up some sort of fixed location for receipt of the goods in country S will it be in danger of having a permanent establishment. For example, in a US administrative ruling, the right to use part of a terminal was sufficient to satisfy the "fixed place of business" test resulting in a permanent establishment.[295] Thus, merely making arrangements for the shipping of the purchased goods will not constitute a permanent establishment.

A survey conducted in 39 countries around the world by Coopers & Lybrand concerning the permanent establishment implications of the wide range of telecommunications services indicates that no permanent establishment is likely to exist for the following services[296]:

- the provision of long-distance telephone services by a foreign company to local customers, without any local presence;
- the licensing by a foreign enterprise of technology and know-how to a local company, if there is no local presence;
- the leasing of telecommunication equipment to the local company, with no local supporting activity;
- the provision of call turnaround services if the telephone cards are marketed through an independent agent and if there is no substantial presence of the foreign enterprise by way of equipment, office space or employees;
- the provision of internet access services and computerised information; except that in some countries (*e.g.*, Austria) the ownership of

---

[294]*See,* SKAAR, *supra* note 272, at 134. ("[A] PE is not constituted if the enterprise solely delivers goods at different places in the country, as long as the transporter does not have right of use to a fixed place of business.").

[295]IRS Ltr. Rul. 8026004.

[296]COOPERS & LYBRAND, "GLOBAL TELECOMS TAX PROFILES" (1997). There is an absence of case law so the survey represents the opinions of contributors based on experience.

local telecommunications equipment through which the service is provided may well result in a taxable activity.

In several countries the services, if they do not create a permanent establishment, may still create a liability of withholding tax with respect to the royalty, rental or service fee paid to the foreign company.

4.2.1.2.3.1.2. Agency

Articles 5(1) through (4) of the OECD Model deal with whether a permanent establishment exists in situations where the enterprise has a place of business of some sort in the source state. In contrast, Article 5(5) describes situations in which an enterprise will be deemed to have a permanent establishment whether or not it maintains a physical place of business in the source state.[297]

Under Article 5(5), an enterprise will be deemed to have a permanent establishment in the source state if it utilizes a person (other than an independent agent described in Article 5(6)) for the purposes and in the manner described therein, even if the enterprise does not have a fixed place of business in the source state. In effect, Article 5(5) describes an agency relationship between a person in the source state and the enterprise in the state of residence. Because independent agents described in Article 5(6) are expressly excluded in this context, Article 5(5) applies only to dependent agents of the enterprise.[298] Article 5(5) is intended only to apply to enterprises that participate in the economy of the source state in a special way based on the nature and the scope of the authority they grant to persons in the source state to act on their behalf.[299]

Article 5(5) focuses on dependent agents of the enterprise. A dependent agent generally is subject to extensive control by the principal who generally bears the entrepreneurial risk.[300] Ordinarily, the dependency requirement will be met in the case of an employee of the enterprise, and normally it will not be met in the case of a self-employed person who performs similar activities for more than one principal. However, if an independent agent performs activities for an enterprise outside the normal course of the

---

[297]OECD Commentary, 1997, Art. 5, para. 31.
[298]OECD Commentary, 1997, Art. 5, para. 32.
[299]*Id.*
[300]OECD Commentary, 1997, Art. 5, para. 38.

agent's business, the agent may be a dependent agent of the enterprise with respect to such extraordinary activities.

The authority to contract on behalf of the enterprise must relate to the business activity of the enterprise itself. Authority to conduct internal administration (hire personnel, order office supplies) on behalf of the enterprise would not constitute a permanent establishment under Article 5(5).[301] For a permanent establishment to exist under Article 5(5), the agent must have authority to conclude contracts that bind the principal. Whether the requisite authority exists, however, does not depend on the mere legal authority of the agent actually to sign the contract on behalf of the enterprise. For example, the OECD Commentary provides that an agent has and exercises the requisite authority if the agent negotiates contracts on behalf of the enterprise that are actually signed in the state in which the enterprise is located.[302] Otherwise, it obviously would be easy to avoid permanent establishment status by imposing a mere signing formality.[303]

To constitute a permanent establishment, the agent must not only have authority to contract on behalf of the enterprise, but he must also habitually exercise that authority. The requirement that the authority be "habitually exercised" reflects the "permanence" aspect of the permanent establishment concept.[304] The OECD Commentary provides that the determination of whether the authority to contract is habitually exercised by the agent must be decided by examining the facts and circumstances involved in each case.[305] For example, the determination will depend in part on the nature of the business of the enterprise. In addition, the habitual nature of

---

[301] OECD Commentary, 1997, Art. 5, para. 33.

[302] *Id.*

[303] Nevertheless, the OECD Model provides that the agent must have authority to "conclude" contracts. This suggests that something more than mere negotiation by the agent is necessary to generate a permanent establishment. Neither the OECD Commentary nor case law provides additional assistance in determining how much contracting authority is necessary to generate a permanent establishment. As a practical matter, however, a permanent establishment should be deemed to exist where it may be presumed that the agreement negotiated by the agent will be accepted by the enterprise. This will depend on the particular facts and circumstances involved. For example, if the enterprise routinely accepts and signs contracts negotiated by the agent, the requisite authority should be deemed to exist.

[304] OECD Commentary, 1997, Art. 5, para. 33.

[305] *Id.*

the exercise of contracting authority should be examined in a manner analogous to the permanence requirement in Article 5(1).

An agent who acts on behalf of an enterprise and has the authority to conclude contracts and habitually exercises such authority will not constitute a permanent establishment of the enterprise if the agent's activities are limited to activities of a preparatory or auxiliary character as set forth in Article 5(4).[306] The mere possibility to conclude contracts with respect to activities beyond those mentioned in Article 5(4) is irrelevant, unless the agent exercises that authority habitually.

As a counterpart to Article 5(5), Article 5(6) of the OECD Model provides that an independent agent in the source state who acts on behalf of an enterprise of the state of residence and who meets the requirements of Article 5(6) will not cause the enterprise to be deemed to have a permanent establishment in the source state. The specific examples of independent agents listed in Article 5(6) are brokers and general commission agents. However, even brokers and general commission agents qualify as independent agents under Article 5(6) only if they otherwise satisfy the requirements of that provision. That is, a broker or general commission agent will be an independent agent under Article 5(6) only if his activities are legally and economically independent of the principal and he acts for the principal in the ordinary course of his business.[307]

---

[306]OECD Commentary, 1997, Art. 5, para. 28, 33.

[307]Whether an agent is independent of its principal depends on the nature and extent of the agent's legal and economic obligations to the principal. OECD Commentary, 1997, Art. 5, para. 38. An agent is legally independent of the principal if the contractual relationship between the agent and the principal does not allow the principal to dictate in detail the activities of the agent or otherwise supervise closely those activities. Obviously, no bright line approach can apply here and the facts and circumstances of each case must be carefully examined, including the nature of the business activity of the principal and the general practice in the industry. However, generally the more the principal/agent relationship resembles an employer/employee relationship, the more likely it will be that the agent will not be considered to be legally independent.

In examining the economic independence of an agent, an important factor to consider is the allocation of entrepreneurial risk. OECD Commentary, 1997, Art. 5, para. 38. Generally, the success of an independent agent's business will not depend primarily on the success of the business of the principal, although the success of either can influence the success of the other. For example, an economically independent agent generally should be in a position to allocate his efforts more to other principals if the business of one principal deteriorates.

4.2.1.2.3.1.2.1. Personal agents

In the electronic commerce hypothetical set forth in section 4.2.1.1, R Corp. has not engaged any agents — independent or dependent — that habitually exercise an authority to conclude contracts binding on R Corp. All products and/or services that are sold by R Corp. are distributed pursuant to contracts executed by R Corp. employees operating in country R. It is true that R Corp. may have some contractual relationships with other persons who are not customers but who facilitate the performance of R Corp.'s functions. For example, R Corp. may have concluded contracts with internet service providers to provide assistance to customers seeking to establish internet access. Just because a contract has been concluded does not make the internet service provider an agent of R Corp. Rather the internet service provider is a supplier of services to R Corp.

Even if an internet service provider were considered to be an agent of R Corp., contracts concluded by the internet service provider are not contracts on behalf of R Corp., which is not in the business of providing internet access. As stated by the OECD Commentary, "The authority to conclude contracts must cover contracts relating to operations which constitute the business proper of the enterprise."[308] If an internet service provider were deemed to function as an agent of R Corp., the agent's activities would still not constitute a permanent establishment under Article 5(5) of the OECD Model if it were merely carrying on functions specified in Article 5(4). Arranging for R Corp.'s potential customers to obtain internet access so that they can view R Corp.'s web page would appear to be arranging for the "display or delivery"[309] or more generally an activity that is "preparatory or auxiliary"[310] to R Corp.'s business of selling goods or services.

If R Corp. has any agency relationships, they would seem to fall squarely within Article 5(6) of the OECD Model — independent agents operating in the ordinary course of their own businesses. Similar reasoning leads to the conclusion that companies that might provide a credit check on the customers of R Corp. or other banking services would not constitute

---

[308] OECD Commentary, 1997, Art. 5, para. 33.
[309] OECD Model, 1997, Art. 5(4)(a).
[310] OECD Model, 1997, Art. 5(4)(e).

agents creating a permanent establishment for R Corp. under Article 5(5) of the OECD Model.

4.2.1.2.3.1.2.2. Software agents

Article 5(5), the agency permanent establishment provision in the OECD Model, is premised on the fact that even though a principal may not have a physical permanent establishment in the source country, the nature and level of the activities conducted by the principal's agent are sufficient to subject the principal to the source country's taxing authority. If contracts which bind the principal are concluded habitually in the source country, it is availing itself of the economic infrastructure in a sufficient manner to justify taxation. This result occurs whether the agents are employees of the principal or non-employee, dependent agents.

Suppose, though, that upon the request of a potential customer, who clicks on a hyperlink on the image of R Corp.'s web page that the customer has displayed on her monitor, R Corp.'s server dispatches a mobile software agent to the customer's browser. The intelligent software agent is able to answer questions, display products, provide pricing information, negotiate terms of payment, and conclude a contract of sale that binds both the customer and R Corp. All of this is done without any additional human input.[311] If the software agent does all of this on a regular basis in country S, might R Corp. have an agency permanent establishment in country S? After all, the software is accomplishing precisely the same functions that any person acting as an agent might accomplish and which would constitute a permanent establishment of R Corp. if accomplished by a personal agent. But perhaps "[t]here is a danger . . . in ascribing too much when borrowing terms from the human sphere."[312] A software agent is confined to decision-making based on a limited set of instructions.

Notwithstanding what the software agent does, as a technical matter the software agent cannot constitute a permanent establishment under Ar-

---

[311]Of course, the parameters within which the software agent acts are determined along with the other features of the agent by programmers.

[312]Krogh, *The Rights of Agents* in WOOLDRIDGE, MÜULLER AND TAMBE, INTELLI-GENT AGENTS II, PROCEEDINGS OF THE 1995 WORKSHOP ON AGENT THEORIES, ARCHI-TECTURES AND LANGUAGES, http://www.informatics.sintef.no/~chk/krogh/index.html

ticle 5(5) of the OECD Model as currently written. That provision refers to a "person" acting on behalf of an enterprise. The term "person" is defined in Article 3(1)(a) to include "an individual, a company and any other body of persons." A software agent is not a "person" within the meaning of the OECD Model. As a matter of tax policy, if the reason for Article 5(5) of the OECD Model is the nature (*i.e.,* concluding contracts) and the level (*i.e.,* habitually) of the activities in country S, it seems irrelevant to country S's taxing authority whether those activities are conducted by a personal or software agent. In any case, the debate may be more theoretical than real. Even if Article 5(5) of the OECD Model did encompass software agents that habitually concluded contracts in the name of a principal, technologically there is no difficulty in arranging for the conclusion of the contract to take place on R Corp.'s server in country R or elsewhere rather than on a customer's computer in country S.

4.2.1.2.3.2.   "Attributable to"

In the electronic commerce hypothetical set forth in section 4.2.1.1, if neither R Corp. nor ZISP Corp. is deemed to have permanent establishments in country S, it is unnecessary to determine under Article 7 of the OECD Model what business profits are subject to the taxing authority of country S because country S does not have the authority to tax business profits without a permanent establishment in country S. However if a permanent establishment does exist in country S, it is necessary to determine the business profits that result from that permanent establishment.

The second sentence of Article 7(1) of the OECD Model allows the state of the permanent establishment to tax business profits, "but only so much of them as is attributable to that permanent establishment." Thus, the OECD Model rejects the "force of attraction" principle for taxing permanent establishment income.[313] In general, profits are "attributable to" a permanent establishment if they result from the economic activities of the

---

[313]Under the "force of attraction" principle, if an enterprise of a Contracting State maintains a permanent establishment in the other Contracting State, the state in which the permanent establishment is located is entitled to tax all income the enterprise derives from sources within that state as permanent establishment income (business profits) whether or not that income is connected with the permanent establishment. OECD Commentary, 1997, Art. 7, para. 5.

permanent establishment. The OECD Commentary explains that the principle underlying the "attributable to" requirement is that a source country's taxing authority over business profits derives from the presence of the permanent establishment and not from the enterprise as a whole.[314] Thus, Article 7(1) draws a distinction between the activities of the permanent establishment and those of the head office or other parts of an enterprise. Taxation of business profits of the enterprise in the state in which the permanent establishment is located is permitted only where there is a connection between the activities of the permanent establishment and the profit the enterprise derives.

If R Corp. is deemed to have a permanent establishment in country S, the fiscal authorities can tax the business profits of R Corp. that are attributable to that permanent establishment. This raises a host of factual issues that illustrate the difficulty of applying the "attributable to" concept generally and to business profits that are generated through electronic commerce specifically. If R Corp. is deemed to have a permanent establishment by virtue of arrangements it makes with internet service providers to provide local access numbers, are all of R Corp.'s business profits from sales to customers in country S attributable to that permanent establishment? It may be true that in the absence of local access numbers, customers in country S would not be able to purchase the goods/services from R Corp. But it is also true that in the absence of R Corp.'s server in country S, there would be nothing for country S customers to access. Moreover, the internet connection permits country S customers to participate in only part of the sales cycle — obtaining information, placing an order, payment, shipping arrangements. The actual production of the goods/services sold (or their acquisition) may be independent of the means (e.g., the internet) by which they are sold. Accordingly, some of the profits generated by R Corp. may be attributable to a permanent establishment, but some of the profits are attributable to the activities taking place in country R.

This type of allocation problem is not unique to transactions over the internet. Allocation problems permeate international taxation. However, to the extent that the internet offers new ways of doing business that facilitate multi-jurisdictional participation, the allocation issues may become more difficult. For example, a country R company may have a manufacturing facility in country S. But the design of the manufacturing plant, the manu-

---

[314]OECD Commentary, 1997, Art. 7, para. 5.

facturing process, and the manufactured goods might have the joint input of engineers and others in many countries, communicating through video conferencing or various design programs over a network. Allocating the business profits resulting from such a manufacturing process where the manufacturing inputs are found in many jurisdictions will compound the allocation issues that exist under traditional forms of commerce. Legal principles may provide general guidance. But, tax authorities are going to have to deal with these issues on a case-by-case basis.

One of the paradigmatic changes arising out of electronic commerce is the very real change in the relationship between source and residence country in the contribution of those countries to the production and sales processes. In many cases, the profit attributable to the marketing and sales functions (typically incurred in the source country) declines relative to the production or manufacturing function that might take place in the residence state. It is now possible to do a large volume of business on the internet without making investments in office space, marketing and sales personnel, or distribution. Because investment in these functions has declined, the percentage of a company's profit allocated to these functions perhaps also should decline. On the other hand, where the use of the internet has made the production and dissemination of information easier for consumers, perhaps the profit allocated to those functions should reflect the value added by internet availability.

4.2.1.3.   *Independent services*

The tax issues that surround the performance of services can arise in a variety of contexts including electronic access to: the internet and on-line information services (*i.e.*, ISP's and OSP's); proprietary databases and/or on-line publications; consulting and other services; and software. In the electronic commerce hypothetical above in section 4.2.1.1, assume that in addition to ZISP Corp. providing internet access, ZOSP Corp., a country Z resident, offers on-line services along with internet access.[315] ZOSP Corp., like ZISP Corp., offers internet access, but also offers access to proprietary services, such as "chat rooms,"[316] discussion groups, email, assorted publi-

---

[315]ZOSP Corp. might charge more than ZISP Corp. to customers for the enhanced services.

[316]A "chat room" is an online real-time exchange of electronic messages, usually organized around specific topics.

cations, or various travel, banking, or financial services. Assume that R Corp., is a financial consulting company that offers: 1) a research database of companies, the shares of which are traded on the country R national stock exchange; 2) an on-line subscription to the weekly R Corp. newsletter filled with investment advice; 3) access to a bulletin board maintained by R Corp. for its subscribers; 4) on-line personal consulting through video conferencing or electronic messaging; and 5) investment software that customers can download electronically.

Income from transactions like those entered into by ZISP Corp., ZOSP Corp., and R Corp. may conceivably be classified as income from services, rental income, licensing income (*i.e.*, royalties), or income from the sale of property (tangible or intangible). Historically, international tax rules — both domestic and treaty — have classified income into categories with different rules applying to different categories of income. The parameters of these artificial categories are under extreme pressure as a result of electronic commerce.

Differences in the treatment of distinct categories of income might affect: tax base (*e.g.*, gross or net base); tax rates; administrative provisions (*e.g.*, withholding provisions); source rules; and treatment under anti-deferral regimes. For example, a country where services are performed by a nonresident may be able to fully tax the services income (*e.g.*, at rates that may typically be in the 35-50% range) while royalty income arising in that country may be subject to only a 15% or lower rate.[317] Moreover, services income may be taxed on a net basis while royalty income is taxable on a gross basis. Royalty income might be subject to a withholding requirement on the part of the payor while income from services or from a sale of goods may not. The significance of different source rules associated with different types of income might be that under one source rule a country would not be permitted to tax while under a different source rule taxing authority is permitted. For example, in *Karrer v. United States*,[318] a Swiss national, a scientist, maintained that he was compensated for services performed in Switzerland by a Swiss corporation for work culminating in several patents. The taxpayer maintained that the payments received were foreign source income not subject to US taxation even though the payments were based on US sales of the synthetic vitamins developed from his work. The IRS argued

---

[317]*See e.g.*, OECD Model, 1997, Art. 12 which does not permit source state taxation.

[318]152 F. Supp. 385 (Ct. Cl. 1957).

unsuccessfully that the appropriate source rule was the one dealing with royalties[319] and that the payments received for the use of a patent in the United States were US source income. The court determined that the payments were for the performance of services that were not performed in the United States.

Uncertainty over the correct source rule might lead to double taxation where, for example, country R, a tax credit country, does not consider the income in question to be sourced in country S while country S, applying a source rule for a different category of income, considers the income to be from sources in country S. Finally, the difficulty of classifying income may also affect the application of a country's anti-deferral provisions. For example, suppose that R Corp.'s wholly-owned country S subsidiary, S Corp., conducts the financial services activities listed above. If some of those activities are deemed to produce royalty income, country R may tax R Corp. on the royalty income earned by S Corp.[320] If the income were considered income from the performance of services, the income may not be taxable to R Corp. when earned by S Corp. in country S.

These kinds of problems arise because of the difficulty of distinguishing income from services from other types of income. That problem is explored below in the context of the electronic commerce hypothetical in section 4.2.1.1. Even if a particular item of electronic commerce-generated income is treated as income from services, it is not always easy to determine the source of the income produced. After considering the types of transactions that give rise to these issues, legal principles under national and treaty law are considered.

4.2.1.3.1. Problems presented

4.2.1.3.1.1. What are services

It seems likely that fees received for access to the internet provided by ZISP Corp. and ZOSP Corp. would be treated as income from the performance of services. It is true that both ZISP Corp. and ZOSP Corp. normally

---

[319] IRC § 861(a)(4).

[320]For example, in the United States, IRC § 954(c) may treat royalty income as subpart F income that is taxable to R Corp. when earned by S Corp. *But see* IRC § 954(c)(2)(A). If the income were considered income from the performance of services in country S, subpart F may not apply.

would, in effect, sublease to customers access to telecommunications lines that they have leased from the telephone company, perhaps suggesting that customers are paying rent for the subleased lines. But more accurately ZISP Corp. and ZOSP Corp. are providing an overall access service to customers, and to render that service the providers lease telecommunications capacity. In addition to internet access, ZOSP Corp. offers what in the industry is generally referred to as "on-line services."[321] The income generated by ZOSP Corp. is likely to be characterized as income from the performance of services, rather than fragmenting the income produced into component parts (*e.g.*, royalty payment for the use of a database).[322] This conclusion is supported by the fact that typically on-line service providers bill customers monthly based on usage, the arrangements can be easily terminated by either contracting party, there are few restrictions (*i.e.*, other than copyrights) and the service provider continually updates the information made available to customers. Some of the issues raised if each of the activities offered by ZOSP Corp. were considered separately are considered in connection with the activities of R Corp.

Turning to the activities of R Corp., the payments[323] it receives for providing a database, on-line subscriptions, and a bulletin board might be considered income for the performance of services or might be considered royalty income for the use of a copyrighted intangible. Perhaps the income might be considered income from the sale of an information product. For example, if the database or the electronic publication contains financial material that is also published as a book, magazine, CD, cassette, etc., dispositions of those items might give rise to income from the sale of products. However, access to a database, on-line subscription, or bulletin board is in many ways similar to a license — users are given the right to use the electronic material rather than to purchase it. Suppose a customer makes a search request to the financial database (*e.g.*, please provide the price/earnings ratios of all banks with assets of more than $1 billion and indicate whether to buy, sell, or hold shares in such banks) which produces the re-

---

[321]The services might include chat rooms, discussion groups, email, assorted publications, or various travel, banking, or financial services.

[322]*See* Cigler, Burritt and Stinnett, *Cyberspace: The Final Frontier for International Tax Concepts?* J. INT'L TAX. 340, 344 (August 1996).

[323]Typically, the fees might be based on a variety of factors such as time spent accessing the central processing unit, the number of searches made, or the number of files searched.

quested information in the form of a report. If the same request were made to an R Corp. employee, it is likely that the income received by R Corp. would be income from the performance of services. Indeed, the on-line consulting income R Corp. generates either through video conferencing or electronic messaging would be classified as income from the performance of services. Should the result change if R Corp. uses software that enables the automatic preparation of the same material from its database?

Many of the most difficult classification of income problems arise with respect to income generated by the acquisition of computer software. Suppose that R Corp. permits customers to download investment software. If the software were "shrink-wrapped" software sold through a store, the income produced would likely be treated in the same manner as the sale of a book — income from the sale of a tangible good. But suppose that the downloaded software is subject to a variety of restrictions with respect to the use of the software (*e.g.*, on what machine it can be used), the software is customized for each customer and the customer can use the downloaded software for a limited time. Faced with these factors, a taxing authority might determine that the customer licensed the software so that payments to R Corp. would constitute royalties. If the computer program is considered to be tangible personal property, the license of the program would give rise to rental income.[324] Finally, depending on the nature of the software downloaded and the support that accompanies the software, taxing authorities might treat payment for the software as a payment for the provision of services.[325] For example, if R Corp. promises customers that when they download the generic investment software, R Corp. programmers will modify the software in accordance with specifications provided by customers, payments received by R Corp. may be treated as income from the performance of services.[326]

---

[324]For example, if R Corp. leased hardware including a central processing unit (CPU) that contained computer instructions, the payment would likely be treated as rental income.

[325]*See e.g.,* Notice 702/4/94, "Importing computer software," HM Customs and Excise (UK) (1 Sept. 1994).

[326]The classification conflict between royalty and services income is illustrated by *Boulez v. Commissioner,* 83 TC 584 (1984). *See also Ingram v. Bowers,* 57 F.2d 65 (2d Cir. 1932). In *Boulez,* a musical conductor residing in Germany was subjected to double taxation on payments he received from CBS for recordings made of his performances in the United States. The amount of the payments was calculated based on the proceeds CBS received from sales of the recordings. Germany treated the payments as royalties, which

4.2.1.3.1.2. Where are services rendered

Even assuming that difficulties of characterizing income can be overcome, services income produced by electronic commerce generally must be sourced in order to determine whether a country has taxing authority under domestic law. For example, if R Corp. produces services income from its on-line or video conferencing activities, is that income generated in country R where R Corp. operates or country S where customers access the services through the browser on their computers? There are at least three reasonable source rules that could be implemented with respect to income from the performance of services. First, income from the performance of services could be deemed to arise where the services are performed. Second, if different from the place where services are performed, services income might be sourced where the benefit of the services is received. Finally, income from the performance of services might be sourced where the benefit of the services is utilized, which may or may not be where the services are received.

Typically, all three of these possible source rules arise in a single country. For example, if R Corp. generated financial consulting income by sending employees to country S to meet with country S customers, the place where services were performed, where services were received or where services were utilized would be in country S. Even in this traditional mode of producing services income, there may be some uncertainty concerning the source of the services income. For example, R Corp.'s employees may think about a country S customer's needs and even devise strategies to meet those needs while sitting in an office in country R after meeting with the customer in country S and before meeting again with the customer to plan a course of action in country S. In this situation, arguably at least some of the services are rendered in country R, although the benefit of those services would be received in country S.[327] Suppose that the customer travels to country R to receive the advice of R Corp. employees and then returns to

---

under the applicable treaty were taxable exclusively in Germany. The United States, however, treated the payments as services income which was subject to US taxation. Based on the language of the contract between Boulez and CBS, the US tax court determined that the parties intended to establish a contract for personal services, thereby allowing source state taxation of the income from services by the United States under the then-existing treaty between the United States and Germany.

[327] Alternatively, R Corp. may provide financial consulting advice over the telephone to a customer in country S.

country S to implement the investment advice. Now the services are rendered and received in country R but are utilized in country S. Conceivably, both country R and country S might, relying on source jurisdiction, claim the authority to tax the income generated by the services income.

Conflicts over source which can arise under traditional methods of commerce may become more prominent as electronic commerce spreads. If R Corp. renders financial consulting advice through an exchange of electronic messages or through video conferencing, should the source of the income be in country R or in country S? In some cases, a customer in country S may click on a hyperlink on the customer's browser in country S causing the downloading of an interactive program from R Corp.'s server in country R.[328] The interactive program provides advice to the country S customer based on the responses received. Assuming that payment for the use of this program is considered a payment for services, where are the services rendered — in country R where the programmers and financial advisers work or in country S where the program interacts with the customer?

Turning from the content provider, R Corp., to the service providers, ZISP Corp. and ZOSP Corp., it is likely that some or all of the income generated by ZISP Corp. and ZOSP Corp. would be treated as income from the performance of services. However, in some countries an issue may arise concerning the correct source rule to employ even if the income is characterized as income from the performance of services (*e.g.*, different source rules for different types of services). For example, under US law, international communications income of a nonresident is generally deemed to be from foreign sources unless attributable to an office or other fixed place of business in the United States.[329] If ZISP Corp. (or ZOSP Corp.) does not have an office or other fixed place of business in country S and if the international communications source rule were to apply, then country S would not be able to tax the income earned by the provider from providing internet access and other services to customers in country S. On the other hand, if a more general source rule for services applied rather than the international communications source rule, then perhaps country S would have taxing authority because the provider was rendering its access services in country S.

---

[328]The downloaded program may be an ActiveX program. *See supra* text accompanying notes 112-113.

[329]IRC § 863(e)(1)(B).

4.2.1.3.2. National law

The United States has grappled with the question of whether income is generated from the performance of services or falls into another income category in a variety of circumstances.[330] In some cases, Congress has entered the fray. For example, in Code section 7701(e), Congress has set forth the following factors for determining whether a transaction which purports to be a service contract shall be treated as a lease of property:

- the service recipient is in physical possession of the property,
- the service recipient controls the property,
- the service recipient has a significant economic or possessory interest in the property,
- the service provider does not bear any risk of substantially diminished receipts or substantially increased expenditures if there is nonperformance under the contract,
- the service provider does not use the property concurrently to provide significant services to entities unrelated to the service recipient, and
- the total contract price does not substantially exceed the rental value of the property for the contract period.

This formulation typifies the general approach — that where elements of the provision of tangible property and the performance of services are intertwined, the transaction is generally classified depending on the predominant nature of the transaction. For example, if a consultant is hired, ultimately culminating in the presentation of a written report to the client, the payment received by the consultant normally would be income from services.[331] In contrast, if a customer purchases a washing machine which is installed by the seller, the payment received by the seller will normally be treated as gain from the sale of property.[332]

---

[330]See e.g., Bank of America v. United States, 680 F.2d 142 (Ct. Cl. 1982) (commissions on letters of credit were in the nature of interest not services); Cook v. United States, 599 F.2d 400 (Ct. Cl. 1979) (sculptor's income on sale of a sculpture was services income rather than income from the sale of property).

[331]See e.g., Rev. Proc. 71-21, 1971-2 CB 549. US Treasury Report, supra note 217.

[332]See e.g., Reg. § 1.451-5.

In the case of R Corp.'s activities, it is not clear how the payments would be treated under US law. If R Corp. charges users a general fee that provides access to all that R Corp. offers, the entire payment may be classified as a service, particularly if R Corp. is constantly updating its database, bulletin board, newsletter, etc. There is little guidance under federal law. Under state tax law, many states treat the electronic transmission of information as a taxable service.[333] While the statutory wording differs from state to state, fees for the use of R Corp.'s financial database, on-line subscription to the newsletter, access to the bulletin board, and on-line video conferencing would all be treated as "services."[334]

The US Treasury has addressed the treatment of income from the investment software that R Corp. makes available for customer downloading. The Treasury formulation is too broad to provide a high degree of certainty but highlights: 1) the intent of the parties; 2) which party owns the copyright in the computer program; and 3) how the risks of loss are allocated.[335] For example,[336] suppose that a country S customer commissions R Corp. to

---

[333] See Frieden, *The Taxation of Cyberspace: State Tax Issues Related to the Internet and Electronic Commerce,* available in LEXIS/NEXIS, 96 STN 221-57 (14 November 1996).

[334] Some states treat the electronic transmission of information content as a taxable "information service." *See e.g.,* D.C. Code Ann. § 47-2001(n)(B); N.Y. Tax Law § 1105(c)(1). In *Mark S. Klein,* TSB-A-93(65)S (Dec. 1993), an investment advisor was subject to sales tax on receipts from the sale of its online news service. *See also Quotron Systems, Inc.,* TSB-A-93(61)S (Nov. 1993) (out-of-state corporation that electronically transmitted financial information to its New York subscribers was selling an information service).

Some states treat electronic transmission of information as a taxable "electronic information service." *See e.g.,* Ohio Rev. Code § 5739.01(c).

Some states treat electronic transmission of information as a taxable "computer service." *See e.g.,* Conn. Agencies Regs. § 12-426-27(b)(1); Pa. Pronouncement § 60.13(a) and (b)(1).

Not all states treat the transmission of electronic information as production of services income. For example, cities in Arizona treat the electronic transmission of magazines and pictures as the sale of tangible personal property. Frieden, *supra* note 333, at 19. The city of Chicago taxes the electronic transmission of information as the lease of tangible personal property if the information is accessed from a computer in Chicago. See Chicago Personal Property Lease Transaction Tax Ordinance.

[335] Reg. § 1.861-18(d).

[336] Reg. § 1.861-18(h) Ex. 15.

create financial software pursuant to the instructions of the customer. Upon completion, the copyright in the program would belong to the customer. The customer pays R Corp. a fixed amount during the software development. The customer can cancel the contract at any time, but upon cancellation R Corp. retains all payments and the customer retains any work that has been done. There is no provision between the customer and R Corp. for any future work. Under these circumstances fees received by R Corp. would be fees for services. On the other hand, if the customer pays R Corp. for the right to download "canned" software, the transaction is likely to be treated as a purchase of goods.[337]

Individual US states do not treat the electronic transmission of software in a consistent manner. Some states treat the software as tangible personal property.[338] Others treat the software as electronic services.[339] Some states distinguish between standard software, which is treated as tangible personal property, and custom software, which is treated as intangible personal property.[340] Some states treat custom software as a taxable service.[341]

If it is determined that some or all of the income generated by R Corp., ZISP Corp., and ZOSP Corp. is income from the performance of services, it is necessary to determine where the services are performed. Under Code section 861(a)(3), rents from human capital (*i.e.*, income from the performance of services) are sourced where the services are rendered. This can be contrasted with some of the source rules for other types of rental income, such as those rules governing rents for the use of intangible property (*i.e.*, royalties) which are sourced according to where the intangible (*e.g.*, a copyright, patent) is used. The significance of this dichotomy is fully illustrated by *Karrer*.[342] Under US law, it is not where the services are received or uti-

---

[337]Reg. § 1.861-18(h) Ex. 2. Existing, prepackaged programs of general application not created for any particular user, but instead to be sold to many different users are referred to as "canned" software. *Comptroller of the Treasury v. Equitable Trust Co.,* 464 A.2d 248, 250 (Md. 1983). Custom software, on the other hand, is developed, at least in part, specifically for the party acquiring the software. Scott, Scott on Computer Law, at 10-2 (1993).

[338]*See e.g.,* Ill. Admin. Code tit. 86, § 130.1935(a).

[339]*See e.g.,* Pa. Revenue Pronouncement § 60.13(c)(iii).

[340]*See e.g.,* Pa. Rev. Pronouncement § 60.13(c)(iii).

[341]*See e.g.,* Me. Rev. Stat. Ann. tit. 36, § 1752(17-A).

[342]*See supra* text accompanying note 318. The source of income from the performance of services can also determine whether a US shareholder must recognize subpart

lized but rather where the services are rendered that is solely determinative. That is why in cases like *Ingram v. Bowers*[343] and *Boulez v. Commissioner,*[344] once the courts determined that the income generated was services income rather than royalty income, there was no issue concerning the source of the services rendered (*i.e.,* United States) even though the result of those services (*i.e.,* recordings) were purchased and utilized outside the United States.[345]

As to the various activities of R Corp., *Commissioner v. Piedras Negras Broadcasting Co.*[346] may offer the closest US authority concerning the source rules for services rendered. In *Piedras Negras,* a Mexican corporation received advertising income from advertisers in the United States where the advertisements were directed largely to a US audience. The court of appeals affirmed that the source of the income from advertising services was in Mexico stating:

> If income is produced by the transmission of electromagnetic waves that cover a radius of several thousand miles, free of control or regulation by the sender from the moment of generation, the source of that income is the act of transmission.[347]

Although R Corp.'s server does not transmit until a country S customer initiates a request for one of R Corp.'s services, that act of transmission would determine the source under US federal law.

ZISP Corp. and ZOSP Corp., which provide access services for customers in country S, would be taxable on the access services where they are performed. It is likely that the US taxing authorities would source the income based on where the customer is provided internet access. The internet service providers, however, might be able to show that part of the service

---

F income generated by a controlled foreign corporation. Subpart F income includes services which "are performed outside the country under the laws of which the controlled foreign corporation is organized." IRC § 954(e).

[343] 47 F.2d 925 (S.D.N.Y. 1931), *aff'd.* 57 F.2d 65 (2d Cir. 1932).

[344] 83 TC 584 (1984).

[345] *See also Cook v. United States,* 599 F.2d 400 (Ct. Cl. 1979), where a sculptor's services income was deemed to be foreign source even though title to the finished sculpture passed in the United States and the sculpture was purchased by a US customer.

[346] F.2d 260 (5th Cir. 1942).

[347] *Id.* at 261.

they are providing is worldwide access to the internet for country S customers. Consequently, some of the fees paid for access might be allocated to where the provider's servers, routers and other equipment are located.[348] However, consistent with the reasoning of the Supreme Court decision in *Goldberg v. Sweet*,[349] the IRS may determine that the source of all fees received for internet access services is where users can access the internet (*i.e.*, the local access node). In *Goldberg*, the Supreme Court determined that a state tax on the entire charge of a telephone call that either originated or terminated in the taxing state (and that was billed to an in-state billing address) did not violate the "fair apportionment" requirement of the Commerce Clause, even though the telephone access provided service beyond the tax state's border.[350] The Court reaffirmed its decision in *Goldberg* in *Oklahoma Tax Commission v. Jefferson Lines*.[351] There, the taxing state imposed a sales tax on the entire price of a bus ticket purchased in the taxing state, although a portion of the bus service was to be performed out-of-state.

If the internet access provided by ZISP Corp. and ZOSP Corp. is considered to be international communications income, the services income would be foreign source income except to the extent that the income is attributable to an office or other fixed place of business in the United States. The term "international communications income" is defined as "income derived from the transmission of communications or data from . . . any foreign country (or possession of the United States) to the United States."[352] Depending on how that term is interpreted, it could cover only telecommunications companies or it could apply to internet access providers as well.[353]

---

[348]*See* Reg. § 1.861-4(b)(1)(i).

[349]US 252 (1989).

[350]The Court determined that the tax satisfied all prongs of the *Complete Auto* test. *See infra* text accompanying note 588.

[351]US 175 (1995).

[352]IRC § 863(e)(1)(B).

[353]A similar issue arises under state tax law. Most US states tax telecommunications services. It is clear that residential telephone calls and cellular communications are covered. There is a difference among the states concerning whether enhanced services such as internet access, email, and bulletin boards are subject to the tax on telecommunications sales. A number of states (*e.g.*, Indiana, Kansas) impose a sales or use tax on "basic" transmission services, but not "enhanced" (or "value added") services, as those

In Japan, a foreign corporation's domestic source personal service income is not generally taxable in the absence of a permanent establishment. However, income from certain special types of personal services will be subject to net base taxation even in the absence of a permanent establishment.[354] These types of personal services include income derived from a "business which consists principally of providing the services of an individual possessing expert knowledge or special skill relating to scientific technology, management control, and other fields by putting that knowledge or skill to practical use."[355] Because providing access to internet-based and on-line information services is not the same as providing the services of an individual possessing expert knowledge or special skill, income derived from the provision of such services will not be subject to Japanese taxation in the absence of a permanent establishment, unless some other business factors are substantially involved. Thus, the taxation of internet and on-line services hinges upon whether the operator in question has a permanent establishment in Japan.

4.2.1.3.3.   Treaty law

Assume in the electronic commerce hypothetical set forth in section 4.2.1.1 that the activities of R Corp., ZISP Corp., and ZOSP Corp. produce services income under applicable domestic tax law. If an OECD Model

---

terms are defined under federal regulatory guidelines. 47 C.F.R. § 64.702(a). The term "basic services" refers to the pure transmission capability over a communications path that is virtually transparent in terms of its interaction with customer supplied information. This would include local exchange and long-distance phone calls. The term "enhanced service" is any service offered over a telecommunications network that: (a) employs computer processing applications that act on format, content, code, protocol or similar aspects of the subscriber's transmitted information; (b) provides the subscriber additional, different, or restructured information; or (c) involves subscriber interaction with stored information. This would appear to cover the type of services rendered by ZISP Corp. and ZOSP Corp. Other states define telecommunications services broadly to include more than the basic services such as internet access or database access. *See generally* Frieden and Porter, *The Taxation of Cyberspace: State Tax issues Related to the Internet and Electronic Commerce,* available in LEXIS/NEXIS, 96 STN 221-57 (14 Nov. 1996); Grierson, *Tennessee, Connecticut Step Up Efforts to Tax Internet Service Providers,* STATE TAX NOTES 410 (5 Aug. 1996).

[354]Corporation Tax Law, Art. 141(iv)(a).
[355]Corporation Tax Law, Art. 141(iv)(b).

treaty applies, how should the income be treated? Article 14 provides that income derived by a resident of a Contracting State (*e.g.*, R Corp.) in respect of professional services or other activities of an independent character shall be taxable only in that state. However, income may be taxed in the other Contracting State (*i.e.*, country S) to the extent attributable to a fixed base in that state.

The OECD Commentary provides that the principles of Article 7 can be used as guidance for interpreting Article 14.[356] The terms "permanent establishment" and "fixed base" are used in the same manner, namely, to determine when the state of residence and when the state of source have primary taxation rights.[357] An activity exercised abroad does not justify taxation by the foreign state unless there is a sufficiently intensive economic connection. The presence of a permanent establishment or a fixed base is the criterion for assuming that such an intensity of economic connection exists. The criteria are similar, regardless of whether business enterprises or personal services are involved.[358]

However, the fixed base must be "regularly" available to the person performing the independent personal services. In this regard, a fixed base differs from a permanent establishment. For a permanent establishment to exist, it is required that the business of the enterprise be "carried on" in the fixed place of business. In contrast, the fixed base only needs to be available to the person performing the services. It is not required that the fixed base be used continually; permanent use of the fixed base could not be required because of the very nature of independent personal services. Thus, the principles developed for determining whether a permanent establishment exists cannot completely be transferred to the same determination in respect to a fixed base, since the continuity of operation is critical in determining the existence of a permanent establishment, but of little importance for determining the existence of a fixed base.

More fundamental than the differences between "fixed base" and "permanent establishment" is whether Article 14 even applies to any services income produced by R Corp., ZISP Corp., or ZOSP Corp. It is likely that any services income generated by R Corp. or the access providers would fall under Article 7 rather than Article 14. The OECD Commentary does not de-

---

[356]OECD Commentary, 1997, Art. 14, para. 4.

[357]*See* Michaux, '*Fixed Base' and Its Relation to 'Permanent Establishment*,' INTERTAX 68 (1987).

[358]OECD Commentary, 1997, Art. 14, para. 3.

fine "professional services" which might well include financial consulting or granting access to financial databases. However, the OECD Commentary notes that Article 14 "excludes industrial and commercial activities."[359] It seems likely that the activities of R Corp. and the access providers would be considered commercial activities.

If Article 7, rather than Article 14, applies to the income generated by the rendering of services, country S will only be able to tax income generated from services if the income is attributable to a permanent establishment in country S. Whether R Corp. or the internet service providers have a permanent establishment in country S is discussed above.[360] If there is a permanent establishment, only the income attributable to the permanent establishment is subject to tax in country S. Determining that income and the expenses associated with that income poses the same types of problems that non-electronic commerce poses.

4.2.1.4. Dependent services

4.2.1.4.1. Problems presented

Many of the issues raised in the context of dependent personal services are the same as or are variations of the issues raised with respect to the rendering of services in general. To focus the discussion, suppose that R Corp., a country R resident, hires E, an employee, located in country Z. E performs the work required by R Corp. through "telecommuting." That is, from E's home, or perhaps an office, in country Z, E logs in to the R Corp. computer intranet through R Corp.'s server in country R. On the R Corp. intranet, E might engage in a variety of functions, including video conferencing, analyzing data and preparing reports or other documents. How E accomplishes the work depends on the nature of R Corp.'s network.

There are at least four possible ways of interfacing with R Corp.'s server depending on how R Corp. configures its network. First, E might use E's computer as a "dumb terminal" connected to R Corp.'s central computer. Think of R Corp.'s central computer as having a very long cord that connects the central computer and E's remote keyboard and monitor.

---

[359]OECD Commentary, 1997, Art. 14, para. 1.
[360]See supra section 4.2.1.2.3.1.

Stated differently, E would transmit characters from the keyboard but all processing would be accomplished in the memory of the central computer and any storage would occur on the hard drive of the central computer. Second (and conversely), if R Corp. uses a "file server" model for its network, all of the processing would take place on the central processing unit (CPU) of E's remote terminal although storage would normally be on the hard drive of R Corp.'s server. Third, in a true client-server network, the processing of information can be shared between the server and the client. For example, if a client sends a request to search a database on the server, the processing of that request takes place on the CPU of the server. Once the requested records are found, normally they would be downloaded to E's remote computer where E would manipulate them on the CPU of the remote computer. They would then be sent back to the server for storage. Finally, in a distributed processing model, any processing that is requested of the server by E might be done on the CPU of the R Corp. server or might be done on the CPU of any computer that is connected to the server (*e.g.,* other remote computers). Stated differently, distributed processing allows a network to make more efficient use of all the processing capacity that is available on the network.

The central issue raised by these technological possibilities is determining where the employee is rendering services. In the example above, does E render services where E is physically located or should the services be sourced where the processing takes place?[361] Note that in the case of a distributed processing network, that processing could conceivably take place in any country that has computers that are connected to the R Corp. network.

If country R does not tax E on the services performed because E is in country Z when performing them, country R may nevertheless be able to tax the value that E has added to R Corp. Suppose that E receives 100u for the services performed in country Z and that the services performed for R Corp. enable R Corp. to earn an additional 120u.[362] R Corp. normally would deduct the 100u cost of earning the 120u in calculating the income

---

[361]There are other possibilities as well. For example, E's services could be sourced where they are utilized.

[362]Assume that there are no other fixed costs (*e.g.,* secretary, plant, equipment) or marginal costs (*e.g.,* telephone toll charges, supplies, electricity) associated with E's work.

to be reported to country R.[363] Assuming that country R does not tax E on the 100u that E earns, country R would collect a tax on 20u, the value added to R Corp. Some countries might regard this result as a leak in the system, depriving them of the authority to tax the full 120u of wealth created as a result of E's services and R Corp.'s value added. This view stems from the fact that it is the R Corp. server in country R that allows E to produce value and that E owes an economic allegiance to country R as a result. Tax laws that reflect this view might determine that E's services were rendered where the processing takes place which, depending on the nature of R Corp.'s network, may be in country R.

Of course, it might be appropriate to allocate the income in some fashion. Suppose that E stood on the country Z side of the border that separates country Z from country R. With arms extended over the border, E opens various books and files, turns pages, locates the information desired, and writes a report all the while standing in country Z. The hands are writing in country R but the head is thinking in country Z. A variation might be that E is situated entirely in country Z, operating a robotic arm that does the research and writes the report. Perhaps a more realistic situation is where E phones from country Z to country R to do research and then dictates findings to someone in country R. Or E accomplishes the same tasks through video conferencing. In these situations, should the income generated by E be allocated in some fashion, on one hand, to the thinking that went on in country Z and, on the other hand, to the physical manipulations in country R?

It is worthwhile to point out that historically, there have always been situations where a corporation in country R paid employees who rendered dependent personal services in country Z. In these traditional situations, it may be easier to see that it is country Z to which E owes economic allegiance because country Z provides the infrastructure that makes E's work possible. Telecommuting may make it possible for more employees to render more services while situated outside country R (*i.e.*, a difference in degree) than have done so traditionally. Moreover, telecommuting blurs the geographic boundaries, making it difficult to determine which jurisdiction has provided the infrastructure giving rise to E's creation of wealth (*i.e.*, a difference in kind).

---

[363] Assume that the 120u earned by R Corp. is attributable to R Corp.'s home office and not some presence in country Z or elsewhere.

4.2.1.4.2.   National law

Under US law, sourcing income produced by the rendering of dependent personal services is no different from sourcing income produced by the rendering of independent personal services.[364] It is the situs of performance that is determinative.[365] While no case or ruling directly confronts the situation where a person situated in one country is able to manipulate data in another country (*e.g.*, by accessing a server), it seems likely that the place where services are utilized does not, under current law, determine source.[366]

If a search of a database in country R by E, situated in country Z, did constitute the performance of services in country R, presumably the compensation income earned by E would be allocated in accordance with the services performed.[367] Typically, allocation might be based on the number of days E spends in country Z and country R,[368] but allocation based on time spent is not the only means of allocation.[369] In the case of E, would the allocation be based on the amount of time E accesses the R Corp. server in country R compared with the amount of time E spends in country Z working for R Corp.?[370] Administration of such a source rule would be problematic.[371]

---

[364]IRC § 861(a)(3).

[365]Reg. § 1.861-4(a)(1)

[366]*See e.g., Piedras Negras Broadcasting Co. v. Commissioner,* 43 BTA 297 (1941) (fees for broadcasting advertisements sourced where broadcasting facilities were located, not where consumers heard the advertisements).

[367]Reg. § 1.861-4(b)(1).

[368]*See e.g., Stemkowski v. Commissioner,* 690 F.2d 40 (2d Cir. 1982).

[369]Reg. § 1.861-4(b)(1)(i) (last sentence).

[370]Note that when E accesses the server in country R, E is also performing services (*e.g.*, thinking and typing commands) in country Z.

[371]It should be noted that there is some support in US law for the notion that physical presence in a country is not a prerequisite for determining that an employee's income from service-like payments should be sourced in that country. In *Korfund Co., v. Commissioner,* 1 TC 1180 (1943), the court determined that payment for a promise not to compete should be sourced in the jurisdiction where the taxpayer promised not to compete. A payment for an agreement not to compete is a payment for an agreement not to render services. The court sourced the income in the jurisdiction where the ser-

Because cross-border activity in Switzerland is substantial, the Swiss have introduced special provisions for frontier workers in its treaties and in ad hoc agreements with most countries bordering on Switzerland.[372] The aim of these agreements is to avoid double taxation, often giving one state full right of taxation and providing the other state with an equitable compensation. Generally speaking, frontier workers are employees who commute daily between their place of residence in one state and their place of employment in another state.[373] One interesting question is whether rules applying to employees commuting daily from one state to another could or should be extended to telecommuters.

4.2.1.4.3. Treaty law

The term "dependent personal services" found in the OECD Model refers to services performed by a resident in an employment capacity, where an employee-employer relationship exists between the resident performing the services and the person or entity paying for those services. This is to be contrasted with "independent personal services" which refer to services performed by an individual for that individual's own account, where the individual receives the proceeds or bears the losses arising from those activities.

Unlike independent personal services, the income of which is generally taxable exclusively in the state of residence of the person performing those services,[374] income from dependent personal services is taxable in the state

---

vices were not performed according to the agreement even though the taxpayer was not present in that jurisdiction. However in reaching its decision, the court clarified that it was not treating the income for the covenant not to compete as income from services. *See also* Rev. Rul. 74-108, 1974-1 CB 248 (similar analysis for a sign-on bonus); *Linseman v. Commissioner*, 82 TC 514 (1984) (sign-on bonus sourced in the same way as services income). Perhaps read very broadly, *Korfund* stands for the proposition that when a person is compensated for some action or inaction (*i.e.,* rendering services or refraining from rendering services), it is the location of the effect of the person's action or inaction that determines source for tax purposes.

[372]Switzerland IFA Branch, *Comments on Electronic Commerce Report* (1998) (on file with the authors).

[373]Supreme Court Judgment of 19 June 1984, 55 Archives de droit fiscal at 585.

[374]This assumes that the income is not attributable to a fixed base in the source state.

where those services are performed (state of employment).[375] The general rule that dependent personal services are taxable in the state where performed is subject to certain exceptions, which are listed in Article 15(2) of the OECD Model. If employment is exercised in the state of employment, that state has the primary right to tax remuneration, but only if the employee is present in that state for more than 183 days in the taxable year concerned or if the remuneration is paid by, or on behalf of, an employer resident in the state of employment or the remuneration is borne by a permanent establishment or fixed base of a non-employment state established in the state of employment.[376] If the employee is not present in the source state for more than 183 days during the taxable year and the payor does not satisfy the other requirements of Article 15(2), then the residence state has exclusive taxing authority. This principle is based on the consideration that a person should be taxed by a state to which his economic allegiance is higher, and, moreover, that the state of residence is likely to be in a more favorable position to tax income from both domestic and foreign sources. Taxation by the residence state continues to be the rule even when employment is exercised in the other Contracting State if all three tests of Article 15(2) are satisfied. This facilitates sending abroad qualified personnel, a practice which is becoming more important with growing economic interdependence.

The income E earns as a telecommuter is clearly income from dependent personal services. The primary issue that arises under the OECD Model treaty with respect to this income is the same one that arises under domestic law — where are the services exercised. If they are deemed to be exercised in country R, country R has the authority to tax the income from the services under Article 15(1). Employment is considered to be exercised where the employee is personally present.[377] However, there is German case law that supports the notion that services, other than manual labor, may be considered to be performed where the services become effective rather than where performed.[378] In a 1971 decision, the Federal Finance Court (BFH) held that two Swiss residents who were general managers of a German corporation (GmbH) performed their services at the place of management of the GmbH (*i.e.*, in Germany) even though they were rarely present in that

---

[375]OECD Model, 1997, Art. 15(1).

[376]OECD Model, 1997, Art. 15(2).

[377]K. VOGEL, DOUBLE TAX CONVENTIONS, Art. 15, m. no. 17.

[378]K. VOGEL, DOUBLE TAX CONVENTIONS, Art. 15, m. no. 19.

jurisdiction.[379] The GmbH with its seat and place of management in Germany had two general managers who were both residents of Switzerland. Although one of the managers never went to Germany, and the other spent only a few days there, the German Finance Office asked the GmbH to withhold salary tax on their compensation. The GmbH objected on the ground that the managers had been active in Switzerland, not Germany, and that under the 1931 Germany-Switzerland tax treaty, Switzerland had the exclusive right to tax the general managers' salaries. The BFH conceded that a general manager (or other executive of a corporation) renders personal services where he or she is personally present. However, because part of a general manager's duties include giving orders and directives, the personal services are completed only when the orders and directives are received. In other words, it is not at the moment when an order is issued but rather when it is received that the services of a general manager are fully performed. According to the BFH, the place where the orders and directives of a general manager are received is the "seat" of the corporation.

In a more recent decision, however, the BFH held that a German resident who was president of a Canadian corporation rendered employment services at the place where he was personally present.[380] The 1994 case concerned a German resident (petitioner) who was the president of a company (R-Ltd.) incorporated under the laws of the province of Alberta, Canada. The company had two other directors, both of whom were Canadian attorneys. The shares of R-Ltd. were held by a Luxembourg corporation (S-S.A.). The purpose of R-Ltd. was the construction of an office building in a Canadian town. Petitioner contended that Canada had the exclusive right to tax his income because he had performed the services in Canada. After an unsuccessful appeal to the German Finance Office, the petitioner turned to the courts. The Finance Tribunal of Düsseldorf concluded that Canada had the exclusive right to tax the petitioner's personal services income. Upon the Finance Office's appeal, the BFH annulled the decision and remanded the case to the Finance Tribunal for further findings. The BFH pointed out that the Finance Tribunal had correctly concluded that the income in dispute came under article 15 of the Germany-Canada tax treaty, the provision covering

---

[379]Decision of 15 Nov. 1971, Gr.S. 1/71, BStBl.II 1972, 68. This decision followed a long-standing German judicial doctrine. RFH (Reichsfinanzhof — Imperial Finance Court), decisions of 25 Apr. 1933, VI A 988/31 and 1252/31, RStBl.1934,417; BFH, decision of 12 Aug. 1960, VI 300/58 S, BStBl.III 1960, 441 (443).

[380]Decision of 5 Oct. 1994, I R 67/93. BStBl.II 1995, 95.

dependent personal services.[381] According to this provision, the state where the services are performed is entitled to tax the income derived from such employment. The BFH held that the 15 November 1971 decision was not applicable, because its scope was limited to the former Germany-Switzerland treaty. Moreover, the BFH apparently believed that the place where the activity was exercised was related to the physical presence of the petitioner.

The concept that income from the performance of services might be taxable by a Contracting State even though the person performing the services is situated in another Contracting State is not beyond the contemplation of the OECD Model. In Article 16 of the OECD Model, directors' fees and other similar payments derived by a resident of a Contracting State in his capacity as a member of the board of directors of a company which is a resident of the other Contracting State may be taxed in the state where the paying company is resident even if the services are not rendered in that state.[382]

The likelihood of double taxation if services are considered to be performed where exploited would be substantially increased. Both the state where the services are performed and the state where the services are exploited might both claim primary taxing authority. Where the source rule is the location of the person rendering services, disputes between countries is limited to the relatively concrete concept of physical location. But if exploitation becomes a touchstone for taxing authority, there will be more room for inconsistent treaty application.

4.2.1.5. Capital income

The widespread use of computers has had an impact on virtually all phases of commercial and investment activity. It is not only business profits and income from the performance of services that are affected by the use

---

[381] Article 16 of the treaty was not applicable, because it applies only to members of supervisory boards. The BFH stated that, under Canadian law, corporations have only one board, which has both management and supervisory functions, whereas German corporations have both a managing board and a supervisory board. Hence, only the fees of directors who are members of a supervisory board, or who exercise supervisory functions, are included under article 16 of the Germany-Canada tax treaty. The remuneration of a managing president, however, is considered dependent personal services income within the meaning of article 15 of the treaty.

[382] OECD Commentary, 1997, Art. 16, para. 1. The United States has entered a reservation, believing that the rule should apply only to services performed in the State where the paying company is resident. *See* US Model, 1996, Art. 16.

of computers but also investment income generated by capital. However, this report focuses on income from electronic commerce rather than investment income. Consequently, the effects of the digital revolution on dividend and interest payments are not considered. However, the treatment of royalty income and gains from the sale of computer software are an inextricable part of electronic commerce and are, therefore considered below.

4.2.1.5.1. Dividends and interest

For tax purposes, different types of returns on investments are treated differently for tax purposes. For example, dividends, which are returns on equity investment, have different tax implications than interest which is the return on a debt investment. The ability of investors to arbitrage differences in tax treatment has been greatly aided through the use of computers. This ability to arbitrage has given rise to an assortment of new financial vehicles. The term "derivative financial instruments" is used to describe the array of new financial instruments. A consideration of the impact of derivative financial instruments on current tax principles is currently being undertaken under the auspices of the International Fiscal Association.

4.2.1.5.2. Royalties

In the electronic commerce hypothetical set forth in section 4.2.1.1, suppose that R Corp. was not using the server to sell tangible goods that would be delivered to customers by conventional means. Instead, suppose that R Corp. uses a server to disseminate electronic data for a fee paid by customers. In this situation, it may not be clear whether the payment constitutes a royalty for the use of intellectual property in which case the payment would be subject to national and treaty royalty rules. Depending on the circumstances, the fee might alternatively constitute a payment for the performance of services. Still other possible treatments exist. In some cases, a customer may be paying for the right to use tangible property (*e.g.,* a disk or a server) in which case the payment might constitute a rental payment. Finally, if the customer acquires all the rights to property (tangible or intangible), the fee paid may constitute sales proceeds. Any of these characterizations is possible depending on the rights acquired in the transaction.

If the international community cannot reach agreement on these classification of assignment issues, there is a high likelihood of double taxation. For example, if country S treats a fee paid by a country S customer to R Corp. for the use of computer software as a royalty, a withholding tax may apply under country S national and/or treaty law. However, if country R regards the payment as a purchase price, R Corp. may not recognize country S's withholding for purposes of granting relief from double taxation in country R.

4.2.1.5.2.1. National law

In Canada, payments for the use of the computer software, pursuant to a contract under which the seller maintains property rights or the transferee is subject to limitations not usually associated with acquiring full ownership of property, represent payments for the use of a secret formula or process and are classified as royalties for withholding tax purposes.[383] For example, in *Western Electric Company Ltd. v. M.N.R.*,[384] the requirement to supply updated programs subject to a confidentiality agreement was regarded as the provision of a secret formula and the accompanying payments constituted royalties.

According to Canadian tax law, a sale can transpire only where all intellectual property rights in the software are conveyed and the buyer obtains an unrestricted right to sell or lease the software.[385] Thus, a payment for the use of, or the right to use, a custom computer software program for a period of indefinite duration is considered a royalty payment pursuant to

---

[383]Bernstein and Guilbault, *The Taxation of Income Derived from the Supply of Technology*, 82a Cahiers de Droit Fiscal International [Studies on International Fiscal Law] 286 (1997).

[384]DTC 5068 (SCC). Likewise, in its 1992 communications with the OECD, Canada maintained that payments made by a user of computer software pursuant to a contract that required the source code or program to be kept confidential constituted payment for the use of a secret formula or process and thus were to be classified for taxation purposes as royalties. Bernstein and Guilbault, *The Taxation of Income Derived from the Supply of Technology*, 82a Cahiers de Droit Fiscal International [Studies on International Fiscal Law] 286 (1997).

[385]*Window on Canadian Tax* (Don Mills, Ont.: CCH Canadian)(loose-leaf) at para. 2118.

a license, since full rights of ownership have not been transferred.[386] On the other hand, payments for standard software are considered to be income from the purchase of tangible property by Revenue Canada.[387]

Italy recognizes several different forms of technology purchases including: (a) acquisition of ownership of patents, industrial processes, know-how, and formulae; (b) acquisition of the right to use a specific incorporeal property for a specified period of time (where use may be restricted to the purchaser's own production and commercial needs, or may allow the sale of utilization rights); (c) stipulation of a contract for the acquisition of services with a high technology content; and (d) other types of contractual agreement.[388]

Of primary importance, under the Italian tax law, is determining what form of purchase took place. In deciding this issue, the method of payment is not determinative. A lump sum payment does not automatically make the transaction a sale, nor does a series of payments, related to the number of units sold or produced, automatically make it a license transaction. In some cases, a licensing agreement may provide for the payment of an initial lump sum or a sale transaction for payment to be made in installments, calculated on the basis of the sales made over the years.[389] The breadth of the right of use granted to the purchaser is not determinative either. A transaction is not necessarily an acquisition of a license just because the purchaser may use the property only for its own needs. Neither is a transaction necessarily a sale because the purchaser may copy and market the property.[390]

Instead, under Italian law as stated by the Ministry of Finance, "detailed examination of the individual clauses of the contract and of the true nature of the object of the contract is necessary to establish at the very least the prevalence of the various elements in the individual contract."[391] In es-

---

[386]"Revenue Canada Round Table", in *Report of Proceedings of the Forty-Fifth Tax Conference,* 1993 Conference Report (Toronto: Canadian Tax Foundation, 1994) at question 31.

[387]*Id.* at question 29.

[388]Bennani, *The Taxation of Income Derived from the Supply of Technology,* 82a CAHIERS DE DROIT FISCAL INTERNATIONAL [STUDIES ON INTERNATIONAL FISCAL LAW] 471 (1997).

[389]*Id.* at 472.

[390]In fact, some licensing agreements even allow the licensee to sell utilization rights to third parties. *Id.*

[391]Circular no. 41 of 12 December 1981.

tablishing the "prevalent economic content," a central factor to be considered is the length of time that the purchaser is allowed to use the rights. If the time period is unlimited, the arrangement is considered a sale of incorporeal property.[392] On the other hand, if the time period for use of the rights is limited, the arrangement is held to be a license.[393]

In some cases, the supplier may retain identical utilization rights. While it would seem that this would prevent characterization of the transaction as a sale, under Italian law such a contract instead establishes a form of common ownership, regulated by the parties to avoid the potential conflict. However, in the opposite case, where the agreement prohibits the licensor from using the incorporeal property for the entire term, the transaction is characterized as an exclusive licensing agreement.[394]

Businesses desiring to use a specific incorporeal property may either obtain full ownership or only license rights, and payments under a license agreement are considered royalties.[395] In Italian law, software falls into the category of "original works," and is therefore considered to be "incorporeal property."[396] Thus, the rules set forth above regarding incorporeal property are applicable to software. Also, Italy is one of the few countries with extensive and detailed guidelines specifically for the taxation of income from the purchase of software, which includes computer programs under Italian law. Software is defined as that information needed to run computers, and a distinction is made between system software and application software.[397]

Four basic situations are recognized and addressed by Italian law re-

---

[392]Whereas many other countries use the terms "intangible property" or "intellectual property," Italian law refers to "incorporeal property." For purposes of this section, all three terms are interchangeable.

[393]Bennani, *The Taxation of Income Derived from the Supply of Technology*, 82a CAHIERS DE DROIT FISCAL INTERNATIONAL [STUDIES ON INTERNATIONAL FISCAL LAW] 472 (1997).

[394]*Id.* at 472-73.

[395]*Id.* at 471.

[396]D. Legs. no. 518 of 29 December 1992.

[397]Bennani, *The Taxation of Income Derived from the Supply of Technology*, 82a CAHIERS DE DROIT FISCAL INTERNATIONAL [STUDIES ON INTERNATIONAL FISCAL LAW] 474 (1997). System software consists of the operating system that interfaces with and supports the processing operations performed by the various applications. It usually accompanies the computer at the time of acquisition and the combined cost of the hardware and the software constitutes the overall cost of the corporeal property. Since the two parts (software and hardware) cannot be divided the entire transaction is deemed

garding application software. First, where the software is acquired for an unlimited period of time, but exclusively for the personal use of the purchaser, the purchaser is considered to have acquired ownership of the property (disk) that contains the program (incorporeal property). Thus, the purchase price is characterized as sales income. Where the software is acquired for an unlimited period of time, and the purchaser has the right to reproduce and trade it, the purchaser is considered to have purchased an original work. As above, the purchase price is classified as income pursuant to a sale. Third, where the software is acquired for a specified period of time, exclusively for the personal use of the purchaser, the arrangement is regarded as a lease of movable property (the disk) and the payments, though rental payments, are like sales income in that they are not subject to taxation in Italy when received by a nonresident. Lastly, where the software is acquired for a specified period of time, and the purchaser has the right to reproduce and trade it, the purchase is considered a license to use an original work, since the software can be reproduced and traded for a specified period of time. Payments in this case are regarded as royalties.[398] Thus, if reproduction and marketing rights are acquired for a limited period of time, the agreement is regarded as a license.

In Japan, there is an issue concerning whether an amount paid by a customer for the use of downloaded software or music constitutes a royalty. Japanese law taxes domestic source royalty income which is defined as a royalty from "a person performing business in Japan" and which pertains to that business.[399] When a Japanese customer uses downloaded software for personal use, the customer may not be "performing business."

The US Treasury has addressed aspects of the classification issue through the issuance of proposed Regulations.[400] The Regulations treat a

---

to be a sale. *Id.* at 475. Since the primary focus of this section is application software, system software will not be addressed.

[398]Bennani, *The Taxation of Income Derived from the Supply of Technology,* 82a CAHIERS DE DROIT FISCAL INTERNATIONAL [STUDIES ON INTERNATIONAL FISCAL LAW] 475 (1997).

[399]Corporation Tax Law Art. 138, No. 7 and Income Tax Law Art. 161 No. 7.

[400]*See,* Internal Revenue Service, *IRS Publishes Proposed Regs Classifying Transfers of Computer Programs — Classification of Certain Transactions Involving Computer Programs,* available in LEXIS/NEXIS, 96 TNI 225-21 (20 Nov. 1996); Pearlman & Berman, *Attorneys Recommend Changes to US Computer Program Regs.,* available in LEXIS/NEXIS, 97 TNI 40-27 (28 Feb. 1997); Karlin, *Computer Program Prop. Regs, are a Good but Cautious Start,* 8 J. INT'L TAX. 64 (1997).

transfer of a computer program as a transfer of a copyright right if the transferee acquires one or more of the following rights: 1) the right to make copies of the program for distribution to the public by sale, by other ownership transfer, or by rental, lease, or lending; 2) the right to prepare derivative computer programs based on the copyrighted program; 3) the right to make a public performance of the program; or 4) the right to publicly display the program.[401] Accordingly, a transfer of a computer program without any of these rights will be treated as the transfer of a copyrighted article.[402] For ex-

---

The Regulations do not address the treatment of all transactions involving electronic data. For example, the Regulations do not address the treatment of a payment for the right to access data online or for the right to download or print such data. Similarly, characterization of payments for internet access or web hosting are not directly addressed by the Regulations.

[401]Prop. Reg. § 1.861-18(c)(2).

[402]The Copyright Act of 1976, as amended (17 USC. § 101 *et seq.*), provides protection against infringement of the exclusive rights of the owner of a copyright in original works of authorship, fixed in any tangible medium of expression, including literary works. 17 USC. § 102. The term "literary works" includes: ". . . numbers, or other verbal or numerical symbols or indicia, regardless of the nature of the material objects, such as books, periodicals, manuscripts, phonorecords, film, tapes, disks, or cards, in which they are embodied." 17 USC. § 101. Computer programs are literary works for purposes of the Copyright Act. *See also* EC Directive on Legal Protection of Computer Programs, 1991 (91/250/EEC); and the Berne Convention (Paris Text, 24 July 1971).

The Copyright Act grants five exclusive rights to a copyright owner. The proposed Regulations focus on three with respect to computer programs: the right to reproduce copies of the copyrighted work (17 USC. § 106(1)); the right to prepare derivative works, which may themselves be separately copyrighted, based upon the copyrighted work (17 USC. § 103 and § 106(2)); and the right to distribute copies of the copyrighted work to the public by sale or other transfer of ownership, or by rental, lease or lending (17 USC. § 106(3)). Additionally, in certain circumstances, the right to publicly perform the copyrighted work (17 USC. § 106(4)) and the right to publicly display the copyrighted work may also be relevant (17 USC. § 106(5)).

Under US copyright law, the user of a computer program who does not possess any of those five rights (or parts of them) has obtained only rights to use the copyrighted article it possesses. Generally, that user is treated as having only received a copy of the copyrighted work. Under US copyright law, a copy is a material object in which a work is fixed by any method now known or later developed, and from which the work can be perceived, reproduced, or otherwise communicated, either directly or with the aid of a machine or device (17 USC. § 101.). In these proposed regulations a copy is also referred to as a "copyrighted article." The distinction between copies and copyrights is made most clearly in § 202 of the Copyright Act which provides:

ample, the sale of a "shrink-wrap"[403] computer program to the general public, even though documented as a license, would be treated as the transfer of a copyrighted article since the customer would not normally have the right to make copies for distribution to the public and would not have the right to prepare derivative programs.

Once the analysis is complete as to whether the transfer consists of a copyright right or a copyrighted article, a determination must be made as to whether the transaction is a sale or exchange or a license or lease. This analysis is important, as dramatically different tax consequences can arise. The standards to be used differ depending on whether the transaction is the transfer of a copyright right or a copyrighted article. In the case of the former, the question is whether there has been a transfer of all substantial rights in the copyright. If so, there will be a sale or exchange. If less than all substantial rights are transferred, the transaction will be regarded as a license. In the case of a transfer of a copyrighted article, the test is the standard applicable to transfers of tangible property (*i.e.*, whether the benefits

---

Ownership of a copyright, or of any of the exclusive rights under a copyright, is distinct from ownership of any material object in which the work is embodied. Transfer of ownership of any material object, including the copy or phonorecord in which the work is first fixed, does not of itself convey any rights in the copyrighted work embodied in the object; nor, in the absence of an agreement, does transfer of ownership of a copyright or of any exclusive rights under a copyright convey property rights in any material object.

Certain rights pass to the purchaser of a copy of a computer program. The most important of these is the right to sell (but not, without permission, to lease, rent, or lend) the copy to another person. (17 USC. § 109.) Additionally, the owner of a copy of a computer program has the right to make a copy of that copy as an essential step in the utilization of the program (*e.g.*, copying to the memory of the computer) and may also make a copy for archival purposes. (17 USC. § 117.) If, however, the owner of the copy sells that copy, all copies made pursuant to the 17 USC. § 117 right must be destroyed.

Although the proposed Regulations are guided by copyright law principles in determining whether a copyright right or copyrighted article has been transferred, the regulations depart in some cases from a strict reliance on copyright law in order to take into account the special nature of computer programs and to treat functionally equivalent transactions in the same way. For example, the proposed regulations do not treat the transfer of a right to copy as the transfer of a copyright right, unless it is accompanied by the right to distribute the copies to the public.

[403]The term "shrink wrap" refers to the plastic covering used to wrap mass-produced software that is widely available for public purchase.

and burdens of ownership of the article have been transferred). If such rights have been transferred, a sale or exchange will have taken place. If not, the transaction will be regarded as a lease.

In some situations, a transaction involving computer software may not be treated as a sale, license, or lease of a copyright right or copyrighted article, but rather as a transfer of services. Whether a transaction involving computer software is treated as the provision of services (or is characterized in some other fashion) is a facts-and-circumstances inquiry that takes into account the intent of the parties with respect to who will own the copyright rights and the allocation of the risk of loss.[404] The provision of information with respect to a computer program will not be treated as the provision of know-how unless the information (1) relates to computer programming techniques; (2) is not capable of being copyrighted; and (3) is subject to trade secret protection.[405]

In a series of examples, the Proposed Regulations illustrate these principles. Suppose that R Corp., a country R corporation, owns the copyright in a computer program, Program A. It copies Program A on to disks. The disks are placed in boxes covered with a wrapper on which is printed what is generally referred to as a shrink-wrap license. The license is stated to be perpetual. Under the license no reverse engineering of the computer program is permitted. The transferee receives, first, the right to use the program on two of its own computers (for example, a laptop and a desktop) provided that only one copy is in use at any one time, and, second, the right to make one copy of the program on each machine as an essential step in the utilization of the program. The transferee is permitted by the shrink-wrap license to sell the copy so long as it destroys any other copies it has made and imposes the same terms and conditions of the license on the purchaser of its copy. These disks are made available for sale to the general public in Country S. In return for consideration, C, a country S resident, receives one such disk. Taking into account all of the facts and circumstances, C is properly treated as the purchaser of a copyrighted article.[406]

---

[404]Prop. Reg. § 1.861-18(d).

[405]Prop. Reg. § 1.861-18(e).

[406]Prop. Reg. § 1.861-18(h) Ex. 1. The proposed Regulations contain other examples of a sales transaction involving copyrighted articles. For example, S Corp., a distributor in country S, enters into an agreement with R Corp., a country R corporation, to purchase as many copies of Program A on disk as it may from time to time request. S

The same characterization is appropriate under the proposed Regulations if, instead of selling disks, R Corp. decides to make Program A available, for a fee, on a world wide web home page on the internet. C, the country S resident, in return for payment made to R Corp., downloads Program A (via modem) onto the hard drive of her computer. As part of the electronic communication, C signifies her assent to a license agreement.[407]

Suppose instead that R Corp. allows C, the country S resident, to use Program A for only one week. At the end of that week, C must return the disk with Program A on it to R Corp. C must also destroy any copies made of Program A. If C wishes to use Program A for a further period she must enter into a new agreement to use the program for an additional charge. Whether the program is acquired by purchase of a disk or downloading from a web site, C has received no copyright rights. Nor is C treated as the

---

Corp. will then sell these disks to retailers. The disks are shipped in boxes covered by shrink-wrap licenses. S Corp. has not acquired any copyright rights with respect to Program A. It has acquired individual copies of Program A, which it may sell to others. The use of the term "license" is not dispositive; S Corp. has acquired copyrighted articles by purchase. Prop. Reg. § 1.861-18(h) Ex. 7.

Suppose that R Corp., a country R corporation, transfers a disk containing Program A to S Corp., a country S corporation, and grants S Corp. the right to load Program A on to 50 individual workstations for use only by S Corp. employees at one location in return for a one-time per-user fee (generally referred to as a site license). If additional workstations are subsequently introduced, Program A may be loaded on to those machines for additional one-time per-user fees. The license which grants the rights to operate Program A on 50 workstations also prohibits S Corp. from selling the disk (or any of the 50 copies) or reverse engineering the program. The term of the license is stated to be perpetual. The grant of a right to copy, unaccompanied by the right to distribute those copies to the public, is not the transfer of a copyright right. Rather, it is the transfer of a copyrighted article by sale. Prop. Reg. § 1.861-18(h) Ex. 10-11.

Assume the same facts, except that S Corp. pays a monthly fee to R Corp., calculated with reference to the permitted maximum number of users and the computer power of S Corp.'s computer. In return for the fee, S Corp. receives the right to receive upgrades of the program. Upon receipt of the upgrades or upon termination of the agreement, S Corp. must return the program disks to R Corp. Under these facts, S Corp. has not received any copyright rights. Instead, S Corp. has received a copyrighted article. Because S Corp. is making monthly payments and must return the disks if the agreement terminates, there has been a lease of the copyrighted article. Prop. Reg. § 1.861-18(h) Ex. 12.

[407]Prop. Reg. § 1.861-18(h) Ex. 2.

owner of a copyrighted article. Rather, there has been a lease of a copyrighted article, not a sale.[408]

Consider the following example of a sale of the copyright itself. Suppose that R Corp., a country R corporation, transfers a disk containing Program A to S Corp., a country S corporation, and grants S Corp. an exclusive license for the remaining term of the copyright to copy and distribute an unlimited number of copies of Program A in the geographic area of country S, prepare derivative works based upon Program A, make public performances of Program A, and publicly display Program A. S Corp. will pay R Corp. a royalty for three years, which is the expected period during which Program A will have commercially exploitable value. Under these facts, R Corp. will be treated as having sold copyright rights to S Corp. S Corp. has acquired all of the copyright rights in Program A within a geographic area, has received the right to use them exclusively, and has received the rights for the remaining life of the copyright in Program A. The fact that the agreement is labeled a license is not controlling (nor is the fact that R Corp. receives a sum labeled a royalty). This would also be the case if the copy of Program A to be used for the purposes of reproduction were transmitted electronically to S Corp.[409]

Suppose that R Corp., a country R corporation, transfers a disk containing Program A to S Corp., a country S corporation, and grants S Corp. the non-exclusive right to reproduce and distribute for sale to the public an unlimited number of disks at its factory in country S in return for a payment related to the number of disks copied and sold. The term of the agreement is two years, which is less than the remaining life of the copyright. As in the previous example, the transfer of the disk containing the copy of the program does not constitute the transfer of a copyrighted article because S Corp. has also acquired a copyright right. Unlike the previous example, here there has been a license of Program A to S Corp., and the payments made by S Corp. are royalties. There has not been a transfer of all substantial rights in the copyright to Program A because R Corp. has the right to enter into other licenses with respect to the copyright of Program A, in country S (or even to sell that copyright, subject to S Corp.'s interest). S Corp. has acquired no right itself to license the copyright rights in Program

---

[408]Prop. Reg. § 1.861-18(h) Ex. 3-4.
[409]Prop. Reg. § 1.861-18(h) Ex. 5.

A. Finally, the term of the license is for less than the remaining life of the copyright in Program A.[410]

Under some circumstances, payments received with respect to computer software may be treated as payment for services rather than as a payment for the copyright (*i.e.,* sale or license) or the copyrighted article (*i.e.,* sale or lease). Suppose that S Corp., a country S corporation, enters into a license agreement for a modified version of Program A only if R Corp., a country R corporation, makes substantial modifications to the program. Only the core idea of Program A will be used and a considerable amount of labor will be expended in rewriting Program A, which as a derivative work under applicable copyright law will be a separate, new program. R Corp. and S Corp. agree that R Corp. is modifying Program A for S Corp. and that, when modified Program A is completed, the copyright in the modified program will belong to S Corp. S Corp. gives instructions to R Corp. programmers regarding program specifications. S Corp. agrees to pay R Corp. a fixed monthly sum during development of the program. If S Corp. is dissatisfied with the development of the program it may cancel the contract at the end of any month. In the event of termination, R Corp. will retain all payments, while any procedures, techniques, or copyrightable interests will be the property of S Corp. All of the payments are labeled royalties. There is no provision in the agreement for any continuing relationship between R Corp. and S Corp., such as the furnishing of updates of the program, after completion of the modification work. Taking into account all of the facts and circumstances, R Corp. is treated as providing services to S Corp. because S Corp. bears all of the risks of loss associated with the development of modified Program A and is the owner of all copyright rights in modified

---

[410]Prop. Reg. § 1.861-18(h) Ex. 6. *See also* Prop. Reg. § 1.861-18(h) Ex. 8-9. The tenuous nature of these classification issues is illustrated by comparing Examples 8 and 9. In Example 8, a US corporation acquires one copy of the program and is permitted to install the program on the hard-drive of computers it sells. The term of the agreement is less than the remaining life of the copyright. The Regulations conclude that the arrangement is a copyright license. But in Example 9, the US corporation acquires one disk with the software on it for each hard drive it manufactures and sells. The software from each disk is copied on to the hard drive. Under these circumstances the payment is considered to be the purchase of a copyrighted article. The actual result is exactly the same as in Example 8, but the classification for tax purposes is different — the inevitable problem where artificial categories are created.

Program A. The fact that the agreement is labeled a license is not controlling (nor is the fact that R Corp. receives a sum labeled a royalty).

Under some circumstances, a payment associated with the transfer of computer software may be treated under the proposed Regulations as a payment for know-how. For example, suppose that R Corp., a US corporation, and S Corp., a country S corporation, agree that a development engineer employed by R Corp. will travel to country S to provide know-how relating to certain techniques which are not generally known to computer programmers, which will enable S Corp. to more efficiently create computer programs. These techniques represent the product of experience gained by R Corp. from working on many computer programming projects. Such information is not capable of being copyrighted, but it is subject to trade secret protection. Accordingly, the transaction will be classified as the provision of know-how.

The US regulations address the treatment of computer programs. They do not address the treatment of other types of electronic data that may be accessed on-line.[411] For example, a customer in country C may for a fee access a website on R Corp.'s server in country R. Should the fee from reading data on-line be treated as a royalty? A service? Does it matter if the customer downloads or prints the material? Consider also other transactions such as fees paid for email or bulletin board access or for web hosting or fees paid for short-term use of electronic data. These issues are not easy to sort out. Payments for reading data on-line might be considered a payment for a service. Perhaps, an analogy might be made to paying a library to read materials housed within. If the user is free to download or print the accessed material, the transaction more closely resembles a sale. However, if the ability to download and/or print were regarded as incidental to the ability to access, characterization as a service may still be appropriate. In any case, solutions to these and other characterization issues must be developed.

The distinctions that the US Regulations wrestle with are important because in many countries different tax consequences attend different characterizations. However, in those countries where territorial tax principles require withholding on all outbound payments, the characterization issues

---

[411]Deloitte & Touche, *Letter to Joseph Guttentag (International Tax Counsel) and Bruce Cohen (Attorney-Advisor), Department of the Treasury, dated 9/15/97,* Tax Notes Int'l 1483 (3 November 1997).

are not as important.[412] In Brazil for example, payments made by a resident to nonresidents are subject to withholding whether the payments derive from the transfer, the license, or the supply of technology.[413]

In Japan, the term "royalty" is defined in an extremely broad manner. A royalty is any consideration which is received: (a) from industrial property rights and other rights concerning technology,[414] production formula

---

[412]Even in these situations, the characterization may be important if different withholding rates apply to different types of income.

[413]Pasqualin, *The Taxation of Income Derived from the Supply of Technology*, 82a CAHIERS DE DROIT FISCAL INTERNATIONAL [STUDIES ON INTERNATIONAL FISCAL LAW] 261 (1997). Under its industrial and tax legislation, Brazil has set forth a basic list of potential types of technological and copyright (computer program) transactions which may occur and assigned a different tax category treatment to each area of related income. When the right for exploitation of patents is transferred, income to the transferor is classified as sales income, but when the right for exploitation of patents is only licensed, income to the licensor is classified as royalty income. Similarly, when the right for the use of trademarks is transferred, income to the transferor is classified as sales income, but when the right for the use of trademarks is only licensed, income to the licensor is classified as royalty income. When technical, scientific, administrative, or other assistance (usually that associated with the supply of non-patented technology and with the supply of know-how which may or may not be associated with trade secrets) services are rendered, income to the transferor of the technology is classified as fees. Likewise, when technical services are rendered, income to the performer of the services is also classified as fees. When franchising rights are granted, income obtained by the franchiser may be of different classifications. For example, royalties may be received for the licensing of the trademark and patents, fees collected for the rendering of technical assistance and services, and sales income acquired for the supply of raw material and equipment. When the copyright of a computer program is fully transferred, any income to the holder of such copyright is classified as sales income, but when the copyright is only licensed, income to the holder of the copyright is classified as royalty income. Also, when the program is distributed by the holder or the licensee of the copyright, income to the distributor is classified as sales income. However, if a computer program is purchased outside Brazil from a program distributor that is not the author, and subdistribution in Brazil is not authorized, the payment for such purchase will be classified as sales income instead of as a royalty payment.

[414]"Industrial property rights and other rights concerning technology" include patent rights, utility model rights, trademark rights and registered design rights, and applications therefor or licenses thereto. Such rights may also include a right to merchandise a design or animated character. Kamiya, *The Taxation of Income Derived from the Supply of Technology*, 82a CAHIERS DE DROIT FISCAL INTERNATIONAL [STUDIES ON INTERNATIONAL FISCAL LAW] 492 (1997).

by special technology, or rights similar thereto,[415] or consideration derived from the transfer thereof; (b) from copyrights (including publication rights and other similar rights) or payments derived from the transfer thereof; and (c) from machines, devices, vehicles, transport methods, tools, instruments and equipment.[416] Any consideration received will be classified as royalties if the type of technology being transferred falls under any of these categories.[417] Japanese tax law thus holds that any payment received for the grant of a license or transfer of a copyright is considered to be royalty income.[418] Under Japanese copyright law, computer programs and databases are both deemed to be copyrightable.[419] Databases are copyrightable in Japan when they exhibit sufficient creativity in their choice of information or their systemic structures.[420] Thus, it would be difficult to consider that a simple informational interface, like a shopping mall on the internet could be copyrightable. On the other hand, a database for trademark searches is considered to be copyrightable because it may contain the requisite creativity in both its choice of information and its systemic structure for the provision of the requested information.

---

[415]"Production formula by special technology or those similar thereto" refers to inventions or ideas which have not been registered as patent rights, utility model rights, trademarks, or registered design rights. It includes any production formula using a special raw material, process, machinery, or equipment, any similar secret skill or recipe, and other knowledge or design of special technical value. "Know-how" (trade secrets and technical knowledge) falls within this category. Income Tax Basic Circular, section 161-22; Corporationn Tax Basic Circular, section 20-1-21.

[416]Income Tax Law, Art. 161(vii), Income Taxation Enforcement Order, Art. 284(1); Corporation Tax Law, Art. 138(vii), Income Tax Law Enforcement Order, Art. 181(1).

[417]Kamiya, *The Taxation of Income Derived from the Supply of Technology,* 82a Cahiers de Droit Fiscal International [Studies on International Fiscal Law] 493 (1997).

[418]Any payment for reproduction, public performance, musical performance, broadcasting, exhibition, screening, translation, arrangement, adaptation, cinematography and any other form of use of a copyrighted work, and for transfer of copyright is considered a royalty by Income Tax Basic Circular, section 161-23; Corporationn Tax Basic Circular, section 20-1-22.

[419]Effective as of 1 January 1986, computer software is protected by "copyright" under the Japanese copyright law. Chosakukenho (Copyright Law) Law No. 48 of 1970, as amended, art. 10 (1) [9], art. 12-2.

[420]Copyright Law, Art. 12-2(1).

Also, although computer programs are generally copyrightable, it is questionable whether payments received for providing access to information on the internet would constitute a royalty. This would be analogous to an entrance fee at a movie theater for seeing a copyrighted movie. It would be difficult to consider that such a fee is a royalty. The use of a computer is always associated with the use of some kind of computer programs. It would not be a reasonable result to consider all uses of computer programs to be subject to royalty payments. The payment of a fee to a provider by a consumer (from among the general public) for the use of the internet-based services should be distinguished under Japanese law from that of a fee paid to the creator of the relevant system by a person who is licensed to utilize the internet-based service concerned for the purpose of providing access to that service to others. It is an established Japanese interpretation that payments for the use of copyrighted databases offered on-line are treated as royalties.[421]

It should be noted that the mere fact that computers are used for on-line services would not prevent a payment made in exchange for their use from being considered a royalty. In the Tokyo High Court Judgment of 25 September 1997, a payment made by a Japanese TV system to a foreign corporation that had granted live broadcasting rights through an international communication satellite for sporting events (along with the right to record them) was held to be a royalty for a copyrighted movie. The use of a communication satellite did not affect the Court's conclusion.

It has been a subject of argument as to whether consideration paid for the purchase of a computer program constitutes a royalty in Japan arising from the "transfer of copyright." The Japanese tax administration takes the position that a payment for the purchase of a computer program is a royalty,[422] but at the same time, it recognizes the possibility that the purchase

---

[421]Y. WATANABE, KONSARUTANTO KOKUSAI ZEIMU JIREI (Consultant International Tax Cases), 807 (1996)

[422]Some commentators have argued that payment for the purchase of computer software to be used itself, but that may not be duplicated and resold by the purchaser, should be classified as payments for the purchase of property, and thus constitute business profits income, rather than royalties. Tax authorities have decided instead to carefully review the terms of the contract and the actions of the parties in the transaction. *See, e.g.* Okamoto, *Hikyojyushawomeguru Kokunaigensenshotokuno Jireikento (Review of Cases of Domestic Source Income concerning Nonresident)*, 15 INT'L TAX. (No. 2) 33-34 (1995); Fujieda, *Konpyutasofutoweano Taikanoshirharaito Gensenchoshunikansuru Ichi-*

of a standard software package may be the equivalent of the purchase of an item of personal property (*i.e.*, a copyrighted article) and, thus, payment for such a purchase might not really be best characterized as a royalty.[423] The tax treatment in this area is by no means settled yet in Japan.

Under this definition of royalties, considerably broader than that adopted by most countries, Japanese tax authorities consider all payments for implementation, use, adaptation, provision, technical assistance, or grant of a license or assignment of the technology concerned to be royalties.[424] Even consideration paid in such a manner as to appear on its face to be sales income (*e.g.*, lump sum), will still automatically constitute royalty income. And payments for costs incurred in connection with the actual transfer of the technology or for the performance of technology-related services will be characterized as royalties.[425] Thus, unlike the situation in other countries, no determination needs to be made regarding the amount of rights transferred, length of time they may be used, or even if any rights were transferred — so long as the arrangement is technology-related, all transactions result in royalty income.

Research and development ("R&D") activity is the one situation where payments are not automatically deemed to be royalties (technology-related services), but may instead be classified as independent personal services income. It is common for Japanese corporations to hire foreign corporations to perform R&D for them. Since the result of such R&D would be "technology," a situation arises where a determination must be made regarding the nature of the payments.[426] Japanese tax authorities, though taking the position that determinations in such situations will be made on a case-by-case basis, have stated that the payments will not be classified as royalties if: (a) when the agreement for R&D was executed, it was unknown whether the

---

kosatsu (*A Review of Payment of Consideration for Computer Software and Withholding of Tax*, 15 INT'L TAX. (No. 3) 31-40 (1995).

[423]K. OKAMOTO AND M. SUGIO, GENSEN SHOTOKUZEI NO TORIATSUKAI (Treatment of Withholding Tax) 759 (1995).

[424]Income Tax Basic Circular, section 161-23; Corporationn Tax Basic Circular, section 20-1-22.

[425]Income Tax Basic Circular, section 161-7; Corporation Tax Basic Circular, section 20-1-25.

[426]Kamiya, *The Taxation of Income Derived from the Supply of Technology*, 82a CAHIERS DE DROIT FISCAL INTERNATIONAL [STUDIES ON INTERNATIONAL FISCAL LAW] 497 (1997).

results of the R&D would be fruitful; and (b) the amount of costs for the R&D to be paid by the Japanese resident party is equivalent to the amount of R&D expenses incurred by the non-resident party.[427]

In India, the definition of royalty is also very broad. Like most other countries, in making classifications of income derived from the transfer of computer software, Indian courts look to whether transfer of the rights is more akin to actual "parting of an asset" or simply a partial transfer for the assets' "employment in trade."[428] The former is considered a sale and the payments associated therewith are capital gains.[429] The latter is a license and the accompanying payments are royalties.[430]

Indian law defines licensing as a grant of partial rights for use, usually with periodic or lump sum payments made based on the value of the benefit passed on. In determining if a transaction constitutes a license and thus, the payments are royalties, Indian courts look at all the circumstances. Licensing can occur with regard to property rights (copyrights, patents, trademarks, etc.) or exclusive information and knowledge (i.e. know-how). The actual terminology used by the parties in the transaction is unimportant — a payment will be considered a royalty if in substance it is a royalty.[431]

The Indian definition of royalty covers all payments made for the transfer of all or any rights in copyrights, literary, artistic, or scientific work, or other industrial property rights,[432] and those for use of copyrights or other industrial property rights. Royalty also includes consideration for services connected with licensing rights and know-how and the imparting of information concerning technical, industrial, commercial or scientific knowledge, experience or skill (know-how),[433] and services associated with

---

[427]See, e.g. Hikyojyushanozeimu (Taxation for Nonresident) 154, 309 (1991).

[428]*CIT v. Cilag Ltd.* 70 ITR 760, 767 (Bom).

[429]*Evans Medical Supplies Ltd. v. Moriarty* 35 ITR 707 (HL). *CIT v. Ralliwolf Ltd.* 143 ITR 720 (Bom).

[430]*CIT v. Cilag Ltd.* 70 ITR 760 (Bom), *CIT v. Gilbert & Barker Mfg. Co.* 111 ITR 529 (Bom). *Rolls-Royce Ltd. v. Jeffrey* 56 ITR 580 (HL).

[431]Although the agreements used the terms "research contribution" (*CIT v. Ahmedabad Mfg. & Calico Printing Co.* 139 ITR 806 (Guj)) and "commission" (*N.V. Philips v. CIT* 172 ITR 521 (Cal)), both were held in substance to give rise to royalties.

[432]For example, patent, invention, model, design, secret formula or process, trademark, or similar property.

[433]Thus, training of Nigerians in manufacture and sale of products was held to be imparting of information. CBDT v. HMT 199 ITR 144 (Kar). Datta, *The Taxation of In-*

any of the above.[434] The term "royalty" does not include consideration for software supplied along with computers or computer based equipment.[435]

A distinction is made between royalties paid in a licensing arrangement and fees paid for technical services. Licensing enables the licensee to use the technology transferred. A fee for technical services, on the other hand, is consideration paid where one party provides his services using his own skill to perform a service for another party without involving transfer of skill to the latter. Thus, in the case of fees for technical services, the owner of the technology uses his own technology to perform a service for a fee.[436]

Characterization of a payment as a royalty in Mexico at least in theory is not affected by how property is transferred (*i.e.*, through traditional means or electronically). In a case where customers in Mexico download software that R Corp. maintains on a server located outside Mexico, the nature and tax treatment of such payments will be determined in the same manner as when such assets used or purchased are delivered through more traditional methods (*i.e.*, when the software or database diskettes are physically purchased and imported). The download of software for private use will be categorized as a partial transfer of a copyright right for an unlimited period of time and the revenue will be treated as income from the sale of a right, therefore, it will not be regarded as a royalty. If payments are made for the right to develop or exploit the software itself commercially, *i.e.*, obtaining the right to use it to create a new commercial product, then such payments will be treated as a royalty[437] and will be subject to a 15% with-

come Derived from the Supply of Technology, 82a CAHIERS DE DROIT FISCAL INTERNATIONAL [STUDIES ON INTERNATIONAL FISCAL LAW] 414 (1997).

[434]Expln. 2 to sec. 9(1)(vi) of ITA 1961.

[435]Usually software imports are under license from the foreign licensor and payments are characterized as royalty. However, under a special ruling, software that accompanies computers or computer based equipment supplied by non-resident manufacturers is considered income from a sale. Second proviso to sec. 9(1)(vi) of ITA 1961.

[436]The distinction has little significance as royalties and fees for technical services are treated alike under the domestic law. Datta, _The Taxation of Income Derived from the Supply of Technology_, 82a CAHIERS DE DROIT FISCAL INTERNATIONAL [STUDIES ON INTERNATIONAL FISCAL LAW] 414 (1997).

[437]The Mexican Federal Fiscal Code, _Codigo Fiscal de la Federacion_, in effect since 1 January 1982, defines royalties as payments of any kind received as a consideration for the use or temporary exploitation of any patent, trade mark, commercial name, copyright of literary, artistic or scientific work, including cinematography films and recordings for radio or television, any design or model, plan, secret formula or process and for

holding tax at source. These payments will be deemed to be of Mexican source if the rights are exploited in Mexico or the payments are made by a Mexican resident or a Mexican permanent establishment of a foreign resident. When the beneficial owner of such payment is a resident in a tax treaty country the withholding rate is usually reduced to 10%. When customers in Mexico purchase access to databases that R Corp. maintains on a server located outside Mexico, the payment will be categorized as a compensation for services rendered by R Corp. and income tax will not be caused in Mexico if such services are performed in their entirety outside the country.[438]

4.2.1.5.2.2. Treaty law

Article 12 of the OECD Model addresses the taxation of royalties received by a resident of a Contracting State. The article addresses only royalties arising in a Contracting State (source state) paid to a resident of the

---

the right to use industrial, commercial or scientific equipment, as well as payments made for the transfer of technology or information concerning industrial, commercial or scientific experience or any other similar right or property. Article 15-B specifies that the use or temporary exploitation of copyrights related to scientific works includes any program or set of instructions for computers required for the operational functions of such equipment or to carry out any application, notwithstanding the method by which they are delivered. Included in the royalty definition are any payments for the right to receive for retransmission any video image, sound or both, or any payment for the right to give access to the public to such audio or video images, when such signals are transmitted by satellite, cable, fiber optics or any other similar method. The Code excludes from the royalties' definition any payment for technical assistance, which is defined as 'independent personal services' by which knowledge which is not able to be patented is shared and such knowledge does not include the transmission of any confidential industrial, commercial or scientific experience. To be classified as technical assistance, the provision of services must continue during the application of such knowledge.

[438]In accordance with Article 2 of the MITL, any foreign resident that provides independent services will only be subject to tax in Mexico if it provides such services through a fixed base. Fixed bases are subject to the same rules as permanent establishments. Independent personal services are subject to a 21% withholding tax at source if such services are performed in Mexican territory and the person performing such services remains in the territory for more than 183 days in any twelve month period. (Article 147).

other Contracting State (residence state), granting exclusive taxing authority to the residence state. Royalties arising in either the residence state or in a third state are not addressed by Article 12. Instead, Article 7 may apply. Because Article 12 specifically addresses royalty payments, it takes precedence over Article 7, which deals generally with business profits. However, if the royalties are attributable to a permanent establishment in the state in which the royalties arise, Article 7 rather than Article 12 applies. If the royalties are attributable to a fixed base, then Article 14 will apply.

Article 12(2) contains a special treaty definition of the term "royalties." This precludes any interpretation of the term solely by reference to domestic law. But domestic law principles may play a role in interpreting the treaty definition under Article 12(2).

The term "royalties" means all payments made as consideration for the use of (or right to use) copyrights, industrial property rights, other like rights or property, or information pertaining to the foregoing. The consideration that is covered by Article 12 of the OECD Model includes payment in money or in money's worth. Moreover, the payment can be recurring or in a lump sum. The payment must pass from the licensee to the licensor (i.e., the beneficial owner). Exploitation of the payment by the licensor in any other way would not fall within the scope of Article 12. For example, if the licensor sold a royalty contract to a third party, the payments received from the purchaser would not constitute royalties within the meaning of Article 12(2) of the US Model.

Article 12 does not require the royalties to be computed based on any particular formula or in any particular manner. For example: royalties do not have to be based on sales or profits; the payments can be recurring or made in a lump sum; and the payments can be proportionate, progressive, or regressive. Whether the royalty payments are appropriate is solely an issue of the maximum amount allowed under Article 12(4) or the transfer pricing rules of Article 9. Even within the scope of these two special provisions, the parties are free to agree on a royalty formula.

The payment must constitute the economic consideration for the licensed subject matter described in Article 12(2). The treaty definition covers both payments made under a license and compensation payable for infringing a right. However, interest payable on the sum of any damages paid would fall under Article 11 rather than Article 12. Costs awarded in addition to damages (*e.g.*, attorneys' fees or court fees) are not royalties within the meaning of Article 12(2), but might nevertheless be considered ancillary to the compensation and be treated as royalties for purposes of Article 12.

Article 12(2) defines royalties as payments received as consideration "for the use of, or the right to use" specified property or rights. A distinction must be made between licensing rights to an underlying asset on the one hand and the alienation or transfer of the underlying asset on the other hand. The former certainly constitutes the "use" of the assets in question. The latter will not constitute "use." In some countries (*e.g.*, the United States), the gains derived from such alienation may, nevertheless, be considered royalties under the second sentence if they are contingent on the productivity, use, or disposition of the asset.[439] The decisive difference between a license and a sale is the degree of change in the attribution of the asset from licensor to licensee.

There is another distinction to be made concerning the term "use." If the potential licensor uses the royalty property within the framework of an advisory activity, fees paid for the services are not royalties within the meaning of Article 12(2). The concept of "use" lies somewhere between outright alienation for a single, fixed amount and the complete retention of the property in question by the owner who, by using it, renders services for a customer. However, if a licensee makes a payment for the right to use royalty property but does not in fact use the property, the payment will nevertheless constitute a royalty under Article 12(2). This "right to use" language should cover any amounts paid for an option to use royalty property regardless of whether the royalty property is in fact used.

Neither Article 12 nor any other treaty provision contains a definition of "use." Moreover, there is no reference to the law of the source state (in contrast to the definition of "dividend" in Article 10(3), which specifically invokes the domestic law of the source state). Before resorting to domestic law under Article 12(3) of the OECD Model, the context of the treaty must therefore be considered.

The OECD Commentary offers some observations on the difficult issues surrounding classification of income with respect to computer software. First the Commentary defines "software" as follows:

> Software may be described as a programme, or series of programmes, containing instructions for a computer required either for the operational processes of the computer itself (operational software) or for the accom-

---

[439]*See e.g.,* US Model, 1996, Art. 12(2).

plishment of other tasks (application software). It can be transferred through a variety of media, for example in writing, on a magnetic tape or disc, or on a laser disc. It may be standardized with a wide range of applications or be tailor-made for single users. It can be transferred as an integral part of computer hardware or in an independent form available for use on a variety of hardware.[440]

The OECD Commentary recognizes that transfers of rights in software can occur in many different ways ranging from the alienation of the entire rights to the sale of a product which is subject to restrictions on the use to which it is put. The consideration paid can also take numerous forms. These factors may make it difficult to determine where the boundary lies between software payments that are properly to be regarded as royalties and other types of payment.[441]

In trying to provide guidance with respect to different methods of transfer, the OECD Commentary considers three situations. The first situation involves a payment where less than the full rights in software are transferred.[442] In a partial transfer of rights the consideration is not likely to be considered a royalty.[443] Instead, the payment will then be dealt with as commercial income in accordance with Article 7 or 14.[444] It is of no relevance that the software is protected by copyright or that there may be restrictions on the use to which the purchaser can put it.

The second situation is where the payments are made as consideration for the alienation of rights attached to the software.[445] Where consideration is paid for the transfer of the full ownership, the payment does not repre-

---

[440]OECD Commentary, 1997, Art. 12, para. 12.

[441]*Id.*

[442]OECD Commentary, 1997, Art. 12, para. 13.

[443]However, payment for such a transfer may be considered a royalty where the transferor is the author of the software (or has acquired from the author his rights of distribution and reproduction) and he has placed part of his rights at the disposal of a third party to enable the latter to develop or exploit the software itself commercially, for example, by development and distribution of it. It should be noted that even where a software payment is properly to be regarded as a royalty there are difficulties in applying the copyright provisions of the Article royalties because paragraph 2 requires that software should be classified as a literary, artistic, or scientific work. None of these categories seems entirely apt but treatment of software as a scientific work might be the most realistic approach. OECD Commentary, 1997, Art. 12, para. 13.

[444]OECD Commentary, 1997, Art. 12, para. 14.

[445]OECD Commentary, 1997, Art. 12, para. 15.

sent a royalty and the provisions of Article 12 are not applicable. Difficulties can arise where there are extensive but partial alienation of rights involving:

- exclusive right of use during a specific period or in a limited geographical area;
- additional consideration related to usage;
- consideration in the form of a substantial lump sum payment.

Each case will depend on its particular facts but in general such payments are likely to be commercial income within Article 7, or Article 14, or a capital gains matter within Article 13, rather than royalties within Article 12. That follows from the fact that where the ownership of rights has been alienated in full or in part, the consideration cannot be for the use of the rights. The essential character of the transaction as an alienation cannot be altered by the form of the consideration, the payment of the consideration in installments or, in the view of most countries, by the fact that the payments are related to a contingency.[446]

The third situation is where software payments are made under mixed contracts.[447] Two examples of such contracts are the sale of computer hardware with built-in software and the transfer of software combined with the provision of services. Where necessary the total amount of the consideration payable under a contract should be broken down on the basis of the information contained in the contract or by means of a reasonable apportionment with the appropriate tax treatment being applied to each apportioned part.

The principles articulated in the OECD Commentary are not universally accepted.[448] Some countries articulate a broad standard of what constitutes a royalty so that negotiated withholding taxes may be applied to payments received by a nonresident that would not otherwise be taxable in the source country under Article 7 or Article 14. For example, Spain holds the view that payments relating to software are governed by Article 12 where less than the full rights in the software are transferred, either if the payments are in consideration for the right to use a copyright on software

---

[446]OECD Commentary, 1997, Art. 12, para. 16.

[447]OECD Commentary, 1997, Art. 12, para. 17.

[448]*See* Lainoff and Vaish, International Fiscal Association, General Report, *The Taxation of Income Derived from the Supply of Technology,* 82a CAHIERS DE DROIT FISCAL INTERNATIONAL [STUDIES ON INTERNATIONAL FISCAL LAW] 34-35 (1997).

for commercial exploitation or if the payments relate to the software acquired for the use of the purchaser.[449] Accordingly, transactions that some countries might consider a sale of software might be characterized as a royalty by Spain. In Canada, payments by a user of computer software pursuant to a contract that requires that the source code be kept secret are treated as royalties.[450] India imposes a withholding tax on outbound payments related to software unless the software is supplied as part of a hardware sale.[451] Korea provides that outbound payments for software are treated as royalties if the source code is provided, the software is transferred pursuant to a Korean importer's custom order, of if the consideration paid is based on usage of the software by the transferee.[452]

These principles that are set forth in the OECD Commentary may need to be more clearly articulated in order to provide guidance for taxpayers. The failure to articulate clearly may result in double taxation. For example, suppose R Corp. allows customers in country S to access data on R Corp.'s server in country R. Assume that R Corp. does not have a permanent establishment in country S and that the R-S treaty generally complies with the OECD Model, except that the treaty permits 10% source state withholding of royalties. If country S regards payments made by country S customers to R Corp. as a royalty under its view of Article 12, then country S may require withholding. However, if country R views income received by R Corp. as income from the sale of data or the performance of services that is not attributable to a permanent establishment, R Corp. may not be willing to grant relief from double taxation under Article 23 in keeping with its view of the treaty.

Problems could multiply if more than two countries are involved. Suppose that the server is located in country Z, which determines that R Corp. has a permanent establishment in country Z to which the income is attributable. Country S may not recognize the permanent establishment

---

[449]OECD Commentary, 1997, Art. 12, para. 28.

[450]OECD Commentary, 1997, Art. 12, para. 27.

[451]Lainoff and Vaish, International Fiscal Association, General Report, *The Taxation of Income Derived from the Supply of Technology,* 82a CAHIERS DE DROIT FISCAL INTERNATIONAL [STUDIES ON INTERNATIONAL FISCAL LAW] 34 (1997).

[452]Kim, *The Taxation of Income Derived from the Supply of Technology,* 82a CAHIERS DE DROIT FISCAL INTERNATIONAL [STUDIES ON INTERNATIONAL FISCAL LAW] 518-519 (1997) (citing *Payments to a Foreign Corporation as Consideration for Imported Software* — article 6-1-13 (55) (1 August 1996)).

and require withholding of what it considers to be royalty income. Country Z may not grant relief from double taxation for withholding on what it considers to be business profits under Article 7. Country R may not grant double taxation relief for either the withholding by country S or the tax imposed in country Z on the business profits, because Country R does not consider the earnings to be royalties and does not consider the server in country Z to constitute a permanent establishment.

4.2.2. Application of traditional residence rules in the context of electronic commerce

While the growth of electronic commerce tests traditional notions of source-based taxation, it also raises questions with respect to the adequacy of historical formulations of "residence" for tax purposes. Traditional residence concepts are based on physical location, which in the world of electronic commerce may not be easy to determine.

4.2.2.1. Problems presented

The residence of a company has always been an artificial construct because a company is an artificial construct — nothing more than a nexus of contractual relationships among shareholders, employees, suppliers, creditors, and customers.[453] The artificiality of a company's residence is heightened where managers and employees of a company can reside in different jurisdictions, doing their work and communicating through the internet or other electronic means. Indeed, the activities of a company may not have any central location. Instead the components of the business may be scattered among several countries, linked together through a network. For example, suppose that R Corp., a company incorporated in country R, produces and distributes financial and investment information and services. R Corp. has no office or other premises. Its business activities are carried out on a server which is located on an offshore island which is a low tax jurisdiction. R Corp. is managed by directors who live in countries R, S, and Z. R Corp. employees are scattered throughout the world but have access to

---

[453]Lambooij, *Rethinking corporate residence,* Symposium on the Internet and the Taxation of International Electronic Commerce, Leiden 6 June 1997, http://www.lovotax.nl/tax/onderwerp5.

the R Corp. server through an intranet. The directors of R Corp. do not conduct meetings in person but rather videoconference from their respective home bases. What country has residence-based taxing authority over the income that the virtual company, R Corp., generates?

Determining the country that has residence-taxing authority is only the first step. Allocating income and deductions from R Corp.'s far-flung activities to the residence country may prove to be increasingly difficult. Even for those countries that tax a resident on worldwide income, determining the proper allocation of income and expenses may be necessary in order to determine appropriate relief from double taxation (*e.g.*, whether to grant a foreign tax credit with respect to net income that another country taxes).

Even individual residence principles may not be sufficient to cope with technological change. For example, it is possible for C, an individual who physically is domiciled in country S, to use the internet to shop, bank, go to school, work, travel, and recreate all through internet sites located on servers outside of country S.[454] Should C be treated as a resident of country S because of physical presence even though much of C's economic activity takes place over the internet outside of country S? Indeed, some internet companies have built on-line communities where "homesteaders" pick a neighborhood based on their interests, setting up a web page as a cyber-home.[455]

The definition of residence for individuals is further tested by the ability to telecommute. Individuals can more easily avoid numerical residency rules based on a period of physical presence by absenting themselves from a jurisdiction for the necessary number of days while still maintaining employment through telecommuting. In this manner, it may be easier for an individual to have no residence for tax purposes while continuing to work for the same employer in an uninterrupted fashion.

4.2.2.2. National law

There are two basic approaches to corporate residence. Some countries, like the United States, determine residence by looking to where a corporation is incorporated.[456] This is an artificial approach in that in-

---

[454]The physical location of these sites may also be outside country S.

[455]Sreenivasan, *Internet Companies Build Free On-line Communities,* NEW YORK TIMES (17 March 1997).

[456]*See* IRC § 7701(a)(4)

corporation can be a completely ministerial act requiring no corporate presence. A corporation which files articles of incorporation in country R may have its center of operations in country S. While the "place of incorporation" test may be artificial, it provides objective certainty.

The other approach used in determining residence sacrifices the certainty of "place of incorporation" for a more realistic determination of the corporation's presence. Bearing different monikers, this "place of central management and control" or "place of effective management" test focuses on determining the jurisdiction where corporate decisions are made. The landmark case of *De Beers Consolidated Mines v. Howe*,[457] typifies this approach. De Beers was a company registered in South Africa that was involved in diamond mining. The company's head office was located in South Africa, but it maintained other offices in both South Africa and London. Day-to-day decisions were made in South Africa where the diamond mines were located. Major decisions were made in London. In determining the company's residence, the Court reasoned:

> In applying the conception of residence to a Company, we ought, I think, to proceed as nearly as we can upon the analogy of an individual. A Company cannot eat or sleep, but it can keep house and do business. We ought, therefore, to see whether it really keeps house and does business.[458]

The Court ruled that the place of central management and control was in London where the Board made its major decisions. Determining at which meetings the effective management of a corporation takes place is a fact intensive inquiry that is difficult enough. But determining where a meeting takes place when the participants make decisions in cyberspace pushes beyond the developed jurisprudence.

The impact of the internet on determining the residence of individuals may be less troubling. In the United States, an individual is considered a resident if the individual has a "substantial presence" in the United States.[459] Under this test, an individual is a resident of the United States if he is present in the United States for at least 31 days during the current year, and 183 days for the three-year period ending on the last day of the current

---

[457]TC 198 (1906).

[458]*Id.* at 212-213.

[459]IRC § 7701(b). There are two other means of qualifying for US residence — the "green card" test and a special first-year election.

year using a weighted average.[460] The test is based on physical presence. Accordingly, a taxpayer who is physically domiciled in country R but who spends much of his time meeting life's needs connected to US internet sites would not be considered a US resident. Many other countries use a subjective test that focuses on the "facts and circumstances" such as the maintenance of a dwelling, the location of immediate family, the location of personal property, postal address, telephone number, and locus of banking activities.[461] Conceptually, a country using a subjective facts-and-circumstances test might claim that an individual who is working, shopping, recreating, etc., on web sites situated on servers within that country might be said to reside there. While such a conclusion would almost certainly be controversial, it would also be impractical. There is no practical way for the tax authorities of a country to ascertain to what extent someone is accessing web sites within that country. Consequently, it seems likely that current definitions of residence for individuals may not need rethinking in light of technological change.[462]

4.2.2.3. Treaty law

The continuing development of electronic commerce does not raise issues with respect to the treaty treatment of "residence" beyond those raised under national law definitions. Article 4 of the OECD Model does not define the term "resident," leaving that to national law definitions.[463] However, the OECD Model does contain treaty tie-breaker provisions to deal with multiple claims of the right to impose a comprehensive residence-based tax. The tie-breaker provision for competing claims with respect to corporate residence is the "place of effective management."[464] The same problems that this phrase presents under national law are present under treaty law. For example, if the managers of R Corp. are scattered in different jurisdictions, making decisions through video conferencing, more than one

---

[460]IRC § 7701(b)(3).

[461]*See e.g., Thomson v. Minister of Nat'l Revenue,* 2 DTC 812 (Can. Tax Ct. 1946).

[462]It is true that individuals may try to escape high residence based taxation by relocating to low-tax jurisdictions. But to do so involves very real physical consequences (*e.g.,* where an individual is domiciled, banks, socializes, goes to the market). If an individual is willing to undertake these consequences, it is appropriate that the tax laws recognize the decision to relocate.

[463]OECD Commentary, 1997, Art. 4, para. 3.

[464]OECD Model, 1997, Art. 4(3).

country may under applicable domestic law claim the right to impose a comprehensive tax on R Corp. If that occurs, Article 4(3) will do nothing to resolve the conflicting claims of taxing authority.

Because the "cyberresident" issue with respect to individuals probably will not present serious problems under national law, it is not likely that the treaty residence tie-breaker provision will cause any difficulties. Article 4(2) of the OECD Model contains a series of tie-breakers, the first of which focuses on a taxpayer's "permanent home." So if an individual maintains a home in one Contracting State but the other Contracting State deems that individual to be a resident because of extensive internet activity, including telecommuting, shopping, and banking, the taxpayer would be considered a resident of the former Contracting State. However, if an individual has a permanent home in neither or in both Contracting States, the treaty tie-breaker focuses on the individual's "centre of vital interests." Determining to which Contracting State an individual's personal and economic relations are closer may be more difficult where an individual has extensive internet activities (*e.g.*, shopping, banking, working).

4.2.3. Transfer pricing

The rules governing the allocation of intra-group business profits (*i.e.*, transfer pricing rules) are as important in international tax law as the permanent establishment and source of income rules or the residence rules. Both domestic tax legislation and treaty law address the transfer pricing issue. Article 9 of the OECD Model Treaty provides for the right of contracting states to adjust profit transferred to an associated enterprise by means of pricing not in accordance with the arm's length rule. Article 7 provides for the direct (and under some conditions indirect) method of intra-company profit allocation requiring separate accounts for the permanent establishment and likewise imposes the arm's length principle to the relations between head office and permanent establishments (or between separate permanent establishments).

In its Guidelines[465] the Committee on Fiscal Affairs recommends the use of standard methods for evaluating whether transfer pricing complies

---

[465]OECD Committee on Fiscal Affairs, *Transfer Pricing Guidelines for Multinational Enterprises and Tax Administrations* (1995).

with the arm's length principle. The Guidelines conclude that "to date practical experience has shown that, in the majority of cases, it is possible to apply traditional transaction methods." However, they also conclude that "the complexities of real business life situations may put practical difficulties in the way of application of the transactional transaction methods. In those exceptional situations, where there are no data available or the available data are not of sufficient quality to rely solely or at all on the traditional transaction methods, it may become necessary to address whether and under what conditions other methods may be used" (paragraphs 3.49 and 2.49).

The Guidelines thus allow the combining or aggregation of transactions where it is more reasonable to assess the arm's length terms for the transactions together rather than individually, and further allow, as a method of last resort, the transactional profit split and transactional net margin methods. The global formulary apportionment approach and other non-arm's length methods of group profit allocation are "sometimes mentioned as a possible alternative (but) would not be acceptable in theory, implementation or practice" (paragraph 1.14).

The OECD Guidelines do not expressly deal with arm's length pricing of electronic commerce. However, the global trading of securities may offer some guidance.[466] The tax treatment of global trading is the subject of a

---

[466]The communications revolution and financial deregulation are largely responsible for globalizing financial markets. To meet the global demand of borrowers and investors, financial houses developed innovative financial instruments which are traded on a global basis. Financial institution MNE thus maintains a portfolio of proprietary positions (forward transactions, currency options, etc.) in several locations in a 24-hour global trading process. The process involves the originating office (*e.g.,* X Corp. in London) but also branch offices or affiliated companies covering the other time zones: Y Corp. (*e.g.,* in New York) and Z Corp. (*e.g.,* in Tokyo). Those trade centers perform front office functions (trading, risk management, funding) and back office functions (accounting, product control, development of computer-based systems, credit exposure, regulatory compliance, etc.). In an integrated trading model, X Corp, Y Corp. and Z Corp. split the functions among them. While the market is open in the first time zone, X Corp. trades. As the market closes in its location, X Corp. closes the positions and transfers the authority for trading with respect to the securities to Y Corp. which opens new positions. At the closing of the market in its time zone, Y Corp. passes on the trading book to Z Corp, etc. Especially in case of derivatives, the transaction may be unbundled and the responsibility of the different risks of the book assigned to different trading centers of the group. It is difficult to apply traditional transactional methods to the transac-

special OECD discussion draft.[467] Where there is a high level of integration between the various functions and trading locations — typically the case of centralized product management and integrated trading — traditional transaction methods may not be adequate for allocating the profit of the transactions among associated enterprises or branches considering the various functions involved (trading, risk management, funding, sales and marketing, intangibles development and other back office functions).

Accordingly, a more appropriate approach may be the profit split method. It would be applied on a case-by-case basis, determining the profit share of each branch or affiliate with the profit experience of independent traders and risk managers in similar circumstances. The profit split method may be the best approach, but leaves open the question of which factors and what weighting should be used to attribute income according to arm's length standards. The Discussion Draft makes reference to IRS Notice 94-40[468] which focuses on value, risk and activity factors measured by reference to the compensation paid to key support people or to the net present value of transactions executed at each of the trading locations. In the absence of consensus on the concrete application of this method and criteria of transactional profit splitting, the OECD Draft suggests that bilateral or multilateral Advance Pricing Arrangements or bilateral mutual agreement procedures may provide the certainty needed by a taxpayer and by taxing authorities.

Global trading and electronic commerce have similarities. Indeed, global trading can be viewed as one form of electronic commerce. As in the case of global trading of securities, the issues raised by the application of transfer pricing rules to electronic commerce are not unique or novel, but

---

tions among X Corp, Y Corp. and Z Corp. as they closely cooperate to manage the risk and perform the functions and to close the integrated transaction. The arm's length allocation of taxable income (profit share, commission, service fee, split hedge fee, internal payments of interest or for intangibles) attributable respectively to X Corp, Y Corp, Z Corp. and the other trade centers involved, is also tricky where a model of centralized or pooled product management is applied. In such a model, X Corp, being the natural home, takes the full responsibility for hedging and trading and compensates Y Corp. and Z Corp. and other centers of the group for the functions and risks which X Corp. centrally delegated to them.

[467]OECD Committee on Fiscal Affairs, *The Taxation of Global Trading of Financial Instruments: a Discussion Draft* (97)29 (1997).

[468]1994-1 CB 351.

highlight the existing problems of applying the arm's length principle and traditional transactional analysis when branches and associated companies located in different tax jurisdictions deal with each other on a highly integrated basis. Such advanced transactional integration can be present in electronic commerce. The use of the new information and communication technologies in business increases the speed and borderless mobility of the transactions making it difficult for tax administrators to identify and measure contributions and functions of the single participating undertakings to this unitary business or contract performance. It becomes also very difficult to find comparables for determining the economic value of the single contribution to the highly integrated internet transaction in view of its unique features.

The business integration resulting from intranetworking also exarcerbates the particular issue of the inter-jurisdictional allocation of the benefits of the increased group productivity, synergy effects and strategic bundling of MNE-resources. It is not an easy matter to apply to highly integrated business-to-business electronic commerce a comprehensive functional analysis of the functions performed, risks borne and assets held by each of the single participants. How should source state S determine arm's length profit — only on the basis of the limited technical functionality of the infrastructure (server, switching and cabling and possible software agents) in S, taking the view that the economic value derived from the software data, patents, trademarks belongs to the owner in R? Or, alternatively, should state S take the view that the new medium permits the enterprise in residence state R to access and develop the market in S and by the same token to develop the profit potential of its trademarks, or to develop over the intranet engineering, design, research and other profitable business projects by means of a highly integrated and specialized multi-jurisdictional cooperation which justifies the holistic view that those benefits should accrue to each and every tax jurisdiction in which participants operate?

The OECD-CFA document reflects many of those concerns:

- "This development is an occasion to step back and evaluate the rules of Article 7(. . .) and consider whether they are appropriate for purposes of electronic commerce or whether refinements or changes may be in order. Electronic commerce constitutes an environment where automated functions, by their very nature, can undertake a significant amount of business activities in a source of jurisdiction with little or no physical activity in that jurisdiction" (paragraph 103).

- "These ways of sharing workloads among related corporations in the form of collaborative projects can make it difficult to evaluate the contribution of each related corporation to the overall project. They also raise the issue of how to allocate any synergetic benefits among the participants."

Issuance of specific guidelines cannot be expected soon in the absence of further study and international consensus. In the interim, national administrations may apply existing transfer pricing guidelines to electronic commerce along the following lines. Where transactions over the internet (or intranet) are not closely integrated and comparables are available (*e.g.,* in many manufacturing, distribution and support activities), it may be possible and appropriate to apply traditional standard methods (*e.g.,* CUP, cost plus, resale minus). Where the electronic commerce among specialized MNE-undertakings is integrated and the performance unitary, the aggregation of continuous transactions may be the most appropriate approach and the application of transactional profit split formulae the most fitting valuation method. As in the case of global trading, the profit split method may become a standard method for integrated electronic commerce rather than a method of last resort.

The Committee on Fiscal Affairs appropriately points to the dangers of waiting too long to provide guidance for difficult transfer pricing issues arising from electronic commerce. Legal certainty and uniformity in the methodology are needed by multinational enterprises, by national tax authorities and national courts as well as by the arbitration commissions that are established under the European Convention (90/326/EEC) on the elimination of double taxation in connection with the adjustment of profits of associated enterprises. Common guidelines and criteria would also help administrations to enter into mutual agreements under Article 25 of OECD Model-based agreements and advance pricing agreements and to issue rulings and safe harbors circular letters providing administrative simplicity and certainty.

The results of transfer pricing uncertainty are rarely neutral to the MNE's and the tax authorities involved. MNE's, especially if they deal in information products or other portable on-line business, may use the difficult application of the current OECD Guidelines to electronic commerce but also the safe harbor determinations thereunder by some national authorities for the purpose of shifting profits to low tax jurisdictions. The use of the new technologies make the decision to locate or relocate activities such as financial services very elastic and sensitive to tax arbitrage. While the OECD Guidelines do not favor safe harbors, they also point out that it is for a country to decide whether it is prepared to suffer some erosion of its tax base in implementing a safe harbor provision.

Consider the case of call centers and other intelligent service centers and their use in transfer pricing practices of MNE's. Call centers may be established around the world to satisfy the growing need of cost effective formulae for customer contact and sale of products and services — the complexity of which requires a high level of support and the marketing of which requires a wide-regional interface with the customer. Electronic communication is the key tool of this formula based on the use of telephone line, the internet, email, teleconferencing and such other media as the customer may prefer to communicate. The communication with the customer may cover a wide range of inbound-mode and outbound-mode contacts: advertisement, news of product launches, product information, pre-sale services, post-sale services, payments. The activity covers a global or wide regional market segment, (*e.g.,* Europe). The center is staffed with multilingual labor and equipped with an adequate telecommunications infrastructure. Its location is mainly selected on the basis of those availabilities.

In an advanced organizational structure, the call center and its communications are established and managed on a centralized basis often organized in the form of a worldwide "hub and spokes" system. The main investment is in a global or centralized unit, thereby reducing significantly the investment in resources of the decentralized call centers which operate as spokes depending for their services on an intranet connection with the hub. The global unit maintains the server, database and staff. It communicates directly with customers' computers, providing internet access to high technical quality, high value-added services. Low margin mass services are left to be handled by the responsible spoke (*e.g.,* the European center), to which the hub routes all calls involving mass services. The center will often work for the account of companies of its own group, posing directly the transfer pricing issue for business-to-business charges. It may, alternatively, work on an independent basis for third party vendors, in exchange for a commission fee for its external contribution to their sales activity, posing the transfer pricing issue of the internal allocation of this fee.

The following illustrates how a call center operates. Suppose that X Corp. is an MNE (airline, bank, etc.) consisting of a group of companies selling products or services to customers in Europe. Other companies of the same group (e.g., A Corp. and B Corp.) sell other products or services to customers in the same European region. Instead of entrusting the full gamut of sales activities and related customer contacts to its country subsidiaries selling via traditional channels or of relying on outsourcing from a telemarketing firm, MNE operates its own call center (C Corp.) which it locates in European country C and staffs it with a dedicated specialized team operating 24 hours a day and 7 days a week. C Corp. employees sitting at their computer terminals receive calls from prospects dialing from all over the European region in response to an advertisement. The incoming calls may be routed intelligently by a C Corp. operator to another call center or work station of the group (e.g., D Corp.). The operators access or input information into the MNE private database and exchange information on line with the correspondent in a customized manner. Using an automatic dialing program, the C Corp. operator contacts the correspondent and transmits to him the information for the account of A Corp. and B Corp. or of TH Corp. in a tax haven country, which eventually conclude the sale with him with the logistical support of C Corp.

This call center activity poses practical tax problems of arm's length allocation of income and expenses when it comes to splitting the group commission fee between the hub (C Corp.) and the spokes cooperating with it over the intranet to render the integrated service. It also poses a tricky transfer pricing issue when call center C Corp. operates in support of client-group members X Corp, A Corp, B Corp. selling the goods or services to the external correspondent.

The tax problem begins with the issue of permanent establishment — does C Corp. create a permanent establishment for X Corp, A Corp, or B Corp? Is the establishment taxable or exempt under the C-X, C-A, or C-B treaty because the commercial and highly productive contacts of the center with the customers of those client-group companies qualify as preparatory of auxiliary services provisions under those treaties? If C Corp. would give rise to a taxable establishment, on what basis should it share in the sales profit of X Corp, A Corp, B Corp? If the call center activity of C Corp. does not give rise in C to a permanent establishment of its client-group members, how is the arm's length nature of its own fee determined? Should the fee for the services of C Corp. for X Corp, A Corp, B Corp. be determined by reference to the commission fee earned by independent call centers performing a more or less similar service for third party vendors or, in the absence of a comparable, by the use of traditional transaction methods? Does it make a difference that C Corp. functions as a central trading company of the group located in a low tax jurisdiction with little mainstream activity and operational substance of its own other than that over the MNE intranet? Taking into account the high degree of integration and productivity of the call center services and the limited effective mainstream activity of the client-group members, one view is that the traditional cost plus compensation of support services is not an adequate evaluation of the contribution of the center and that the transactions of the center, and the client-group members should be combined in view of the allocation of the aggregate profit by a split on the basis of a functional analysis of the activities.

Belgium has issued a Circular Letter on 26 July 1996 to provide for a safe harbor profit determination for such centers. The Circular describes the authorized special services as "intellectual services." Referring to their intensive and productive use of electronic tools, they can also be described as "intelligent" services. Their main role is that of interface between external customers and the companies of the group. Independent call or service centers rendering interface services to companies which do not belong to the group, are excluded from the special tax regime.

For purposes of determining the tax regime and hedging against transfer pricing adjustments, the Circular Letter distinguishes in particular four categories of center service activities, taking into account the nature of their respective support function and different contribution to the realization of the profit of the client-group members.

(i) activities having a purely preparatory or auxiliary character

These activities may not directly add value to the goods sold or the services rendered to the customers. They might include: the management for the benefit of a group of airlines of a database containing the mileages of their customers, the logistic operations inherent to the permanent professional training of the staff of the group companies, the management of the flow of operational communications within the group or with public

209

authorities, the centralization of purchases or goods on behalf of the group members, operations in the field of scientific research, services of providing to group companies information, coordination and advice concerning organization, sales techniques, legal affairs, etc.

(ii)   activities relating to providing information to customers of group members

These activities focus on requests of the customers (*e.g.,* a helpline for repairs by telephone of data-processing equipment or other technical operation assistance) or information regarding goods sold or services rendered by group companies (*e.g.,* availability of a product, delivery time, etc.).

(iii)   activities contributing in a passive way to sales operations of group members

A passive contribution implies that the center cannot decide autonomously — acting instead only on behalf and for the account of the sales companies of the group. It may register and confirm orders emanating from persons who are not group members but, being a go-between or interface for group members, cannot negotiate nor accept the offer to buy itself.

(iv)   activities contributing in an active way to operations of group members

In this case, the center operates as an intermediary in the selling of goods or services of group members. It acts for their account but in its own name. The center is, for example, empowered to accept orders, the conditions of which (price, quantity, terms, etc.) have been fixed in advance. It may send out order confirmations, (re-)invoice and carry out administrative and tax formalities. Customer contacts thus include a wide range of subsidiary MNE-activities: advertisement, pre-sale information, after-sale help lines, commissionaire sales, management of receivables. The center may not itself engage in the business of active solicitation of customers, telemarketing, autonomous selling, bearing commercial risks (other than minor risks), material handling activities, distribution of products.

The special tax regime detailed in the Circular is based on the administrative fiction that the center conforms to the arm's length principle if the profit realized by it amounts to no less than the minimum tax basis laid out in the Circular with respect to those four categories of activity. The tax administration will not challenge the arm's length character of the center's dealings with its client-group companies if the amount of its net profit as a percentage of costs relating to its operation reaches the following safe haven levels:

(i) The percentage can vary from 5% to 15% and is fixed for each service center based on the relative importance of the kind of activity performed.[469] The percentages are:
 • 5% for activities having a preparatory or auxiliary character;
 • 10% for activities relating to informing the customers;
 • 15% for activities contributing in a passive way to sales operations.

(ii) If the service center performs activities which amount to an active intervention in sales operations, its minimum remuneration (commission) is determined in accordance with the resale minus method at a margin of the sales of goods and services in which the center participated for the account of the group members. The percentage is fixed case by case, depending on the nature of the contribution of the service center and the risk borne by it. It does not exceed 5% of the amount of sales.

The Belgian Circular thus offers an application of the arm's length principle laid down in national law (Article 26 ITC), to various forms of support by intelligent centers contributing to the multi-jurisdictional marketing activities of their group with the help of the new information and communication technologies. It is uncertain that the application will also be accepted for purposes of bilateral treaties (Article 7(2) and 9 of OECD Model-based treaties) and European law (Article 4 of European Tax Arbitration Convention).

The income determination resulting from the application of the Circular is characterized by two features. In the first place, the Circular provides safe harbors assuring simplified compliance with the arm's length principle, which is particularly elusive when it is applied to the activity of interfacing via the new medium between the mainstream activity of the

---

[469]Some costs do not require a percentage net profit (e.g., telecommunication costs resulting from free telephone calls to the call center incurred for the benefit of the companies of the group).

client-group members and their customers. The traditional transactional methods of cost plus and resale minus are often best suited for support activities. The Circular does not employ a profit splitting method. That method is better suited for core activities which contribute significantly to an integrated transaction.

The Circular also applies to cases in which the mainstream sales activity is carried out by virtual companies located in tax haven countries. This broad scope may explain the Circular's other feature. It functions as a fiscal instrument in the Belgian government policy attracting such activities thereby increasing the country's fiscal competitiveness. MNE's may, because of this tax incentive, want to locate their special service (call) center in Belgium and entrust the formal selling and decision-making responsibility to a regional or world trading subsidiary in a low or zero tax jurisdiction with limited operational substance and staffing but closely integrated with the Belgian center with the help of electronic communication and banking tools. The offshore central trading company fixes pricing conditions in advance, depends on advertisement on the internet for soliciting orders and unbundles its marketing function, leaving customer information, interface, order acceptance, invoicing and receivables collection in the hands of the Belgian service center.

In many cases of electronic commerce, the existing transfer pricing issue is thus greatly exarcerbated by the high degree of integration making the aggregated transaction instantaneous and borderless. The evaluation of individual core transactions (as in the case of global trading in the financial sector) and even of individual services of marketing support to sales activities, for instance if the website is operated by such support facilities for the account of the vendor (as in the intelligent services industry) is troublesome. Also the lack of comparables in terms of functions, intangibles used and risks assumed pose a problem as transactions become increasingly unique with the help of the new information and communication technologies. In many cases of electronic commerce, the application to such cases of traditional transactional methods recommended by current OECD Guidelines may therefore not be adequate. Interpretations and applications by national authorities risk being divergent, giving rise to problems of profit reallocation and double taxation but also to tax planning opportunities for MNE's and fiscal competition among national authorities. Common guidelines and models dealing specifically with highly integrated and complex cases of business to business electronic commerce within MNE's or other forms of crossborder cooperation over a private intranet should now be developed by the OECD Committee on Fiscal Affairs and specifically by its Electronic Commerce Working Group of WP6.

4.2.4. Controlled foreign corporations

To prevent or limit the reduction, deferral, or avoidance of taxes through the use of controlled foreign corporations set up in low tax jurisdictions, more and more countries are enacting specific anti-tax-haven legislation[470] whereby the undistributed income of a controlled foreign company is not deferred, but is taxed to its domestic shareholders on a current basis.[471] The legislation all follows the same basic pattern. Deferral of

---

[470]While many countries use the term "controlled foreign corporation (CFC)" in their tax-avoidance legislation, a few do not, though the provisions operate in relatively the same manner. To avoid confusion, this report will often use the broader term "anti-tax-haven legislation" to include all countries with such measures, whether or not they specifically reference controlled foreign corporations. Factual information in OECD member countries is discussed in OECD, CONTROLLED FOREIGN COMPANY LEGISLATION: STUDIES IN TAXATION OF FOREIGN SOURCE INCOME (1996).

[471]Although it had foreign personal holding company legislation since 1937, the United States was the first country to pass legislation dealing with controlled foreign companies. In 1962, the United States enacted legislation which subjected specified income of certain foreign corporations controlled by US shareholders to US taxation when earned by such corporations. The legislation was aimed at curbing "tax deferral." Before the enactment of the controlled foreign corporation provisions, foreign corporations, even though controlled by US shareholders, were not subject to US tax laws on foreign source income. As a result no US tax was imposed with respect to the foreign source earnings of these corporations until dividends were paid by the foreign corporations to their US parent corporations or to their other US shareholders. The tax at that time is imposed with respect to the dividend income received by the American shareholder, and if this shareholder is a corporation it is eligible for a foreign tax credit with respect to the taxes paid by the foreign subsidiary. In the case of foreign subsidiaries, therefore, this means that foreign taxes are paid currently, to the extent of the applicable foreign income tax, and not until distributions are made will an additional US tax be imposed, to the extent the US rate is above that applicable in the foreign country.

Former President Kennedy questioned the desirability of providing tax deferral with respect to earnings of US-controlled companies except in the case of investments in less developed countries. However, his primary emphasis was on removing tax deferral in the case of what have been called "tax havens." In this respect he stated:

The undesirability of continuing deferral is underscored where deferral has served as a shelter for tax escape through the unjustifiable use of tax havens such as Switzerland. Recently more and more enterprises organized abroad by American firms have arranged their corporate structures — aided by artificial arrangements between parent and subsidiary regarding intercompany pricing, the transfer of patent licensing rights, the shifting of management fees, and similar practices which maximize the accumulation of profits in the tax haven — so as to exploit the multiplicity of foreign tax systems and international agreements in order to reduce sharply or eliminate completely their tax liabilities both at home and abroad.

In this area the President recommended the:

* * * elimination of the tax haven device anywhere in the world, even in the underdeveloped countries, through the elimination of tax deferral privileges for those forms of activities, such as trading, licensing, insurance, and others, that typically seek out tax haven methods of operation. There is no valid reason to permit their remaining untaxed regardless of the country in which they are located.

The resulting legislation did not go as far as the President's recommendations. It did not eliminate tax deferral in the case of operating businesses owned by US residents which are located in the economically developed countries of the world. Testimony in congressional hearings suggested that the location of investments in these countries is an important factor in stimulating American exports to the same areas. Moreover, it appeared that to impose the US tax currently on the US shareholders of US-owned businesses operating abroad would place such firms at a disadvantage with other firms not subject to US tax located in the same areas. The resulting legislation ended tax deferral for US shareholders in certain situations where the multiplicity of foreign tax systems has been taken advantage of by US-controlled businesses to siphon off specified types of income.

Using the US legislation as a model, in 1972 Germany enacted its own equivalent to the US controlled foreign corporation legislation, Aussensteuergesetz (AstG), Sections 7 to 14 contain detailed rules under which income realized by foreign controlled corporations is included in the taxable income of their German shareholders. Strobl & Fuger, International Bureau of Fiscal Documentation, THE ACQUISITION OF ASSETS BY A BASE COMPANY, Volume 31 1991 No. 5 (1 May 1991). Like the United States, Germany attributes only passive income and certain base company income of the CFC. Passive income is defined in the negative, in that it is income which is not described in an enumerated list. SANDLER, PUSHING THE BOUNDARIES: THE INTERACTION BETWEEN TAX TREATIES AND CONTROLLED FOREIGN COMPANY LEGISLATION 19-21 (1994).

Using as models the legislation of the United States, Germany and Canada which was then in effect, Japan adopted its anti-tax haven measures in 1978 as part of the Special Taxation Measures Law, Arts. 40-4 through 40-6 (individuals) and Arts. 66-6 through 66-9 (corporations). What was different from the aforementioned countries' legislation was that the application of Japan's measures was based on an exhaustive blacklist of tax haven countries. Japan eliminated this blacklist in 1992, replacing it with domestic taxation on the income of a controlled foreign corporation until it distributes dividends to its shareholders is eliminated. The existence of the foreign corporation is ignored for specified purposes. The resident shareholder of the controlled foreign corporation is taxed directly on a pro rata share of the corporation's undistributed income.[472]

Anti-tax-haven legislation operates to distinguish a foreign corporation whose undistributed income should be taxed currently to its domestic shareholders from a foreign corporation whose income should be taxable to its domestic shareholders only when distributed to them. Usually three factors are used to make this distinction: (1) The domestic shareholders must control or have a significant ownership interest in the foreign corporation; (2) The geographical location of the controlled foreign corporation — where it is established or does business — is suspect; and (3) The nature of the activities engaged in by the foreign corporation and the character of the income derived by it are used to distinguish between controlled foreign corporations engaged in bona fide business operations and those used primarily to defer or avoid domestic tax.[473]

---

a test based strictly on the comparative effective tax rate (25 percent or less) of the foreign country concerned.

Modeled, with substantial modifications, on the original Japanese anti-tax-haven measures, the UK's controlled foreign corporation legislation was enacted as part of the 1984 Finance Bill. Like the United States, the United Kingdom has had certain limited anti-haven measures aimed at incorporated pocketbooks since the 1930's. The UK controlled foreign corporation legislation, found in Part XVII, Chapter IV (ss. 747-56) and related Schedules of the Income and Corporation Taxes Act 1988, as amended (TA 1988), does not apply to companies on the UK Excluded Countries list (*i.e.,* a "white list"). United Kingdom IFA Branch, *Comments on Electronic Commerce Report* (8 April 1998) (on file with the authors).

Norway's controlled foreign corporation legislation, Chapter 7 of the Company Tax Act, became effective from 1 January 1992. Also similar to the original Japanese model, it applies where the controlled foreign corporation is established in a low-tax jurisdiction.

The controlled foreign corporation legislation incorporated in article 18(2) of Indonesia's Income Tax Law (ITL) was introduced with the amendment of the ITL at the end of 1994. Like the original Japanese model, Indonesian controlled foreign corporation rules apply to corporate entities established in countries or territories designated on a black list. Hilders & Murata, *CFC Legislation in Indonesia and Japan,* available in LEXIS/NEXIS, 97 TNI 6620 (7 April 1997).

[472]ARNOLD, THE TAXATION OF FOREIGN CONTROLLED CORPORATIONS: AN INTERNATIONAL COMPARISON 131 (1986).

[473]ARNOLD, *supra* note 472, at 407.

Countries with anti-tax-haven legislation define a controlled foreign corporation (CFC) in much the same manner. A controlled foreign corporation is a foreign corporation more than 50% of whose shares, voting power, or value is owned by domestic shareholders. Beyond this general principle, however, each country's definition appears to differ in minor ways. For example, to be considered "shareholders" for purposes of the above definition, some countries require a certain percentage of share or vote ownership. US shareholders are defined as US persons owning stock with at least 10% of the voting power.[474] As a result, US persons owning less than 10% of the voting stock are not counted for purposes of determining controlled foreign corporation status, nor are they taxed on their shares of the controlled foreign corporation's subpart F income ("tax haven income") prior to receipt of it as a dividend.[475] Indonesia has no minimum ownership rules, but only includes those who are direct shareholders in its 50% calculation.[476] It is expected that the ownership threshold in the United Kingdom will be raised from 10% to 25% in 1998.[477]

The geographic location requirement is aimed at identifying those countries which impose little or no tax on income generated in their territory — "tax havens." The OECD report defines a tax haven as "a jurisdiction actively making itself available for avoidance of tax which would otherwise be paid in relatively high tax countries."[478] To be useful to nonresident individuals and corporations, tax havens usually have the following characteristics which bolster their appeal as a location for commercial

---

[474]Under Japanese law, a resident individual or corporation must own 5 percent or more of the issued shares in the foreign corporation. Specified Foreign Subsidiary Corporation, Arts. 40-4(1) and 66-6(1).

[475]DELOITTE AND TOUCHE LLP, UNITED STATES, 13.09 Controlled Foreign Corporations, PART 6 CORPORATE INCOME TAXES, Chapter 13 Special Corporate Tax Situations.

[476]Hilders & Murata, *CFC Legislation in Indonesia and Japan,* available in LEXIS/NEXIS, 97 TNI 66-20 (7 April 1997).

[477]United Kingdom IFA Branch, *Comments on Electronic Commerce Report* (8 April 1998) (on file with the authors).

[478]International Bureau of Fiscal Documentation, OECD, Reprinted from No. 145 OECD Observer, AprilMay 1987 with permission of the OECD, Paris TAX HAVENS, Volume 27 1987 No. 5 (1 May 1987) (citing International Tax Avoidance and Evasion: Four Related Studies, Paris Organization for Economic Cooperation & Development (1987) — setting up base companies in such tax havens which have no real economic activity (second study)).

enterprise, while at the same time allowing a reduction or avoidance of tax in the individual or corporation's country of residence: low taxes (or none at all) on certain types of income and capital; high levels of banking and commercial secrecy; absence of exchange controls on foreign deposits of foreign currencies; a disproportionately large financial sector; modern communications facilities, including sea and air transport; selfpromotion as an offshore financial center; and few or no tax treaties providing for exchange of information.[479]

Because legislation for taxation of controlled foreign corporations is primarily aimed at those entities established in tax havens, many countries have written their legislation to apply only to those controlled foreign corporations located in defined tax havens. Under this "designated jurisdiction" approach, the taxing authorities in a country issue a list of tax haven or non-tax haven countries and the anti-deferral measures either do, or do not apply, respectively. The tax haven lists may be issued as part of the legislation itself or as an administrative pronouncement.

Several methods have been used to categorize taxing regions under the designated jurisdictional approach. The simplest designates by name those jurisdictions in which there is no income tax or the income tax rate is low compared to that of the home country.[480] This type of list, termed a "black list," is exclusive, meaning that if a jurisdiction is not on the list, then a corporation organized in that jurisdiction is not subject to controlled foreign corporation taxation even if, for some reason, no tax ends up being paid there. An official black list precludes arguments by taxpayers that a controlled foreign corporation in a listed country was actually subject to a high rate of tax. Although it no longer uses such a list, this method was created and first utilized by Japan, where the Ministry of Finance designated 33 jurisdictions (subsequently increased to 41 jurisdictions) as having low tax regimes. Currently, Indonesia has such a black list naming more than 30 tax haven countries.[481]

Similar in function, but opposite in form, is what is known as a "white

---

[479]Gordon, *Tax Havens and Their Use by United States' Taxpayers — An Overview* (US Treasury 1981).

[480]There are three general approaches to defining a tax haven in terms of a comparison of domestic and foreign tax rates: (1) a comparison on the basis of nominal tax rates (Germany); (2) a comparison on the basis of effective tax rates (Japan); and (3) a comparison on the basis of actual taxes paid (United Kingdom, Norway). ARNOLD, *supra* note 472, at 429-430.

[481]For a list of the countries, *see* Hilders & Murata, *CFC Legislation in Indonesia and Japan*, available in LEXIS/NEXIS, 97 TNI 6620, Appendix A (7 April 1997).

list." This type of list designates jurisdictions in which the tax rate is not significantly below the rate of the home country. Taxpayers may have additional jurisdictions added to the list by proving that the tax burden in the jurisdiction in question meets the relevant tests. An official white list of non-tax-haven countries precludes arguments by the tax authorities that a controlled foreign corporation in a listed country was actually subject to low taxation.[482] Unofficial lists (usually white) serve as simple guidelines for the taxpayer and taxing authorities as to the status of certain foreign countries and only establish a presumption about a listed country. This presumption may be rebutted by either the taxpayer or the tax authorities with respect to a particular controlled foreign corporation.[483]

A similar, but less specific, approach adopted by many countries is to set a particular tax rate as defining the boundary of a "low-tax" jurisdiction.[484] All countries with a nominal rate below the designated rate automatically qualify as a "tax haven" under the controlled foreign corporation provisions. A secondary determination made by some countries is whether in fact that tax rate was in fact paid. For example, Germany designates any jurisdiction with a nominal rate below 30% as a low tax jurisdiction, but then examines in particular cases whether the foreign corporation in fact paid a rate above 30%.[485] To aid in the determination, the German tax authorities recently published an exhaustive list of countries that are deemed to have a lowtax regime.[486] Under its new tax haven provision, Japan also employs an income tax rate test. Unlike Germany, however, it uses an "effective income tax rate" of 25% or less.[487] Norway and the United Kingdom regard a country as a lowtax jurisdiction if the taxes payable on the income derived by the entity in the country are less than a set percentage amount of the tax that would have been payable if the entity had been domestic.[488] The

---

[482]ARNOLD, *supra* note 472, at 434.

[483]However, as a practical matter, judging from the experience of Germany, an unofficial list has a tendency to operate as an official list. ARNOLD, *supra* note 471, at 435.

[484]Often a country will issue a corresponding list (white or administrative) to aid taxpayers and tax authorities in their analysis of a particular tax jurisdiction.

[485]*See* ARNOLD, *supra* note 472, at 246.

[486]DELOITTE AND TOUCHE LLP, GERMANY, 11.06 Controlled Foreign Companies, PART 5 INCOME TAXES, Chapter 11 Special Corporate Tax Situations.

[487]SANDLER, *supra* note 471, at 131.

[488]For Norway, the amount designated is less than ⅔ of the Norwegian tax rate. For the United Kingdom the amount is less than ¾ of the UK tax rate. The United Kingdom also has a published white list. *Id.* at 133.

United States has no definition of a tax haven in its Subpart F legislation.[489] However, one of its provisions does exempt Subpart F income that is subject to actual overall foreign taxes of at least 90% of the US rate from being currently taxable to the domestic shareholders.[490]

Even after it has been determined that a controlled foreign corporation exists in a tax haven/low-tax jurisdiction it is often still necessary, under various countries' legislation, to determine if the income earned falls within the definition of income which is attributed to domestic shareholders on a current basis. Where the provisions apply only to special kinds of attributable income, usually only certain types of passive income and/or foreign base company sales or services income are included.

There are some countries (*e.g.,* Japan and Indonesia) that do not distinguish between the type of income (passive income, active income, sale and/or services income from relatedparty transactions, or a combination of the above) generated by the foreign corporate entity, but instead consider all income attributable.[491] The United Kingdom attributes all income, except it does not include capital gains.[492] Norway, on the other hand, has a rather unique way of determining which profits are attributable. Where the controlled foreign corporation is resident in a country without a treaty with Norway, all profits are attributed. Where the controlled foreign corporation is resident in a country with a treaty with Norway, only profits from "passive" activities are attributed.[493]

Passive income generally refers to investment income. It is easily diverted to a controlled foreign corporation established in a tax haven to avoid domestic tax. Thus, most countries that attribute only certain types of income, apply their anti-tax-haven measures to passive income.[494] The main point in defining passive income is to distinguish it from income derived from an active business which, except for certain base company income, is not attributed to the domestic shareholders of a controlled foreign corporation.[495]

---

[489]*Id.*

[490]IRC § 954(b)(4).

[491]*See* SANDLER, *supra* note 470, at 137; Hilders & Murata, *CFC Legislation in Indonesia and Japan,* available in LEXIS/NEXIS, 97 TNI 6620 (7 April 1997).

[492]SANDLER, *supra* note 471, at 139.

[493]*Id.* at 138.

[494]ARNOLD, *supra* note 472, at 450.

[495]There are two primary ways of defining passive income. (1) Such income can be

Rents and royalties may be either active business income or passive income, depending on the circumstances.[496] In the United States, royalties are considered active if the controlled foreign corporation developed or added substantial value to the licensed property in the regular course of its business or entered into the license as a result of marketing functions performed by the controlled foreign corporation through a staff of employees in a foreign country.[497]

The term "base company income" generally refers to income of a controlled foreign corporation, other than passive income, which is attributed to the corporation's domestic shareholders. Most definitions include two basic requirements: (1) the income must be derived from transactions between the controlled foreign corporation and a related party; and (2) the income must arise from sales made or services rendered outside the country where the controlled foreign corporation is located (unless an exemption is allowed).[498] Thus, where a subsidiary is incorporated in a tax haven, sells only products acquired from its parent or related corporations, sells such products outside the country in which it is incorporated, and does not

---

defined generally or specifically by listing the common types of investment income, such as dividends, interest, rents, royalties, and capital gains from the disposition of securities and other investment property. The United States defines it this way. (2) Passive income can be defined indirectly or negatively as the total income of a controlled foreign corporation less the corporation's active business income. Germany uses this method of defining passive income. ARNOLD, *supra* note 472, at 450.

[496]In IRC § 954(c)(3)(A), the United States excludes "rents and royalties which are derived in the active conduct of a trade or business" from its definition of passive income. However, even rents and royalties that are considered passive under that definition are specifically excluded from passive income if they are received from a related person for the use of property in the country in which the controlled foreign corporation is established. IRC § 954(c)(4)(C).

[497]Reg. § 1.954-2(d).

[498]Germany, Japan, and the United Kingdom provide exemptions for corporations engaged in active business or business with unrelated parties only if the foreign corporation has a "substantial and independent" business operation in the foreign country. This usually means that the corporation must be independently managed, and have a fixed place of business, with a sufficient amount of employees and facilities to carry on its business. ARNOLD, *supra* note 471, at 465. No exceptions are recognized by Japan, the United Kingdom, or the United States to the treatment of related-party transactions outside the local market as income taxable in the hands of shareholders. ARNOLD, *supra* note 472, at 462.

have a substantial or genuine presence in that country, the subsidiary may appropriately be viewed as a vehicle to avoid domestic tax, and the income should be currently taxable to the domestic shareholders.[499]

As a general rule, income derived by a controlled foreign corporation from selling property or rendering services is considered to be active business income; accordingly, such income is not attributed to its domestic shareholders.[500] However, where a controlled foreign corporation established in a tax haven is used to perform services in the country in which its controlling shareholder is resident, whether such services are performed for related or unrelated persons, the arrangement may be viewed as an artificial reduction of domestic tax.[501]

Also, in situations where a related party provides substantial assistance to the controlled foreign corporation in earning its sales or services income, it may be appropriate for the income to be attributed to the parent corporation if the income could not have been earned by the controlled foreign corporation on its own.[502] However, if the assistance provided by the re-

---

[499]ARNOLD, *supra* note 472, at 456. The United States has enacted a special incentive to encourage the use of foreign sales corporations (FSCs) by US exporting corporations. IRC §§921-927. As a result of this incentive, income that might normally be taxable in the United States as a result of the US controlled foreign corporation provisions is exempt from US taxation. The Taxpayer Relief Act of 1997 has clarified that computer software that is produced in the United States and is licensed for reproduction abroad is considered export property entitled to FSC benefits. HR 2014, 105th Cong. 1st Sess. §1171 (1997).

The existence of incentives like the FSC provisions reveals a degree of schizophrenia on the part of the United States. On one hand, the United States has well-developed controlled foreign corporation provisions intended to prevent US corporations from using foreign subsidiaries to shield foreign base company income from US taxation. On the other hand, the FSC provisions explicitly exempt income that would otherwise be subject to US taxation. Moreover, while there is concern that controlled foreign corporation provisions may not fully address the challenge of electronic commerce, at the same time Congress specifically makes it easier for certain income related to electronic commerce to be exempt from US taxation.

[500]ARNOLD, *supra* note 472, at 458.

[501]ARNOLD, *supra* note 472, at 459.

[502]ARNOLD, *supra* note 472, at 464. It is not hard to imagine a controlled foreign corporation that provides services to third parties receiving financing, employees, technical expertise, equipment, materials, and/or supplies from its parent corporation to aid it in rendering the services.

lated person is insignificant or incidental to the subsidiary's business, the subsidiary's income should not be treated as base company income.[503]

4.2.4.1. Problems presented

The ability of taxpayers to sell digitized information and services electronically may require a re-examination of controlled foreign corporation provisions to see if they are sufficient in their current form to achieve the intended purposes. If controlled foreign corporations can engage in extensive electronic commerce in information and services through web sites or computer networks located in a tax haven, it may become increasingly difficult to enforce existing controlled foreign corporation legislation, in part because of the difficulty of detection.[504] Some persons engaged in electronic commerce may already be locating their businesses offshore.[505]

It is likely that more controlled foreign corporation arrangements will appear in the next few years because of the portability of many forms of electronic commerce. Incorporating a server in a tax haven so that customers can download the parent company's product (*e.g.,* software), may be much easier than incorporating a more traditional business establishment in the tax haven country.

The growth of electronic commerce should not pose any major problems with regard to which corporations are classified as controlled foreign

---

[503]ARNOLD, *supra* note 472, at 464. Even if a foreign company is resident in a low-tax country for a particular year and the other conditions for the imposition of a tax charge apply, it may nevertheless be excluded from the anti-deferral provision under a series of exemptions provided by some countries for controlled foreign corporations. There are five exemptions commonly found in anti-deferral legislation for controlled foreign corporations: (1) engaged primarily or exclusively in genuine business activities; (2) that distribute a certain percentage of their attributable income; (3) whose shares are publicly traded on a stock exchange; (4) that are not used for the purpose of avoiding or reducing tax (motive exemption); or (5) whose income does not exceed a defined amount. ARNOLD, *supra* note 472, at 472-473.

[504]US Treasury Report, *supra* note 217, Section 8.

[505]Murphy, *Cooling the Net Hype,* WIRED 86 (Sept. 1996). ("Companies selling information over the internet can call any place home, and the savvy ones are choosing jurisdictions with low or no taxes, financial privacy, governmental stability, and decent communications systems. (Warm water and sandy beaches are also a plus.)")

corporations,[506] or which jurisdictions qualify as tax havens. However, electronic commercial transactions may create confusion in determining where transactions took place and what type of income was produced. For example, income from the performance of services is generally sourced to where the services are performed. However, electronic commerce blurs the geographic issue. On-line databases and video conferencing can often substitute for many facetoface meetings.[507] Thus, it becomes difficult to determine where the service was actually performed, and particularly whether it was outside the country where the controlled foreign corporation is located. The same problem arises in the sales context where customers can download software and other products over the internet rather than actually having a physical location where buyer and seller come together. A corresponding problem raised by electronic commerce is determining what is purchased — tangible/intangible goods or services — and, if goods are involved, whether the goods are licensed (*i.e.*, intangible), leased (*i.e*, tangible), or sold outright. That characterization may be crucial in determining whether a controlled foreign corporation regime applies.

Finally, the policy underlying the creation of anti-deferral legislation is called into question. In enacting such measures, countries were attempting to curtail the schemes being employed by corporations to avoid domestic tax. Thus, many of the rules are restricted in that they apply only in circumstances where the corporations took actions which appeared to be designed to avoid domestic tax. However, the rules may not be so restrictive when they include corporations doing business electronically, and may apply even when a corporation has a legitimate purpose for its corporate setup. This is possible since many countries require some sort of physical presence in the low-tax jurisdiction or the anti-tax-haven rules automatically apply.[508]

---

[506]However, the creation and use of the internet may encourage more businesses to develop which are owned by shareholders residing in a number of countries, thus exempting the corporation from the definition of a controlled foreign corporation altogether.

[507]It may be argued, however, that these technological developments are only extensions of existing communications devices. For example, a video conference is likely to be a substitute for a conference telephone call. Downloading is analogous to a mail order purchase. US Treasury Report, *supra* note 217.

[508]For example, all the income and expenses of a foreign company can be trans-

4.2.4.2. National law

Suppose that CFC Corp., resident in a tax haven (TH) sells software created by R Corp., its parent corporation, resident in country R. Customers in country S purchase the software by accessing CFC Corp.'s web site and downloading the software to their own computers. First of all, it should be noted that some countries like Japan, Indonesia, and the United Kingdom (except for capital gains), do not distinguish between types of income. Instead, all income is considered attributable to the domestic shareholders if it is produced by a controlled foreign corporation. Likewise, Norway attributes all income derived by controlled foreign corporations located in countries with which it does not have a treaty. (Otherwise, if there is a treaty, it attributes only passive income.) For these countries, the income resulting from CFC Corp.'s activities may be taxable by country R, unless an exemption is applicable.[509]

For countries, like the United States, which assert tax jurisdiction only when income is considered base company income, CFC Corp.'s purchase of software from a related party, R Corp., and its sale to customers in country S would generally constitute base company income under traditional principles. But suppose that employees of CFC Corp., perhaps residing in country R, develop the software which is then sold to country S customers. In this situation, because CFC Corp. is not itself purchasing the software from a related party but rather is developing the software, under some controlled foreign corporation regimes, the income may not constitute base company income.[510]

---

ferred to its Norwegian owner if "the foreign company has no intrinsic value or economic reality of its own. If a foreign company has no employees and if all or most of the decisions relating to it are made in Norway, the tax authorities are likely to assess its profits and tax them as if they had been made directly by the Norwegian owner." DELOITTE AND TOUCHE LLP, NORWAY, 13.06 Controlled Foreign Corporations, PART 6 CORPORATE INCOME TAXES, Chapter 13 Special Corporate Tax Situations.

[509]Due to the wide variety and differences in each country's exemption rules, a complete analysis of applicable exemptions will not be made here. Instead, they will only be addressed to the extent that several countries might adopt the same approach with substantially the same result.

[510]See e.g., IRC § 954(d). Of course the compensation paid to the state R programmers must be arm's length in accordance with IRC § 482.

In Japan, a CFC's income is not subject to taxation if the CFC: 1) has substance (*i.e.,* fixed facilities necessary for conducting its business in the CFC's country of residence; 2) itself administers, controls and manages its business; and 3) does not conduct its main business with its affiliated persons in the wholesale, banking, trust, securities, insurance, water transportation or air transportation business, or conducts its business in the CFC's country of residence in other businesses. When this legislation was enacted, the legislators did not anticipate electronic commerce. Accordingly, how this type of CFC is treated, particularly under the third test, is not clear.

Suppose that instead of selling software to customers in country S, CFC Corp. licenses the software to customers in exchange for a royalty. The initial issue, of course, is whether the transfer of the software should be characterized as a sale of goods or licensing of an intangible. Many countries would adopt the latter view since no physical product is changing hands.[511] Under this view, the income received from the transaction would be royalty income. If the royalty income is considered to be passive, some controlled foreign corporation regimes would permit country R to tax the income. If CFC Corp. merely purchases the software from R Corp. and then licenses the software to customers in country S, royalty income received would likely be treated as passive income that could be taxed by country R.

However, a different result might be reached if the software is created, or substantially modified (after receipt by R Corp., but prior to license) by CFC Corp. Now the royalties may constitute active business income that cannot be taxed by country R when earned.[512] This is a situation that tests the purpose of controlled foreign corporation legislation. It is not difficult for R Corp. to arrange its affairs so that CFC Corp. develops or substantially modifies the software it licenses. The ease with which this can be accomplished may cause some countries to rethink whether income from an active licensing business perhaps should constitute income that is taxed by the country of the parent corporation.

Suppose that instead of selling or licensing intangible goods, CFC Corp. operates a server that advertises and electronically sells tangible goods. The goods, produced by R Corp. in country R, are shipped from R

---

[511] *See supra* the discussion in section 4.2.1.5.2.1.

[512] *See e.g.*, Reg. § 1.954(2)(d).

Corp. directly to the customers, paying a fee to CFC Corp. commensurate with its function. This fact pattern does not pose any unusual problems under most controlled foreign corporation regimes. Where CFC Corp. is performing services on behalf of a related party for customers in country S, generally the income produced by CFC Corp. would be considered base company income.[513] It does not matter whether the services are rendered through a web page or by employees located in the tax haven.

Suppose instead of providing services for a related party in connection with a sale, CFC Corp. maintains an investment information database. It charges fees to country S customers for access to this database. Employees providing the information found on the database are located in country R. Services can constitute base company income. In this case, CFC Corp. is rendering services for R Corp. in the tax haven.[514] The first determination that must be made is whether the income received is for the right to access the information database (*i.e.*, for services rendered), or for the information contained on the database (*i.e.*, for a license). Assume the only income received by CFC Corp. from the customer is from access fees for services rendered. Because the payments received are for services rendered by CFC Corp. on its own behalf, it is unlikely that most controlled foreign corporation legislation would permit country R to tax them. Germany's controlled foreign corporation legislation is a case on point, stating that income derived from services rendered by a foreign corporation is excluded from the anti-deferral measures unless the services are provided by or for a German shareholder or affiliated person subject to tax in Germany.[515] Thus, where CFC Corp. provides services to customers other than German shareholders or other related persons, the income derived is not subject to German controlled foreign corporation legislation.

Some countries may not be happy with this result because, as in the licensing situation discussed above, R Corp. can easily arrange its affairs to isolate services income in a tax haven without making any physical com-

---

[513]*See e.g.*, IRC § 954(d).

[514]The United States considers services to be performed on behalf of a related person where: (1) the CFC is paid or reimbursed by a related person for performing the services; (2) the CFC performs services that a related person is obligated to perform; or (3) the CFC performs services in connection with the sale of property by a related person when the performance of the service is a condition of the sale. IRC § 954(e).

[515]ARNOLD, *supra* note 472, at 251.

mitment (*e.g.*, the presence of employees) to that jurisdiction. Similar possibilities of isolating services income outside of country R exist under more traditional methods of commerce, but are made more likely by the portability of electronic commerce.[516]

If R Corp, a Mexican resident company, sets up a subsidiary (CFC Corp.) in country TH and CFC Corp. operates a server in country TH which is accessed by customers in country S, the recently enacted Mexican controlled foreign corporation provisions will apply and all income earned by CFC Corp. becomes taxable in Mexico to the extent that country TH is considered a low tax jurisdiction in accordance with Article 17(xi) of the MITL. Otherwise, no tax will be payable in Mexico until income is distributed to R Corp. Mexican resident companies are required to include each year all taxable income derived from any company, trust or other entity located in a low tax jurisdiction in which they are shareholders, beneficial owners or have the right by any other means to participate in the profits of such entities.[517]

However, the controlled foreign corporation provisions have been substantially amended by Regulations issued by the Mexican Ministry of Finance and Public Credit (*"Secretaría de Hacienda y Crédito Público."*)[518] These Regulations exclude from the Mexican controlled foreign corporation regime all business profits derived by any low tax jurisdiction entity when its fixed assets, immovable property and inventories used for the business activities of such entity represent no less than 50% of its total assets, and any income from the rental of property, dividends, interest or royalties represent 20% or less of the total income of the entity in any taxable year.[519] Therefore, income derived by CFC Corp. for the activities previ-

---

[516]*See generally* Cigler, Burritt, and Stinnett, *Cyberspace: The Final Frontier for International Tax Concepts?*, 7 J. INT'L TAX 340, 350 (August 1996).

[517]Article 17(xi) allows such Mexican residents to reduce the includible income from such low-tax jurisdiction entities with any deductible items or carry forward losses incurred by such entities only if the books and records of such entities are made available to the Mexican tax authorities upon request. The MITL contains a list of the countries that are considered low-tax jurisdictions (Article 4 (viii) of the MITL Transitory Articles in effect since 1 January 1997).

[518]*Cuarta Resolución Miscelánea Fiscal para 1997* published in the Official Gazette of the Federation on 23 June 1997.

[519]Rule 3.6.16 of the *Cuarta Resolución Miscelánea Fiscal para 1997*. Rule 3.1.6 also excludes from the controlled foreign corporation regime all income derived by a low-tax

ously described will not be taxable in Mexico in accordance with the above-mentioned regulations, even if CFC Corp. is located in a low-tax jurisdiction.

This result will not be altered even if: (i) country S customers log on to the CFC Corp. server and order the merchandise from CFC Corp. which is produced and shipped from R Corp.'s home office in Mexico; (ii) CFC Corp. purchases the merchandise at an arms length price from R Corp. and resells it to customers, (iii) CFC Corp. is paid a commission for arranging sales from R Corp. to country S customers; or (iv) country S customers log on to the server and order merchandise (*e.g.*, software) or services (*e.g.*, access to a database) that is downloaded from the server.

4.2.4.3. *Treaty law*

Treaties following the OECD Model do not directly address domestic controlled foreign corporation provisions. Whether domestic controlled foreign corporation legislation violates treaty commitments has been raised by commentators.[520] However, the OECD Commentary seems to implicitly recognize that controlled foreign corporations do not raise treaty problems.[521] In any case, the rise of electronic commerce does not pose any additional treaty problems with respect to controlled foreign corporations than does more traditional forms of commerce.

4.3. VAT AND SALES TAXES

4.3.1. The general challenges of electronic commerce and telecommunications services to VAT

4.3.1.1. *Systems of indirect taxation*

In countries like Canada and the United States, consumption-based taxation is in the form of sales or turnover taxes. In the other OECD Mem-

---

jurisdiction entity when its stock is traded in a recognized stock exchange and the Mexican taxpayer does not have the ability to control or influence such entity.

[520] *See e.g.,* SANDLER, *supra* note 471, at 112-118.

[521] OECD Commentary, 1997, Art. 10, para. 37.

ber States, consumption taxation is in the form of VAT.[522] The VAT has seen its most complete development in the context of the EC; the development and harmonization of VAT rules are subject to its legal framework. This discussion, therefore, will focus on the regulation and experience of the EC, since it is extensive and deals with issues which may arise elsewhere.

4.3.1.2.   Direct and indirect electronic commerce and telecommunications services

Electronic commerce is defined in the EU Esprit Programme as "any form of business transaction in which the parties interact electronically rather than by physical exchanges or direct physical contact." It is, in essence, a business use made of the new information and communication technologies involving, as in any international commerce pattern, a seller established in one country (R Corp.) and a customer established in another one (S Customer).

The VAT discussion that follows focuses on the direct configuration of electronic commerce. (i.e., downloading digitized goods and services).

Electronic commerce involving the delivery of tangible goods (indirect electronic commerce) is not emphasized in the following VAT discussion because application of the VAT rules to the off-line delivery of such goods raises fewer VAT challenges. Consider the sale of digitized goods (direct electronic commerce). Tangible goods crossing international borders can always be subjected to tax, although inevitably there will be some avoidance with cross border shopping and postal delivery. However, the case of indirect commerce is still relevant for the VAT discussion where it highlights certain issues such as the characterization of the transaction (e.g., is software a good or a service or is a good intangible because it is downloaded or what is the characterization of composite supplies involving goods coupled with services?). Also the costs and administrative burdens of fiscal controls at the border are particularly onerous for a transaction which is partly electronic (the order being placed over the internet) or which competes with soft products (e.g., sale of the book in printed versus book in electronic form).

Electronic commerce may not involve the traditional intermediaries (retailers, warehouses, transporters, forwarders, bank agencies, insurance

---

[522]Outside the EC, VAT has not been the subject of bilateral or other treaties.

brokers, etc.). However, it involves new intermediaries — such as internet service providers. Basic telecommunications services are thus essential to electronic commerce. While telecommunication services may be considered one aspect of electronic commerce, they are also examined in the VAT discussion. Mainly in connection with their global and portable nature, the problems of applying traditional VAT rules and concepts to electronic services are highlighted by a consideration of telecommunications services. They even gave rise, in the EC VAT context, to the first application of specific rules, which may eventually inspire the VAT rules (of place of supply) for soft goods. The VAT discussion will therefore involve telecommunications services and indirect and direct electronic commerce, but the focus will be on direct electronic commerce.

The need to recognize, in the VAT system, the particular features of the supply of goods in digitized form and of electronic services can technically be satisfied in several ways:

- a flexible application of present VAT rules and concepts. Some relevant rulings of national VAT authorities and decisions of national VAT courts and of the European Court of Justice are discussed in section 4.3.4.4.
- special rules adapting the tax treatment of electronic commerce and telecommunications services within the existing general VAT framework. The adaptation of the tax regulations, to telecommunications services in particular, is discussed in section 4.3.3.
- tax reform which carves out telecommunications services and electronic commerce from the scope of the general VAT legislation, with the goal of applying alternative forms of special indirect taxation in lieu of, or as a supplement to, the application of existing VAT principles to electronic commerce. New ideas of alternative, special consumption taxes, in particular the bit tax, are discussed in section 5.3.

4.3.1.3. Official VAT Working Groups

Twenty-seven of the 29 OECD Member States apply a system of VAT taxation. The 15 Member States of the EC apply a common ("Community") VAT system. Both official international organizations (OECD and EC) are, therefore, taking an active interest in the issues posed by the application of a general VAT system to electronic commerce and telecommunications services.

In its 22 July 1996 Communication, proposing a definitive common VAT system, the European Commission recognized the distinctive features of electronic commerce and its inability to respond to these features under the current VAT system. It concludes that the current rules, a heritage from the past, are ill-suited to the new challenges of modern business practices, in particular the challenges of the new information and communication technologies:

> The present system is poorly suited to the development of the most buoyant segment of the European and world economy, *i.e.,* those international services which evade or increasingly might evade VAT on consumption within the Community. Current legislation is incapable of ensuring correct taxation in areas such as telecommunications, in which very rapid technological developments have occurred. Likewise, activities which were previously the exclusive domain of public services are increasingly being taken on by private firms: the derogations introduced for the private sector have thus become obsolete and give rise to competitive disadvantage which are increasingly damaging to both the public and private sectors.[523]

It is no longer correct for the Commission to conclude that current legislation within the EU is incapable of ensuring correct taxation in the telecommunication area, although it is true in countries which still tax telecommunications companies according to the origin principle. EU businesses have to account for VAT on telecommunications services purchased both within and from outside the EU. Non-EU suppliers have to VAT register and account for VAT on supplies to final consumers resident within the EU. (*see infra* section 4.3.3.3).

On 15 April 1997, the Commission released its Communication, *A European Initiative in Electronic Commerce,* in which it summarized its tax position as follows:

> To allow electronic commerce to develop, it is vital for tax systems to provide legal certainty (so that tax obligations are clear, transparent and predictable), and tax neutrality (so there is no extra burden on these new activities as compared to more traditional commerce). The potential speed and anonymity of electronic transactions may also create new possibilities for tax avoidance and evasion. These need to be addressed in order to safeguard the revenue interests of governments and to prevent market distortions. Indirect taxation,

---

[523]Commission of the European Communities, *A Common System of VAT. A program for the Single Market,* Com (96) 328 fin., 22 July 1996, para. 1.2 and 1.3.

and particularly VAT, is the area in which the Community is most harmonized. Electronic trade in goods and services clearly falls within the scope of
VAT, in the same way as more traditional forms of trade do. However, thorough analysis is needed to evaluate the possible impact of electronic commerce on present VAT legislation (on issues such as definition, control and
enforceability) and to judge if, and to what extent, present legislation needs
to be adapted, while ensuring tax neutrality.[524]

The Commission concludes the action-oriented discussion of its European
Initiative by proposing key actions which should be completed by the year
2000, with a mid-term review. However, when it comes to the taxation of
electronic commerce, the action proposals are weak and inarticulate. There
is a need for further initiatives covering direct and indirect taxation. International consensus should be reached, in the appropriate multilateral and
bilateral forums, concerning an adequate global regulatory framework for
the appropriate taxation of electronic commerce. The proposals are not yet
included in the current Information Society Action Plan of the Commission. Likewise, in its Monti Report on Taxation in the European Union, of
22 October 1996, the Commission did nothing more than put issues relating to the "taxation of international services and the impact of the new
technologies" on the agenda of the Taxation Policy Group.[525] In its 1998
Communication *E-Commerce and Indirect Taxation,* the European Commission offers guidelines for EU taxation of electronic commerce which
form the basis of the EU's input in the OECD Ministerial Conference *A
Borderless World: Realizing the Potential of Electronic Commerce* which will
take place on 6-8 October 1998.

The work of the OECD's Committee on Fiscal Affairs was described by
Mr. J. Owens, Head of Fiscal Affairs, in his presentation to the 5 April 1997
Harvard Symposium on Multi-Jurisdictional Taxation of Electronic Com-
merce.[526] In June 1996, the Committee on Fiscal Affairs considered a note,

---

[524]Commission of the European Communities, *A European Initiative in Electronic
Commerce,* Com (97) 157 of 15 April 1997, para. 56, 57, 59 and Conclusion II.

[525]Commission of the European Communities, *Taxation in the European Union —
Report on the development of tax systems,* Com (96) 546 final of 22 October 1996, para.
6.6.

[526]Owens, *The Tax Man Cometh to Cyberspace,* TAX NOTES INT'L 1833 (2 June
1997).

Tax Policy and Administrative Implications of the Communication Revolution, and decided that its subsidiary bodies would examine the impact in their respective areas of competence. Dealing in particular with the challenge to consumption tax, Mr. Owens reports that:

> [T]he sub-group of the Special Session on Consumption Taxes is examining whether, as in the case of the Model Convention for the definition of 'permanent establishment,' the concept of 'fixed establishment' for VAT purposes is or is not sufficiently comprehensive to deal with electronic commerce since services can be supplied without the service provider setting up [a] traditional 'establishment' (from which) customers may receive the services. The sub-group is focusing on the following main issues: the distinction between goods and services provided over the internet since goods are losing their physical identity; the distinction of different types of services; the changes to the place of supply and place of establishment rules for telecommunication services; more uniformity and updating of technical terminology in the definition of telecommunication services; extension of reverse charge/self-assessment mechanisms when appropriate; audit trail difficulties and other control issues (in close contact with the sub-group of Working Party No. 8) and developing increased international mutual assistance.

The flaws of existing VAT legislation, in terms of facing the challenges of the new technologies, are thus identified by the responsible working groups of the EC and OECD. They recognize the immediate need to deal with the specific problems of telecommunications as they relate to VAT and the more general need to update the current VAT regulatory and administrative framework so as to make it effective in a globally networked economy.

4.3.2. Hypothetical case

The following case illustrates the complexities of Community VAT when its rules, concerning categorization and place of service, are applied to telecommunications, and other intangible performances, supplied to customers (private and business) in the various countries of the four corners of the world (within and without the Community and possibly out of some tax haven location) using different new technologies (*e.g.,* satellite, cable, internet).

Suppose a company is set up, in the British Virgin Islands (BVI), to start a new television channel showing pictures of tropical islands, around the clock and around the world, with a background of soft music. BVI has no production team, no marketing team and no foreign sales offices. BVI concludes a contract with another company, based in the Cayman Islands (CI) and operating an advanced system of satellite broadcasting that can film tropical islands from space. Transponder capacity on another satellite is leased from another satellite operator.[527] BVI sells its worldwide rights to cable companies based in New Jersey and Hong Kong. The cable companies offer the channel to hotels, hospitals, dentists and private homes on a pay-per-view or subscription fee basis. The cable companies are also licensed by BVI to operate a virtual travel advisory office under the name Tropical Islands Channel Travel Advisory. This service is advertised on the channel and sold to users as an on-line service over the internet.

VAT issues arise with respect to the categorization of the different services involved: Basic telecommunications services? Content services? Lease? Entertainment? Issues also arise regarding their taxable place of supply:

1. the services of satellite operator CI
2. the lease of transponder capacity from the other satellite operator
3. the license of channel broadcasting rights by BVI to the cable companies
4. the distribution of a commercial television program to hotels, homes, dentists and other customers accessing the channel by the payment of subscription fees or pay-per-view charges
5. the subscription fees or use charges for on-line travel advisory services
6. the provision of access to the internet and on-line service to hotels, homes, etc. in exchange for the payment of a subscription fee to the access provider.[528]

---

[527]A transponder is a device on a telecommunications satellite receiving a weak signal from the transmitting satellite station and sending back a strong signal to the receiving satellite station. For a discussion of the issue of VAT classification of transponder services, *see infra* section 4.3.3.5).

[528]Other examples dealing more specifically with direct electronic commerce are found *infra* in section 4.3.4.

4.3.3. Telecommunications services[529]

4.3.3.1. Need of specific regulation

The need for specific VAT regulation of basic telecommunications services arises from a number of factors:

- the global growth and innovative technological developments of the telecommunications industry, making the commercial telecommunications business portable, fluid and borderless as they do not necessitate extensive infrastructure in the individual Member States;
- the liberalization and commercial deregulation of the national telecommunications markets and the dismantling of the national monopolies of the public sector permitting new operators, especially US telecommunications companies, to penetrate EC markets;
- the active use made of the telecommunications infrastructure to provide a broad range of intangible content services, raising questions about the categorization of the broad range of telecommunications services;
- the highly competitive nature of basic telecommunications services, making the VAT cost to private users, banks and insurance companies a critical factor;
- the privatization of postal and telecommunications operators (PTO's), raising questions about the Community law basis for the application of the VAT exemption to the settlement payments between recognised private sector operators in Member States.

4.3.3.2. Public and private telecommunications operators

In its 1996 Program for a definitive common system of VAT, the European Commission concluded that the need for a re-examination of the Community VAT approach taken in the Sixth Directive (1977) is necessary,

---

[529]See Ogley A., *VAT and Telecommunication Services in the European Union*, TAX NOTES INT'L 1155 (7 April 1997); *VAT implications of business on the Internet*, Andersen Worldwide SC/The European-American Tax Institute, Seminar, Brussels 26 March 1997.

particularly in the area of derogations for public postal and broadcasting services. The Commission referred to the fact that activities, which were previously the exclusive domain of the public sector, are being taken on by private firms and that the telecommunications market will be deregulated by 1998. Existing VAT derogations have thus become obsolete and give rise to distortions of competition.

In Article 4(5) of the Sixth Directive and in Annex D, governmental authorities and other public bodies are considered taxable persons in relation to telecommunication activities. However, there are public interest exemptions, in Article 13A(a) and (g), for the services of the public postal office, other than telecommunications services, and for the activities of public radio and television bodies, other than those of a commercial nature. The transitional provisions of Article 28(3)(b) and Annex F(5) allow Member States to continue to exempt the reception of broadcasting services and public postal services under existing conditions. However, the derogation in Annex F(5), for telecommunications services supplied by public postal offices, is no longer applied by Member States, resulting in the application of VAT to all telecommunications services, whether provided by public or private operators.

At the international level, it was agreed at the 1988 Convention of Melbourne (Final Act of the World Administrative Telegraph and Telephone Conference) to exempt financial settlements, dealing with revenues from telecommunications services, between public national operators of telecommunications networks (PTO's). In the framework of the deregulation of the telecommunications market, and the admission of private telecommunications companies to the market, several Members give a liberal interpretation to their obligation under the Melbourne Convention. These Members do not to apply VAT to settlements between large telecommunications companies even if they are not public. Other Members conclude that VAT should be applied to settlements effected by private companies under the international clearance system.[530]

---

[530]This restrictive interpretation is based on the view that Article 30 of the Sixth Directive only authorizes derogations granted by the Council. The legal issue would have been resolved by the 3 February 1997 proposal for a Council Directive regarding the application of VAT to telecommunications services. The Commission proposed to delete the provision of Annex F(5) in the Sixth Directive and to add to the list of the other exemptions of Article 13 B: "the supply, between communications network oper-

4.3.3.3. Place of supply

The place of supply is the principal VAT issue concerning telecommunications services. The rules evolved from the original version under the 1997 Sixth Directive (hereinafter (i)) to that of the 1997 derogation (hereinafter (ii)), with the prospect of moving to definitive rules by 1999 according to the 1997 Commission proposal of directive amendment (hereinafter (iii)). The evolution highlights the problems of jurisdiction to tax telecommunications services. Those problems primarily involve dealing with VAT avoidance, but they also involve dealing with double taxation. The experience may also offer ideas for dealing with the jurisdictional issues of electronic commerce.

(i) Under the 1997 Sixth Directive, telecommunications services are subject to Article 9(1). They are thus taxable at the place where the supplier (*i.e.*, the telecommunications company) has established its business or has a fixed establishment supplying services. The choice of this basic rule was generally justified by its simplicity. It was intended to avoid the problems of interpretation that were likely to arise if the test had been the place of performance, utilization and exploitation. It follows that operators of telecommunications services, which have established their business in a Member State, must apply the VAT of that Member State, irrespective of the location and VAT status of their customers. It also follows that non-EC-based operators are not liable for Community VAT.

This solution leaves private consumers and exempt or mixed taxable persons in the Community better off using the services of non-EC based operators. This competitive disadvantage may lead EC-based companies to operate from an establishment in a non-EC country, where they supply the telecommunications service free of VAT under Article 9(1). This is sometimes referred to as the "American route," as many of the telecommunications companies taking advantage of this loophole are based in the United States. Member States view this situation as unsatisfactory. It affects the competitiveness of EC-based telecommunications companies. It encourages them to set up businesses outside the Community. It also leads a grow-

---

ators, of telecommunications services relating to the routing and termination of telephone calls." It would thereby apply on a Community level the exemption now laid down in the Melbourne Convention. As the Commission proposal was not approved, the issue of the lack of a legal basis for the VAT exemption still exists.

ing number of European consumers (private customers but also banks and insurance companies which cannot fully recover their input VAT) to procure their telecommunications services outside the EC. The problem was exacerbated by the development of call-back cards. These cards allow non-EC telecommunications operators, via a toll free call center, based in a third country, to short circuit the local telecommunication services providers. The overseas operator sells a phone card, to an EC customer, which can be used to make calls through the overseas operator. Alternatively, the telecommunications service of the overseas operator is charged to the customer's credit card or is charged by separate invoice. No VAT is charged because the supply is deemed to take place where the supplier is located, *i.e.,* overseas. EC-based consumers may thus circumvent Community VAT by subscribing with US (*e.g.,* America Online or CompuServe) or other non-EC providers at international tariffs. This may save as much as 25%, depending on the Member State.

(ii) In order to remedy this arbitrage opportunity and prevent revenue loss, Member States were authorized, by the EC Council, to derogate from the rule of Article 9(1) of the Sixth Directive. The derogation is legally based on Article 27(1) of the Sixth Directive. This Article allows the Council to authorize any Member State to introduce special measures, derogating from the Directive, in order to simplify procedures or to prevent certain types of tax evasion or avoidance. The preamble to the 15 Council decisions, of 17 March 1997,[531] concluded that these conditions were met:

> Whereas the measure is necessary to counter the tax avoidance effects that have led a growing number of Community taxable and non-taxable persons to purchase telecommunication services outside the Community in order to avoid payment of VAT; whereas the measure is furthermore necessary to discourage suppliers of telecommunication services established in a Member State from establishing themselves outside the Community; whereas the measure is also necessary to simplify the procedure for charging the tax insofar as it provides the same tax obligations for customers of telecommunications services regardless of whether these services are performed by suppliers established inside or outside the Community.

---

[531] Council decisions of 17 March 1997 authorizing (each of the Member States) to apply a measure derogating from Article 9 of the Sixth Directive 77/388/EEC on the harmonization of the laws of the Member States relating to turnover taxes (97/200/EC) O.J. 28 March 1997 NO L 86/5.

The Council decisions authorize each of the 15 Member States to include telecommunications services within the scope of Article 9(2)(e). Their place of supply thus becomes the customer's business establishment or the fixed establishment where the telecommunications services are supplied. Under this derogation regime, EU-based business customers must apply a reverse-charge VAT to the services, irrespective of whether they receive them from a provider based in another Member State or outside the Community.

The 1997 derogation also provides for the application of Article 9(3)(b) to the telecommunications services of overseas providers. According to this provision, Member States may, with regard to the supply of services referred to in Article 9(2)(e), deem the country where the services are effectively used and enjoyed as the place of supply. This provision can be applied to avoid situations of tax avoidance or competitive disadvantage. It means that telecommunications services, which were not previously taxable (because the customer was a private consumer in the Community — no taxation under Article 9(2)(e) — and the supplier was an overseas operator — no taxation under Article 9(1)), become taxable in the Member States where they are used and enjoyed. The Council decision, however, does not provide mechanisms for VAT accounting and collection. Applying, therefore, standard VAT procedural rules, the overseas telecommunications companies are required to register as traders in the consumers' Member State. This means that a US telecommunications operator selling international phone cards, dial services, etc., to private consumers in all 15 Member States, must register in all 15 Member States, pay 15 different VAT rates and adhere to 15 different sets of VAT rules. Under this system, the "American route" only works if operated illegally (*i.e.*, if the US telecommunications company fails to VAT reister in the EU).

The derogation had to be implemented by 1 July 1997 but its introduction was staggered.[532] The derogation applies until 31 December 1999

---

[532]The United Kingdom IFA Branch concludes that if there is a lesson to be learned from the derogation which was implemented by the 15 Member States on different dates. Such a staggered procedure and without harmonization of the detail has lead to anomalies and practical problems in implementation. If a similar procedure is to be followed for electronic commerce, then international solutions are potentially better than those adopted in isolation by individual countries. United Kingdom IFA Branch, *Comments on Electronic Commerce Report* (8 April 1998) (on file with the authors).

or, if a Directive altering the place of taxation of telecommunication services enters into force at an earlier date, until that date. The transitional feature is designed to allow the Council to adopt a general and definitive Community solution based on a Commission proposal for a directive.

(iii) The 17 March 1997 Council decisions were more of a reflection of the views and preferences of the Member States than those of the Commission. According to the Commission proposal, Member States would be authorized, in a transitional period, not to apply Article 9(1) to basic telecommunications services, but to consider them to fall within the scope of Article 9(2)(e), *i.e.*, to be content services supplied in the country of the establishment of the customer, if it is an EC-based business. If the customer is a private person, telecommunications services are taxable if they are used and enjoyed in the Community. Their overseas supplier would be required to register as a trader in each of the Member States in which the supplier's services are used. However, a problem arises where the non-EU supplier has no establishment as some Member States do not accept the concept of fiscal agency constituting an establishment. For example, a US supplier with human resources in the United Kingdom would become an EU supplier thus needing only one registration.

By 1 January 1999, at the latest, new provisions of Article 9 should be enacted by all Member States, forming their definitive VAT system. To this effect, the Commission, on 3 February 1997, submitted a proposal for a Directive amending the Sixth Directive.[533] It provides a legal basis for the VAT exemption for services between (private) telecommunications network operators, defines basic telecommunications services and deals with the problems of competitive disadvantage and loss of tax revenue. These changes would be effected through a new article, 9(2)(f), dealing with the place of the taxable supply of telecommunications services. Under 9(2)(f), it would be the place where the customer has established a business, a fixed establishment where the services are supplied, or, in the absence thereof, a permanent address or usual residence. A telecommunications services provider established outside the EC, identified for VAT purposes on account of having supplied telecommunications services, will be deemed to

---

[533] Proposal for a Council Directive amending Directive 77/388/EEC as regards the value added tax arrangements applicable to telecommunications services (97/C 78/05), submitted by the Commission on 3 February 1997.

be established in the Member State where customers are located. Like the EC-based provider, it would only be required to register as a trader in one Member State, irrespective of the number of Member States in which services are sold.[534]

4.3.3.4. Definition of telecommunications services

The 1977 text of the Sixth Directive contains no definition of telecommunications services. The Council decisions of 17 March 1997, authorizing Member States to derogate from Article 9, regarding telecommunications services, provide for the same definition as the one proposed in the 3 February 1997 Commission proposal to amend the Sixth Directive with respect to the place of supply rule. It refers to "the transmission, emission or reception of signals, writing, images and sounds or information of any nature by wire, radio, optical or electromagnetic systems, including the transfer or assignment of the right to use capacity for such transmission, emission or reception." This definition is similar to that of the Melbourne Convention.

Being essentially the provision of electronic means of transmission, "telecommunications services" include not only the provision of cable or satellite networks, but also additional services, such as access to the internet and data networks. The reference to the provision of access services was found in the original text of the definition and is still found in the Explanatory Memorandum. It was deleted in the final text, but the deletion was probably justified because an express reference in the text was unnecessary. Also, the reference, in the initial draft, to the broadcasting of television programs through cable or satellite was deleted. If the distribution of television programs through satellite or cable is thus excluded from the definition, the 1997 changes to the place of supply rules, as regards telecommunications services, do not apply to them. Telecommunications services probably also include "enhanced services," such as email or voice mail, because they have as their essential feature that of connecting parties, even as they add to the

---

[534]Under Article 9(3)(a), EU VAT does not apply to supplies made outside the EU. The article has not been commonly adopted under the telecommunications derogation. The United Kingdom is a significant exception which is why many US telecommunications companies have chosen to VAT register there. United Kingdom IFA Branch, *Comments on Electronic Commerce Report* (8 April 1998) (on file with the authors).

value of the transmission by additional linkage and extra facilities, such as storage of messages. Do they include teleconferencing and electronic courier services as well? An electronic newspaper is normally not a basic telecommunications service, but an information-content providing service and is excluded even if it is transmitted through satellite or cable. Does it become a transmission service if an electronic newspaper is downloaded onto the computer of a third party vendor who resells it to customers who actually read it?

Another definitional issue arises from the characterization of satellite transponder services. In some Member States (*e.g.,* France, Belgium) transponder services are considered a rental of a tangible, movable good (transmission equipment) falling within the scope of Article 9(2). In other Member States (*e.g.,* the United Kingdom) they are considered to be more than a simple lease arrangement; being a means of transmission, but not exactly a telecommunications service, the right to use transmission capacity is not itself a transmission activity. Where no clear categorization can be applied, a service falls within the scope of the general rule of Article 9(1). It appears, however, that transponder services should qualify as telecommunications services. This interpretation results from the definition found in the 1997 Council decisions expressly treating the right to use capacity for transmission as a telecommunications service.

With respect to the interpretation of other services, constituting borderline cases in the range of telecommunications services, the VAT Advisory Committee should endeavor to arrive at a consensus among Member States. The issue of the categorization of basic telecommunications services as distinct from other services, intangible content services in particular, was mainly relevant for purposes of determining their taxable place of supply. It lost some, but not all relevance in this respect as a result of the new place of supply rule in the 1997 derogation.

4.3.3.5.   *The Community VAT experience with telecommunications services*

The rules concerning place of supply of telecommunications services were seemingly simple in the pre-1997 system developed by the Sixth Directive. Being considered ordinary services, falling within the scope of the general rule of Article 9(1), they were subject to only one criterion — the place of the operator's establishment. However, the application of this rule to basic telecommunications services raised problems of definition and de-limitation.

Definitional problems may create situations of double taxation, non-taxation and competitive disadvantage. They are illustrated by the case of transponder services. In the United Kingdom, they are deemed to fall within the scope of the general provision of Article 9(1) and to take place in the United Kingdom if the supplier is established there. In France, follow-ing Article 9(2)(e), they take place where the business customer is estab-lished. The UK based supplier is at a competitive disadvantage vis-à-vis a French based supplier because the customers outside the Community will not be liable for French VAT. Non-EC-based business customers may ad-mittedly recover the UK VAT, but the experience with refund claims, under the Thirteenth Directive, is often frustrating.

Furthermore, Article 9 does not define the concepts of a company's primary place of business or its fixed establishment or the relationship be-tween the two criteria for purposes of applying the Article (*see infra* section 4.3.4.4.1). With the proliferation of global telecommunications operations, the risk of the double or multiple taxation of these services is very real. Ar-ticle 9(3)(a) responds to the risk by providing the option of foregoing EC VAT under Article 9. The measure, however, is not commonly exercised in the case of telecommunications services.

The transitional system was designed to close the "American route" loophole, in the pre-1997 place of supply rules, and to eliminate the VAT handicaps of EC-based operators vis-à-vis their overseas competitors. However, it raises practical enforcement problems. Effective tax collection and controls are less of a problem where the operator and customer are es-tablished in different Member States. If a telecommunications company is established outside the EC and the recipient of its services is a business es-tablished in a Member State, the tax is due and collected at the level of the latter business under the reverse charge system. The problem of compliance and enforcement is much greater if an overseas operator supplies them to a private customer established in a Member State or a private customer who uses the services within a Member State. They are taxable under the respec-tive tests described in the 1997 derogation and in the drafted permanent so-lution. How effective is it to place the tax burden on final consumers? If the operator does not withhold tax, there are no effective mechanisms for en-suring compliance. The OECD, the Council of Europe Multilateral Con-vention on Mutual Administrative Assistance on Tax Matters and the corresponding articles in tax treaties based on the OECD Model Tax Convention on Income and Capital Article 26 do not provide solutions to the problem of compliance.

The tax is payable by the overseas operator, who must register as a trader in each of the Member States where the services are used. How practical is this rule and collection mechanism? If a US tourist visits all Member States and calls home every day during his 15-day trip, with a GSM (Global System for Mobile Communications), the calls result in the application of VAT at 15 different rates and under 15 different sets of rules. Moreover, the overseas operator is obliged to register in each Member State, provide a breakdown of the calls in his US administration and settlements of client accounts. This collection system problem would be less acute if Member States would agree to interpret the undefined expression "effective use and enjoyment of telecommunications services" as a reference to the use and enjoyment by residents of Member States. This restrictive interpretation would be easier to administer and in accordance with the primary concern of dealing with the loophole of the "American route."

The overseas operator can simplify the administrative burden of registering in every Member State by setting up a fixed establishment, in a Member State, which supplies services throughout the Community. In the Commission proposals for a definitive system, EC- and non-EC-based operators would only be required to register once and pay one VAT rate. Under that system, overseas operators would have the attractive alternative of registering in the EC country with the lowest rate. If, by that time, VAT rates are approximated in accordance with the Commission proposal for a definitive VAT system, overseas telecommunications operators would not register according to the lowest VAT rate (now ranging from 15 to 25%). Registration choices, however, might reflect an assessment of the impact of the different VAT rules and regulations applied by the Member States.

The derogation regime and the drafted permanent solution may not adequately address the concern of revenue loss until EC VAT rates are standardized. Under the interim regime, revenue income from telecommunications services is re-allocated to the states in which third country operators set up fixed establishments and to the states in which EC operators have establishments. Under the Commission's draft proposal a fixed establishment will not be required. While the interim decisions provide pragmatic solutions for the short term, the revenue consequences for individual member countries must, for the long term, be clarified with political solutions requiring standardization.

4.3.4. Electronic Commerce

4.3.4.1. *Range of internet activities and VAT distinctions*

Electronic commerce (which for the purpose of this section does not include basic telecommunications services) involves the use of information and communication technologies in carrying out the wide range of exchanges of goods and services. To the extent electronic channels are used, electronic commerce includes the production and distribution of tangible, movable goods and material services. Retail stores and mail order firms, selling and delivering physical goods and tangible services, may thus use the new medium for marketing and advertising. Customers may use it in the selection, ordering and payment process (*e.g.,* electronic cash). Those activities are sometimes described as "Wehkamp-activities" and "indirect electronic commerce."[535] They give rise to VAT liability in accordance with the general rules and procedures for the supply of (tangible) goods and services and for internet services used to effect the sale of goods and services.

Other goods and services, in digitized form, can be acquired directly from the internet. They are sometimes referred to as "City-activities" and more often as "direct electronic commerce." Music, videos, newspapers, software, betting, games, advice, etc. can be sold in digitized form. The consumer simply downloads the good or service onto his PC. Under VAT rules such supply is typically not considered a (physical) good, but a service. VAT is applied in accordance with the rules and procedures concerning the particular service in question.

The VAT distinction among internet activities is not purely academic. There are several differences between the treatment of goods and services throughout the VAT system. Differences may involve a taxable event (*e.g.,* import from non-EC supplier applies to goods — not to services), the place of taxable supply (*e.g.,* intra-community acquisition deals with goods — not with services), exemptions (*e.g.,* distance selling rule applies to goods — not to services), formalities (*e.g.,* reverse charge procedure applies

---

[535]EC Commission, Communication *A European Initiative in Electronic Commerce,* Com (97) 157: "Indirect electronic commerce – the electronic ordering of tangible goods, which must be physically delivered using traditional channels such as postal services or commercial couriers; and direct electronic commerce — the online ordering, payment and delivery of intangible goods and services such as computer software, entertainment content or information services on a global scale."

to services — not to goods) and applicable rates (*e.g.*, zero-rate may apply to books in printed form — not in digitized form).

It is important, for purposes of determining the applicable rate, exemption, place of supply, mechanism of VAT collection, etc., to distinguish between services according to their type. For different services there are different VAT rules, particularly with respect to the place of supply. Article 9(2)(c) applies to cultural, scientific, entertainment and similar services. Article 9(2)(e) applies to consulting and other intellectual performances, including data processing and the supply of information, banking, financial and insurance transactions. Article 9(1) applies to other services which do not fall in any special category. Article 9(3) applies to services such as telecommunications, supplied to private users, by overseas operators.

In the absence of a specific global framework for categorizing electronic transactions, the application of VAT rules, with respect to the place of supply, requires categorizing transactions carried out through electronic commerce. However, there are problems with such classifications. Transactions are less identifiable and their distinctions more easily blurred when the internet is involved. The same electronic channels of production or distribution also blur the VAT distinctions regarding the place services are supplied. The concepts of fixed establishment, use and enjoyment, location of property, the place where services are performed and distance covered by transport were developed for tangible goods and services in a different technological era.

The application of the current EC VAT place of supply rules to telecommunications services and direct electronic commerce thus involves several challenges: categorization of services or of combinations of different services being supplied; the determination and apportionment of composite service charges; and the identification and interpretation of the application of the criterion for determining taxable place of supply.

4.3.4.2. Characterization of a service

4.3.4.2.1. Supply of goods or of services?

There is no contextual, conceptual or practical merit in the approach of some authors who conclude that all internet transactions and telecommunications services should be treated as a supply of goods. These commentators justify their interpretation on the inclusion of "electricity and the like" in the definition of "goods" in the Sixth Directive.[536]

The supply of a service such as a legal opinion or advertisement advice is generally taxed as a service, irrespective of the form in which it is supplied (*i.e.,* over the internet or traditional methods). In some cases, the distinctions between goods and services are not clear and classifications by Member States are not uniform. This is the case with computer software. For VAT purposes it is often categorized as a physical good if it is supplied off-the-shelf (mass-marketed, shrink-wrapped). If it is developed for consumer needs, it is often categorized as a service. Does mass-marketed software still constitute a good where it is downloaded from the internet? The French Tax Administration ruled that software, downloaded onto a purchaser's computer, constitutes a service, irrespective of its customized development. Bourtourault points out the practical problems of applying the French VAT rule:

> When the supplier is established outside the EU, French VAT should apply to all deliveries. This raises an important practical problem, as it may be difficult for a software supplier established outside the EU to identify transactions with non-VATable purchasers located in France to charge, collect and repay VAT to the French Tax Administration, and also it is quite doubtful that non-VATable purchasers will take the initiative to pay VAT.[537]

In the United Kingdom, software which is downloaded from the internet is not treated as imported for customs and VAT purposes. The Finance Bill contains provisions imposing a VAT charge on telecommunications services provided by overseas companies with no fixed establishment in the United Kingdom.[538]

---

[536]Houtzager & Tinholt, *E-Commerce and VAT,* in Caught in the Web: the Tax and Legal Implications of Electronic Commerce 99, Fed-Fiscale actualiteiten 32 .

[537] Bourtourault, *International Tax Issues in Cyberspace: Taxation of Cross-border Electronic Commerce,* (France) Intertax, 139 (April 1997). The French Tax Administration also ruled that (1) the installation of software on a computer in France must be characterized as an intangible service subject to specific VAT rules when this installation is done through telecommunication systems; and (2) maintenance is also an intangible service when not physically performed in France (*e.g.,* assistance by telephone or over the internet).

[538]Kay, *International Tax Issues in Cyberspace,* l.c. (UK), Intertax, 142 (April 1997).

Under Switzerland's (EC inspired) VAT rules, mass-marketed software is treated differently by different administrative bodies depending on the form of delivery. If it is downloaded from the internet, it is treated as a service by the Federal Tax Administration. If it is imported in CD-rom or disk form, it is treated as a good by the Federal Custom Administration.[539] The EC VAT Committee agreed to a specific guideline setting out its views on the distinction between software qualifying as good and software qualifying as service.

The categorization issue raises the problem of consistency in application among countries and also in nature of delivery. Why should the form of the delivery be determinative in the case of software and newspapers, but not for legal services or advertisement advice? Arguably, the classification of a good changes if its fundamental nature changes, not because of a change in its mode of storage and transmission. The European Court of Justice seems to hold the view that characterization of a good or service should not depend on the mode of distribution. In the *Datacenter* case, it found that the mode of distribution was irrelevant for purposes of defining tax exempt services.[540] However, the progressive blurring of the nature of a good is also confusing for purposes of VAT categorization: from record to audiotape, to CD combining sound, image and text, to the interactive CD permitting the input of the consumer.[541]

Products purchased in digitized form are treated differently than products purchased in traditional forms. If a Belgian consumer downloads an electronic newspaper or magazine, the transaction is treated as the supply of a service rather than a good (Article 5 of the Sixth Directive of goods as tangible property). The applicable VAT rule, concerning place of supply, is probably found in Article 9(2)(e). If the service is supplied electronically or by mail order firm, the distance selling exemption does not apply. In some Member States the applicable rate is also different for electronic transactions (*e.g.*, zero for books — not in electronic form). If the supply is made via the internet, to a business customer established in a Member State, the Member State is responsible for collection in accordance with the

---

[539]Switzerland IFA Branch, *Comments on Electronic Commerce Report* (20 April 1998) (on file with the authors).

[540]E.C.J., Case C-2/95 of 5 June 1997, *Sparekassernes Datacenter (SDC) v. Skatteministeriet.*

[541]Stevens, *internet en belastingen*, WEEKBLAD VOOR FISCAAL RECHT, 1996/6222 1723 (21 November 1996).

reverse charge procedure. Other VAT problems arise with the uncertainties of categorization. Is VAT on imported mass-marketed software packages collected at the border or is it collected when they are downloaded onto the customer's home computer? If such software is supplied by a business established in one Member State to a private customer in another Member State, under distance sales conditions, the supplier will be required to register as a trader and pay VAT in the other state. The supplier does not register and pay VAT in that other state if the (customized) software qualifies as a service. A US supplier licensing such software to private EC consumers via the internet does not apply VAT to that service under Article 9(1).

Another tax issue (rate, place of supply, collection mechanism) is the lack of tax neutrality when a good or service is treated differently depending on the channel of distribution (electronic or non-electronic). If a Belgian consumer goes to a retail store, or a mail order firm in another country, and purchases a book, CD, or off-the-shelf computer software, the transaction is treated as the sale of a good. If the store, or mail order firm, is established in another Member State, VAT is due in that other state (or in Belgium if the value of the Belgian sales of that mail order firm exceeds the threshold of 1.5 million BF).[542] If the book or CD is purchased from a US bookstore, or mail order firm, and imported into Belgium, VAT and the applicable customs duty are due in Belgium (even if their effective collection will often depend on the mail order firm reporting the content (CD) and full value of the package and on examination (opening the package) by the Belgian Customs Office or by the Belgian Post Office).

Should the sale of the same good or service receive different treatment depending upon the channel of distribution? Should there be a difference in tax treatment between the sale of a book or newspaper (*i.e.*, the supply of a physical object) in a retail outlet and one delivered onto the consumer's computer screen (the supply of a service)? Considering the principle of tax neutrality (the same product is involved whether distribution takes place via traditional channels or via electronic commerce) and the concern that trade distortions may occur where switching between the two distribution forms — a technicality — is easy, it would be appropriate to reduce the risk of inconsistent treatment. This can be done by taxing electronic and non-electronic transactions at the same VAT rate or by questioning the logic of different categorizations of certain products/services when the fundamental nature of the content is the same. However, inconsistent treatment in-

---

[542]*See supra* section 2.2.4.1 for rules concerning distance sales.

volves VAT rules as well as rates. These rules include administration and accountability procedures and place of supply rules, especially goods or services supplied from non-EC countries.

VAT policy regarding the characterization of electronic transactions is discussed in section 5.2.2.8. The European Commission, in its 1998 Communication, *E-Commerce and Indirect Taxation*, proposes the following uniform guideline: "A supply that results in a product being placed at the disposal of the recipient in digital form via an electronic network is to be treated for VAT purposes as a supply of services (. . .) Products that, in their tangible form, are treated for VAT purposes as goods are treated as services when they are delivered by electronic means."

4.3.4.2.2. Categorization of composite supplies (goods and services)

Another classification or allocation problem arises with respect to composite supplies — the simultaneous supply of goods and services. Should bundled fees be apportioned or should they be categorized by reference to the predominant feature? For example, what if a taxpayer purchases vegetables via the web site of a grocery store? Should the purchase be treated as the sale of goods (vegetables) or should it be broken down into a charge for goods with a separate charge for services (the delivery)? Vegetables may be taxed at a reduced rate, whereas the delivery of services is taxed at the standard rate.

In an international context, the place of taxable supply rules are likely to vary with the categorization of a transaction. For different types of supplies different rates or exemptions might be applicable. The legal consequence is that each type of supply should be treated separately. This is problematic, however, with composite supplies — when the components are normally not sold separately. If there is a prominent feature (*e.g.*, a good), the consideration shall not be apportioned. If, on the other hand, there are distinguishable elements, the consideration shall be apportioned.[543] Goods or services — or any combination thereof — must, there-

---

[543]Swedish IFA Branch Comments, *Comments on Electronic Commerce Report* (1998) (on file with the authors), referring to Westberg, Björn, *Mervärdesskatt* (1997), at 86-87, at 120-121, at 130-131, at 269 and 299.

fore, be characterized to determine whether the principal supply method or the apportionment method should be applied. Although the Sixth Directive does not deal with the matter explicitly, Article 17(5), in conjunction with Article 19, deals with the apportionment of input tax for taxable and non-taxable supplies.

The principal supply method was applied by the European Court of Justice in *Faaborg-Gelting Linien A/S.*[544] In that case, German authorities took the view that German VAT applied to meals provided on board a ferry in German territorial waters. The Danish authorities, on the other hand, considered them a composite supply with the predominant feature being service. They believed the services were subject to Danish VAT because the suppliers were Danish:

> In order to determine whether such transactions constitute supplies of goods or supplies of services, regard must be had to all the circumstances in which the transaction in question takes place in order to identify its characteristic features. (. . .) Restaurant services are characterized by a cluster of features and acts, of which the provision of food is only one component and in which services largely predominate. They must therefore be regarded as supplies of services within the meaning of Article 9(1) of the Sixth Directive. The situation is different, however, where the transaction relates to "take away" food, and is not coupled with services designed to enhance consumption on the spot in an appropriate setting.

Accordingly, the European Court held that the services were subject to Danish VAT.

The Swiss IFA Branch reported a recent decision by the Swiss Supreme Court which is relevant to an analysis of EC VAT because the Swiss VAT system is derived from the EC VAT system.[545] The case involved a Swiss company supplying pizzas within Switzerland. The issue was the VAT rate. The applicable rates were 2% for a good and 6.5% for a service. For a service, the restaurant must have an installation allowing consumers to eat the prepared pizzas on the premises. The reduced rate for goods is only applicable if it is effectuated by an organization separate from the restaurant. It can be concluded that, at least in Switzerland, food should not be characterized

---

[544]E.C.J., Case C-231/194 of 2 May 1996, *Faaborg-Gelting Linien A/S v Finanzamt Flensburg.*

[545]Supreme Court of Switzerland, 31 January 1997, AFT 123 II 16.

differently if it is purchased from home via the website of a grocery store. If there is no installation for food consumption at the seller's premises, it is treated as a supply of goods.

The *Faaborg-Gelting Linien A/S* case and the discussion of the categorization of composite supplies may not be directly relevant to electronic commerce, regardless of the categorization. However, the case may provide some guidance for the European Court when it has to resolve electronic service issues, *e.g.,* how to determine the place of supply for the contributions of different businesses and software data banks, in different jurisdictions, involved in the production and sale of the same service to the customer. According to the predominant business contribution? Under a system of apportionment? The place of the data bank, if the business input is limited? There may be an even greater level of complexity. For instance, what if a vacation package is purchased over the internet? Is it a good or a composite supply? Is it supplied where the supplier is located, or where the main component (*e.g.,* transport) is supplied? If there is more than one good or service, how will the transaction be characterized to ensure appropriate apportionment? Similar issues arise for combined telecommunications, on-line information and broadcast services. The characterizations of individual countries will not be consistent because of different tax rates and interpretations. Simpler tax structures and more international agreements are, therefore, required. The neutrality policy should be that electronic commerce is not taxed more heavily than traditional methods of commerce.[546]

4.3.4.2.3. Categorization of services according to type of service

VAT categorization is also not always easy where scientific, educational or entertainment services are supplied over the internet or by satellite telecommunication. Are they subject to VAT in the Member State of performance (Article 9(2)(c)), VAT in the Member State of the supplier (Article

---

[546]Ireland IFA Branch, *Comments on Electronic Commerce Report* (on file with the authors); United Kingdom IFA Branch, *Comments on Electronic Commerce Report* (8 April 1998) (on file with the authors).

9(1)) or VAT in the customer's Member State, being intellectual services not unlike the supply of information (Article 9(2)(e))?

In June 1994, a ruling under the pre-1997 system, dealing with the application of VAT to telecommunications services, was rendered by the UK VAT Tribunal, in *British Sky-Broadcasting v. Commissioners of Customs and Excise*. The case involved TV programs broadcast by satellite, from the United Kingdom, to subscribers, including residents of the Channel Islands (*i.e.*, non-EC for VAT purposes). The Commissioners concluded that VAT was due under the general rule that the service (broadcasting) was provided from the United Kingdom. Looking at their content (movies and sport), British Sky-Broadcasting argued that the services constituted entertainment, under Article 9(2)(c), in the Member State of their performance because that was the place where the broadcasts (in scrambled form) were unscrambled by decoder equipment; in that case non-EU customers would not be liable for VAT. The Tribunal ruled that the general rule of Article 9(1) applied, rather than the exception in Article 9(2)(c), because entertainment, under Article 9(2)(c), means entertainment before a live audience. The cross-border live transmission of recorded films via satellite TV services could not have been contemplated by the draftsmen of the Sixth Directive (1977). The reasoning of the Tribunal suggests, *a contrario*, that, in an updated version of Article 9 of the Sixth Directive, the rule should be revised to take risks of distortion into account (if EC satellite broadcasters moved their businesses into the Channel Islands to broadcast to EC-based subscribers). The correct rule would, and should, also take into account new technological developments for on-line services: for digital services, such as video-on-demand, the action necessary to obtain the program takes place at the subscriber's end, as the subscriber runs a credit card through a decoder box.

Another decision of the UK VAT Tribunal, *HutchVision Hong Kong Ltd.*, considered the issue of whether broadcasting services should be considered engineering services, subject to VAT in the Member State of the customer's place of business or fixed establishment to which the service is supplied, for customers located outside the Community or for taxable persons established in an EC country different from that of the supplier (application of Article 9(2)(e)). The case involved the transmission of a BBC television signal, via a British Telecommunications center in the United Kingdom, to HutchVision Hong Kong pursuant to two contracts for TV distribution services and for leasing satellite transponder capacity. The charge paid by HutchVision was found to relate to the transmission and to include costs incurred by the British Telecommunications company and its engineers in managing and operating the system. Whereas HutchVision construed its services (of acquiring and transmitting, via satellite, the wireless signal from BBC studios to the Hong Kong receiving station) as engineering services (at that time zero-rated in the United Kingdom). The Tribunal ruled that the supply was not that of engineering services but essentially that of a product (a signal).

4.3.4.3. Determination of taxable charge of a single composite supply

Where a customer is charged a subscription or usage fee, he pays a fee which may be for a well-defined service. It can also be a composite fee for several services having a different nature and treatment for VAT purposes, *e.g.*, for purposes of determining their place of supply. This raises the issue of whether the subscription fee should be apportioned or, alternatively, treated and taxed according to the nature of the predominant service.

In particular, a subscription fee, whether on an ongoing or intermittent basis, may provide for access to the network and for transmission. As such, it is a basic telecommunications service. It may cover additional online services relating to the supply of information, electronic newspapers, entertainment, financial services, insurance or legal advice and similar services. Article 9(2)(e) can be used to determine the place of supply for these on-line services. Some services in the package may be free. A bank may offer its clients free access to electronic banking. Conversely, the subscription fee may be earmarked for the provision of access to the internet with, as an extra on-line service, an offer of free financial advice.

If the place of supply rules are different from the rule that would normally apply to the other component of the subscription fee, the question of whether the fee should be apportioned is raised. If so, each service component is taxed according to its nature and proper rules. On the other hand, should the subscription fee be taxed according to the nature of the predominant feature — presumably that of the information or other content being supplied (electronic newspaper, advice, banking transaction)? Are the parties free to contractually unbundle the fee? The customer would possibly, for VAT cost saving reasons, enter into one contract with the provider of the access and transmission services and a separate one with the vendor of the electronic newspaper or provider of entertainment or information.

The Sixth Directive contains no rules concerning separate billing, unbundling, apportionment of a composite fee for combined services or a determination of the predominant feature of a service. These rules should be made on rational grounds. Omitting them increases the risk of inconsistent taxation by the revenue authorities of the Member States concerned.

4.3.4.4. Problems of defining the place of supply of services

4.3.4.4.1. Place of business and of fixed establishment

In this context, Article 9 of the Sixth Directive provides for two categories of place of supply rules: the first is based on the identification of the place of business of the supplier or the customer, depending on the service. The second is based on the place of effective use and enjoyment, irrespective of the place of business. The criterion of place of business establishment is twofold. It involves the primary establishment as well as the secondary establishment.

The place of supply of a service is, under the general rule of Article 9(1), deemed to be the place of the supplier's business or fixed establishment from which the service is supplied. For services covered by Article 9(2)(e) — in particular the services of data processing and the supply of information and similar intellectual or intangible services, including telecommunications services (under the 17 March 1997 derogation) — it is the place of the customer's business or fixed establishment to which the service is supplied, or, in the absence thereof, the place of the customer's permanent address or usual residence.[547]

The expressions "place of business," "fixed establishment," and "permanent address or usual residence" are not defined in the Sixth Directive. The terminology is not found in the OECD Model Convention-based income tax treaties which use terms such as "permanent establishment" and "fixed base." This raises the issue of whether the corresponding notions in

---

[547]French text: "siège de son activité économique, établissement stable, domicile ou residence habituelle"; German text: "Sitz seiner wirtschaftlichen Tätigkeit, feste Niederlassung, Wohnort oder üblicher Aufenthaltsort"; Dutch text: "zetel van bedrijfsuitoefening, vaste inrichting, woonplaats of gebruikelijke verblijfplaats"; Italian text: "sede della attività economica, centro di attività stabile, domicilio o residenza abituale"; etc.

the two tax systems should be coordinated. Whether there is merit in trying to arrive at uniform concepts in the two autonomous systems is a matter of policy and legislative change, not of interpretation of the concepts as they are traditionally applied.

The first issue relates to the interpretation of the place where the supplier — or the customer — has a place of business. According to Advocate–General Mancini, in the *Günther Berkholz v. Finanzamt Hamburg-Mitte-Altstadt case*, and, implicitly, Advocate–General La Pergola, in the *DFDS A/C case*, the expression designates the registered office of the company. It is the place where the business is managed, irrespective of the place where it carries on its business activities. This interpretation is not shared by all commentators. Some believe that the place of business is not necessarily the registered office when no significant business is carried out through the registered office.[548] The latter interpretation offers a more appropriate criterion for purposes of the VAT concept designating the taxable place of supply of services. A virtual company supplying computer information products without any significant operational substance or staffing has a main place of business under either interpretation.

The more critical issue relates to the term "fixed establishment." There have been no serious attempts to bring it into line with the definition of the term "permanent establishment" in Article 5 of the OECD Model Convention and its interpretation in the OECD Fiscal Committee Commentary. However, some analogy can be found in the interpretation by the European Court that the VAT concept also apply in the case of local subsidiaries and agents which are not sufficiently independent and that no fixed establishment is created by ancillary activities and circumstances (*e.g.*, the selection by customers of cars at a local dealer or their temporary storage and repairs by local servicemen if car leasing is the core activity).

Different proposals have been made for defining a supplier's fixed establishment. In its Second Report, the Commission submitted two possible definitions to the VAT Committee: The first is a place where taxable transactions can be performed. The second is that the fixed place does not nec-

---

[548]De Broe, *Cross-border leasing of cars into Belgium: issues of VAT and the freedom to provide services — analysis of and comments on the European Court's holding in Aro Lease,* EC Tax Review 219 (1997/4). However, the Belgian Minister of Finance retains the registered office in his answer to a Parliamentary Question of de Clippele of 20 January 1993.

essarily need to be capable of performing the taxable transactions. A majority opted for the second definition.[549] On 5 December 1984, the Commission submitted a proposal for a Nineteenth directive along the lines of the second definition.[550] However, the European Court of Justice held a different view.

In the *Berkholz* case,[551] the European Court ruled that the expression must be interpreted to mean that an installation for carrying on a commercial activity, such as the operation of gambling machines on board a ship, may be regarded as a fixed establishment only if it includes the permanent presence of both the human and technical resources necessary for the provision of those services. The Court also considered the question of when it is inappropriate to deem those services as having been provided from the supplier's place of business. The Court reasoned that one should look for a rational solution. It is for the tax authorities in each Member State to determine, from the range of options set forth in the Directive, which point of reference is most appropriate for determining tax jurisdiction over a given service. The place of the supplier's business is the primary point of reference because it is, essentially, the place where the supplier has headquartered the business. Focusing on a fixed establishment, a secondary point of reference involving the place from which the service is supplied, is appropriate only if the reference to the place of business does not lead to a rational result for tax purposes or creates a conflict with another Member State. In the instant case, the installation and maintenance of the slot machines was performed by employees of Berkholz, which did not have any permanent employees on the ferry. The Court held that there was, therefore, no rational justification for departing from the place of business test.

In the same light, the European Court concluded in *Aro Lease BV* that a Dutch leasing company, which leased cars to customers in Belgium, did not supply services from a fixed establishment in Belgium: (i) customers contacted the leasing company through self-employed intermediaries in Belgium; (ii) customers chose their cars from dealerships in Belgium; (iii) the leasing company acquired and registered the cars in Belgium; (iv) leasing agreements were drawn up and signed at the company's main place of

---

[549]AJ. 1973, c 80/1.

[550]AF. 1984, c 347/5, Art. 1(1)b.

[551]E.C.J., Case No. 168/84 of 4 July 1985, *Günther Berkholz v. Finanzamt Hamburg-Mitte-Altstadt.*

business in the Netherlands; and (v) the leasing company had no storage facilities in Belgium.[552] For purposes of Article 9(1), Aro had no fixed establishment in Belgium because it did not have the staff or technical facilities necessary to conclude leasing agreements. This decision follows the Court's reasoning in *Berkholz*. Services cannot be deemed to be supplied at an establishment other than the place of business unless the requisite degree of stability provided by permanent human and technical resources is present. The existence of other factors and other transactions, such as those which took place in Belgium, being ancillary and supplementary to the leasing services, cannot invalidate that conclusion. The fact that customers were brought into contact with the Dutch company by self-employed Belgian intermediaries or that they chose cars from Belgian dealerships does not have any bearing on the determination of the place of fixed establishment, in terms of permanent human resources. The Court did not consider the fact that the cars concerned were registered in Belgium, where road tax is also payable. Those circumstances relate to the place where the cars are used and are, as such, irrelevant for the purposes of applying Article 9(1), which retains the practical criterion of place of business or fixed establishment: "since forms of transport may easily cross borders, it is difficult, if not impossible, to determine the place of their utilization." The Court confirmed the *Aro* decision in the subsequent case of *Lease Plan Luxembourg.*[553]

In still another case, the European Court, in *DFDS,* examined the intervention of a local agent in the performance of a service by a foreign supplier.[554] The question, referred to the Court for a preliminary ruling, was as follows:

> On the proper interpretation of Council Directive 77/388/EEC of 17 May 1977 and in particular Article 26 thereof, where a tour operator has its headquarters in Member State A but supplies services in the form of package tours to travelers through the agency of a company in Member State B: a) in what (if any) circumstances is the supply of those services by the tour operator taxable in Member State B? b) in what (if any) circumstances can it be said that the tour operator 'has established [its] business' in Member State B

---

[552] E.C.J., C 190/95 of 17 July 1992, *Aro Lease BV v. Inspecteur der Belastingdienst Grote Ondernemingen,* Amsterdam, 17 July 1997.

[553] E.C.J., C 390/96 of 7 May 1998, *Lease Plan Luxembourg SA v. Belgium.*

[554] E.C.J., C 260/95 of 20 February 1997, *DFDS A/S.*

or 'has a fixed establishment' from which [it] has provided the services in Member State B?[555]

DFDS, a shipping company headquartered in Denmark, had designated its English subsidiary, DFDS Ltd., as its general sales and port agent and central booking office for all passenger services. The UK authorities considered DFDS Ltd. a UK fixed establishment. DFDS, on the contrary, considered the services to be taxable in Denmark. DFDS argued that the place of business — or headquarters — is the primary point of reference for levying VAT on services. The Court referred to the *Berkholz* decision and looked for the most rational point of reference for determining tax jurisdiction. In this case, treating all services provided by a tour operator, including those supplied in another Member State, as being supplied from the place of business would have had the clear advantage, as DFDS pointed out, of having a single place of supply for all the business of that operator. However, as the UK government pointed out, that treatment would not lead to a rational result in that it does not take the actual place where the tours are marketed into account.

Member State authorities have good reason to take the place of marketing into account as the most appropriate point of reference, whatever the customer's destination, because of the prospective tax revenue. Consideration of the actual economic situation, however, is a fundamental criterion for the application of the common VAT system. To determine whether DFDS Ltd. was a fixed establishment, the Court examined the issue of whether DFDS Ltd. was in fact independent from the Danish tour operator or an auxiliary organ, or agent. This was not determined by the separate legal personality of the subsidiary, but by the ownership and various contractual obligations imposed on the subsidiary by its Danish parent. The last step was to determine, in accordance with *Berkholz,* whether DFDS Ltd. presented the requisite minimum size in terms of human and technical re-

---

[555]Article 26 of the Sixth Directive lays down a special scheme for travel agents which applies to their transactions and those of tour operators, where they deal with customers in their own name and use supplies and services of other taxable persons in the provision of travel facilities. All transactions performed by the travel agent in respect of a journey constitute a single service which is taxable in the Member State in which the agent has established his business or has a fixed establishment from which he provides the services. The concepts of "place of business" and "fixed establishment" are the same as those used in Article 9(1) of the Sixth Directive.

sources. The Court concluded that DFDS Ltd. displayed the features of a fixed establishment within the meaning of Article 26(3) (and Article 9(1)) of the Sixth Directive.

The UK VAT Tribunal did not contradict the reasoning of the European Court when it decided the *Chinese Channel (HongKong) Limited* case.[556] In *Chinese Channel Limited*,[557] the Tribunal considered whether, under the national provision implementing Article 9(1) of the Sixth Directive, services were supplied from a foreign company's fixed establishment in the form of a branch or agency in the United Kingdom, and whether other services of the foreign company were supplied to a customer's fixed establishment in the United Kingdom, under the national rule implementing Article 9(2)(e). The Tribunal ruled that a Hong Kong company broadcasting Chinese programs in Europe did not carry on its business through a branch or agency or otherwise constitute a fixed establishment in the United Kingdom. Its UK subsidiary marketed subscription contracts, collected subscription fees, received and edited tapes and provided news. Its broadcasts to EC-subscribers were not subject to UK VAT under the applicable rule of Article 9(1) of the Sixth Directive.

In dismissing Customs and Excise Commissioners' appeals from the 1996 decision of the Tribunal, the High Court, applying the reasoning in the *Berkholz* and *DFDS* decisions of the European Court of Justice, found that the facts supported the conclusion that the service was supplied from Hong Kong. Three conditions must be met for a finding of a fixed establishment: (i) there must be a certain minimum size involving the permanent human and technical resources necessary for the provision of the services; (ii) the company operating on behalf of the supplier must not operate, as a matter of substance and function, independently from the supplier; and (iii) the service must be supplied from the fixed establishment.

Considering that the service provided was the broadcast of programs selected by the Hong Kong company, the facts supported the conclusion that the larger part — by far — of the relevant activity (making contracts, arrangement for transmission and selecting programs) took place in Hong Kong. Considering the issue of whether the United Kingdom acted inde-

---

[556]VAT Tribunal, *Chinese Channel (Hong Kong) Limited v. The Commissioners of Customs and Excise,* March 1996 (Case 14,003). The Customs and Excise appeal was dismissed by the High Court, (1998) STC 2347, 26, 27, 28 January 1998.

[557]VAT Tribunal, *Chinese Channel (Hong Kong) Limited v. The Commissioners of Customs and Excise,* March 1996 (Case 14, 003).

pendently, in the light of *DFDS,* the High Court recognized the contribution of the UK company, but the place of business was more directly involved than the fixed establishment. The High Court also considered the fixed establishment test (in the United Kingdom) and the main place of business test (in Hong Kong) with the *DFDS* ruling on priorities in mind: "regard is to be had to another establishment from which the services are supplied only if the reference to the place where the supplier has established his business does not lead to a rational result for tax purposes or creates a conflict with another member state."

For a party relying on *Aro* the main place of business test is appropriate in the interests of simplification, uniformity and clarity. For a party relying on *DFDS,* on the other hand, the main place of business could lead to competitive disadvantage, reflect the economic situation less accurately and might, in a case like *Chinese Channel (Hong Kong) Limited,* lead to non-taxation. The High Court did not resolve the issue of the appropriate test because it found no fixed establishment.

In another case, the Tribunal examined the place of the supply of services, under Article 9(2)(e) (place where the customer has a place of business or a fixed establishment to which the service is supplied).[558] Specifically, the Tribunal examined whether the customer carried on a business through a branch or agency in the United Kingdom and, therefore, had a fixed establishment in the United Kingdom. The alternative was a place of business outside the United Kingdom. The Tribunal based its finding on which establishment was "most directly used" for the services received.

In the *Chinese Channel (HongKong) Limited* case, the High Court was not impressed by the commissioners' arguments that it is not contract, but performance that determines supply, that fixed establishment jurisdiction is evaluated by comparing the importance of activities and staffing in the United Kingdom and Hong Kong and that the rational result for purposes of applying the appropriate test (place of business or fixed establishment) may not be satisfied if the main place of business test may lead to non-taxation and competitive disadvantage.

The concept of fixed establishment was also interpreted in a Ministerial Decree (1994) and in case law in the Netherlands.[559] As a starting point,

---

[558] *W.H. Payne & Co. v. The Commissioners of Customs and Excise* (LON/95/1436 No. 13668).

[559]Vakstudie Omzetbelasing, Art. 6(12), Kluwer.

the Ministry of Finance looked to the decision of the European Court which requires a fixed establishment to have a sufficient degree of permanence and a human and technical resources and capability of supplying goods and services in an independent capacity. It concluded that a fixed establishment must, therefore, carry out its activities in much the same autonomous manner as an independent domestic enterprise. This does not include facilities maintained for the sole purpose of advertising, gathering and disseminating information, research or acting as consignment agent or depot for the account of a foreign vendor.

On 21 September 1994, the Dutch High Court considered the case of a Liechtenstein based company which collected payments via PTT for the operation of 7 erotic chat lines and transferred the amount (less its profit share and costs incurred in Belgium) to a Dutch company which previously operated the same lines. The High Court found a fixed establishment in the Netherlands. The business of the Liechtenstein company was deemed to be a continuation of the Dutch company because the Dutch company transferred its rights, contracts, goodwill, PTT facilities and computer equipment.

On 21 June 1996, the Court of Arnhem examined the case of a Dutch company which allowed a Liechtenstein company to use its computer and telecommunications equipment located in the Netherlands. The equipment was used for the exploitation of erotic lines in the Netherlands. The Court found that the Liechtenstein company functioned as a letter box and had established its business in the Netherlands regardless of its registration in the Netherlands and the channeling of payments and correspondence via Liechtenstein.

The case law determining the meaning of fixed establishment, in the aforementioned circumstances, especially the decisions of the European Court of Justice, offers general guidance for the application of Articles 9(1) and 9(2)(e) to telecommunications services and the provision of various information over the internet. Does the installation of a server with a web site, in Member State S, constitute a fixed establishment? Does it form an appropriate fiscal point of reference for VAT taxation, in S, of the sales and the services of the supplier, established in Member State R, to customers in S? Probably not, as the supplier lacks the permanent presence, in S, of the necessary human and technical resources. Moreover, if the location of a server mattered for VAT purposes, it could easily be located in virtually any location. The presence of infrastructure, such as a web server and routers, does not satisfy the concept of fixed establishment as it is interpreted by the European Court. Neither do local agents offering related services (*e.g.,* free phone facilities). In S, the agents are sufficiently independent from the supplier in R.

The case law offers little guidance, as to the application (or non-application) of the place of fixed establishment rule, if the supplier, R Corp., avoids the need for the permanent presence of technical and human resources, in S, by contractual arrangements for separate services from independent sources. This type of contractual arrangement is an abuse of the fixed establishment rule. National courts increasingly tend to apply abuse doctrines to tax constructions. One commentator suggests that such contractual arrangements may well withstand that challenge.[560] His interpretation may be supported by *Aro.* If the strict interpretation of the concept and its justification in that decision are applied, there is no cause for invoking abuse. A more effective view is adopted by Farmer and Lyal:[561]

> It is submitted that, in a genuine case in which the supplier or customer has several business establishments all capable of performing services, the most appropriate method of determining the place of supply for the purposes of Article 9(1) or 9(2)(e) would be to identify the establishment of the supplier whose resources were primarily used for supplying the service or the establishments of the customer which made primary use of the service (. . .) If formal invoicing and payment arrangements could alter the substantive position, taxable persons would be practically free to choose the jurisdiction in which they wished supplies to be taxed, or even to escape tax altogether by rendering invoices to establishments outside the Community.

Section 4.3.4.7 provides an example of how the scope of tax avoidance or evasion by means of formal arrangements can be extended in the case of electronically communicated digitized information.

It is questionable as to whether the interpretation based on the priority of the main place of business of R Corp., say, in a tax haven country over the fixed place where R Corp. carries out some degree of local activity in S is acceptable to national revenue authorities. In the internet economy, such an interpretation reduces much of the effectiveness of the safety net which

---

[560]Ogley, A., *VAT and Telecommunications Services in the European Union,* Tax Notes Int'l 1157 (7 April 1997).

[561]Farmer & Lyal, EC Tax Law 160 (1994).

the fixed establishment concept was probably deemed to offer to Member State S, where it helps overseas supplier R Corp. to engage in electronic commerce with final consumers in S at no tax cost.

The case law of the European Court may offer a consistent interpretation of the term "fixed establishment," but it has not yet been applied by the Court in the case of electronic commerce. There are, therefore, several unanswered questions and concerns in that area. One general reservation is that the existing interpretation appears to impose more restrictive taxing requirements on the (electronic and other) transactions of foreign vendors, other than manufacturing and those involving physical industries, than it does for domestic vendors or providers. Furthermore, the definition requires a sufficient degree of permanence, size, organization of technical and human resources necessary to provide services, core (as distinct from ancillary) activities, local intermediaries who are not sufficiently independent and reasons for not retaining the vendor's (or customer's) main place of business as the appropriate taxable place. Those are essentially flexible criteria which may leave some room for interpretation when they are applied to a vendor marketing and selling information, products or intellectual services on-line. It can be argued that for such activities the necessity of physical requirements should be less significant than the concern of effective taxation. A fixed establishment, in the Court's narrow interpretation, may be avoided when it is not in the vendor's interest whereas the requirements are easily met if it is in the vendor's interest. The *Aro* case may induce EC-based businesses to locate critical leasing services in Member States with the lowest VAT rate, while keeping sufficient ancillary facilities and servicemen in the market country. The electronic medium may exacerbate this problem. Effective VAT legislation may require that economic substance prevails over formal or elusive arrangements (contract, payment, correspondence and communications over the internet).

The European Court, because of its narrow interpretation in the *Berkholz* and *Aro* line of cases, may have underestimated the productivity of advertisement, storage, payment and interactive communications (so-called ancillary services but closely integrated with transactions such as sales, research, design, etc.) in electronic commerce. Furthermore, the Court may have overestimated the size and needs of local infrastructure, in terms of human and technical resources. The German inspectors conclude"

[the] conventional criteria based on physical criteria run into difficulties in the case of commercial suppliers residing abroad who do not maintain a

fixed place of business in the customary sense within the national territory, since in the internet geographical location is irrelevant. Thus foreign suppliers would escape taxation due to the lack of a traditional permanent establishment. It would seem to be legally defensible to justify the assumption of a permanent establishment by the presence of an internet server installed in the national territory, but it would be easy to get around this, for a server could be moved to another country (perhaps a tax haven) without too much effort. Therefore, we touch inter alia on the possibility of considering a website which when retrieved is copied on the user's immediate access storage as a digital 'sales facility' constituting a domestic permanent establishment under certain conditions (e.g. if complete contractual performance is possible or if there is a certified supplier's identification code). Further study is needed on this.[562]

As the (vendor's) fixed establishment test in the EC is currently very narrow, it is unlikely that the test addresses the case of the electronic business of non-EC suppliers. It thus leaves the origin system of Article 9(1) as the remaining option. If the test is widened, it could result in arguments similar to the nexus arguments in the United States. The alternative is to tax consumption, following the telecommunications example. To do that, questions of definition and discrepancies between residence, billing address and place of use and enjoyment would have to be resolved. In either case, it poses problems of control and enforcement when the vendor is established overseas and the final consumer is established in a Member State.

4.3.4.4.2. Effective use and enjoyment of the services

Article 9(3) allows Member States to retain the right to impose VAT based upon the place of "effective use and enjoyment" of services. It does so only in the context of Article 9(2)(e) (and telecommunications) services and to avoid double taxation, non-taxation or competitive disadvantage. It is commonly used as an anti-avoidance measure, under the 1997 Council derogation, with respect to telecommunications services. No definition of the expression "effective use and enjoyment" is found in the Sixth Directive. The expressions in the different versions are only approximately consistent: in French it is "utilization et exploitation effectives," in German it is "tat-

---

[562]Dittmar & Selling, *How to Control Internet Transactions? A Contribution from the Point of View of German Tax Inspectors,* INTERTAX 92 (1998).

sächliche Nutzung oder Auswertung," in Italian it is "effetiva utilizzazione e impiego," in Dutch it is "werkelijk gebruik en werkelijke exploitatie," etc. In the Nordic countries, there is a difference between the Danish version and the Swedish translation of Article 9(3) of the Sixth Directive on the one hand and Danish and Swedish VAT laws and the Swedish version of the Finnish VAT law on the other hand. The former corresponds to the English, French and German versions of the Sixth Directive and uses a phrase related to effective use and enjoyment. The Nordic laws use a phrase corresponding to exclusive use and enjoyment.[563] The precise meaning of the two distinctive terms in the expression and the use of both the conjunctive, "and," and the disjunctive, "or," creates confusion. There is no merit in defining "exploitation" as business use (by a private or non-taxable person) in an attempt to compare this autonomous VAT criterion with any source rule for services in the OECD Model Convention or its Commentary.

The history of the text of the Sixth Directive may suggest that "use" refers to services involving physical goods (*e.g.,* such as a lease of equipment), whereas "enjoyment" refers more generally to other services (*e.g.,* copyright license, financial services, etc.). If an interpretation according to *ratio legis* is followed, the starting point is the purpose of the provision which is to deal with VAT avoidance and distortion of competition between third country suppliers and local suppliers, if the customer can choose the former for tax reasons. The expression "use and enjoyment" would thus point to the place where the service is consumed. Even so, the expression remains open for interpretation. Where is an advertisement used and enjoyed? Where is the administrative fee, which a Swiss bank charges to a Dutch holding company concerning the management of a Netherlands Antilles company in which the Dutch company holds shares, taxable? The Court of The Hague ruled, on 11 December 1996, that such a fee was subject to Dutch VAT because the user was the Dutch holding company — as little as its Dutch activity may have been — and not the Netherlands Antilles company managed by the Swiss bank.[564]

The expression leaves considerable room for interpretive discretion by each of the 15 Member States. It, therefore, creates risks of uncertainty and

---

[563]Swedish IFA Branch, *Comments on Electronic Commerce Report* (1998) (on file with the authors).

[564]Court of The Hague, 11 December 1996, n° 95/2558, Infobulletin 97/193, V-N 1997, 1773; Wet Omzetbelasting, Art. 6-226.

divergent application and, ultimately, risks of double taxation and competitive disadvantage, which it was intended to cure. It is possible that the European Court accepts the argument that the EC, by using two undefined terms in the expression "effective use and (or) enjoyment," intended to increase the effectiveness of the safety net and to allow a certain degree of flexibility in implementation by the Member States. It is also possible that the European Court, out of respect for the principle of legal certainty and for the stated purposes of the rule of Article 9(3), may want to restrict such discretion by narrowing the contours of this autonomous concept for given services and in typical situations.

Telecommunications services provided by non-EC operators highlight this issue: are calls provided by non-EC operators, and placed by non-EC residents using their GSM while traveling in the EC, to be considered services used and enjoyed in the EC? Or, in order to satisfy the territoriality test for those services, is a VAT applicable only if the users are EC-residents? In the first case, it will be a difficult administrative task to track and bill the cases of telephone card use by non-EC resident travelers. Is it realistic to rely on the effectiveness of the administrative regulatory framework of requiring non-EC companies to become VAT-registered traders, or of requiring EC-business customers to self-account for the VAT in accordance with the reverse-charge rule? It is certainly not realistic to expect that the tax authorities of the overseas provider will resolve the problem of VAT controls and administration for the account of the Member State taxing their residents. Is it justifiable to take account of these administrative and practical problems and of the stated purposes of the test (safety net against "American route" type of situations of non-taxation) in the interpretation of the expression "effective use and enjoyment" and to argue, for instance, that only EC-resident users — not overseas residents who happen to travel in Europe ("oiseaux de passage") — were intended to be covered?[565]

The use of the elusive expression, "use and enjoyment of (intellectual or intangible) services," highlights the problems of interpretation and practical enforcement inherent in any test based on the place of supply of services and stretching the traditional territoriality connection. But then,

---

[565]United Kingdom IFA Branch, *Comments on Electronic Commerce Report* (8 April 1998) (on file with the authors). The UK Comments conclude that the Council derogation does seek to address the effect of the new rules on non-EC residents using GSM or card services in the EC. They should not, in principle, be taxed.

minimum contacts — not earthbound nexus — is a fact of (VAT) life in the networked economy. The concern — from a tax policy perspective, if it's not possible from an interpretative perspective — is different from the earlier question of the application and interpretation of the expression "fixed establishment." The issue is whether tax authorities want an interpretation, of Article 9(3), stressing the taxing right of the Member State where the supplier has its principal establishment or that of the Member State where the supplier maintains a fixed establishment on the basis of links requiring less extensive infrastructure and the less than bright line physical presence of internet activities or, where taxation based on infrastructure alone, such as a server, would not work (*i.e.,* if it would lead to it being located in a tax haven), whether taxing "use and enjoyment" can be given an interpretation which achieves protection and avoids the need of for new taxing concepts.

Article 9(3)(b) deals with situations of non-taxation and the competitive disadvantage of EC businesses. The risk of double taxation, however, is a concern that is no less troublesome for international businesses. This risk of double taxation is real, especially for cross-EC border transactions where the EC VAT system interacts with non-EC tax systems which are often origin-based. To avoid this problem, Article 9(3)(a) provides that (intellectual) services referred to in Article 9(2)(e) which, under Article 9, would be situated within the territory of a Member State, may be considered as being situated outside the EC where the effective use and enjoyment of the services takes place outside the Community.

4.3.4.5. *Overview of VAT applications to electronic commerce and telecommunication services*

The following examples illustrate the application of current EC VAT rules to international electronic commerce.

1. The purchase of a book, ordered via the internet on-line by a private customer in Member State S, from bookstore R Corp. in Member State R, is charged VAT in R. Comparing VAT rates for books in various Member States, customer S goes cross-border shopping via the internet and orders the book, from mail order

store X Corp., in Member State X (*e.g.,* United Kingdom), where the VAT rate is zero. However, if X Corp. dispatches books to S in excess of the applicable annual threshold value of distance sales, it must register in S and charge customer S VAT.

2. If, in (1), instead of buying the book in printed form, private customer S purchases it from bookstore X Corp. in digital form. S downloads it from the internet onto his home PC. It becomes the supply of a service. The zero-rate available in X, to books (in printed form), does not apply to the purchase and its taxable place of supply is determined in accordance with Article 9(2)(e) rather than according to the rule governing situation (1). The distance sales rule does not apply to services.

3. If, in (2), customer S is a taxable person, VAT is chargeable in state S on the intra-Community acquisition (reverse charge). If S Corp. happens to be a bank, or other business without the right of deduction, which uses the book in its (exempt) bank activity, the input VAT is not recoverable. Banks and private persons without a right of deduction are interested in avoiding or reducing the VAT cost by the use of the new medium and its place of supply rules.

4. If R Corp. and X Corp. are the public telecommunications organizations (PTO) of Member States R and X respectively, no VAT is applied, under the Melbourne Convention, to the payments between them in accordance with the clearance system of sharing their revenues from international calls. If R Corp. and X Corp. are private operators, the exemption is, or will be, extended to them under an updated liberal interpretation given to the Melbourne Convention by many Member States and, prospectively, under the post-1999 Directive amendment proposal.

5. If R Corp. is based overseas (in non-EU country R) and provides basic telecommunications services of transmission (long distance telephone services, call turnaround services, internet access services, etc.) to customer S in Member State S, such services were not taxable to their customer established in S (under the general rule of Article 9(1) of the Sixth Directive). However, Member State S (as all other Member States) brought basic telecommunications services furnished by operator R Corp. to S Corp. within the scope of Article 9(2)(e) (under the 1997 derogation). Being a

taxable person established in Member State S, S Corp. is required to apply VAT to the services received from R Corp. under the reverse charge procedure.

6. If, in (5), the customer is a private or other non-taxable person established in S, the telecommunications services effectively used in Member States S, A, B, etc. give rise to VAT liability in S, A, B, etc., if those services are supplied by R Corp. based in the United States or another non-EC country. R Corp. has to register as a trader for VAT purposes in S, A, B, etc. unless it establishes a fixed establishment in any of those Member States from where it supplies its services. In the definitive system, R Corp. US will choose register in whatever Member State it chooses. If VAT rates are not standardized by that time, the US (non-EC) operator may want to register in the Member State applying the lowest rate.

7. If, in (6), the services are not basic telecommunications services but consist in the provision of financial or scientific information, newspapers, music, entertainment or other intangible content goods delivered via the internet to business subscribers established in Member State S, they are subject to VAT in S. Subscriber S Corp. applies the reverse charge procedure.

8. If, in (7), R Corp. provides the services for the account of non-EC based X Corp., to the fixed establishment of X Corp. in Member State S, VAT is charged in Member State S.

9. If, in (7), the newspaper, music, entertainment or other content in digital form is provided by overseas R Corp. and downloaded from the internet onto the PC of private customers or non-taxable persons established in Member State S without thereby creating for R Corp. a fixed establishment in S, no VAT is charged (under Article 9(1)).

10. However, if in situation (9) the digitized products are provided to non-EC based private customers or taxable persons but their effective use and enjoyment take place within the territory of S, A, B, C, etc., VAT may be charged in each of the Member States where Article 9(3)(b) has been adopted and where R Corp. must be registered as a trader for VAT purposes. It is unclear as to whether EC countries will be able to enforce this VAT obligation on the overseas supplier.

4.3.4.6. Regulatory administrative framework and inter-administrative cooperation

When transactions take place over the internet, it becomes difficult for tax officials to track and control parties, to identify the nature and location of taxable transactions and to enforce VAT collection. A sale or service over the internet involves no paper; it offers little information concerning its contents, especially if the message is in encrypted form; the payment permits little verification, especially when electronic cash is used; the electronic medium does away with the need to involve local intermediaries; the global scope of the medium increases the locational elasticity of the underlying transaction and of the supporting infrastructure. The digital signals are transmitted from server installations that can be located anywhere (*e.g.*, in orbit). They are sent via providers and intermediaries who can, likewise, be located in virtually any jurisdiction and have little or no information or control over the transactions that travel over their network system.

Present VAT legislation requires a system of accounting, administration and control that is not easily applied to electronic commerce and telecommunications services. It is based on the registration of taxable persons, the designation of fiscal representatives, the issuance of real invoices containing the required information, the filing of returns and statistical declarations in forms which do not provide for electronic invoicing, reporting, payment and refund claim handling. The application of these requirements and administrative formalities to electronic commerce imposes burdens which risk reducing the productivity of the new medium. A more productive approach is to allow businesses to take advantage of the new technologies in the automated format of their data exchanges and in the electronic processing of payments.

Diverging procedures and administrative practices in the 15 Member States create more burdens and higher compliance costs for businesses as well as competitive disadvantages within the internal market. They risk being particularly harmful for electronic commerce as they restrict its speed, global scope disintermediation and high productivity. Considerable difficulties are experienced by non-resident traders, when they face widely different administrative obligations with respect to the direct registration or appointment of a VAT representative, VAT refund claims and VAT documentation responsibilities (*e.g.*, invoices, periodic returns, etc.). Excessive administrative burdens (billing, etc.) are also experienced, by non-EC telecommunication companies, if the consumption of their services is deemed for VAT purposes to take place in the separate fiscal territories of the 15 Member States and if billing must reflect differences between charges to business and private customers in each of those territories.

Also, compliance with customs and VAT procedures at the border creates problems, especially if the goods, *e.g.*, books, software packages, etc., are dispatched by overseas bookstores or mail order firms. It is estimated that the importation and shipment by courier service, of a book or software package, ordered from a mail order firm outside the EC, is three times more expensive than having that same book or package shipped into the United States.

This situation should improve — and with it, the productivity procured by the new technologies of communication — when in accordance with the 1996 proposals of the Commission a common VAT system replaces the transitional system of taxation of goods which relies on the principle of destination with the system of taxation in the Member State of origin. Such a system will simplify application and leave the responsibility for taxation and deduction with a single administration, thereby avoiding the need and cost of applying the VAT rules of each and every Member State involved in the movement of the goods. This overhaul in the Community VAT system would befit the concept of a true internal market. It would also complement the productivity that can be derived from the communications revolution and electronic commerce (of tangible goods). It is estimated that the cost of administering a sale of goods in another Member State, under the present destination system of taxation, may be as high as 5 or 6 times that of administering the same transaction in the domestic market.[566] However, when an origin-based tax system is applied in the EC, the same communications technologies will also increase the risks of competitive disadvantage, at least if VAT rates and application are not sufficiently standardized to take the tax cost incentive out of any decision to relocate businesses or establishments.

Tax authorities tend to see the new medium as a threat to the effectiveness of their traditional controls, audit trails and to the stability of their

---

[566]European Commission, Communication *A Common System of VAT,* Com (96) 328 final, 22 July 1996, Introduction.

tax revenue. They should consider, however, that the same medium may also be used by tax administrations to improve the efficiency of their rules and practices. In its 1997 Communication, *A European Initiative in Electronic Commerce,* the Commission advocates the adoption of an electronic commerce regulatory framework whilst safeguarding public interests.

The electronic medium does away with the need to involve traditional intermediaries such as retail stores, banks, travel agencies, etc. A number of SME's will act as cross-border intermediaries in relation to trade in goods and services. They may not, however, have any reporting capabilities and may themselves not meet compliance requirements. On the other hand, a number of qualified and financially sound intermediaries (*e.g.,* telecommunications companies, certification authorities, ISP's) appear to have developed new accounting systems (Secure Electronic Payment Systems) involving credit card operators and banks which may function as reporting points.

Intranetworks offer new prospects for more complete exchanges of information between the national tax administrations. In its 1996 proposals for a change-over to the new common system of VAT, the European Commission focused on the renewal of the legal framework for cooperation and on a program to establish a new spirit of administrative cooperation. The Commission stresses "the new collective responsibility" of the national administrations of the Member States. They have the same financial interest in providing cooperation as they have in concentrating on domestic administration. The Commission stresses the administrative merits of its proposal for an origin-based, definitive VAT system:

> Although for tax purposes all transactions will take place in the Member State of registration, physical aspects of the transaction may take place in another Member State. To ensure that the Member State of registration can control all aspects of the transaction, these physical aspects will need to be verified. This requires full cooperation between the Member State of registration and the Member State where the physical aspects of the transaction take place. In short, a level of cooperation between the Member States at least equivalent to that currently achieved within each Member State will be required.[567]

---

[567]European Commission, Communication *A Common System of VAT*, l.c. par. 2.3.4.

In the framework of its 22 July 1996 program for a common system of VAT in the Single Market, the Commission proposes a new Community action program, Fiscalis, to strengthen its present operational systems (VIES, Mattaeus-Tax). The objective is to protect the Member States' financial interests by combating tax evasion, avoiding competitive disadvantage through effective application of Community law and further reducing the burden of administrative charges both for administrations and taxpayers.

The global reach of the new medium and tax authorities' concerns about the adequacy of controls, audit trails and collection mechanisms do not only apply to the Member States using the Community VAT system. The challenge posed by electronic commerce and telecommunications services is just as real for non-EC states applying VAT or another type of turnover tax. Uncoordinated administration and fiscal competition are not an adequate response. The work of the OECD's Committee on Fiscal Affairs, in coordination with that of the Community, should contribute to a wider international consensus on the appropriate procedures and methods of cooperation.

4.3.4.7. *Evaluating the application of EC VAT rules to electronic commerce*

The application of the present EC VAT rules to international electronic commerce entails many risks. It is often a complex and uncertain process. It can result in a distortion of competitive conditions and produce a loss of tax revenue. The EC VAT rules are not easy to apply, control, and enforce. The problems are generally caused or exacerbated by the fact that new information and communication technologies blur traditional transaction and geographical categories. The following issues require clear and uniform answers:

- Should goods that can be transferred in digitalized form, such as CDs and computer software, be defined as goods or services?
- Where should distinctions be made between basic transmission, data processing and similar intellectual services or composite services that combine a transmission service with other service components (*e.g.*, editing, translation, etc.).

- Should free access to the internet offered by a bank to its clients which constitutes a single composite supply be characterized as a transmission or as a banking service.
- When a telecommunications service provider leases a private network linking the worldwide offices of an MNE, involved in global trading, is the VAT applied to the lease charge for the entire circuit or only for the part of the circuit that is used in the EC? Under which formula should the charge be apportioned?
- With the new technologies, the supplier or customer no longer has to be established in the country of consumption. What happens if consumers freely contract with the non-EC place of business of the EC-based supplier for the sole purpose of avoiding the EC VAT? What if the charge is subsequently charged back, as a management charge, to the supplier's main EC place of business? Suppose that there is no actual charge back, but the cost should have been borne by the EC business? Alternatively, should the consideration paid by the consumer be apportioned between the main place of business and fixed establishment? Under which formula?
- Is a fixed establishment, for EC tax purposes, determined according to the tangible fixed criteria imposed by the *Berkholz* line of cases when the services are supplied electronically from the establishment and the company is a virtual company operating with software agents? In such a case, what is the appropriate test: main place of business or fixed establishment?
- Is the use of a GSM, by a US resident traveling in the EC, a transmission service used and enjoyed in the territory of the EC? Is the charge for the service so provided by a US operator subject to EC VAT?

These issues are illustrated by the case of an international business firm or professional partnership, O, P, Q, R and TH, with offices in O (Germany), P (Luxembourg), Q (United States), R (United Kingdom) and TH (a tax haven country, *e.g.*, the Cayman Islands). Experts in those distant offices collaborate closely to perform a contract obligation over the group's intranet. The group is organized according to a hub and spokes system in which R Corp., with the help of software agents, functions as the hub responsible for client communications and billings. The business could be an international law firm operating a European Law Center, or an audit firm reviewing the books of a single client, or an engineering, design or research enterprise with offices in distant locations. The client could be a private individual residing in a Member State (*e.g.,* France (S)) or a (French) bank, insurance company, educational or health institute or a holding company requesting assistance in connection with proposed purchases and sales of shares. The client looks for ways to save on VAT as a deduction of the input VAT is not allowed in this situation.

Under a straightforward application of Article 9(1) (or in this case its implementation under UK legislation), the United Kingdom is the taxable place for the service of R Corp. to S client. The UK VAT rate is 17.5%. The charges to the hub by the offices in O and P are likewise subject to UK VAT under Article 9(2)(e). The parties try to reduce the VAT cost to 15% by arranging for billing out of P Corp. (Luxembourg). Or, to do away with the entire cost, the parties arrange for billing out of the United States or Cayman Islands office. The UK authorities maintain that UK VAT is appropriate, arguing that the determination of the taxable place of supply is a matter of substantive law and not of formal arrangement. On similar grounds (*i.e.,* the substance of the performance matters, not the label), the German and Luxembourg tax authorities argue that R Corp., being a virtual company, has no substance. Accordingly, they apply German (16%) and Luxembourg (15%) VAT and apportion the consideration according to the respective contributions of the local offices. The firm disagrees as it finds the apportionment arbitrary and points out that the human input is limited as the main contribution to the service comes from access to the data base located in the TH office. The French tax authorities apply French VAT (20.6%) under Article 9(1), arguing that the services are supplied from a fixed established in France. R Corp. made its sales pitch by advertising the firm's services on the website of a server located in France which was also used to communicate with the French client and deliver the digital product. Alternatively, they claim the application of the French VAT because the service was used in France. The problem is that France did not implement Article 9(3)(b). Even if it did, how effective are the mechanisms for controlling, collecting and enforcing French VAT when the supplier is based outside the EC?

The example illustrates the wide ranging problems in applying the current VAT rules to electronic commerce — the uncertainties of the conceptual framework, the complexity of application, control and enforcement, the portable nature of electronic transactions in a hub and spoke system, the opportunities to evade or avoid VAT and the associated risks of competitive disadvantage, loss of revenue and multiple taxation. The need for clarification is imperative. While the VAT Committee, the European Commission and the European Court of Justice should be helpful within the EC, the problem of inconsistencies between EC and non-EC VAT rules and interpretations remains.

In a broader context, the OECD Committee of Fiscal Affairs has identified the challenges of applying the place of supply rules to certain supplies of digitized information. The disappearing distinctions between goods and services and the tax mechanism are the main conceptual problems. Seeking consistency and uniformity in the place of supply rules and the related definitions of services, the Committee will examine the issues in close cooperation with the European Commission (paragraphs 142 and 144 of OECD-CFA document).

The European Commission has dealt with the problems and inadequacies of the present system in guidelines set forth in its 1998 Communication. One guideline points to the need for a clear set of rules. For instance, all types of electronic transmissions and all intangible products delivered over the internet or private intranets would be deemed to constitute services, for purposes of EC VAT. The implementation of this guideline may require a legislative change and not simple interpretation after the decision of the European Court in the *Datacenter* case.

Another guideline points to the need for neutrality. Under the neutrality concept, EC businesses would be on a level playing field in relation to non-EC businesses. The EC VAT system should ensure that services, whether supplied via electronic commerce or otherwise, are taxed within the EC when consumed there and without the EC when consumed elsewhere. The VAT system would thus deal with the competitive disadvantage of EC businesses in situations where supplies from non-EC countries to the EC are not taxed and supplies from Member States to non-EC countries are taxed. This is not only consistent with the aims of the EC, but it also allows for a neutral interface with the tax regimes of non-EC countries.

Still another guideline deals with the challenge of ensuring control and enforcement in the case of non-EC based suppliers. The practical implementation of the taxation of non-EC supplies to private consumers within the EC requires further study and consultation with Member States and the business sector.

A final guideline deals with the challenge of making compliance simple and compatible with commercial practices. Paperless electronic invoicing must be authorized. Furthermore, operators engaging in electronic commerce must be allowed to discharge their fiscal obligations through electronic VAT declarations.

The above guidelines are submitted by the European Commission as the EC's contribution to the OECD's Ministerial Conference to be held in Ottawa in October 1998. They should serve as a basis for further discussions within the EC and internationally with all concerned with the development of electronic commerce. The Commission guidelines deal with VAT policies and technical — and fundamental — changes and are, as such, discussed and evaluated in Section 5. The necessity of new policy approaches and legislative changes is highlighted by the difficulties encountered in the application of the current EC VAT rules to electronic commerce. However, at this stage, where electronic commerce technology is still developing and patterns of trade are still unclear, the Commission concludes that it is not necessary or possible to change the existing VAT system immediately. The change may be necessary sometime around the year 2001, when EC consumption attributable to electronic commerce may reach 5 billion ECU. This estimate includes all types of electronic commerce (goods and services ordered and paid for on-line, irrespective of mode of delivery). Only a portion of this total will be attributable to supplies from non-EC countries and only a portion thereof will attributable to direct electronic commerce. It will consist mainly of those services — that pose difficult problems — received by EC private persons from non-EC suppliers; they are not expected to become significant in economic terms before the year 2001.

4.3.5. Other general consumption tax systems

4.3.5.1. Other VAT systems

4.3.5.1.1. Switzerland[568]

Switzerland is not a member of the EC. Since 1995, it has levied a VAT at the federal level which, in substance, follows the general principles em-

---

[568]Switzerland IFA Branch, *Comments on Electronic Commerce Report* (20 April 1998) (on file with the authors).

bodied in the EC's Sixth Directive. However, the Swiss VAT system departs from the EC VAT model in some aspects of its taxation of telecommunications services and electronic commerce.

The place of supply of services is deemed to be the place where the supplier has a registered seat or a permanent establishment from which the services are rendered. Contrary to Article 9(2)(e), Swiss VAT does not provide a specific rule for intangible services. However, intangible services, even if supplied in Switzerland, are zero-rated if they are supplied to recipients with a private domicile or business abroad and are used and enjoyed abroad (Art. 15 para. 2(1) VATO). Under draft legislation designed to coordinate the Swiss and the EC regime, a new place of supply rule will be introduced for advisory services, advertisement, data processing, banking and insurance services and other intangible services. The rule will provide that the taxable place is the establishment of the place of business or the permanent establishment of the recipient of the services.

Following the general EC VAT rule, telecommunications services take place at the place of the principal business or permanent establishment of the operator (Art. 15 para. 2 lit.(f) VATO). However, if they are supplied to Swiss territory from abroad or from abroad, across Swiss territory, to foreign territory (transit), they are zero-rated. The place of access to the network is the relevant criterion. Under this system, a call from abroad is exempt, whereas a call from Switzerland to a foreign country is subject to VAT.

The Swiss system creates risks of double or non-taxation for telecommunications services between EC countries and Switzerland. The Federal Tax Administration has, therefore, by means of Art. 15 para. 2 lit.(f), changed its practice by making it more consistent with the rule of the 1997 EC Council derogation (which applies the rule of Art. 9(3)(b) of the Sixth Directive to telecommunications services when they would be exempt under the rule of Art. 9(1) because they are supplied by non-EU operators to private consumers in the Community). It has been suggested that it would be simpler to delete Art. 15 para. 2 lit.(f) VATO, thus bringing telecommunications services under the regime of Art. 15 para. 2 lit. 1 VATO. Telecommunications services would then be exempt if supplied to customers domiciled abroad and used or enjoyed abroad. Conversely, telecommunications services supplied from foreign operators to Swiss customers would be subject to VAT if used or enjoyed in Switzerland (with an exempt threshold of 10,000 S fr.). It is interesting to note how Switzerland and other countries (*e.g.*, Rumania) aligns its VAT system to that of the EC, whilst departing from it on specific points.

4.3.5.1.2. Israel[569]

While Israel is a leader in the development of internet technology and electronic commerce, the Israeli VAT system has no specific legislation to tackle issues relating to the internet. Israeli VAT is generally imposed on transactions which are undertaken in Israel and on goods imported to Israel. Services provided in Israel or to Israeli residents are subject to VAT.

In the case of international telephone services, involving Israeli residents using a foreign telephone service provider to connect them to the requested overseas number by rerouting the call as an incoming call to Israel, the Israeli VAT authorities have taken the following position: VAT should be imposed on such international telephone services when the call originates in Israel. However, if the call is originated when the Israeli resident is physically outside of Israel, no Israeli VAT is imposed. If the international company uses the services of an Israeli company (for billing, collection, promotion), the services are subject to Israeli VAT. Several practitioners believe the position of the Israeli VAT authorities is overreaching and that services provided to Israeli residents by foreign telephone companies should not be subject to Israeli VAT. The matter has yet to be addressed by the courts.

It can be inferred from this general rule, and from the precedent of the treatment of international telephone services, that Israeli VAT should apply if an Israeli resident purchases merchandise by electronic commerce and the merchandise is shipped to Israel. If an Israeli resident receives services through the internet, such services should be subject to VAT as long as the Israeli resident is in Israel when the services are provided.

4.3.5.1.3. Colombia[570]

The "Impuesto al Valor Agregado" (IVA) is applied, *inter alia,* to the supply of services in Columbian territory. The general rule provides that the taxable place is the one where the supplier is established. However, li-

---

[569]Israel IFA Branch, *Comments on Electronic Commerce Report* (9 April 1998) (on file with the authors).

[570]Colombia IFA Branch, *Comments on Electronic Commerce Report* (on file with the authors).

censing services or the use of intangible goods, professional consulting or auditing services, insurance and intellectual services take place where the recipient is established. Services supplied without Columbia are not taxed under the territoriality principle. If they are supplied abroad and used in Colombia, some commentators claim that they are taxable because such supplies are in the nature of imports.

The Tax Statute imposes the responsibility of collecting the tax on certain persons (mainly traders and importers). Colombian law has adopted a system of tax withholding to accelerate and ensure collection. Fifty percent of the tax will be withheld at the time of the payment by agents, *e.g.*, corporations listed as "grandes contribuyentes," and 100% of the tax in the case of the payment for services of non-resident suppliers without a territorial connection.

4.3.5.2. Non-VAT type consumption tax systems

4.3.5.2.1. Canadian GST

The following description of the GST (Goods and Services Tax) structure is borrowed from the Canadian Report, *Electronic Commerce and Canada's Tax Administration* (April 1998):

> GST is levied on 'taxable supplies' of goods and services that are considered to be made in Canada under the GST rules. Goods are considered to be supplied in Canada when they are delivered or made available to the recipient in Canada. Generally, goods imported into Canada are subject to GST at the border; the tax will be collected by Customs (. . .) Intellectual property, which is considered to be intangible personal property, is considered to be supplied in Canada when it can be used in whole or in part in Canada. Similarly, services are supplied in Canada when they are performed in whole or in part in Canada.
>
> A specific override rule deems a supply to be made outside Canada when the personal property (property other than land or buildings) or service is supplied by a non-resident who is not registered and who is not required to be registered to collect the tax.
>
> When products that will be delivered electronically are acquired, it is likely that these supplies will be correctly classified as services or intangibles rather than goods. When these supplies will be used or consumed by a resident in Canada, specific rules require the purchaser to self-assess the tax (pay

it directly to the government) in situations where the purchaser would not otherwise be able to recover the tax as an input tax credit.

The self-assessment process described above is generally understood and complied with at the business level; however, it is neither well understood nor much used at the consumer level. Consequently, most of the tax revenue loss results from an increased level of purchasers who acquire products electronically from non-residents who are not registered to collect Canadian consumption taxes.

Generally, registration for GST is required of residents who are making taxable supplies in Canada in the course of a commercial activity (subject to a threshold rule for small suppliers). Registration is not required if a non-resident is not carrying on business in Canada. A non-resident will be required to register if contracts are concluded in Canada, or if the operations from which the profits arise are located in Canada. Registration is also required of non-residents who supply prescribed property, mainly publications, for delivery by mail or courier to a location in Canada.

Specific rules determine when a person is deemed a resident. If a non-resident has a permanent establishment (a fixed place of business through which supplies are made) in Canada, the non-resident will be considered a resident with respect to the activities carried out through that establishment. Consequently, not all parties who make supplies electronically to recipients in Canada will be required to register to collect Canadian consumption taxes. The options for tax collection under these circumstances are discussed in the Report.

4.3.5.2.2.   US state sales and use tax

Developments concerning US state tax laws have provided a fertile source of tax jurisdiction jurisprudence, particularly with respect to consumption tax issues. The decisions under state law do not govern US federal determinations, but nevertheless are instructive. The jurisdictional issues are analogous to those considered above in section 4.2.1.2.2 in connection with the federal income tax. With regard to state taxes, however, in personam jurisdictional concerns under the Due Process Clause[571] and inter-

---

[571]The Due Process Clause of the US Constitution provides: "No person shall . . . be deprived of life, liberty, or property, without due process of law." US CONST. amend. V. "[N]or shall any State deprive any person of life, liberty, or property without due process of law. . . ." US CONST. art. XIV, § 1.

state commerce concerns under the Commerce Clause[572] of the US Constitution, rather than US trade or business or "permanent establishment" concepts, set the limits for state jurisdiction to tax.[573] A taxpayer's connection or "nexus"[574] with a state must satisfy both of these constitutional concerns before the taxpayer will be subject to state and local tax laws.

Most US states collect revenue through a sales and use tax regime. A sales tax imposed by a state may be imposed on a sales transaction that takes place within that state. While the tax is imposed on the purchaser, it is the seller who is generally obligated to collect the tax imposed. In the absence of a remedial provision, the mere imposition of a sales tax by the purchaser's state could be easily circumvented by arranging for the sale to take place in the seller's state or a third state even though the purchased item is used in the purchaser's state. Consequently, states that impose a sales tax also impose a use tax for goods purchased outside the state that are used within the state. Like the sales tax, the use tax is imposed on the purchaser who uses the item in the state, but the obligation to collect the tax is imposed where Constitutionally permissible on the seller.

The US Supreme Court has ruled on several occasions that an individual US state cannot constitutionally impose a tax collection obligation on an out-of-state seller who has no physical presence, or nexus with, the taxing state.[575] In *National Bellas Hess, Inc. v. Department of Revenue,*[576] a Delaware mail-order corporation with a principal place of business in Missouri sent catalogs and fliers to Illinois residents by mail and common carrier. There were no other contacts with Illinois, and no agents or sales representatives operated in Illinois. The taxpayer did not have a local Illi-

---

[572]The Commerce Clause of the US Constitution provides that: "The Congress shall have power . . . [t]o regulate commerce with foreign Nations, among the several States, and with the Indian Tribes." US Const. art. I, § 8, cl. 3.

[573]Hellerstein, *Hellerstein's Telecommunications and Electronic Commerce: Overview and Appraisal,* available in LEXIS/NEXIS, 97 STN 37-43 at 36 (23 Feb. 1997).

[574]Nexus is usually created when a taxpayer has a presence and some minimum threshold level of activity within a jurisdiction.

[575]At issue is the Commerce Clause under Article I, section 8 of the US Constitution which, in part, "prohibits certain state actions that interfere with interstate commerce." *Quill Corp. v. North Dakota,* 504 US 298, 309 (1992). Also, *Bellas Hess,* 386 US 753, 756-60 (1967).

[576]*Bellas Hess,* 386 US 753 (1967).

nois telephone number. The Supreme Court struck down the Illinois use tax collection claim against Bellas Hess, ruling that the use tax collection requirement could only be upheld if Bellas Hess had a "physical presence" in Illinois, and use of the mail or common carrier in Illinois was insufficient.[577] In its consideration of the nexus requirement as an element of both constitutional clauses, the Court never indicated that there was any difference in the meaning of the nexus requirement under either clause.[578] However, in its most recent and significant nexus decision, *Quill Corp. v. North Dakota*,[579] the Supreme Court seemed to take a different view; its opinion distinguished the constitutional analyses of the Due Process and Commerce Clauses.

While the Due Process and Commerce Clauses are closely related in their impact on state taxing jurisdiction, *Quill* notes that, because they promote disparate goals, different nexus standards apply under each Clause.[580] Due Process Clause nexus is based on whether a taxpayer's connections with a state are substantial enough to legitimate the state's exercise of power over him.[581] As recently established in the Court's Due Process Clause analysis in *Quill*, this requirement is satisfied if: (a) there is a sufficient and purposeful direction of the taxpayer's activities aimed at a state's residents; and (b) there is a rational relationship between the tax imposed and the benefits the taxpayer received through access to the taxing state's market.[582] Physical presence is not necessary.[583]

Quill was a Delaware corporation with warehouses and offices in Illinois, California, and Georgia. Quill sold office supplies and equipment through catalogs, flyers, advertisements in national periodicals and trade

---

[577]*Id.* at 758.

[578]*See also, Trinova Corp. v. Michigan Dep't of Treasury,* 498 US 358, 373 (1991) (holding the Commerce Clause nexus requirement "encompasses as well the Due Process requirement that there be 'a "minimal connection" between the interstate activities and the taxing State . . .'").

[579]*Quill,* 504 US 298 (1992).

[580]The Commerce Clause serves to promote a stable national economy, while the Due Process Clause serves to insure notice and fair warning to the taxpayer.

[581]*Quill,* 504 US at 312.

[582]*Id.* at 308.

[583]Provided the out-of-state mail-order vendor purposefully directs its solicitation towards residents of the taxing State, "the requirements of due process are met irrespective of a corporation's lack of physical presence in the taxing State." *Quill,* 504 US at 308.

journals, and telephone solicitation of current customers. North Dakota sought to impose a use tax collection obligation on Quill for its sales to North Dakota customers which were delivered by mail or common carrier from out-of-state locations. A "use" tax complements a "sales" tax. A sales tax is imposed on customers who make purchases within the taxing jurisdiction. A use tax is imposed on customers within a taxing jurisdiction who make purchases outside the jurisdiction but "use" the good purchased within the taxing jurisdiction. While both sales and use taxes are imposed on customers, states rely for the most part on withholding by the sellers to enforce these taxes. Conceptually, sales and use taxes are collected only at the retail level while VAT is collected at each stage of production. However, both VAT and sales/use tax systems depend on withholding by sellers to enforce the substantive tax obligations.

In its opinion, the Court noted that the "substantial-nexus requirement" of the Commerce Clause is not the same as the "minimum contacts requirement," of the Due Process Clause and held all that was necessary to satisfy the Due Process standard was that Quill had "purposefully directed its activities at North Dakota residents."[584]

While the Due Process requirement may easily be met by traditional businesses, in the electronic commerce area it appears from recent cases that there has to be some purposeful activity on the part of a person in order to meet the due process requirement. In *Bensusan Restaurant Co. v. King*,[585] the owner of a nightclub in Missouri could not be sued in New York for trademark infringement where the only connection with New York was the owner's web page that could be viewed on browsers located in New York. The owner did nothing affirmatively to avail itself of the benefits of the New York market. In contrast, in *CompuServe, Inc. v. Patterson*,[586] a defendant that distributed software electronically through CompuServe, a major on-line service provider, was subject to a lawsuit in Ohio without a Due Process problem since CompuServe's computers were located in Ohio and the contract between the taxpayer and CompuServe was executed in Ohio.[587]

---

[584]*Id.*

[585] 937 F. Supp. 295 (S.D.N.Y. 1996).

[586]F.3d 1257 (6th Cir. 1996).

[587]However, these cases involved the limits of a state court to impose its jurisdiction on an out-of-state person, not the state's jurisdiction to tax. Steele, *Nexus at the*

Commerce Clause nexus focuses on burdens which the tax collection obligation imposes on interstate commerce, rather than on the fairness of imposing the obligation on the out-of-state vendor. For many years, the Supreme Court held that this meant that the Commerce Clause entirely prohibited states from taxing an interstate transaction.[588] However, after almost a century of being in and out of favor, that ruling met its final demise in *Complete Auto Transit, Inc. v. Brady.*[589] In *Complete Auto,* the Supreme Court determined that a sales or use tax satisfied the Commerce Clause of the US Constitution if the tax:

1. is "applied to an activity with a substantial nexus with the taxing State";
2. is "fairly apportioned";
3. does "not discriminate against interstate commerce"; and
4. is "fairly related to the service provided by the State.[590]

This four-part test was upheld by the Court in *Quill,*[591] which ruled that the substantial nexus requirement of the test's first prong required a physical presence in the state.[592] Therefore, in *Quill,* while the Supreme Court abandoned physical presence as the standard of Due Process Clause

---

Dawn of the Electronic Commerce Revolution, available in LEXIS/NEXIS, 97 STN 67-37 at 18-20 (8 April 1997).

[588]*Leloup v. Port of Mobile,* 127 US 640, 648 (1888) (declaring that "no state has the right to lay a tax on interstate commerce in any form"); *Brown v. Maryland,* 25 US (12 Wheat.) 419 (1827).

[589]US 274 (1977). Complete Auto, a Michigan corporation, transported vehicles to dealers in Mississippi for General Motors, which assembled the vehicle outside Mississippi. The cars were shipped by rail into Mississippi where Complete Auto delivered the autos by truck to Mississippi dealers. Mississippi assessed a sales tax on proceeds of these transportation services.

[590]*Id.* at 279. The Court upheld the tax applied against Complete Auto. For a discussion of the second, third, and fourth factors of *Complete Auto, see Goldberg v. Sweet,* 488 US 252 (1989).

[591]*Quill,* 504 US at 310.

[592]The Court reaffirmed the "physical presence" test first expressed in *National Bellas Hess, Inc. v. Department of Revenue of Illinois,* 386 US 753 (1967).

nexus, the Commerce Clause nexus "physical presence" requirement was reaffirmed.[593] Relying on *Bellas Hess,* the Court found that Quill did not have a sufficient physical presence in North Dakota merely by use of the mail or common carriers to justify the imposition of a use tax collection obligation.[594] The Court also determined that the use of four floppy disks of Quill's proprietary software by a few customers in North Dakota did not satisfy the physical presence requirement. Consequently, an out-of-state mail order catalog company could not be required to collect the use tax imposed on North Dakota customers where the only contact with that state was the use of the mail and common carrier infrastructure.

The taxes at issue in both *Bellas Hess* and *Quill* were use taxes.[595] Whether the US Supreme Court would impose the same standard if the tax involved were an income tax imposed on an out-of-state mail order seller is still an open question.[596] It is possible that a higher Due Process standard may apply to a substantive income tax imposed on a nonresident compared

---

[593]*Quill,* 504 US 298 (1992).

[594]However, many of the reasons the Court gave "for adhering to the physical-presence standard [from *Bellas Hess*] relate principally, if not exclusively, to sales and use taxes on the mail-order industry." Hellerstein, *State Taxation of Electronic Commerce,* TAX L. REV. forthcoming). Thus, *Quill* could be read to have established a "bright-line" physical-presence standard only for sales and use taxes on the mail-order industry, relegating other industries and taxes to "the more flexible balancing analyses" the Court's "Commerce Clause jurisprudence now favors."

[595]Most states impose sales taxes on the sales of goods and services. Generally, retailers and vendors collect and then remit the taxes to the state taxing authority. See Arthur R. Rosen & Walter Nagel, Sales and Use Taxes: General Principles, Tax Mgmt. Multistate Tax Portfolios (BNA) No. 1300, Dec. 22, 1995, at 2. States can only impose a sales tax on intrastate sales transactions. States that impose a sales tax also impose a compensating "use tax" to ensure that residents who purchase goods in or from another state, but use them in-state, will pay the equivalent of a sales tax on the purchase in their state of residence. Committee on Multistate Tax Issues, New York State Bar Ass'n, Request on Guidance on the Application of New York's Sales and Use Taxes to Out-of-State Vendors ¶ 6, reproduced in 96 ST. TAX NOTES 47-47 (8 Mar. 1996).

[596]In previous cases, the Court implied that a higher degree of nexus is required to subject a non-resident taxpayer to direct tax liability than to impose an indirect use tax collection obligation. *See, e.g., Felt & Tarrant Manufacturing Co v Gallagher,* 306 US 62 (1939); *National Geographic Society v. California Board of Equalization,* 430 US 551 (1977).

with the imposed administrative function of collecting an in-state use tax, but it is more likely that it would be the Commerce Clause requirement that would bar a state from taxing internet commerce originating from an out-of-state server. The Supreme Court did address the Commerce Clause issue briefly in *Quill* stating that "[a]lthough we have not, in our review of other types of taxes, articulated the same physical-presence requirement that *Bellas Hess* established for sales and use taxes, that silence does not imply repudiation of the *Bellas Hess* [physical presence] rule."[597] However, since use tax collection requirements may be more burdensome than the imposition of an income tax, it is possible that the Supreme Court might not require "physical presence" in a state before the state can subject an out-of-state person to substantive income tax liability.

While the mere use of the mail or common carriers to make deliveries in a state may not provide sufficient nexus for tax burdens to be placed on residents of another state, the Supreme Court has ruled that it does not take much to establish the required physical presence for state and use tax collection. One way the jurisdictional nexus required for taxation of out-of-state sellers may be found to exist is under a "representational/agency" theory.[598] This concept is based upon Supreme Court cases finding that an out-of-state person had physical presence in the taxing state because it had in-state representatives or agents physically present in the taxing state.

In *National Geographic Society v. California Board of Equalization*,[599] the Court ruled that an out-of-state mail-order seller with two offices in California could be held responsible for collection of the California use tax on its mail-order sales delivered into the state by a common carrier. The fact that the offices conducted business that was unrelated to the mail-order business did not alter the Court's decision.[600] The Supreme Court's reasoning in *National Geographic Society* relied on several of its previous agency

---

[597]*Quill*, 504 US at 314. The Court did note that had *Bellas Hess* been decided "for the first time today," the physical presence requirement might not have been required by "contemporary Commerce Clause jurisprudence." *Id.* at 311.

[598]Grierson, *Constitutional Limitations on State Taxation: States and Use Tax Nexus on the Information Highway,* available in LEXIS/NEXIS, 96 STN 35-38 (21 Feb. 1996).

[599]US 551 (1977).

[600]The Court noted that substantial presence would not exist if the out-of-state seller only had the "slightest presence" in the taxing state. *National Geographic,* 430 US at 556.

case decisions.[601] In *Tyler Pipe Industries v. Washington State Department of Revenue*,[602] the Court held that a single sales representative in the taxing state, whether functioning as an agent or independent contractor, supported jurisdiction to impose a tax on wholesale sales to in-state customers.[603] In some circumstances, the US Supreme Court has expanded the agency concept even further for tax purposes to include "sales representatives" and "independent contractors" whose in-state activities are performed for the benefit of the seller with its knowledge but not necessarily under its direction and or with any specific "agency" authority from the seller in the traditional sense.[604]

States may rely on these agency cases to justify imposing use tax collection responsibilities or income tax liability on out-of-state residents who sell goods or services[605] in-state if arrangements have been made with

---

[601] *Scripto, Inc. v. Carson,* 362 US 207, 211 (1960) (nexus existed where taxpayer had "ten wholesalers, jobbers or 'salesmen' conducting continuous local solicitation" in the taxing jurisdiction); *Standard Pressed Steel v. Department of Revenue of Washington,* 419 US 560 (1975) (single employee of taxpayer in taxing state sufficient to uphold tax on out-of-state company's gross receipts from sales into the taxing state); *Felt & Tarrant Manufacturing Co. v. Gallagher,* 306 US 62 (1939) (in-state exclusive distributors provided sufficient nexus to impose use tax collection responsibilities on out-of-state seller); and *General Trading Co. v. State Tax Commission of Iowa,* 322 US 355 (1944) (traveling salespersons provided sufficient nexus for imposition of use tax collection responsibilities on out-of-state seller).

[602] US 232 (1987).

[603] *Id.* at 251.

[604] See *Multistate Tax Commission Nexus Program Bulletin 95-1 and commentary thereon,* ST. TAX NOTES 973 (March 25, 1996) and *MTC Nexus Bulletin 95-1 Goes Beyond Existing Law,* ST. TAX NOTES 1168 (15 April 1996), referring extensively to *Standard Pressed Steel Co. v. Department of Revenue,* 419 US 560 (1975), *Tyler Pipe Industries v. Washington State Department of Revenue,* 483 US 232 (1987), and *Scripto, Inc. v. Carson,* 362 US 207 (1960). The law is not clear whether such activities must be sales activities in order to trigger nexus. It is clear, though, that the absence of any agents, representatives, independent contractors, or other substantial physical presence prevents a state from obtaining taxing jurisdiction over an out-of-state seller. Interactive Services Association, *ISA Releases Report on US State Taxation of Online and Internet Services,* available in LEXIS/NEXIS, 97 TNI 7-24 at 24 (10 Jan. 1997) (citing *Quill,* 504 US 298 (1992).

[605] The nexus analysis applies to the interstate sale of services as well as products. See *Oklahoma Tax Commission v. Jefferson Lines,* 540 US 175 (1995) (citing *Goldberg v. Sweet,* 488 US 252, 262 (1989)).

telecommunications providers who have a physical presence in-state. Those telecommunications providers might be a company like America Online or a local, regional, or national internet service provider that might provide a means of advertising and/or local access nodes for the out-of-state seller. The Court in *Tyler Pipe* reasoned that "the crucial factor governing nexus is whether the activities performed in this state on behalf of the taxpayer are significantly associated with the taxpayer's ability to establish and maintain a market in this state for the sales."[606] These telecommunications providers, by making access to the in-state market possible, might satisfy the "market maintenance" standard in *Tyler Pipe*.[607]

State tax authorities have also aggressively pushed for expansion of several theories raised in US Supreme Court cases under which third-party activities related to the taxpayer's business may be attributed to the taxpayer for purposes of creating substantial nexus. Under the theory of attributional nexus, even if a corporation itself does not have sufficient presence in a taxing jurisdiction, the jurisdiction may assert nexus by attributing the presence or activity of another person or entity to the corporation.[608] Affiliate nexus, a subcategory of the attributional nexus concept, allows the nexus of one corporation to be imputed to a parent, subsidiary, or other affiliate, at least in some circumstances.[609] However, although several states have tried, none has successfully established taxing jurisdiction over an out-of-state seller on the basis of a relationship with an affiliate that already had a taxable nexus in the state.[610]

---

[606]*Tyler Pipe*, 483 US at 250.

[607]However, the location of these tangible or intangible contacts often will bear little relationship to the location of the essential economic activity that electronic commerce constitutes — the production and consumption of information. Hellerstein, *State Taxation of Electronic Commerce: Preliminary Thoughts on Model Uniform Legislation*, available in LEXIS/NEXIS, 97 STN 82-36, at 14 (29 April 1997).

[608]See, *e.g.*, *Scripto, Inc. v. Carson*, 362 US 207, 211 (1960); *Felt & Tarrant Manufacturing Co. v. Gallagher*, 306 US 62 (1939); *Tyler Pipe Industries v. Washington State Department of Revenue*, 483 US 232 (1987).

[609]*SFA Folio Collections, Inc. v. Tracy*, 652 N.E.2d 693 (Ohio 1995); *Bloomingdale's By Mail v. Commonwealth of Pennsylvania*, 567 A.2d 773 (Pa. Commw. Ct. 1989), *aff'd* 591 A.2d 1047 (1992); *SFA Folio Collections, Inc. v. Bannon*, 585 A.2d 666 (Conn. 1991).

[610]Reid, *Nexus and Electronic Commerce*, Multi-Jurisdictional Taxation of Electronic Commerce Symposium at 6 (5 April 1997) (referencing: *SFA Folio Collections, Inc. v. Tracy*, 652 N.E.2d 693 (Ohio 1995); *SFA Folio Collections, Inc. v. Bannon*, 585 A.2d 666

Economic presence nexus exists if an out-of-state seller's direction of regular and systematic sales solicitation efforts toward a state constitutes a substantial nexus with the state, thereby subjecting the seller to the use tax collection requirements of the state. Support for this doctrine was seen most recently in an argument raised by one of the parties in *Quill*. However, the Supreme Court rejected the argument, reaffirming its repudiation of the theory in *Bellas Hess* twenty-five years earlier.[611] It is likely that the states will present similar arguments and read cases like *Quill* narrowly and cases like *Tyler Pipe* broadly in their attempts to justify an expansion of state taxing authority over out-of-state internet vendors. For example, in the state arena a new theory has already arisen — the possibility that nexus can be established by the mere presence of intangible property within the state. This concept rests primarily on a single case, *Geoffrey, Inc. v. South Carolina Tax Commission*,[612] a state income tax case decided by the South Carolina Supreme Court.

In *Geoffrey*, South Carolina imposed a franchise tax on a nonresident whose only connection with the state was the licensing of various tradenames and trademarks in exchange for a royalty. The Supreme Court of South Carolina held that the licensing satisfied the minimum connection standard of both the Due Process and Commerce Clauses.[613] The court distinguished *Quill* as a use tax case, finding that economic presence, not physical presence, was required to establish income tax nexus. The court held that the economic presence requirement was fulfilled because Geoffrey had purposefully directed its activities at South Carolina's economic forum. Other states have already seized upon *Geoffrey* as presenting a potential theory for expanding their jurisdiction.[614]

In another case, *Orvis Company, Inc. v. Tax Appeals Tribunal*,[615] the court ruled that the "physical presence" requirement of *Quill* need not be

---

(Conn. 1991); *Current, Inc. v. [California] State Board of Equalization,* 29 Cal. Rptr. 2d 407 (1st Dist. 1994)).

[611]*Quill*, 504 US 298 (1992); *Bellas Hess,* 386 US 753 (1967).

[612]S.E.2d 13 (S.C.), *cert. denied,* 114 S. Ct. 550 (1993).

[613]The court ruled that the taxpayer "purposely directed" its activities towards the state even though the licensor had no business activities in the state when the license was entered into.

[614]Hawaii, Maine, Maryland, Missouri, New Hampshire, and Tennessee have reportedly asserted *Geoffrey* in audits of taxpayers. Steele, *supra* note 586, at 17.

[615]N.Y.2d 165 (1995).

"substantial."[616] Occasional visits by a mail order company's sales representatives to solicit orders from retailers, and periodic visits by a computer software and hardware developer's personnel to install software, train employees, and correct difficult or persistent problems, were held sufficient to establish the substantial nexus standards of *Quill.*[617] Under this reasoning, a computer software company that sends its representatives into a taxing jurisdiction to conduct business activities, such as the design and creation of a home page, may be creating nexus for sales and use tax purposes in the taxing jurisdiction.

Other states are also pushing the tax envelope. States have tried to impose a sales tax on the charges to customers for the receipt of electronic financial news and information, claiming that the "transient images" on the screen were tangible personal property.[618] The rental or leasing of computer hardware has provided the nexus for some states to attempt to impose a sales tax on customers receiving electronic information.[619] Some local taxing authorities have sought to impose a use tax on a customer's leasing of a remote database.[620] Even after *Quill,* it is difficult to reconcile cases focusing on the substantial nexus requirement.[621] And in the electronic commerce

---

[616]Direct solicitation by Vermont taxpayer's personnel in New York satisfied *Quill.*

[617]*Orvis,* 86 N.Y.2d 165 (1995).

[618]*Henley Holdings, Inc. v. Department of Revenue,* [2 Fla.] Tax. Rep. (CCH) ¶203-317 (No. 89-4381) (Fla. Cir. Ct. July 22, 1991), *aff'd sub nom,* 599 So. 2d 1282 (Fla. Dist. Ct. App. 1992) (summary judgement in favor of taxpayer); *Department of Revenue v. Quotron Systems, Inc.,* 615 So. 2d 774 (Fla. Dist. Ct. App. 1993) (upholding result in *Henley*).

[619]*Department of Revenue v. Quotron Systems, Inc.,* 615 So. 2d 774 (Fla. Dist. Ct. App. 1993) (leasing equipment was incidental; held, sales tax did not apply); *Quotron Systems, Inc. v. Comptroller of the Treasury,* 411 A.2d 439 (Md. Ct. App. 1980) (same); *Wisconsin Department of Revenue v. Dow Jones & Co., Inc.,* 436 N.W. 921 (Wis. Ct. App. 1989) ("true object" of providing teleprinters was the performance of a service; held, sales tax did not apply). Quotron at 777 ("The plain and common meaning of 'tangible personal property' does not include 'images on a video screen.'").

[620]*Meites v. City of Chicago,* 540 N.E. 2d 973 (Ill. App. Ct. 1989) (searches on out-of-state LEXIS/NEXIS database were considered as a taxable lease of tangible personal property).

[621]*See generally* Harris, *Advising the CyberBusiness: Applying Fundamental Tax Concepts to Internet Sales,* TAXES 709 (December 1996).

The substantial nexus test was satisfied in the following: *Dunhall Pharmaceuticals, Inc. v. Tracy,* 1995 Ohio Tax LEXIS/NEXIS 1289 (Ohio Bd. of Tax App. 1995) (in-state sales force); *Relton Corp. v. Washington Department of Revenue,* Docket No. 93-38

arena, states are likely to start arguing that with changes in technology and the imminent accompanying social and economic changes produced by the information highway, it is unrealistic to apply the physical presence rule to electronic transactions.[622]

Over the past two years, the Multistate Tax Commission (MTC), a quasi-governmental organization, has released several discussion drafts[623]

(Wash. Bd. of Tax App. 1996) (single, part-time out-of-state manufacturer's representative who called on in-state customers 3 or 4 times per year); *Orvis Co. v. New York Tax Appeals Tribunal,* 654 N.E.2d 954 (N.Y. 1995) (out-of-state salesmen visits potential customers occasionally resulting in less than 20 purchases totaling less than $2 million in total sales); *Edens ex rel. Telefile Computer Products, Inc.,* DTA No. 809607, TSB-D-96(19)S (N.Y. Tax App. Tribunal 1996) (sporadic visits by out-of-state field service personnel to install and maintain computer equipment); *Brown's Furniture, Inc. v. Wagner,* 665 N.E.2d 795 (Ill. 1996) (Missouri retailer made 1,000 deliveries in Illinois in a 10-month period, but maintained no Illinois property or operations); *Koch Fuels, Inc. v. Clark,* 676 A.2d 330 (R.I. 1996) (out-of-state company with no Rhode Island contacts made fuel deliveries to Rhode Island utilities using a common carrier); Ill. Priv. Ltr. Rul. No. 95-0339 (10 Aug. 1995) (in-state telephone solicitation firms working for an out-of-state manufacturer).

The substantial nexus test was not satisfied in the following: *Bloomingdale's by Mail, Ltd., v. Huddleston,* 848 S.E.2d 52 (Tenn. 1992) (mail order sales); *In re NADA Services Corp.,* No. 810592 (N.Y. Div. Tax App., 1 Feb. 1996) (20 in-state trips by independent contractors); Ill Priv. Ltr. Rul. No. 95-0346 (15 Aug. 1995) (broadcasting a national home shopping network on in-state television channels); *Care Computer Systems, Inc. v. Arizona Department of Revenue,* Docket No. 1049-93-S (Arizona Bd. of Tax App. 1995) (out-of-state taxpayer who sold computer software and hardware in Arizona did not have substantial nexus where two computers were leased to Arizona customers and sporadic visits were made by sales representatives).

For a sharp comparison of substantial nexus standards in a common fact pattern, compare *Pledger v. Troll Book Clubs, Inc.* 871 S.W.2d 389 (Ark. 1994) (no nexus) with *In re Scholastic Book Clubs, Inc.* 920 P.2d 947 (Kan. 1996) (nexus). In both cases, out-of-state publishers enlisted in-state teachers to solicit and receive book orders. For each order, the teachers received points redeemable for gifts for personal or school use. The different results are explainable by different agency standards in the two states.

[622]Grierson, *State Taxation of the Information Superhighway: A Proposal for Taxation of Information Services,* 16 Loy. L.A. Ent. L.J. 603, 646 (1996).

[623]Multistate Tax Commission, *Nexus Guideline for Application of a Taxing State's Sales and Use Tax to a Remote Seller,* preliminary draft, 25 Jan. 1995; Multistate Tax Commission, *Constitutional Nexus Guideline for Application of a State's Sales and Use Tax to an Out-of-State Business,* preliminary draft, 31 Jan. 1996; Multistate Tax Commission, *Constitutional Nexus Guideline for Application of a State's Sales and Use Tax to an Out-of-State Business,* 1 Nov. 1996; Multistate Tax Commission, *Constitutional Nexus Guideline*

of possible nexus guidelines for the application of sales and use tax laws to out-of-state businesses. These drafts are part of ongoing efforts by the MTC to explore the constitutional and practical limits of extending nexus to remote vendors. Many of the fact patterns explored by the MTC in its January 1996 draft related to electronic commerce.

According to the January 1996 draft, the physical presence requirement is satisfied by a telecommunications linkage associated with the ability of a business to establish and maintain a market in the taxing state. Thus, some of the internet-related business activities it set forth as possibly creating nexus for remote sellers are: (1) ownership, lease, use, or maintenance of computer terminals available for access in the taxing jurisdiction; (2) licensing of proprietary software in the taxing jurisdiction that facilitates use of the on-line service; (3) utilization of a 'cybermall' with a computer server in the taxing jurisdiction that performs various administrative and financial functions on behalf of the remote seller; (4) maintaining a telecommunication linkage by private contract in the taxing jurisdiction that permits the on-line service to establish and maintain a market in the taxing jurisdiction; (5) granting to an in-state person the right to broadcast programming within the taxing jurisdiction; and (6) performing or rendering electronic services in the taxing jurisdiction (*e.g.*, remote computer diagnostics and technical support constituting a 'taxable event').

It is not clear that many of these proffered nexus activities pass constitutional muster. The MTC itself deleted the illustrative examples regarding the internet and electronic commerce in its November 1996 draft, saying that it "temporarily deferred the examples to allow for further examination." However, they illustrate the far-reaching positions that some states may adopt as they attempt to assert their taxing jurisdiction over remote sellers which parallels some of the positions taken by European countries with respect to VAT jurisdiction.[624]

---

for Application of a State's Sales and Use Tax to an Out-of-State Business, initial public participation working group draft, 13 March 1997.

[624]*See supra* section 4.3.4. Further information regarding US state taxation and electronic commerce may be found in the following articles: Cowling & Ferris, *Internet Taxation Reviewed,* available in LEXIS/NEXIS, 97 STN 141-53 (23 July 1997); Hamilton, *US Internet Policy Finally Starts Grabbing Headlines,* available in LEXIS/NEXIS, 97 TNI 129-24 (7 July 1997); Hamilton, *Electronic Commerce Projects in the States: An Update,* available in LEXIS/NEXIS, 97 STN 90-57 (9 May 1997); Brownell, *California Income and Franchise Tax Issues for Electronic Commerce,* available in LEXIS/NEXIS, 97 STN 87-7 (6 May 1997); Hamilton, *Electronic Commerce: The Task Forces Take Shape,* available in

The same concerns that exist on the international front with respect to the implications of electronic commerce for tax systems are played out on the state and local level in the United States with respect to both the income tax and sales and use tax. Many of the state and local income tax issues do not directly correspond to international tax issues because of the reliance by states on a formulary system of allocating income. However, the issues raised by the application of sales and use tax principles within the individual US states are analogous to VAT issues raised in the international arena. While sales and use tax jurisprudence is grounded in the US Constitution, many of the US Constitutional requirements — such as the nexus requirement — find a counterpart under existing VAT legislation. Moreover, the concern of some that electronic commerce threatens source-based tax jurisdiction exists both in the state context and in the international context.

LEXIS/NEXIS, 97 TNI 85-33 (2 May 1997); Hamilton, *News Analysis: Toward More Cogent Policy on Electronic Commerce,* available in LEXIS/NEXIS, 97 TNT 82-5 (29 Apr. 1997); Anderson, *Texas Comptroller's Tax Policy Director Addresses Taxation of Internet — Care and Feeding of the Internet,* available in LEXIS/NEXIS, 97 STN 75-61 (18 Apr. 1997); Ashraf, *Virtual Taxation: State Taxation of Internet and On-Line Sales,* http://www.law.fsu.edu/lawreview/frames/243/ashrtxt.html; Hamilton, *US Lawmakers Introduce 'Internet Tax Freedom Act,'* available in LEXIS/NEXIS, 97 TNT 50-6 (14 March 1997); Eads & Houghton, *Cost Comments on White House Electronic Commerce Paper,* available in LEXIS/NEXIS, 97 STN 37-47 (25 Feb. 1997); Hamilton, *An Electronic Commerce Initiative: The White House Tackles the Beast,* available in LEXIS/NEXIS, 97 TNI 22-39 (3 Feb. 1997); Department of Taxation and Finance, *New York Tax Department Releases Report on Telecommunications Taxes — Improving New York State's Telecommunications Taxes,* available in LEXIS/NEXIS, 97 TNI 12-21 (17 Jan. 1997); Zorn, *Whither Telecommunications Tax Reform?,* available in LEXIS/NEXIS, 96 STN 248-44 (24 Dec. 1996); Information Technology Association of America, *Information Technology Association Issues Paper on Internet Taxation — Straight Talk: Internet, Tax and Interstate Commerce,* available in LEXIS/NEXIS, 96 STN 247-45 (23 Dec. 1996); Hamilton, *States, Industry Consider Seeking US Federal Law on Nexus and Electronic Commerce,* available in LEXIS/NEXIS, 96 TNI 235-26 (5 Dec. 1996); Hamilton, *Uniform State Taxation of Electronic Commerce Urged,* available in LEXIS/NEXIS, 96 TNI 223-9 (18 Nov. 1996); Stein, *US District Court for New York Rules Advertisement on Internet Does Note Establish Nexus,* available in LEXIS/NEXIS, 96 STN 195-52 (7 Oct. 1996); Baker, *State Taxation of On-Line Transactions,* http://www.us.net/~Steptoe/221277.htm; Blum, Comment, *State and Local Taxing Authorities: Taking More Than Their Fair Share of the Electronic Information Age,* 14 J. Marshall J. Computer & Info. L 493 (1996); Edson, *Quill's Constitutional Jurisprudence and Tax Nexus Standards in an Age of Electronic Commerce,* 49 Tax Law. 893 (1996); Hanlon, *MTC Examines Making (Tax) Money on the Internet,* 9 St. Tax Notes 408 (1995).

5

Conclusions and Policy Approaches

The identification and analysis *de lege lata* of the interjurisdictional issues posed by electronic commerce is one thing. The formulation *de lege ferenda* of domestic and treaty policies for dealing with electronic commerce is another, even more controversial challenge. This section will focus on possible approaches to devising an appropriate framework for taxing international electronic commerce.

Any approach must reflect the following considerations: interpersonal and international equity, economic efficiency and competitive neutrality, international acceptance, tax effectiveness, simplicity, low compliance costs, legal certainty and coherence and flexibility in keeping pace with technological and structural development. The OECD document *Dismantling the Barriers to Global Commerce* applies these considerations to electronic commerce as follows: "Whatever the solution adopted, the taxation of e-commerce should be relatively simple, should facilitate voluntary compliance, should not artificially advantage or disadvantage e-commerce over comparable commerce and should not necessarily hinder the development of e-commerce." The document also points to the need for protecting the tax base and of finding international agreement.

Different policy approaches, hereinafter considered, have been put forth in response to these challenges. Some are described in national government reports and official advisory commissions, others in the reports and discussion drafts of international organizations, in particular:

- EC Commission, *A European Initiative in Electronic Commerce* (Green Paper), Com. (97), 15 April 1997.

- EC Commission Communication, *E-Commerce and Indirect Taxation,* Com (98) 374 final, 17 June 1998; the contribution by the EC and its Member States on indirect tax issues for the OECD Ministerial Conference, *A Borderless World: Realizing the Potential of Electronic Commerce,* in Ottawa on 6-8 October 1998.
- European Ministerial Conference (Ministers from EC, of European Free Trade Association, Central and Eastern Europe and Cyprus), *Global Information Networks: Realizing the Potential,* Bonn, July 1997.
- OECD, second conference held in Turku, Finland on 18 November 1997, *Dismantling the Barriers to Global Electronic Commerce* (hereinafter OECD-Turku document).
- OECD Committee on Fiscal Affairs, *Electronic Commerce: the Challenges to Tax Authorities and Taxpayers. An informal Round Table Discussion between Business and Government* (hereinafter OECD-CFA discussion draft, preparing the Turku conference).
- United States Department of the Treasury, Discussion paper, *Selected Tax Policy Implications of Global Electronic Commerce,* November 1996; Executive Office of the President of the United States, *A Framework of Global Electronic Commerce,* 1 July 1997.
- Japan, Electronic Commerce Strategy, *Towards the Age of the Digital Economy for Rapid Progress in the Japanese Economy and World Economic Growth in the 21st Century,* May 1997.
- Australian Taxation Office, Electronic Commerce Project, *Tax and the Internet,* August 1997.
- Canada, a Report to the Minister of National Revenue from the Minister's Advisory Committee on Electronic Commerce, *Electronic Commerce and Canada's Tax Administration,* April 1998.
- Report to the Underminister of Finance from the Dutch Advisory Committee, *Notitie belastingen in een wereld zonder afstand,* May 1998.

The debate over how international tax principles ought to be reevaluated and maybe reformed to cope with electronic commerce is still in its formative stages. While it is true that some businesses at the vanguard of the digital revolution may already be engaged in substantial electronic commerce, for the most part the growth of electronic commerce, which is still in its infancy, will continue to be a steady rather than "bursty" phenomenon.[625] In keeping with evolutionary development of commercially feasible technology solutions, perhaps taxing authorities should proceed in a steady, principled manner to make whatever changes are necessary to existing international tax norms.[626] Starting with incremental steps or measures to accommodate the rise of electronic commerce does not preclude making more significant changes in the future if necessary.

Electronic commerce with its own futuristic vocabulary, including terms such as "cyberspace", can at times carry us away with its exotica. Many commentators, including the authors of this report, have talked about transactions taking place "in cyberspace" as if cyberspace refers to a foreign planet or outer space. Satellite communications aside, electronic commerce takes place here on earth. Transactions taking place in "cyberspace" are taking place in some country. Servers, routers, switches, and "pipes" (*e.g.*, telephone wires and cables) are located somewhere on this planet. To the extent that international tax principles allocate taxing authority among countries, those rules could be applied to income from electronic commerce. The difficulty is not that cyberspace is some otherworldly realm but rather that an international consensus has yet to develop concerning how to determine in what country income from electronic commerce is produced.

Perhaps the most fundamental threat to the international tax system posed by electronic commerce is the erosion of the worldwide tax base. Because technological advances have made certain business functions more mobile, it is increasingly possible for a company to try to divert income to a tax haven by locating servers there. It also is increasingly possible given current residency tests to render a company a resident of a tax haven. As suggested below, these possibilities may require a re-examination of the rules governing CFCs as well as the rules governing residence. The threat to the tax base is not just an income tax phenomenon. To the extent that non-VAT countries sell to VAT countries electronically, it grows increasingly difficult for VAT countries to protect their tax bases.

---

[625]The actual technological advances may indeed be episodic, but their implementation in the commercial world takes time and tends to be more measured.

[626]The German IFA Branch has noted: "The development of electronic commerce constitutes merely a change in the way in which international business is conducted, it is not a revolution, which requires introduction of a new tax regime." German IFA Branch (Portner), *Comments on Electronic Commerce Report* (5 May 1998) (on file with the authors).

Even if it is determined that there is no threat to the overall tax base or that the threat can be dealt with by adjusting current international tax norms, claims on the existing tax base may be altered as a result of the rise of electronic commerce. The growth of electronic commerce may signal an economic realignment of the role of source and resident countries compared with their roles in traditional commerce.[627] A typical traditional commercial transaction might involve R Corp., a country R company, producing goods in country R and marketing and selling the goods through a country S permanent establishment or subsidiary. In this scenario, country S might tax income attributable to the permanent establishment or subsidiary, and country R might tax any income attributable to the production process. Countries have relied on this basic division of tax jurisdiction for most of the 20th century. To the extent that electronic commerce replaces traditional commercial patterns, the tax balance between countries is threatened. Through the use of the internet, R Corp., which still may produce its goods in country R, now can market and execute sales in country S without the need for a presence in country S. Even if R Corp. must maintain a presence in country S, it is likely that the presence will be much more limited and that the income attributable to such a presence will likewise be limited. Consequently, the balance between country S and country R with respect to imposing income tax on R Corp.'s income or VAT on its sales may be altered as a result of the growth of electronic commerce.

For example, in a traditional commercial transaction, suppose that R Corp., a country R company, spends 500 to produce its inventory which it sells through a permanent establishment in country S. R Corp. also incurs 500 of production and marketing expenses that are attributable to the permanent establishment. R Corp. sells a unit of inventory for 1800. Assuming that an arm's length price for the manufactured inventory is 900, then country S may tax 400 of net income attributable to the permanent establishment. Country R may also tax 400 of net income. Suppose instead, that as a result of marketing and distribution over the internet, the production and marketing expenses are reduced to 200 because there is no need for a physical presence in country S (*e.g.*, a retail establishment, country S employees). Suppose that in light of the reduced marketing expenses, competition reduces the price that R Corp. can command for a unit of its

---

[627] *See e.g.*, Discussion Report of the German Tax Office Electronic Commerce Project, *Tax and the Internet* (August 1997).

inventory to 1200. If there is no permanent establishment in country S, then country R may tax the entire 500 of net income.[628] While the per unit profit for the inventory may, in some cases, decrease as a result of electronic commerce, R Corp. may in fact make up for that decrease by increased sales at the reduced price. If that occurs, all of R Corp.'s profits are subject to tax in country R whereas a traditional commercial transaction would have allowed country S to tax 50% of R Corp.'s profit.

Even if R Corp. is deemed to have a permanent establishment in country S (*e.g.*, because R Corp. locates a server in country S), that determination by itself does not restore country S's base to that which existed under traditional commerce. In the example above, R Corp. would generate 1200 of gross income that is attributable to R Corp.'s permanent establishment in country S. The expenses incurred by the permanent establishment in producing the income would consist of 200 of marketing expenses and a 900 deemed, arm's length payment to R Corp.'s home office. Accordingly, on a per unit basis, country S may be able to tax 100 of net income while country R will tax 400 of net income.[629] If R Corp. earns the same total income from its sales, country S has taxing authority over 20% of the income rather than taxing authority over 50% of the income which was the case under the more traditional mode of commerce.

Any change in the balance of taxing authority between country R and country S under existing international tax principles may lead countries — particularly those likely to be source countries (*i.e.*, country S) — to call for new international tax principles or at least for a reinterpretation of existing tax principles in a manner that will restore the preexisting tax equilibrium. A consideration of the political factors that might motivate such a call is beyond the scope of this report. The following discussion will present, however, a number of possible approaches to the issues raised by electronic commerce.

---

[628]R Corp. has income equal to 1200 of gross income minus 500 production expense and 200 of marketing expense.

[629]R Corp. has income equal to 1200 of gross income minus 500 production expense and 200 of marketing expense. If country R is an exemption country, then country R can tax 100 of income. The same result obtains if R Corp. is a credit country if country S's tax is creditable and the country S effective tax is equal to or greater than the country R effective rate.

5.1. INCOME TAX

5.1.1. Source-based versus residence-based taxation — a new balancing of taxing authority

5.1.1.1. *Taxation based on source*

Perhaps the central international tax issue arising out of electronic commerce is the allocation of business profits between the residence and source countries and leakage to tax havens. If R Corp. sells goods or services to customers in country S, determining whether R Corp. has a permanent establishment in country S may be the key issue in determining whether country S has any taxing authority over the business profits. Set forth below are a list of different possibilities for allocating taxing authority between country S, the source state, and country R, the residence state, with respect to R Corp.'s electronic commerce activities. The possibilities are set forth without recommendation and recognizing that some of the possibilities may not be practical. Nevertheless, an approach which one country may dismiss as impractical may be seen by another country as necessary in order to fairly allocate profits generated through electronic commerce.

5.1.1.1.1. Status quo

Inertia has its benefits. Often the devil we know is preferable to the devil we do not know. The permanent establishment concept has been a mainstay of international tax law for approximately 70 years. Notwithstanding inevitable disputes about what constitutes a permanent establishment, the permanent establishment concept has served the international community well.[630] Applying current permanent establishment principles to electronic commerce most likely would favor residence state taxation.[631] There is no reason for R Corp. to locate a server in country S even if the customers are there. The server can be located in country R, in a low-tax offshore jurisdiction or "out of this world" in orbit. Consequently, keeping

---

[630]It is the sense of many IFA member countries that current principles with some minor modifications can meet the challenge of electronic commerce. *See e.g.,* German IFA Branch (Portner), *Comments on Electronic Commerce Report* (5 May 1998) (on file with the authors); U.S.A. IFA Branch, *Comments on Electronic Commerce Report* (5 May 1998) (on file with the authors).

[631]US Treasury Report, *supra* note 217.

current permanent establishment principles and faithfully applying them would favor residence state taxation for companies that have traditionally sold goods and performed services through a permanent establishment but can now conduct the same business over the internet.

Even if R Corp. locates the server in country S., the server may not constitute a permanent establishment, particularly if the server is only facilitating preparatory and auxiliary activities. Even if the server would constitute a permanent establishment, it seems likely that the income "attributable to" that permanent establishment will be much less than would be attributable to the same business conducted through a traditional "bricks and mortar" permanent establishment. That is, as the cost of marketing and sales goes down, the profits allocated to those functions may also decrease. Compared with an investment in a retail presence, a marketing and sales staff, and other marketing and sales requirements, the cost of a server may not justify country S in taxing a significant level of business profits.

Others will disagree with this approach and argue that inertia (status quo) is not an available option, given the fast growing significance of electronic commerce, and the impact of its special characteristics, which was not considered when the rules of international income taxation were designed. Some who think that electronic commerce will require changes in taxing rules think that it is premature to consider such changes at this point with electronic commerce in its infancy.[632] Under this view, only when we have gained some experience with the tax problems associated with electronic commerce should change be considered.

5.1.1.1.2. Enhanced residence-based taxation

As early as 1819 the Netherlands exempted from the business tax (patentrecht) foreign ships of countries which made reciprocal allowances.[633] The first shipping treaty in 1843 between France and Belgium also exempted shipping from source-based taxation.[634] World War I led to similar legislation, with the United States abandoning source-based taxa-

---

[632]*See e.g.,* German IFA Branch (Portner), *Comments on Electronic Commerce Report* (5 May 1998) (on file with the authors).

[633]Seligman, Double Taxation and International Fiscal Cooperation 52 (1928).

[634]*Id.*

tion of shipping enterprises from foreign countries with reciprocal provisions.[635] The exclusive residence state taxation of shipping profits found favor in the early League of Nations efforts that ultimately resulted in Article 8 of the current OECD Model treaty. Air navigation was added to shipping in 1928.[636]

Article 8, which denies taxing authority to a source state with respect to shipping or air transport profits, was born out of a recognition that the peripatetic nature of shipping and air transport would mean that enterprises conducting such business might be subject to tax in multiple jurisdictions with the attendant likelihood of double taxation. Accordingly, under the OECD Model, taxing authority is limited to the Contracting State in which the place of effective management of the enterprise is situated.

Some may look to Article 8 as an analog for the concept that profits generated by electronic commerce should be taxable only in the residence state. Once a company establishes an internet presence (e.g., a web site), customers throughout the world that are connected to the internet can access that site. Like shipping or air transport, electronic commerce has the potential of eliciting multiple taxation because of the number of countries that may be involved. Article 8 principles could apply to income generated by both internet service providers and content providers.[637] Alternatively, the principles of Article 8 might be extended solely to internet service providers, which like shipping and air transport companies, may provide internet communications globally.

Where Article 8 deals specifically with shipping and air transport and may be based on specific jurisdictional fictions (ship/aircraft constitutes territory), the application of the analogous reasoning would probably warrant a separate treaty provision which would deal with electronic commerce and would carve such business income out from the scope of Articles

---

[635]*Id.*

[636]THE JOINT COMMITTEE ON INTERNAL REVENUE TAXATION, 4 LEGISLATIVE HISTORY OF UNITED STATES TAX CONVENTIONS 4170 (1962).

[637]Article 8 principles could also apply to telecommunications companies. However, telecommunications companies generally have more of a physical presence in source countries (*i.e.,* telecommunications infrastructure) than do internet service providers or content providers. In some cases, telecommunications companies may not have a strong physical presence in source countries as the increasing use of telecommunications satellites may lessen the need for physical infrastructure.

7 and 5 dealing with conventional ways of doing business and generating profits.

Some might suggest that the problems posed by electronic commerce are just the tip of the iceberg. The underlying problem is the challenge created by attempting to allocate taxing jurisdiction between residence and source states in a global economy. Inevitably, double taxation results from conflicting jurisdictional claims. Because of the difficulty of determining what income arises in the source state, assigning exclusive taxing authority to residence countries may offer the hope of avoiding double taxation. This possibility essentially takes the Article 8 analog and applies it not only to income from electronic commerce, but all income. This proposal has a better chance of acceptance from developed countries which can rely on residence to provide a sufficient tax base. Developing countries may not have that luxury. Taxing the profits of electronic commerce is another possibility. This proposal should be considered for the same reasons that led Mr. A. Wiedow, Tax Director at the European Commission, to consider it for mobile income in a Community and global context:

> The initiatives the Commission has taken, either by way of the Parent/Subsidiary Directive or the proposal on interest and royalties, demonstrate quite clearly the kind of withholding taxes we would like to abolish. They are those withholding taxes which add to the normal taxation in the country of residence of the beneficiary. Historically, the justification for giving a share of the residence State's taxation right to the source country was based on the consideration that the economic activity had taken place in the source country and that the country of residence had only provided the capital or know-how. However, this sharing of taxation rights is out of date in a worldwide, 'global' economy and this is reflected in the general tendency towards a reduction of withholding taxes between industrialized countries (. . .) This is why the author is personally convinced that a real Internal Market implies that it is taxed exclusively in just one Member State.[638]

Of course, such a rule, applied in an ordinary international context, would be a radical shift of taxing authority as we now know it. Taxing authority would move from source countries to residence countries. Placing all taxing authority in the residence country would eliminate conflicting

---

[638]Wiedow, A., *To withhold or not to withhold*, EUROPEAN TAXATION 294 (September 1994).

claims. Aside from problems relating to the distribution of tax revenue, this exclusive residence-based possibility places great emphasis — which may not be warranted — on the definition of residence. The same forces that question the permanent establishment concept, and other source-based taxation concepts, also call the adequacy of the residence concept into question — particularly the residence of a company.[639] If the definition of residence is artificial and easily manipulated, granting exclusive taxing authority to residence countries is not a good solution. Moreover, for an exclusive residence-based system to function smoothly, there would have to be international consensus concerning the definition of residence. This may not be easy to accomplish.

5.1.1.1.3. Enhanced source state taxation

The possibility of moving to a system of taxation based exclusively on source has been explored by Professor Klaus Vogel, who set forth the historical lineage of this basis for international taxing jurisdiction.[640] This view is based on the concept that it is the "place of income-generating activity"[641] rather than the jurisdiction where the income producer resides

---

[639]Lambooij, *Rethinking corporate residence,* Symposium on the Internet and the Taxation of International Electronic Commerce, Leiden 6 June 1997, http://www.lovotax.nl/tax/onderwerp5.

[640]*See* Vogel, *Worldwide vs. Source Taxation of Income — A review and re-evaluation of arguments (I-III),* 8-9 INTERTAX 216 (1988), 10 INTERTAX 310 (1988), 11 INTERTAX 128 (1988). Professor Vogel credits Georg von Schanz as being one of the early writers advocating economic allegiance based on business and economic activities; he proposed that the source state should levy its tax at ¾ of the normal rate and the residence state should levy its tax at ¼ the normal tax rate. Vogel also points out that Latin America has historically emphasized territoriality in its tax system. *See e.g.,* First Latin American Tax Law Convention, "Declaration of Principles" (1956). On the international front, the International Chamber of Commerce adopted a resolution advocating that the source state have "the sole right" to tax international income. *See* International Chamber of Commerce, *Avoidance of Double of Taxation: Exemption versus Tax Credit Method,* Resolution of ICC Council and Report of Commission on Taxation (1955). The International Fiscal Association also considered this concept favorably in 1961 and 1984.

[641]Musgrave & Musgrave, *Inter-Nation Equity* in MODERN FISCAL ISSUES: ESSAYS IN HONOR OF CARL S. SHOUP 71 (1972).

that economically contributes to the production of income and should be compensated for that contribution. Those who believe technological change wreaks more havoc with the definition of residence than with the effect on the determination of source may find the exclusive source-based approach promising. As many companies continue to become global enterprises, the accuracy of determining the place of effective management declines. There may not be a single locus where management decisions are made. They may be made in many jurisdictions or through video conferencing in cyberspace (*i.e.,* in a jurisdiction or jurisdictions that cannot easily be determined). Perhaps focusing on where income-generating activity takes place offers a better chance for international taxing authorities to collect an appropriate tax and not inflict double taxation on entrepreneurs. Aside from any difficulties in determining residence, some countries may favor exclusive source state taxation because they are more likely to provide markets for consumption than they are likely to be places where entrepreneurs reside.

In the absence of any change in the definition of a permanent establishment or if Article 8 (of the OECD Model) principles were expanded to apply to income from internet activities, source countries may forego taxing authority over income generated by electronic commerce. Not surprisingly, those countries that see themselves as markets for electronic commerce (*i.e.,* source countries) rather than as residence countries for electronic commerce entrepreneurs will almost certainly push hard to assert a taxing right over some of the profits generated by this new and profitable means of conducting business.

Source countries that find current international tax principles too confining might look to Article 17 of the OECD Model as an analog for the taxation of electronic commerce. Article 17, which applies to artistes and sportsmen, authorizes source state taxation even in the absence of a permanent establishment in the source state. The justification for this treaty provision is a recognition that artistes and sportsmen are able to earn large incomes from source countries even though the artistes and sportsmen do not have a permanent establishment anywhere. For example, a popular rock-and-roll band in country R on a two-week tour in country S can earn millions of dollars, even though the band does not earn its income through a fixed place of business in country S. By analogy, some countries might view entrepreneurs engaged in electronic commerce in the same way. R Corp. may be able to sell its goods or services to country S customers, earning significant income, even though R Corp. has no permanent establishment in country S. Like the rock-and-roll band, R Corp. is able to move around in country S and reach customers without having a fixed place of business. Some countries may look to Article 17 principles to reach otherwise unreachable business profits generated by electronic commerce.[642]

Here again the analog reasoning does not mean that profits of electronic commerce would actually be brought within the limited scope of Article 17 but means that the same principles of source taxation would be applied to it in a separate article which would distinguish profits derived from electronic commerce from profits generated by conventional ways of doing business, dealt with in Articles 7 and 5. The specific provision would also deal with income from the electronic exercise of independent professions. To make such a system workable, perhaps there would be a *de minimis* amount that would essentially replace the permanent establishment concept as a threshold. Entrepreneurs earning less than the *de minimis* amount in the source country would not be subject to source country taxation.

Of course a source-based system is not a miracle answer to the problem of double taxation of business profits. For this standard to work efficiently, there would have to be international understandings of how source is determined. From the perspective of source countries, switching to a source-based system may allow taxing authority over income generated by electronic commerce that arises in the source country but is not generated through a permanent establishment. Even if the substantive jurisdictional issues can be resolved through international understanding, there may be significant enforceability issues where a nonresident does not have a permanent establishment or other physical presence in a source state that essentially can serve as collateral for any tax liability.[643]

---

[642]There may be enforcement difficulties of expanding the Article 17 concept to electronic commerce. It is often the case that a promoter resident in the source state is in a position to collect a withholding tax on nonresident artistes or sportsmen. There is no comparable withholding agent in the case of electronic commerce.

[643]Discussion Report of the Australian Tax Office Electronic Commerce Project, *Tax and the Internet* (August 1997).

5.1.1.1.4. Adapting the permanent establishment concept

Perhaps a better approach to the challenge of extending source taxation of the profits of international electronic commerce is that of adapting the permanent establishment concept.[644] The permanent establishment concept was designed some 100 years ago in a physical economy. It connoted a structure of "bricks and mortar" at a geographic point in the territory of the taxing state. The history of the concept is described by Professor Skaar.[645] The expression "stehendes Gewerbe" (trade with fixed place of business) first emerged in the mid-nineteenth century when it designated full-source taxation as a remedy against double taxation in Prussia's inter-municipal relations. The German judiciary introduced the requirements of a fixed physical location ("Betriebstätte") and of a recognizable business activity in the source state. Both requirements became the core elements of the permanent establishment concept, introduced in the first general international tax treaty between Austria-Hungary and Prussia (1899). At that time, it designated full source state jurisdiction.

In the 1923 report of its Group of Economists, its 1927 draft and 1946 London Model, the League of Nations imposed a permanent establishment test for source taxability because "it is extremely difficult to tax foreign enterprises efficiently and equitably when they do not possess a permanent establishment in a country." The Fiscal Committee of the OECD favored residence state taxation by the permanent establishment definition, in its 1963 Model Convention. Its requirements of fixed place of business and recognizable activity became increasingly restrictive as businesses became more mobile and technology more advanced.

The development of the permanent establishment as a jurisdictional framework for source taxation of business profits was not acceptable to

---

[644]It is accomplished either by an expansive interpretation of the existing definition or by an overt revision of that definition.

[645]SKAAR, *Permanent Establishment. Erosion of a Tax Treaty Principle* in SERIES ON INTERNATIONAL TAXATION, Kluwer VOL. 13 (1991). The discussion that follows is taken from Hinnekens, *Looking for an Appropriate Jurisdictional Framework for Source-State Taxation of International Electronic Commerce in the Twenty-first Century,* 26 Intertax, 192 (1998).

everybody. In its 1955 policy resolution, the International Chamber of Commerce justified the change in its traditional preference for residence state taxation in favor of extensive source state taxation as follows: "The claim of the country of residence to tax income derived from the country of origin rests largely on historical grounds which are out of keeping with existing conditions; at the most the country of residence is only entitled to a proportionate share of the total tax of the income which is commensurate with the contribution it makes to the production of the income." Other signals pointed to a reevaluation and erosion of the permanent establishment concept, such as the 1980 Model Convention of the Group of Experts of the United Nations introducing permanent establishment fictions in the rules governing business relationships between developed and developing countries. In the Andean Pact Model, the permanent establishment was only one example of source taxation of business profits. Moreover, some treaties between industrialized countries (*e.g.,* between the United Kingdom and Norway) provide for extensive source state taxation of the business profits of petroleum-related offshore industries, thereby deleting the requirement of fixed place of business.

The OECD Commentary concerning automated vending or gaming equipment concludes that the presence of personnel is not necessary.[646] Examples of a permanent establishment, without personnel, have been found in a German case, Belgian case law (real estate companies owning, leasing or selling property) and some treaties (dealing with insurance companies selling policies in the other Contracting State).

Those definitions and interpretations point to a process involving a reevaluation of the permanent establishment concept that questions the requirement of a fixed place of business in the ethereal world of business in cyberspace. The issue of the permanent establishment concept in the transition from the physical to the digital economy is recognized and taken seriously in the OECD-CFA Discussion Draft (1997): "This development is an occasion to step back and evaluate the rules of Articles 5 and 7 (on the definition of, and allocation of income to, permanent establishments) and consider whether they are appropriate for purposes of taxing electronic commerce or whether refinements or changes are in order. Electronic commerce constitutes an environment where automated functions, by their very nature, can undertake a significant amount of business activity in a

---

[646]OECD Commentary, Art. 5, para 10

source jurisdiction with little or no physical activity in that jurisdiction. These are questions that the Working Group on Permanent Establishment is exploring." (para. 103).

History has thus shown that there is nothing sacred about the legacy of the permanent establishment as a fixed place of business in a changing economy. It started with the idea of taxation of business profits on the basis of economic allegiance to the taxing state and distinguished (taxable) core business activities from ancillary activity. A possible policy approach to the taxation of profits from electronic commerce is, therefore, to re-invent or re-source the permanent establishment concept and look for a permanent establishment fiction, e.g., a virtual permanent establishment. This permanent establishment fiction would lower the threshold by deleting the requirement of fixed place of business and by adapting the scope of the excluded ancillary activities. The OECD-CFA discussion draft points to this challenge of redefining the delimitations of auxiliary versus core business activity when it is carried out over the internet. It does so in the following terms:

> The question has to be addressed with respect to the various functions that can be automated, such as advertising, ordering, payment, storage and digital delivery as well as with respect to various combinations of these functions. It also requires a determination of the extent to which a data base of digital contents may be said [to be] a stock of goods and, if that is the case, whether the data base may be said to be maintained solely for the purpose of storage, display or delivery if it also has a search and reporting facility. (para. 97).

Many governments and tax experts will not agree with this "virtual permanent establishment" approach. It raises a number of problems.

1. Some take the view that the advent of electronic commerce is merely a further step in an ongoing natural process of economic development which does not warrant a change in the jurisdictional tax rules, e.g., permanent establishment.[647] Query whether the acceleration of the trend involving the erosion of source state taxation makes it acceptable to electronic commerce net importing states who, as electronic commerce grows, lose income tax revenues. Instead of being located in industrialized coun-

---

[647]German IFA Branch (Portner), *Comments on Electronic Commerce Report* (5 May 1998) (on file with the authors).

tries of residence, the profits may flee to tax havens with the help of the new technologies.

The tax base, to the extent it is based on traditional international tax notions, appears to be eroding. The extent of the erosion may be an important consideration in the evaluation of any change in the permanent establishment rule.

2. The territorial theory of economic allegiance justifying the permanent establishment rule was developed in 1892 by Georg von Schanz.[648] In 1934, Allix, of France,[649] took over where von Schanz left off: whoever benefits from an economic community ought to pay tax to that community. This idea made much sense originally, when the economy was earthbound. It became difficult to apply when business became mobile and more difficult when it became digital. At this stage, reevaluation has become a political necessity. The problem is finding the basis of an agreement for sharing taxing authority, between the state of residence and of the state of source, which satisfies both electronic commerce exporting and importing states.

3. Professor Skaar suggests that the permanent establishment treaty rule may be sufficiently flexible to permit treaty partners to interpret the permanent establishment concept in accordance with the need to respond to a digital economy. However, the need to re-invent the rule by deleting the fixed place of business requirement and redefining the scope of the exclusion of ancillary business would appear to require an overt change in the traditional rule. Such a treaty change would not be an easy process. At any rate, the proliferation of interpretations in national case law and bilateral treaty amendments would have an interim detrimental effect on international trade.

An interpretation by the OECD Committee of Fiscal Affairs would be a practical and tactical approach. The Committee could include a discussion of electronic commerce in its aforementioned Commentary.[650] However, depending on the outcome of the reevaluation, a definition of a

---

[648]Von Schanz, *Zur Frage der Steuerpflicht,* 9 Finanzarchiv 356 (1892).

[649]Allix, *La Condition des Etrangers au Point de vue fiscal,* 61 RdC (1937): "L'Etat a jurisdiction fiscale, en vertu de l'allégeance économique, sur tous ceux qui participent à sa vie économique ou sociale."

[650]OECD Commentary, Art. 5, para. 10.

different taxing nexus (permanent establishment fiction) may require a change in the present treaty definition of permanent establishment.

Even if the Committee cannot find a consensus among OECD Member States, individual states would still be free — through unilateral legislative action — to expand the scope of the permanent establishment definition as it applies to electronic commerce. The source state would thus deal with the erosion of its tax base if profits move to non-treaty countries, particularly tax havens. Currently, several countries bolster their domestic permanent establishment definition by extending it to activities which do not involve a fixed place of business, *e.g.*, the taxation of Andorra-based radio-broadcasting companies selling advertisement contracts for messages sent through the ether to French listeners.[651]

4. The challenge of adapting the permanent establishment threshold to a level which constitutes an appropriate jurisdictional framework for the source-based taxation of electronic commerce is a daunting task. How should the virtual permanent establishment be defined both from a conceptual and practical point of view? If it would no longer require a fixed place of business, it would still require a connection of the business to the territory of the source state that is sufficiently close, effective and rational. The term "business" is usually defined by reference to qualitative and quantitative criteria. A mere significant volume of sales in a market would not be sufficient to constitute a taxing nexus. The virtual permanent establishment would imply a continuous, purposeful, systematic and focused performance of core business activity in the market of the taxing country. The OECD-Turku document[652] hints at a solution: "Jurisdictional concepts based on physical geography, such as (. . .) permanent establishment, may require modifications to fit the world of electronic commerce (. . .) Consequently, computer servers or websites may have to be included in the notion of what constitutes a permanent establishment." Some commentators also make the argument — in the context of VAT — that websites should be deemed permanent establishments, when accessed, because they are copied to the user's immediate access storage. Similarly, a digital sales facility constitutes a domestic permanent establishment under certain circum-

---

[651]French Conseil d'Etat, 13 July 1968, No. 66503.

[652]OECD, second conference held in Turku, Finland on 18 November 1997, *Dismantling the Barriers to Global Electronic Commerce.*

stances, *e.g.*, if complete contractual performance is possible or if there is a certified supplier's identification code.[653]

However, the reevaluation of the permanent establishment concept in relation to electronic commerce would involve more than a simple test involving the location of a server with a commercial website. When, then, are the links sufficiently close, clear, effective, rational and politically acceptable to a sufficient number of electronic commerce importing and exporting countries?

A suitable permanent establishment definition (or fiction) should take the unique characteristics of electronic commerce into account. In particular, the productivity of the medium and the disintermediation permitting greater cooperation and contact in both business to business and business to customer relationships. The experience with the constitutional nexus necessary to legitimize a US state's authority to tax out-of-state vendors over the internet may be helpful in determining the nature and level of the connection. Harris reports that US courts examine Due Process nexus by asking the following three questions: "Did the taxpayer 'purposefully avail' itself of the benefits of a taxing state? Did the taxpayer's conduct and operations in the taxing State rise to a level where it should have reasonably anticipated being haled into court? Were the taxpayer's in-state activities a continuous and systematic part of its general business in the state?"[654]

5.   It is clear that an elaboration of this approach requires further study, experience and political acceptance. The same caveats also apply to the issue of determining the amount of profit generated by businesses under any new concept of international taxation. The interjurisdictional allocation of profits, including the benefits of increased group productivity resulting from information sharing, cooperation and centralized services, is particularly difficult with electronic commerce because of its vertical integration. The OECD-CFA discussion draft acknowledges this issue, in the case of business to business collaboration, as follows (para. 128):

> Through the information-sharing system and co-operative work system of the Internet and intranets, it is possible for many of the corporations within

---

[653]Dittmar & Selling, *How to Control Internet Transactions? A Contribution from the Point of View of German Tax Inspectors,* INTERTAX 88-92 (1998).

[654]Harris, *Advising the Cyberbusiness. Applying Fundamental Tax Concepts to Internet Sales,* TAXES 713 (1996).

a MNE group to act more like a division or segment of a single corporation (...) These ways of sharing workloads among related corporations in the form of collaborative projects can make it difficult to evaluate the contribution of each related corporation to the overall project. They also raise the issue of how to allocate any synergistic benefits among the participants in any such project.

5.1.1.1.5. Increased reliance on source state withholding

The rise of electronic commerce threatens to upset the tax balance that exists between importing and exporting states.[655] Consider a typical traditional transaction where R Corp., a resident of state R manufactures widgets in state R for sale to state S customers. After production, the widgets are transferred to a facility (*e.g.,* a retail establishment) in state S where a state S sales force markets and distributes the widgets to state S customers. By international consensus, the income that is produced by the sale of the widgets is allocated between states S and R so that state S has primary taxing authority with respect to the income attributable to the marketing and distribution in state S while state R has taxing authority with respect to the income attributable to the manufacturing.[656]

Now consider the same transaction in the world of electronic commerce. The widgets are still manufactured in state R but now can be marketed and sold to state S customers through an internet web page that might be located on a server in state R.[657] The goods would be shipped to state S customers and payment would be made electronically when the purchase was made. If the widgets were digital in nature (*e.g.,* investment ad-

---

[655]The discussion that follows is taken from Doernberg, *Electronic Commerce and International Tax Sharing,* Tax Notes Int'l 1016 (30 March 1998). For an explanation of the technical aspects of electronic commerce, *see* Abrams & Doernberg, *How Electronic Commerce Works,* Tax Notes Int'l 1573 (12 May 1997).

[656]These results can be achieved under the exemption or tax credit mechanisms. Essentially, under the exemption method, the income earned in state S is exempt from taxation in state R. Under the tax credit mechanism, R Corp. is taxable on worldwide income (*i.e.,* the income generated in state S) but R Corp. receives a tax credit against state R taxes for income tax paid in state S on the state S income.

[657]The R Corp. server could be located virtually anywhere with little difficulty. Indeed, it is not inconceivable that the server could be located on a satellite in orbit or that the data could easily moved from server-to-server.

vice, a video), delivery could be made through the internet. Of course, it has always been possible for R Corp. to sell to customers in state S without having a physical presence there. Sales through mail order or telephone order sales may permit R Corp. to penetrate markets in state S. However, the rise of electronic commerce through the internet makes it possible for out-of-state vendors such as R Corp. to reach customers in state S with greater ease and in far greater numbers than was previously possible. Accordingly, what may have been a *de minimis* trading pattern historically has become and will become a substantial trading pattern. Electronic commerce also in some cases allows the delivery of goods and services electronically which may result in a deemphasis of physical presence and also poses enforcement problems for tax administrators because of the lack of an audit trail.[658]

In the traditional transaction, the wealth (*i.e.,* increased widget value) that is created from manufacturing occurs in state R; the wealth that is created from marketing and sales occurs in state S. For example, suppose that R Corp. spends 100u to produce manufactured widgets that at the wholesale level have a fair market value of 300u. After spending 50u on marketing and sales, the goods are sold to retail customers for 500u. Of the 350u of wealth created (500u [sales proceeds] — 150u [costs]), 200u was created in state R and 150u was created in state S. Divided tax authority seems appropriate. In the digital transaction, all of the wealth is created in state R. Not only does the manufacturing take place there but programmers in state R have created the web page that facilitates the marketing, sales and payment functions. The only contribution of state S is the customer base.

The digital transaction poses a variation of the old philosophical conundrum: if a tree falls in the forest and no one hears it does it make a sound? In the electronic commerce context, the issue might be posed: if all widget value is created in state R but all the customers that determine value are in state S, where is the income generated? From an economic standpoint, one might suggest that only state R should have income taxing authority because all of the wealth was created in state R. Certainly, under traditional international income tax principles, state S which boasts only of a customer base, would have no income taxing authority.[659]

---

[658] *See e.g.,* Discussion Report of the Australian Tax Office Electronic Commerce Project, *Tax and the Internet,* http://www.ato.gov.au (August 1997).

[659] *See* Forst, *The Continuing Vitality of Source-Based Taxation in the Electronic Age,* 15 TAX NOTES INT'L 1455 (1997). However, under a Value Added Tax (VAT) or retail

Even if historically and economically income taxing authority should reside in state R, politically and financially many S states of the world are unlikely to embrace or even grudgingly accept such a conclusion. To do so might signal a dramatic shift in the tax base, as compared with traditional commerce, from those states who import electronic commerce to those states that export electronic commerce. One way or another, the electronic commerce importing states (*e.g.,* state S) are going to lay claim to what they regard as their share of income generated over the internet and through other digital means. Their claim may result from a creative (or some may argue distorted) view of source-based taxation.[660] Or perhaps, state S may place greater reliance on consumption-based taxes (*e.g.,* VAT) which focus on the consumer rather than where wealth is created. Or perhaps, state S may abandon the permanent establishment concept in favor of other tax regimes that guarantee income taxing authority to the state of the customer.

Aside from differences in determining what constitutes a permanent establishment, state R and state S may also disagree about allocation of the tax base resulting from other definitional differences. For example, suppose that R Corp. makes available to state S customers accounting software which can be downloaded for a fee from R Corp.'s web page on its server in state R. State R might view the transaction as a sale that is only taxable in state R in the absence of a state S permanent establishment. Or state R might view the transaction as a performance of services taxable only in state R in the absence of a state S permanent establishment or fixed base. However, state S may view the payment by a state S customer as a royalty that may be subject to a state S withholding tax. If state R does not recognize the taxing authority of state S, state R may be unwilling to relieve double taxation by granting a tax credit for any withholding tax imposed.

To the extent that the tax treatment of electronic commerce transactions is unclear, failure of state R and state S to resolve these and other differences may result in double taxation. Those who toil in the international tax vineyard are beginning to suggest approaches to the uncertainties and the potential tax base shift occasioned by the rise of electronic com-

---

sales tax the focus is on where consumption takes place (*i.e.,* state S) not on where income is created (*i.e.,* state R).

[660] States may claim that a server or the telecommunications infrastructure could constitute a permanent establishment.

merce.[661] Proposals run the gamut from the status quo to revolutionary overhaul. For example, the US Treasury takes the position that existing international tax principles will be able to apply adequately to electronic commerce transactions.[662] This approach may not command an international consensus if it results in an important tax base being subject to taxation disproportionately by electronic commerce exporting states. If the US Treasury advocates the status quo, proponents of a "bit tax" suggest a totally new approach for taxing income generated from electronic commerce where users of electronic commerce would be taxed based on the number of bits generated.[663]

This approach is premised on the maintenance of the permanent establishment principle which has the advantage of longevity and familiarity. Under the current permanent establishment principle, R Corp. which has no presence in state S other than a customer base would not be subject to income tax in state S merely because R Corp. reaches customers in state S through a web site or through some other means of electronic commerce. Even if a server were located in state S, a server alone is not likely to constitute a permanent establishment.[664] Nor would the use of a telecommunications network or the shipping of goods from state R to state S constitute a permanent establishment.[665]

---

[661] *See e.g.,* Hinnekens, New Age International Taxation in the Digital Economy of the Global Society, 25 INTERTAX 116 (1997); Powers, et al., *International Tax Issues in Cyberspace: Taxation of Cross-border Electronic Commerce,* 25 INTERTAX 120 (1997); Mall, Leow & Murata, *Taxation of Cross-Border Internet Transactions in Australia, Japan and Singapore,* available in LEXIS/NEXIS, 97 TNI 36-2 (24 Feb. 1997); Glicklich, Goldberg & Levine, *Internet Sales Pose International Tax Challenges,* J. TAX'N 325 (June 1996); Glicklich, Levine, Goldberg and Brody, Electronic Services: *Suggesting a Man-Machine Distinction,* 87 J. TAX 69 (1997).

[662] Department of the Treasury Office of Tax Policy, *Selected Tax Policy Implications of Global Electronic Commerce,* http://www.ustreas.gov/treasury/tax/internet.html (22 Dec. 1996) (hereinafter sometimes referred to as "US Treasury Report").

[663] CORDELL, IDE, SOETE & KAMP, THE NEW WEALTH OF NATIONS: TAXING CYBERSPACE (1998).

[664] However, the OECD Commentary takes the position that vending machines and other automated devices could constitute permanent establishments if the enterprise engages in business beyond the mere installation of such machines. OECD Commentary, 1997, Art. 5, para. 10.

[665] *See* Forst, *The Continuing Vitality of Source-Based Taxation in the Electronic Age,* 15 TAX NOTES INT'L 1455, para. 70 (1997).

Keeping the permanent establishment principle intact may be widely viewed by electronic commerce importing states as unacceptable because they will not be able to share in the tax base generated by electronic commerce income. Consequently, for electronic commerce importing states to continue to accept the permanent establishment principle as presently constituted, it may be necessary for electronic commerce exporting states to make concessions in other areas that will permit sharing of the electronic commerce tax base with electronic commerce importing states.

Currently under income tax treaties and the international tax provisions of most countries, income is categorized and different treatment may apply to different categories of income. For example, under the OECD Model treaty, sales proceeds, income from the performance of services, royalties, dividends and interest may all be treated differently. Categorization of income from an economic standpoint is inherently artificial. In the marketplace, a seller does not care (aside from tax considerations) how a payment received is categorized as long as the payment is fair value for what was sold. The artificiality of categorization has manifested itself in the growth of derivative financial instruments which can turn one category of income into a category that is more tax-favored (*e.g.*, dividends into interest).[666] Similarly, determining the difference between a royalty and the sale of an intangible or the sale of a tangible disk may be untenable.[667] Problems of categorization are likely to intensify as electronic commerce becomes more widespread.

As a modification of the current system, suppose that international consensus could be reached on a single withholding rate for any payment borne by a state S payor to a state R beneficial owner that had the effect of eroding the state S tax base. What the single rate should be would be determined by empirical information, international consensus and negotiation but a 3 percent rate may be reasonable and will be used for purposes of discussion.

---

[666]*See e.g.*, Ring, *Risk-Shifting Within A Multinational Corporation: The Incoherence of the U.S. Tax Regime*, 38 Boston College L. Rev. 667 (1997).

[667]For example, in Prop. Reg. § 1.861-18, Exs. 8 and 9, the category of income received by a vendor depends upon whether the vendor transfers a master disk to the purchaser which is in then copied on to computers for resale or whether the vendor transfers a separate disk for each computer to be resold. In the former, payment is treated as a royalty and in the later, payment is treated as proceeds from the sale of tangible goods.

This 3 percent rate would be applied to any payment that is borne by a state S payor to a state R beneficial owner that erodes the state S tax base. That is, if the payment is deductible by a state S purchaser or goes into the cost of goods sold (thereby decreasing gain on the sale of goods) of a state S reseller, it is subject to withholding regardless of the category of income to the recipient. Consequently, payments that may be categorized as royalties, interest, compensation, cost of goods sold would all be subject to withholding. Dividends would not be subject to withholding because typically dividends are not deductible and do not erode the tax base of the payor's state. Payments made by state S consumers to state R vendors would not be subject to withholding because the consumer does not deduct the cost of consumption.

The withholding tax imposed by state S must be creditable in state R for this approach to work. That is, this approach is intended to allocate the tax base among states, not raise the overall level of taxation. If this approach worked seamlessly (and little in life does), R Corp. would be indifferent because the overall level of tax would be unchanged although the withholding by state S may result in a transfer of tax revenue from state R to state S.

Even a 3 percent gross base withholding tax may disguise a much higher rate of net taxation on R Corp. Certainly, this may be true where the tax is imposed on inputs or services purchased by a state S business from R Corp. In this situation, R Corp. will have its own cost of goods sold and other expenses so that the amount received for the inputs is not all income. In order to ameliorate double taxation, R Corp. should have the right to file in state S as a net basis taxpayer, receiving a tax refund of the withholding tax where appropriate.[668] That is, R Corp. should be given an election to file in state S as if the income were attributable to a state S permanent establishment. If the withholding tax rate is kept low, the incidence of net basis taxation will be minimized. However, the burden associated with R Corp. in some cases having to file in state S as a net base taxpayer is a cost of this ap-

---

[668]For example, suppose that a state S customer pays $100 to R Corp. for a component that S incorporates in goods it sells to customers. Because the $100 payment is part of S's cost of goods sold, it would be subject to a 3 percent withholding tax of $3. However, if R Corp.'s cost of goods sold for the component is $95, the 3 percent nominal rate on gross income becomes a 60 percent effective rate on R Corp.'s $15 of income. Under these circumstances, R Corp. should be able to file in state S as a net basis taxpayer. If state S's general tax rate is 40 percent, R Corp. should be able to file for a refund of $1.00 ($3 withholding — $2.00 net tax).

proach, although one that can be justified by the overall benefits of a single withholding rate to all deductible cross-border payments.

A 3 percent tax on the cost of cross-border purchased inputs may look very much like an excise tax which would inhibit international trade, but it differs in two significant ways. First, the tax would be creditable in state R so the withholding tax should not increase R Corp.'s overall tax burden. Second, R Corp. retains the right to file on a net basis in state S if the withholding tax burden exceeds the tax burden on net income attributable to activities in state S.

This approach has some positive and negative implications. On the positive side, whether a payment is a royalty, a payment for services, a lease payment or a payment for goods becomes irrelevant for international tax purposes. The test for withholding on a cross-border transaction at a single rate becomes whether the payment erodes the state S tax base (*i.e.*, is deductible or added to cost of goods sold). Because of the link between withholding and deduction, the approach may be enforceable. To the extent that a state S business tries to take a deduction or other tax benefit for a payment to R Corp. and cannot show that its withholding obligation has been discharged, no deduction will be permitted.

Because of the link between withholding and deduction, state S consumers will not have a withholding obligation because typically no deduction is permitted for consumption.[669] From an administrative point of view, this is a desirable result because compelling consumers to withhold would be logistically difficult and politically unpopular. It is true that not requiring consumers to withhold means that state S will not share in the portion of the tax base attributable to R Corp. sales to state S consumers where R Corp. does not have a permanent establishment in state S. However, there are two observations to make concerning this. First, the overwhelming amount of electronic commerce is business-to-business electronic commerce rather than business-to-consumer.[670] Consequently,

---

[669]If a deduction were permitted under state S law (*e.g.*, an interest payment), withholding would be required on interest payments to R Corp. in order for a consumer to qualify for the deduction.

[670]*See e.g.*, Kane, *Year in review: Cyber commerce,* http://www.zdnet.com/zdnn/content/zdnn/1229/266738.html (29 Dec. 1997) (in 1997, $1.4 billion in merchandise and services sold online; however, $5 billion spent by companies purchasing in business-to-business transactions); Duvall, *Businesses Buy Into E-Commerce,* http://www.zdnet.com/intweek/printhigh/20298/extra202.html (2 Feb. 1998*); World Wide Web-based trade set*

state S's inability to share in this portion of the tax base generated by electronic commerce may not be as significant as first may appear. Second, state S may be compensated for that loss of tax base by the withholding tax on business-to-business transactions. For example, under current international tax principles, there is no withholding on payments for inputs sold by R Corp. to a state S business where R Corp. does not maintain a permanent establishment in state S. If state S is permitted to collect a withholding tax on the amount paid for such inputs even in the absence of an R Corp. permanent establishment in state S, that allocation of this new tax base to state S may be acceptable as a proxy for the lost tax base on sales by R Corp. directly to consumers. Similarly, a withholding tax on interest and royalty payments in the business-to-business context may provide an allocation of the tax base that will be acceptable to state S.

If the state S withholding is creditable in state R, there should be no additional cost to R Corp. from this approach.[671] Of course, the withholding rate can be adjusted to achieve a tax base sharing between states R and S that is acceptable to both states. Note also that under this approach, state S maintains its right to tax any income generated by R Corp. that is attributable to a permanent establishment in state S.

Neither this approach nor any approach is likely to clear up all the problems that are raised by electronic commerce. For example, the need to determine source of income does not totally disappear. If state R is going to credit the withholding tax imposed by state S on a deductible payment to R

---

to explode, http://www.zdnet.com/zdnn/content/reut/1201/252283.html (1 Dec. 1998) ("business-to-business as the dominant force" according to International Data Corp. forecast); Jones, *Business-To-Business E-Commerce market To Double,* http://www.zd-net.com/intweek/daily/9802191.html (19 Feb. 1998) (possible doubling of business-to-business electronic commerce in next six months according to survey conducted by Information Technology Association of American and Ernst & Young LLP); Nairn, *Future of Electronic Commerce,* The Financial Times (London) 6 (2 July 1997) (business-to-business activities will dominate); *Euro Internet Commerce Research Reveals Business-to-Business Transactions Will Dominate,* 38 EDP Weekly 3 (4 Aug. 1997).

[671] In some cases where the gross base withholding tax result in a higher state S tax burden than would be the case if the taxpayer paid taxes on a net basis, a net basis election is available. Filing as a net basis taxpayer may impose burdensome compliance costs on a nonresident taxpayer doing business in many countries. This compliance cost burden would have to be addressed.

Corp., state R must conclude that the income is generated in state S. Stated differently, state R will not give a credit for state S taxes that are imposed on what state R under its domestic rules considers to be state R income. So if state R receives payment from state S customers for access to data on state R's server located in state R, state S may impose a withholding tax that state R may not credit if it deems the source of income to arise in state R where the server is located. State R may be reluctant to condition creditability upon whether state S permits a deduction for the payment.[672]

This approach may not be conceptually pure. In an income tax system, why should R Corp. be taxable in state S on sales to a business that can deduct the cost of the input but is not taxable on the sale to a consumer who cannot deduct the payment? But this approach is premised on the idea of finding an overall compromise between electronic commerce exporting and importing states that is simple, equitable and enforceable. If state S is willing to cede a tax base (*i.e.,* electronic commerce sales to customers that may be difficult to collect) to state R in exchange for the right to withhold on payments that are not presently subject to withholding, perhaps no great inefficiency is created. After all, R Corp.'s total tax burden on income generated by electronic commerce should be the same whether state R collects the tax or the tax is shared between states R and S. So any impurities in this approach should have minimal efficiency implications.

5.1.1.1.6. Unitary taxation

At an IFA-/VNO-NCW seminar held in Amsterdam, on 23 December 1997, the head of fiscal affairs of a Dutch multinational suggested that the answer to the interjurisdictional issue of electronic commerce may be to allocate the profit of MNE's among the states in which the consumption takes place. The fact that the new medium also makes it easier for SMEs to engage in integrated multi-jurisdictional business activities may justify the application of the consumption profit tax to them. It would be a simple but

---

[672]There is also the possibility that a customer in state S may withhold on a payment that is not deductible and pocket the withheld amount. This, of course, is a problem between the customer and R Corp. which might just as easily overcharge even in the absence of a withholding tax.

crude method of formulary apportionment. It is not a plausible assumption that the receipt of each dollar through electronic (and conventional) sales in each jurisdiction reflects an equal contribution to the worldwide profit of the group. Other pre-determined criteria and indicators of activity within individual participating states as well as minimum thresholds may have to be included in the formula.

This is not the place to relive in detail the ongoing debate between adherents of the arm's length method and those who support formulary apportionment.[673] However, the problems posed by the growth of electronic commerce do nothing to quiet the debate. Those who favor formulary apportionment based on criteria such as property, payroll and sales might suggest that the wisdom of such an approach is made more obvious by the rise of electronic commerce. The blurring of geographical boundaries makes it more difficult to determine arm's length transactions.[674]

Of course, the overall effect of a formulary system, under which profits of a company or related companies are allocated according to a specified formula depends on the formula selected. For example, if the formula is comprised of factors based on property, payroll, and sales, R Corp. with its property and employees in country R may still have a tax liability in country S based on the sales that take place there. This would require an understanding that sales in fact do take place in country S because customers

---

[673]See e.g., Hubbard, *MTC Urges Switch from Arm's Length to Formulary Apportionment Method,* available in LEXIS/NEXIS, 93 TNT 112-11 (26 May 1993); Fernandez, *Dorgan Blasts Arm's Length Transfer Pricing Method,* available in LEXIS/NEXIS, 96 TNT 249-4 (24 Dec. 1996); Avi-Yonah, The Rise and Fall of Arm's Length: A Study in the Evolution of U.S. International Taxation, *15 Va. L. Rev., No. 1 (1995);* Hellerstein, Federal Income Taxation of Multinationals: Replacement of Separate Accounting with Formulary Apportionment, *Tax Notes, 23 Aug. 1993; Langbein,* The Unitary Method and the Myth of Arm's Length, *30 Tax Notes 625 (1986);* Kauder, Intercompany Pricing and Section 482: A Proposal to Shift from Uncontrolled Comparables to Formulary Apportionment Now, *Tax Notes, (25 Jan. 1993).*

Material advocating the arm's length method includes: Coffill & Willson, Federal Formulary Apportionment as an Alternative to ALP: From the Frying Pan to the Fire, *Tax Notes (24 May 1993); Wilkins & Gideon,* Memorandum to Congress: You Wouldn't Like Worldwide Formula Apportionment, *Tax Notes (5 Dec. 1994).*

[674]It would not be necessary to use formulary apportionment between unrelated entities. Rather the arm's length method could still be used. Formulary apportionment could be used to allocate income among related entities.

located in country S make the purchases, even though the marketing, the order taking, the payment system, and shipment all take place outside of country S. If the weight of these non-country S activities resulted in the sales component of the formula not being assigned to country S, the formulary approach would not produce a result any more satisfactory to source countries than current tax principles when no permanent establishment exists.

Electronic commerce poses a serious challenge to traditional arm's length pricing. In the 1990's, consumers are less patient than ever before — they want everything yesterday — and with its speed, the internet is one of the fastest means of concluding transactions. For this reason it is likely that the volume of electronic commerce will increase dramatically. However, the potential number of transactions, if actually realized, will make it much harder for taxing authorities to apply separate transactional pricing. Also, it appears it will be more difficult to apply functional analysis to the activities of a company doing business via the internet (*e.g.*, R Corp.), since any given function may be performed in several places. For example, to the extent that R Corp., in country R, is selling tangible goods via the internet, the goods may have been designed in country A (by designers located in countries X, Y, and Z), manufactured in country B, offered for sale through a server located in country C, which server is run by an internet service provider located in country D, and shipped by a country E company to a purchaser in country S. If R Corp. is selling intangibles or services, the breakdown can become even more complex, as consultants or programmers residing all over the world may contribute to R Corp.'s web site and multiple servers in various tax jurisdictions may be involved in the purchase and downloading, or performance of services.[675] For these reasons, many authorities feel that an alternative to arm's length pricing is needed, and that some form of formulary apportionment is the proper replacement.

---

[675]One other difficulty arises out of the development of corporate intranets. Intranets will allow multinationals to conduct their businesses internally, as a single, more unified entity. Fewer transactions with outside parties will make it more difficult to use the arm's length pricing method since one of the components of the calculation is based on comparable transactions between unrelated parties. Avi-Yonah, *International Taxation and Electronic Commerce* Tax L. Rev. (forthcoming).

One general formulary apportionment method that is currently being advocated is for tax authorities to negotiate advance pricing agreements that apply to specific types of operations by specific taxpayers.[676] While there are some apparent obstacles to such a scheme, such as a lack of an appropriate forum for all of the countries involved and the fact that a large number of agreements would be required, potential solutions to such problems are also being presented.[677] A concurrent default rule would apply for those smaller companies subject to tax in more than one jurisdiction, whereby profits would be equally allocated between the location of production and consumption — 50% of the income by the sales factor, and 50% by the location where the costs of production were incurred, although it may be difficult to identify those locations.[678]

It is argued that this proposed formula may be applied to income from the purchase/sale of intangibles by distinguishing between the value of the intangible derived from research and development activities (which are performed using tangible equipment and human capital) and from marketing activities, and referencing those values either in the cost of production (research and development intangibles) or in sales (marketing intangibles). To the extent that these amounts do not account for the full value of the intangible, the extra value is deemed likely to derive from the existence of the multinational itself, in the sense that it would be lost if the transactions were conducted at arm's length between unrelated parties. In such a case, no country would have a right to the intangible, and any for-

---

[676]See, e.g., Avi-Yonah, *International Taxation and Electronic Commerce, supra* note 675.

[677]It is first suggested that a multilateral forum be established for the negotiations. As to the second issue, it is argued that it is not as difficult a problem as it seems at first blush, since there is a limited number of very large multinationals. Currently, the top 350 multinationals own about one-sixth of the world's productive assets, and a third of world trade takes place among their affiliates. Avi-Yonah, *supra* note 675.

[678]The sales factor would be broadly defined to include both royalties and income from services. Costs of production would include payroll, depreciation, and other payments to unrelated parties.

Costs are advocated as the appropriate device for allocating income because: (1) costs of production are a reasonable proxy for source; (2) costs to unrelated parties are market-based and thus less subject to manipulation; and (3) if an enterprise shifts deductible costs to low-tax jurisdictions because of the resulting shift in profits, the deductions will also be worth less, which somewhat limits that type of tax avoidance.

mula that is generally agreed upon may be used to allocate the residual.[679] Therefore, whether R Corp. is a large or small company making/selling computer programs, the income it derives should be allocated between the production costs — *e.g.*, hiring computer programmers, buying/leasing computer-related machinery, and advertising — and sales. If R Corp. is a large corporation, however, the formula used for such allocation would be found in agreements pre-negotiated by the taxing authorities. If it is a small company subject to tax in more than one jurisdiction, there would be an equal 50%-50% split between production costs and sales.

A throwback rule is advocated as the appropriate solution for situations where the formula allocates some of the income to a tax haven. If income is allocated to a jurisdiction with a tax rate below a specified acceptable minimum, the income would be "thrown back" into the general pool to be divided pro rata among the other producing countries. Such a system would deter any attempts to manipulate the factors to allocate income to tax havens.[680] Thus, if R Corp. employs computer programmers residing in the Cayman Islands, the production costs associated with those programmers (*e.g.*, salaries) would not be allocated to the Cayman Islands, but instead divided on a pro rata basis between the other countries where production costs were incurred.

The use of formulary apportionment may or may not offer a better method of allocating income than the arm's length method. But regardless of the general approach to allocation issues, difficult definitional issues would remain and lines would have to be drawn. To the extent that formulary apportionment depends on determining the source of income or the location of an intangible, that method may not make the job of tax collec-

---

[679]In *Bausch & Lomb, Inc. v. Commissioner*, 933 F.2d 1084 (2d Cir. 1991), B&L (US) imported contact lenses that were manufactured by B&L in Ireland using know-how that significantly reduced its cost of manufacturing, and was unavailable to B&L's competitors. Most of the profit from the transaction resulted from this know-how, and depended on B&L's ability to keep it inside the multinational and not engage in arm's length dealings with an outside contract manufacturer. Since the residual did not "belong" to either the US or to Ireland, the IRS' argument that it must be allocated to the US merely because it was originally developed there was rejected.

[680]However, if sales into a country fall below the taxable threshold, the throwback rule should not be applied so that the income is taxed somewhere else since that would deprive small businesses from the protection of the threshold. Avi-Yonah, *supra* note 675.

tors any easier than trying to cope with existing allocation methods. This observation is particularly true if widespread agreement on a formulary apportionment method cannot be achieved by taxing jurisdictions.

5.1.1.1.7. Transactional taxes

If tinkering with the permanent establishment concept represents one of the least radical approaches to the issues raised by electronic commerce and moving from arm's length principles to a formulary approach is more radical, then abandoning or de-emphasizing the income tax is perhaps the most radical approach. The income tax is not an easy tax to administer because the tax is a net tax that is collected periodically. Although withholding obligations help tax authorities collect the income tax, there is often a dependence on voluntary compliance, particularly with respect to business profits and deductions. Even if it were possible to audit all businesses, the difficulty of determining with accuracy that all income has been reported is compounded as the physical manifestations of business activity disappear or become more difficult to detect. When R Corp. conducts its commerce through traditional means, there is visible evidence of business activity (*e.g.*, a building, a sales force, paperwork). When R Corp. conducts its commerce electronically, it may be much more difficult for taxing authorities to discern that commerce has taken place. There may be fewer physical signs of commercial activity — no building, no sales force, no paper trail. The income tax enforcement difficulties that will arise as electronic commerce grows may cause countries to emphasize other forms of taxation.

In a situation where all of the value of a transaction (*e.g.*, production, distribution, marketing, sales) arises in a single jurisdiction, and the only contact with another jurisdiction is the presence of a customer base for that product, conceptually it may be difficult to discern the production of any income in that other jurisdiction. In an income tax, the significance of a customer base is taken into account when those customers earn the income that makes a purchase possible. To permit a jurisdiction income taxing authority solely on the basis of providing a customer base may distort beyond recognition the concept of an income tax. On the other hand a consumption tax rightfully focuses on where consumption takes place — where the customer base is located.

The extension of a VAT to a foreign telecommunications company that does not have a permanent establishment in any EC country may portend a more general approach to electronic commerce. The use of a VAT to provide taxing authority over a foreign taxpayer that does not have a permanent establishment may permit source countries to capture tax revenue generated by electronic commerce that might otherwise escape under the income tax. The growing interest in some type of "bit tax" to impose on those involved in electronic commerce stems from the same concern — collecting a share of the revenue generated by electronic commerce. Enforcement problems relating to income generated by electronic commerce may also arise in attempting to impose transactional taxes. Collection of a VAT from nonresident entrepreneurs without a physical presence in a country may not be any easier than collection of income tax from such entrepreneurs.

If a VAT or a bit tax were to replace the income tax as a method by which source states could subject profits from electronic commerce to source state taxing authority, entrepreneurs may experience punishing tax liabilities, particularly if the residence state continues to impose an income tax. Although the imposition of a source state transactional tax and a residence state income tax may not be double taxation in a conventional sense, in terms of the marginal effects on entrepreneurs, transactions may not be undertaken if the overall tax bite is too high. If such a situation were to arise, it might be advisable for residence countries to think about granting relief from double taxation even though the source state is imposing a transactional tax rather than an income tax.[681] A tax credit country might consider giving a foreign tax credit for any VAT or bit tax that might be imposed in the source state. An exemption country might exempt income subject to a VAT or other transactional tax in a source country even though the income is not attributable to a permanent establishment in the source state. Under current tax principles, double taxation relief is simply unavailable between different (*e.g.,* direct and indirect) types of taxes. But perhaps this principle might be reevaluated.

---

[681]In order to compute a tax credit limitation, a country might have to convert the transactional tax base into an income tax base or perhaps determine creditability by treating a transactional tax as an income tax and then applying existing credit limitation criteria.

Alternative consumption tax formulations are briefly reviewed and evaluated in section 5.3.

5.1.1.1.8. Domestic tax considerations

In considering international principles to deal with alternative approaches to taxation of electronic commerce, it is appropriate to think in terms of OECD Model Convention articles. However, the issue of tax jurisdiction starts at home and should also encompass domestic rules determining whether income derived from international electronic commerce is taxable. While national authorities increasingly also take into account the jurisdictional practices and tax rights of other countries and of treaty law, they may still want to provide in their domestic tax laws for criteria with a long or flexible jurisdictional arm to deal with the intangible and global features of electronic commerce and the risk of their abuse by offshore and other constructions. They would leave to treaty law the task of resolving overlapping taxation which may result from such domestic taxation.

Should the criterion for source-based taxation of business profits provide for a lower threshold? That is already the case in countries which apply the test of the place where trade or business is carried on (*e.g.*, the United Kingdom). Other countries utilize the permanent establishment test, but may extend the tax liability of non-residents in their domestic legislation to non-permanent establishment or lower permanent establishment threshold situations. For instance, under the Belgian Income Tax Code non-resident companies are liable for tax with respect to rental income and capital gains on their real property situated in the national territory. It also provides for the taxation of profits derived as a result of foreign membership in local partnerships and joint ventures or fees derived by foreign directors of local companies, of premium income derived by foreign insurance companies covering local risks, even if policies are sold through independent insurance brokers.[682] The reasoning (that out-of-state profit should be subject to unilateral jurisdictional rules of the long arm type, subject to resolution of double taxation risks by tax treaty provision) may conceivably also be applied to the choice of domestic source rules of profit derived from

---

[682]Article 228 §§2, 3 b), d) and e) Income Tax Code.

electronic commerce, including income derived from independent professions carrying on their activity through electronic tools. Also, the US Treasury appears ready to loosen traditional source concepts: "In devising rules to source this type of income, it may also be necessary to consider the relationship between the service-provider's physical location and other potential indicia of source, such as the location of a computer server or communication link."[683]

5.1.1.2. Taxation based on residence

Much of the attention lavished on the international tax consequences of the rise of electronic commerce has focused on the challenge to source-based taxation. That challenge arises from the ability to carry on commerce in a country electronically without a physical presence. The same technology that makes it possible to carry on commercial activities electronically from a remote location also makes it possible to manage an enterprise from a remote (or more than one remote) location. Indeed, the challenge of technological change to traditional methods of determining residence-based taxation may well be as profound or more profound as the challenge to historical means of source-based taxation.

It is the ability of management to run an enterprise without a consistent physical presence in any single jurisdiction that will test traditional notions of residence. The use of video conferencing and the overall improvements in communications technology allow managers to reside in different jurisdictions and still coordinate management decision-making. The result is that determining the residence of a juridical entity such as a company becomes an even more artificial exercise than it has historically been. Countries are beginning to confront this problem. For example, the Report of the Minister's Advisory Committee on Electronic Commerce has recommended that Revenue Canada issue an interpretation bulletin addressing the significance of modern telecommunications technology on the concept of residence.[684] Set forth below are different approaches to company residence that might be worth considering in light of ongoing techno-

---

[683]US Treasury Report, *supra* note 217, para. 7.4.2.

[684]Report to the Minister of National Revenue from the Minister's Advisory Committee on Electronic Commerce, *Electronic Commerce and Canada's Tax Administration*, http://www.rc.gc.ca/ecomm (April 1998).

logical changes in communications. Some of the issues raised the definition of residence are also discussed below in section 5.1.3.

5.1.1.2.1. Status quo

It has always been possible for managers in different countries to manage a company in a coordinated fashion by using the telephone and by conducting meetings where managers would assemble. Electronic networking makes remote management easier, but some may argue that it does not enable a new form of management. Viewed in this manner, improvements in communications do not necessitate a change in historically proven residence tests such as the "place of effective management."[685]

5.1.1.2.2. Company residence based on other criteria

A company that is incorporated in one country may have directors and managers that reside in a different country (or countries), and they may meet and take action in one or more locations. The company is owned by its shareholders who may reside in many different countries. The company carries on business through its employees who may work in different countries. Corporate books must be kept. Dividends may be paid to the shareholders. Where these factors involve more than one country, determining residence can be complicated.[686] In determining residence, some countries, like the United States, use "a place of incorporation" test. Other countries use a test based on the place of effective management (or central management and control). Different countries use different formulations of this test. Essentially, however, the test focuses on where decisions con-

---

[685]*See* Lambooij, *Rethinking corporate residence*, Symposium on the Internet and the Taxation of International Electronic Commerce, Leiden 6 June 1997, http://www.lovotax.nl/tax/onderwerp5. Those countries that rely on place of incorporation to determine residence do not focus on subjective factors such as where management decisions are made in order to determine residence. Consequently, technological changes that bear on where management decisions are made may not provide a reason to revisit that definition of residence.

[686]*See*, Rivier, *The Fiscal Residence of Companies*, 72a CAHIERS DE DROIT FISCAL INTERNATIONAL [STUDIES ON INTERNATIONAL FISCAL LAW] 47 (1988).

cerning the operation of the business take place. Many countries, like the Netherlands, look at "the circumstances" of a company which might include factors such as: the location of board meetings, the location of the main office building, the place where books are kept, the currency used to keep the company's accounts, where financial documents are drawn up, where the company is registered, and where the statutory seat is located. Some countries, like Australia, look at the domicile of directors as one of the factors to be considered. But no country bases its determination of the residence of a company solely, or even largely on the domicile or residence, of directors, managers, or employees.

The ease with which the place of effective management and the place of incorporation tests for company residence can be manipulated without necessarily substantively altering the way a company conducts its business raises the possibility of using or emphasizing different criteria. If it were deemed desirable to change the definition of residence in light of technological advances, one possibility would be to base a company's residence on the residence of its directors or managers, or perhaps the residence of a specified number or percentage of its shareholders or employees.[687] While, of course, these individuals can also pick up and move to a tax haven or low-tax jurisdiction, any such move will have real consequences in terms of life style. It would require a much greater commitment for a director to physically move than simply to arrange directors' meetings in a low tax jurisdiction. By basing a company's residence on the residence of directors, shareholders, managers, or others who participate in the entity's operations, some of the artificiality of the entity residence definition is eliminated. The "place of effective management" test tries to do that, but still focuses on where decisions are made rather than where the decision-makers actually reside.

By determining the residence of a company using the same tests as determining the residence of individuals, some consistency can be brought to the residence concept. A company is nothing more than a nexus of contracts among participants — perhaps its residence should be determined in the same manner as participants who do not enter into the nexus of contracts but directly operate a business as sole proprietors or through a trans-

---

[687] A publicly-traded corporation might be deemed to be resident where it is traded. However, global trading may mean that a company's shares are listed and traded on more than one exchange.

parent partnership. Of course, there is a wide range between basing corporate residence on the place of incorporation or place of effective management on one hand and ignoring those characteristics in favor of residence based on the residence of the corporation's human participants on the other hand. Traditional residence tests may evolve to more closely consider the residence of participants in determining the residence of the entity without completely forsaking the traditional tests.

5.1.1.2.3. Formulary approach

If international consensus could be reached on a formula for allocating income (*e.g.*, a formula based on sales, property and payroll), then there may be no need to determine residence. All income would be allocated based on the formula. A variation of this approach would be to maintain the existing distinctions between the residence and source concepts, but to determine the state of residence based on a formula. The formula might be based on a composite of the residences of employees, shareholders, or directors. The formula might take into account the location of company property, place of incorporation, or other factors as well. In some respects, the place of effective management already takes into account a variety of factors. A formulary approach might attempt to quantify these factors, resulting in an objective rather than subjective test. The success of a formulary approach to the definition of residence is dependent on a shared acceptance by the international community.

5.1.1.2.4. Full integration

Of course, if the concept of company residence is called into question by advances in communications technology, a direct, albeit radical approach, would be to eliminate taxation at the entity level. Instead, income earned by an entity would in some manner be taxable directly to the shareholders in whatever jurisdictions they reside.[688] For tax purposes, the dif-

---

[688]Further information regarding different methods of corporate tax integration may be found in the following: COMPANY TAX SYSTEMS (Head and Krever eds., 1997); AULT, COMPARATIVE INCOME TAXATION: A STRUCTURAL ANALYSIS (1997); Van Raad, *Observations on Integration of Corporation and Individual Income Taxes Within the European Community*, 9 CONN. J. INT'L L. 763 (Summer 1994); Mcnulty, *Corporate Income*

ference between a partnership and a corporation would become insignifi-cant. This approach substitutes the residence of natural persons for the res-idence of artificial persons (*e.g.*, corporations).

5.1.2. Categorization of income

5.1.2.1.   *Categories of income*

As international tax principles have developed, different tax rules ap-ply to different categories of income. For example, the OECD Model treaty contains different taxing provisions for business profits, income from real property, income from shipping and air transport, dividends, interest, roy-alties, capital gains, income from dependent personal services, income from independent personal services, directors' fees, pensions, etc. Creating sepa-rate categories places a premium on income categorization. In an economic sense, income is income. Vendors rarely concern themselves with the cate-gorization of income before transferring their wares or services for com-pensation. Distinctions between different types of income are artificial. As artificial distinctions are created, it is inevitable that creative tax planners and entrepreneurs will find ways to arbitrage the differences. For example, the growth of derivative financial instruments is due in part to the ability to transform one form of income (*e.g.*, dividends) into another type of in-come (*e.g.*, interest) that may be taxed in a more favorable way.[689]

Tax Reform in the United States: Proposals for Integration of the Corporate and Individual Income Taxes, and International Aspects, 12 INT'L TAX & BUS. LAW 161 (1994); Yin, *Corporate Tax Integration and the Search for the Pragmatic Deal,* 47 TAX L. REV. 431 (Spring 1992); Avi-Yonah, *The Treatment of Corporate Preference Items Under an Integrated Tax System: A Comparative Analysis,* 44 TAX LAW. 195 (1990); Bird, *Corporate-Personal Tax Integration,* in TAX COORDINATION IN THE EUROPEAN COMMUNITY (Cnossen ed., 1987); and U.S. Department of the Treasury, *Report on the Integration of the Individual and Cor-porate Tax Systems — Taxing Business Income Once* (1992).

[689]*See, e.g.,* Avi-Yonah & Swartz, *US International Tax Treatment of Financial De-rivatives,* available in LEXIS/NEXIS, 97 TNT 61-49 (31 March 1997); Lyons, *Innovative Financial Instruments Challenge Tax Systems, According to OECD Official,* available in LEXIS/NEXIS, 96 TNI 192-4 (2 Oct. 1996); Swartz, *ABC's of Cross-Border Derivatives,* Tax Law and Estate Planning Court Handbook Series, 393 PLI/Tax 975 (Oct/Nov 1996); Rosenbloom, *Source-Based Taxation of Derivative Financial Instruments: Some Unan-swered Questions,* 50 U. Miami L. Rev. 597 (April 1996); Kolbrenner, *Derivatives Design and Taxation,* 15 Va. Tax Rev. 211 (1995).

Suppose that R Corp. maintains a database on a server in country R. Country S customers access the server to download information from the database for a fee. The fee might be a payment for services, a royalty, the purchase price of the acquired information, or a rental payment for the use of R Corp.'s server. To the extent that applicable international tax principles dictate different results depending on the characterization, transactions will be designed to exploit the most favorable treatment. This will require more detailed distinctions between different types of income which will open up more planning opportunities for taxpayers, etc. If different countries do not share a common definition of a category of income (*e.g.*, a royalty), the result will be double taxation. For example, suppose that S Corp. determines that the payment is a royalty and under the applicable treaty with country R, country S is permitted to withhold at a 10% rate on royalty payments. If country R does not regard the payment as a royalty but rather treats it as a sale of the data which under the applicable treaty should not be subject to tax in country S, then R Corp. may not permit a credit for the country S withholding. Moving toward fewer categories of income and/or more consistent treatment of income in different categories may be a desirable goal made more urgent by the growth in electronic commerce.

5.1.2.2. *Consistent source rules*

Even if there are fewer categories of income or better international agreement concerning the definition of the categories, little will be accomplished unless there is international agreement on where the defined categories of income arise. For example, suppose that R Corp. receives a royalty for customer C's use of R Corp. software that is maintained on a server in country R. Customer C is a resident of country S and makes use of the data obtained in country S even though the licensed software itself never is downloaded from the R Corp. server. Both country R and country S may agree that the payment by Customer C is a royalty payment and that country S has authority to impose a 10% withholding tax on royalty payments arising in country S. However, country R and country S may not agree on whether the royalty has arisen in country R or in country S. Country S may regard the royalty as arising in the country where the results generated by the intangible are used (*i.e.*, country S). Country R may regard the royalty as arising in the country where the intangibles are actually used, which is country R, or where the server is maintained. The need to synchronize source rules is not a new problem in international tax, but the rise of electronic commerce makes consistency of source rules even more important. Any rethinking of source rules might deal with both the choice of source criteria and their definition. It may result in the application to electronic commerce of more general legal definitions which the courts would clarify when it comes to their application to the various income types of the same family. The US Treasury Paper sees another benefit in such broad formulation of source rules in the digital economy: "The solutions that emerge should be sufficiently general and flexible in order to deal with developments in technology and ways of doing business that are currently unforeseen."

Part of the process of rationalizing and harmonizing source rules should be seeking consistent source rules for different categories of income. For example, in the United States there are different source rules for different types of rents. A rental payment for the use of an intangible (*i.e.*, a royalty) is sourced where the intangibles are used.[690] A rental payment for the use of money (*i.e.*, interest) is sourced where the payor resides.[691] A rental payment for the use of human capital (*i.e.*, compensation) is sourced where services are rendered, not where the payor resides and not where the services are used.[692] In sum, it is desirable to rationalize and harmonize the international understanding of where a particular category of income arises and at the same time to rationalize and harmonize the source rules among different categories of income.

There are, of course, different approaches to the categorization issues that electronic commerce poses. While one approach is to eliminate or reduce the number of categories for different types of rental income, another approach is to create additional distinctions to accommodate income generated by electronic commerce. For example, it has been suggested that services income should be divided into two subcategories with different source rules applying to each category.[693] Services involving human action might be sourced under traditional principles (*e.g.*, under US law, where the services are performed). Services that are purely mechanical (*e.g.*, a database

---

[690]IRC § 861(a)(4).

[691]IRC § 861(a)(2).

[692]IRC § 861(a)(3).

[693]Glicklich, Levine, Goldberg and Brody, Electronic Services: *Suggesting a Man-Machine Distinction*, 87 J. Tax. 69 (1997).

located on a server that accessed by a client) would not be sourced under the place-of-performance principle. Instead, these "Type 2" services would be sourced according to the rules governing the exploitation of tangible or intangible personal property. To the extent that differing source rules for different categories of income is troublesome, this proposal does not address that problem. Rather, the proposal is to move income generated by certain forms of electronic commerce from one category to another.

5.1.3. Policies dealing with abuse of jurisdictional rules and disappearing taxpayers

While it may be true that in the digital economy the jurisdictional rules of residence may be more dependable and less subject to manipulation than those governing source-based taxation, this does not make the corporate residence, especially of companies engaged in electronic commerce and telecommunication services, immune from international manipulation based on location or relocation in jurisdictions with low or zero taxation. For example, a company may set up a subsidiary in a jurisdiction which has a favorable treaty with the source country. In order to counter such constructions, anti-shopping measures often apply extra criteria of residence qualification of the transit company, pursuant to an analytical framework which is partly source-based (*e.g.,* active conduct of business, etc.).

It is the portability of commercial enterprises that can be carried on electronically that will test existing controlled foreign corporation legislation. Those countries that have controlled foreign corporations regimes that tax all income earned by a controlled foreign corporation in tax havens may not have a need to alter existing legislation to deal with controlled foreign corporations engaged in electronic commerce. However, those countries whose controlled foreign corporation legislation does not apply to income produced by an active business may conclude that changes in controlled foreign corporation legislation are warranted. The costs associated with setting up a controlled foreign corporation which then develops software and licenses or sells it to customers (or perhaps renders services over the internet) are quite low when compared to establishing a controlled foreign corporation that conducts a traditional business through a significant physical presence in a tax haven. To the extent that existing controlled foreign corporation legislation does not currently apply to such transactions, countries may consider several approaches.

If the purpose of controlled foreign corporation legislation is to keep domestic enterprises from attempting to isolate income generated by selected segments of its overall business in low tax jurisdictions, then perhaps the rise of electronic commerce poses no threat. If a controlled foreign corporation carries on an entire business (*e.g.*, selling software over the internet) in a low tax jurisdiction and not just one aspect of the business (*e.g.*, marketing), some countries may conclude that income from the entire business should not be subject to controlled foreign corporation legislation. While the portability of businesses conducting electronic commerce may make the use of controlled foreign corporations more prevalent, in the view of some countries that fact alone may not justify extending controlled foreign corporation legislation to cover active business carried on by subsidiaries in other jurisdictions.

However, other countries may see the need to expand their residence tax jurisdiction over income earned by a controlled foreign corporation that carries on electronic commerce — even though it may carry on the entire business actively and not just a portion of the business. The solutions might range from the limited to the expansive. A limited approach might include expanding the concept of foreign base company income to cover automatically all income generated by the sale or licensing of intangibles over the internet even if all business processes are carried on by the controlled foreign corporation. A change of this type would be a recognition of the fact that income generated by intangibles, like interest income, is easily portable and can be moved offshore without the significant physical commitment that would attend moving a traditional "bricks and mortar" business.

In the case of an incorporated presence in a tax haven, perhaps it should be the residence of the programmers and other employees that should be used to determine whether the income earned through a server in a tax haven is considered to be earned in that state.[694] Countries with controlled foreign corporation legislation may want to deny deferral benefits to income earned by a controlled foreign corporation in a tax haven

---

[694]In electronic commerce, it is primarily human capital (*e.g.*, the intelligence and experience of programmers) rather than physical capital (*e.g.*, buildings, equipment) that generates profits for a tax haven controlled foreign corporation.

where the employees do not reside in that state. For example, if a tax haven controlled foreign corporation generates income through a server located in the tax haven but the programmers reside in state R, income attributable to the server would be treated as R Corp.'s income, taxable when earned by TH Corp.

Of course, it is always possible that in the case of a controlled foreign corporation in state TH, the employees may relocate to state TH, thereby achieving tax savings. But if in fact these very real atom-based rather than digital changes are made (*i.e.*, people relocating), tax consequences should reflect these changes. While advances in transportation and communications have made human capital increasingly mobile, relocation of people is not lightly undertaken.

Rather than selectively changing the rules for internet transactions, a more expansive approach would be to end deferral entirely for controlled foreign corporations, taxing all profits of controlled foreign corporations directly to the shareholders. This approach threatens to increase the incidence of double taxation, although any end of deferral would presumably carry with it broadened relief from double taxation (*e.g.*, income taxes paid by a controlled foreign corporation would be directly creditable by the shareholders).

There is much room in the middle of these last two approaches. For example, a country might identify by name or tax structure those countries that are tax havens. Controlled foreign corporations in tax haven jurisdictions would not enjoy deferral on any income. That is, no distinction would be made between income generated through electronic commerce and income generated in a more traditional manner. For controlled foreign corporations outside of these tax havens, controlled foreign corporation legislation would not apply.

In order to avoid piecemeal tax legislation enacted quickly to meet the most recent technological change or craze, taxing authorities may want to use the skyrocketing growth of electronic commerce as an opportunity to carefully review their controlled foreign corporation legislation. Rather than singling out income produced by electronic commerce for punitive treatment merely because of portability, tax authorities may determine that more uniform changes will lead to more rational tax policy and be more easily administered. Focusing on egregious tax havens rather than on income from electronic commerce may present a useful approach.

5.1.4. Administration

Another challenge of electronic commerce relates to tax administration. It is dealt with by appropriate administrative measures adapted to the special characteristics of electronic commerce. Questions must be addressed concerning how taxing authorities should deal with administrative issues associated with electronic money, identity verification, record keeping and information reporting.[695]

Administrative problems raised by electronic commerce also pose issues as to appropriate legislative or treaty rules. Tax rules that may be theoretically sound may, nevertheless, be unsatisfactory from an administrative point of view. It would be inadvisable to design tax rules that can easily be circumvented by available technology. For example, source countries that are seeking to tax income from electronic commerce have to consider how they might enforce any taxing authority they claim. In many cases, an enterprise may not have any physical presence in the country seeking to tax. In such a case, enforcement of any taxing authority by the source state may be virtually impossible. There may be no assets to seize in case of nonpayment and no way of preventing access to the entrepreneur's web site. Moreover, the use of anonymous payment systems may make it even more difficult to trace how much commercial activity is taking place in a source state.[696]

Consistency is just as important as precision. Inconsistencies are a central ingredient to the recipe for double or multiple taxation. It is important that the evolving tax rules are globally consistent as well as simple for both taxpayers and the various tax authorities.[697]

---

[695]For a consideration of some of these issues, *see* Discussion Report of the Australian Tax Office Electronic Commerce Project, *Tax and the Internet* (August 1997).

[696]Of course, if tangible goods are being ordered over the internet, it may be possible for the source state to interdict shipments of an entrepreneur that fails to satisfy its tax liability.

[697]The USA IFA Branch Comments stress in particular the compliance burdens that would occur if countries adopt a source-based approach to taxing electronic commerce. Broader permanent establishment definitions and more pervasive withholding taxes will inhibit the cross-border flow of valuable information and technology, which will be counterproductive to the taxing jurisdictions following this course of action. The Comments likewise stress the importance of uniform rules for intercompany pricing by

While there is no sign that consumers are ready to jettison the acquisition of physical consumer goods, information is becoming an increasingly important part of the economy. The intangible nature of information poses special enforcement problems for taxing authorities. When physical goods are shipped, it is possible to identify where they are from and who they are being shipped to. However, when information is downloaded, the transaction is much more transparent, often leaving a slender audit trail for taxing authorities. While this report will not analyze these problems, they deserve careful study.

5.2. VAT AND SALES TAXES

The special characteristics of electronic commerce create challenges for the application of traditional concepts and rules of VAT and general sales taxation. The issues are not very different in their general nature from the challenges to income taxation. They relate essentially to classification of electronic transactions, interpretation of jurisdictional rules (*e.g.,* the concepts of use and enjoyment of service and fixed establishment), fortifying those rules against risks of manipulation, the challenges of electronic commerce and tax administration. However, the challenges posed by electronic commerce also reflect the particularities of VAT and sales taxation. In the indirect tax area, bilateral tax treaties patterned after an OECD Model Convention would be insufficient for the purpose of international coordination. Among the Member States of the EC, it has been achieved in the past by advanced legislative harmonization and supervision by the European Court of Justice.

5.2.1. Objectives and official positions

The analysis of the application of present VAT and other general consumption tax rules and concepts to the new phenomenon of electronic commerce raises a number of VAT issues which should be resolved. Specif-

all the major taxing jurisdictions. It makes no administrative sense for different countries to apply different standards or rules for taxing the same enterprise engaged in global business. U.S.A. IFA Branch, *Comments on Electronic Commerce* (5 May 1998) (on file with the authors).

ically, the VAT regime of international services has always posed problems with respect to "place of supply" and accountability rules. Those problems are amplified in the case of international electronic commerce. The focus of further analysis thus changes from the application of present rules (*de lege lata*) to the formulation of VAT policy approaches for dealing with those problems (*de lege ferenda*). The specific focus is again on the definition of an appropriate jurisdictional framework. While such a framework would mainly involve "place of supply" rules, the issue cannot be disassociated from the categorization, administration or enforcement issues with respect to electronic transactions.

Official positions concerning possible VAT policy approaches are found in most available reports of national governments, particularly in those of the Executive Office of the President of the United States (1997), of the Advisory Committee to the Canadian Minister of National Revenue (1998), and of the Advisory Committee to the Dutch Underminister of Finance (1998). They are also found in documents of responsible international organizations, particularly those preparing the OECD Ministerial Conference, *A Borderless World: Realizing the Potential of Electronic Commerce*, taking place in Ottawa on 6-8 October 1998. A key issue on the agenda of the Conference is to create a consensus on a global framework of indirect taxation of international electronic commerce. An interactive video conference discussion is planned with the panel of the Seminar on Internet/I.T. Communications Issues, taking place in London during the course of the 1998 IFA Congress. Reference is made hereinafter to three documents relating to the preparation of the Ottawa conference: the VAT-discussions in the OECD-Turku document entitled *Dismantling the Barriers to Global Electronic Commerce* (1997); the OECD-CFA discussion draft entitled *Electronic Commerce: the Challenges to Tax Authorities and Taxpayers. An Informal Round Table Discussion between Business and Government* (1997); and the Communication by the European Commission on *E-Commerce and Indirect Taxation* (1998). EC and OECD recommendations will be submitted to the 1999 WTO Ministerial Conference.

This section provides an overview of VAT policy issues discussed or proposed in the aforementioned documents or resulting from the analysis developed in this study or by other authors. The policies range from "conservative" to "revolutionary" and, in between those positions, from technical legislative adaptations, to more fundamental legislative reform.

Their evaluation is made in keeping with recognized international tax objectives and principles. The OECD-Turku document states them as follows: "Whatever the solution adopted, the taxation of e-commerce should be relatively simple, should facilitate voluntary compliance, should not artificially advantage or disadvantage e-commerce over comparable traditional commerce, and should not unnecessarily hinder the development of e-commerce." The OECD-CFA discussion draft (para. 138) refers to some additional criteria by which to evaluate reform proposals. The system should be effective and minimize the potential for tax evasion and avoidance, thereby contributing to the stability of government revenues. It should be equitable among taxpayers and also ensure a fair sharing of the internet tax base among the participating states. The Communication of the European Commission states them as follows:

> The EU VAT system should provide the legal certainty, simplicity and neutrality required for the full development of electronic commerce. 'Legal certainty' enables commerce to be conducted in an environment where the rules are clear and consistent, reducing the risks of unforeseen tax liabilities and disputes. 'Simplicity' is necessary to keep the burdens of compliance to a minimum. 'Neutrality' means that:
>
> * the consequences of taxation should be the same for transactions in goods and services, regardless of the mode of commerce used or whether delivery is effected on-line or off-line;
> * the consequences of taxation should be the same for services and goods whether they are purchased from within or from outside the EU.
>
> Certainty, simplicity and neutrality are all essential to ensure a level competitive playing field for all traders in the developing global market place, and to avoid market conditions.

The Canadian Report (4.1.2) identifies the following principles of tax policy, providing guidance concerning the appropriate form of taxation of electronic commerce: economic neutrality and equity; ease of administration; no multiple taxation; and fair allocation of the tax base and revenues. The neutrality and equity are defined to require that functionally equivalent transactions be taxed in the same fashion and that customers of these businesses should not be required to pay different kinds and amounts of taxes. While the principles of tax neutrality and equity are thus applied at the level of both businesses and customers, it is submitted that the former application may prevail on the latter in the case of business profit taxation and vice versa in the case of consumption taxation.

In order to encourage further study of methods for adapting the EC VAT system and providing clear and simple rules and global solutions for forming an appropriate VAT framework, the European Commission proposed, in its 1998 Communication, a number of general guidelines for consideration at the OECD Ministerial Conference in Ottawa. Based on the guidelines contained in those position papers and on the analysis of section 4.3 of this Report, section 5.2.2 considers a number of policy approaches to the EC and global VAT framework for international electronic commerce. Here, again, the term "policy approaches" is preferred over "proposals" as any recommended solution would necessitate further study.

5.2.2. VAT policy approaches

5.2.2.1. VAT type approach to general consumption taxation

The short review, in section 4.3.5 of general consumption tax systems of selected non-EC countries, points to a number of international orientations and consistency needs. Aside from the Member States' common VAT system, many non-EC countries — 12 out of the 14 remaining OECD Member States — currently apply a VAT type of general consumption tax. International issues concerning consumption taxation are simplified and more easily resolved by the adoption of a similar system. Because of its wide international acceptance, VAT is an attractive model.

The EC's larger trading partners may want to take EC VAT rules into account in dealing with the jurisdictional issues that arise in cross-EC border transactions. This would avoid the potential of double or multiple taxation. Some countries (*e.g.*, Switzerland, Rumania) have adopted a VAT system that closely follows EC VAT structure, rules, concepts and interpretations.

Other countries designing their own general consumption taxation system will want to participate in international discussions so as to take into account the international tax practices and principles of other jurisdictions, especially when it comes to applying their system to something as global as electronic commerce. The question of what the precise international tax practices and principles are, and whether the growth of electronic commerce justifies their reevaluation, is discussed below.

5.2.2.2. Conservative VAT policy approach

The conservative approach is also described as the "status quo" or "hands-off" approach because it leaves the present VAT system unchanged. The conservative approach is based on the trust that current VAT rules and concepts are sufficiently reliable and flexible for the application to electronic commerce.

The "VAT rules and concepts" relate mainly to the place of supply of services, but also to VAT accountability and collection mechanisms for international electronic services. The taxable place rules are based on the application of essentially three criteria described in three rules which are based on the nature of the service, the country of establishment of the parties, the nature of the establishment and tax status. They are complex and they are not always neutral, effective or consistent.

The need for reevaluation of the principles of the present system is discussed in sections 5.2.2.3 through 5.2.2.6.

5.2.2.3. Origin-based VAT application

In 1996, the European Commission proposed the introduction of a common VAT system of origin-based taxation. It would provide for a single place of taxation — the place where the EC-based trader is established. In that single state, the trader would register, account for and deduct all EC-based VAT. The Commission has estimated that the cost of administering VAT transactions in other states is 5 or 6 times more than the cost for similar transactions conducted in the supplier's home country. It would, therefore, simplify VAT for both EC-based and non-EC operators who would no longer have to divide up their turnover among 15 Member States (assuming business in all 15 States). It would thus do away with the burdensome procedure of multiple registration.

However, the operation of the proposed system implies fundamental changes which are not easily realized:

- a further standardization of rates, preferably into a single rate given the elasticity and tax sensitivity of international electronic trade;

- a uniform application, which would require the transformation of the VAT Committee from an advisory into a regulatory committee;
- the re-allocation, according to consumption, of displaced VAT revenues between Member States so as to guarantee them the same level of current revenue.

It has been suggested that this origin-based tax system should also be applied to electronic commerce across EC-borders. After all, much of the world uses the origin system for sales taxation. However, it is questionable as to whether the application of such a system would be neutral. When the principle of Article 9(1) of the Sixth Directive was applied to telecommunications services — until July 1997 — transactions with EC-based private consumers and non-taxable businesses tended to move to non-EC (*e.g.*, the United States) telecommunications operators, thereby avoiding the cost of VAT both within and without the EC. The origin-based system would, therefore, appear not to be neutral or consistent with the regime retained for basic telecommunications services. However, the idea was proposed by the German Kommission Umsatzbesteuerung in Europa nach dem Ursprungslandprinzip ab 1997 (*See supra* section 2.2.3.3.). Also, one of the Comments of the German IFA Branch (Portner) concludes that the origin method applies to most services. It would be applied under the planned revision charging VAT at the suppliers' local rate and should, therefore, also be applied to electronic commerce, irrespective of the exception relating to telecommunications services and explained by the special circumstances that resulted in discrimination between foreign and domestic suppliers.

5.2.2.4. *Consumption-based VAT application*

The approach is consumption-based when it provides for the taxability of cross-EC border services in the territory where the services are consumed. This is the place of establishment of the customer, his fixed establishment to which the services are supplied or of the place of effective use or enjoyment. It is argued that it is a sound territorial implementation of a consumption tax and is in line with WTO tax principles. This is particularly so where the tax is applied to electronic commerce because, in cyberspace, consumption may provide a more stable tax base.

This principle is endorsed by the European Commission, in its 1998

Communication, *E-Commerce and Indirect Taxation*, "The EU VAT system should ensure that:

- services, whether supplied via e-commerce or otherwise, which are supplied for consumption within the EU, are taxed within the EU, whatever their origin.
- such services, supplied by EU operators for consumption outside the EU, are not subject to VAT in the EU, but VAT on related inputs is eligible for deduction."

The Commission finds that this jurisdictional system would ensure neutrality between EC and non-EC supplies. Furthermore, all services delivered on-line from non-EC sources to private consumers in the EC would be subject to VAT. Conversely, all services exported from the EC to non-EC countries would be tax free. It also ensures neutrality between off-line and on-line deliveries. If services delivered by traditional channels (*e.g.*, telephone, mail) from non-EC sources to private consumers in the EC would be subject to VAT, so would services delivered through electronic channels. The application of this jurisdictional system from non-EC operators to private consumers in the EC raises problems of control and effective collection, discussed in section 5.2.2.6.

The above guidelines concerning cross-EC border commerce do not rule out the application of different rules within the EC in accordance with the Commission's continuing commitment to the introduction of a common VAT system of origin-based taxation.

5.2.2.5.   Consolidating the safety nets

The effectiveness of the criteria used with respect to electronic commerce is a source of concern under either jurisdictional system, especially if the customer is a private consumer (or bank or other non-taxable person bearing the input VAT cost) and the supplier is a non-EC operator. The risk justifies the need for adequate safety nets. While those safety nets are described in the Sixth Directive's place of supply rules, it is noted that the same options are also offered for consideration in the wider context of the OECD-CFA discussion draft (para. 61 *et seq.*).

The rule designating the supplier's place of establishment as the taxable place is complemented by the rule (and safety net) providing for the taxation of the overseas operator supplying the service from a fixed establishment maintained in the taxing state (in the EC context, a Member State). When this safety net is applied to electronic commerce, it may not be effective if the concept of fixed establishment is interpreted to require the permanent presence of human and technical resources or the pre-eminence of a primary place of business. Should fixed establishment, therefore, be fortified by providing for a lower threshold, *e.g.*, the presence of a server and website? This approach may give rise to complications if it means that the definition for internet-related transactions is different from the general definition of fixed establishment as it is applies to other economic activities. The question can also be asked as to whether it is not simpler to rely on the alternative requirement of designation of local representative rather than to lower the permanent establishment threshold.

In a consumption-based jurisdictional system, the place of supply is deemed to be the establishment of the customer. It is fortified by providing for the complementary criterion of taxability of the service in the country of effective use and enjoyment. In a digital environment, consumers are presented with greater choice as to the range of available services and the number of service providers who, with the new technology, are not necessarily established, for VAT purposes, in the country of consumption. Consumption may occur in countries other than the country where the customer resides or where the customer is invoiced. Electronic commerce creates new opportunities for customers, such as final consumers or banking institutions, to evade or avoid VAT by turning to an associate (in this formal arrangement) who assumes billing and communication responsibilities and who is not established in the jurisdiction of the customer. The cost of the transaction may then be charged back to the bank, for example, by means of a management or other service charge not subject to VAT. The additional criterion of effective use and enjoyment should be implemented so as to deal adequately with such abuse.

The US practice of state sales and use taxation is not fully developed in terms of dealing with electronic commerce. A loosening of the traditional interpretation of substantial nexus and of bright line physical presence is required. The outcome, however, may become a source of inspiration for the interpretation of the effective use and enjoyment test found in consumption-based VAT systems, especially in a federal structure (EC). The position that no sales tax can be levied if the out-of-state vendor is not physically present is not relevant in a consumption-based VAT system. Being based on consumption, there should not be a requirement of a fixed establishment in the taxing state if the vendor concludes a deal over the internet.[698]

5.2.2.6. Mechanisms for ensuring VAT accountability and collection

How effective are the mechanisms for accounting for the VAT and for its collection in cross border situations? Where tangible goods are traded across borders, indirect electronic commerce should be physically (import) or administratively (intra-Community transactions) controlled. As compliance burdens pose the risk of slowing the development of indirect electronic commerce at the stage of its off-line delivery, those burdens should be minimized. An increase in the threshold for the small parcel delivery exemption may be considered if this threshold can in practice be controlled and maintained.

When it comes to most EC-based business-users of the internet, the EC VAT system provides an effective mechanism for services: the reverse charge procedure. At least in the Member States where this procedure is applied, the risk is reduced to the case of the supply of services to private consumers, banks and other non-taxable business users of electronic services and digitized goods. The EC VAT system relies, to this effect, on the registration of the overseas (non-EC) operator.

Experience with the reverse charge mechanism should indicate whether the registration procedure is more effective than other mechanisms, *e.g.*, a system of self-assessment (for domestic consumers) fortified by rebuttable presumptions. In the United States, collection solutions are being considered that would enable states to collect use taxes on out-of-state internet sellers. One such solution would rely on Due Process nexus to require sellers to provide customer information to a central clearinghouse, and let the state of consumption collect the use tax directly from the purchaser.[699]

---

[698]German IFA Branch (Prof. Strunk), *Comments on Electronic Commerce Report* (8 May 1998) (on file with the authors).

[699]U.S.A. IFA Branch, *Comments on Electronic Commerce Report* (5 May 1998) (on file with the authors), referring to a paper presented by Mr. Eads to the Multistate Tax Commission. For a discussion of this and other collection solutions *see* Houghton, *How Do We Impose State and Local Taxes on Electronic Commerce?* in COMMITTEE ON STATE TAXATION STATE TAX REPORT, Vol. 97, Issue 6 (1997).

The alternative of a tax withholding approach is proposed as the only effective method by Dittmar and Selling in their article, *How to control Internet transactions? A contribution from the Point of View of the German Tax Inspectors.*[700] For the German inspectors, VAT monitoring and enforcement starts with suppliers, customers and providers are unreliable. Customers may delete the record of their entire internet session, making the origin of supplier and customer unknown. Providers do not always have the tax information, especially if they charge flat rate fees. The only reliable starting point is, therefore, the payment system, especially if fiscal interests are built in a system of payment security. Banks would thus be required to withhold VAT from the compensation of the supplier and transfer it to the tax office. The taxability of the supplies would result from the use of the website. As a digital sales facility, it could also constitute the fixed establishment of a foreign supplier.

This system may not be as effective a collection mechanism as the German inspectors think it is. A server, website and payment flows can be relocated with ease. Moreover, the financial intermediaries may have legitimate reasons for not wanting to serve as tax collection agents. Those responsibilities properly belong to the vendor as the vendor requires information permitting a determination of the nature of the transaction, location, identity and status of parties, VAT calculation, etc. However, vendors could be required to supply to the financial intermediary a copy of the invoice containing the relevant information.

The tax withholding solution is also considered in the Canadian report (para. 4.3.1.):

> One approach that has been suggested would be to make financial intermediaries responsible for collecting sales tax on the transactions that they process for payment. Under this scenario, software could be developed that the financial intermediaries would operate in conjunction with their financial processes. Ideally, this approach would provide a seamless approach to the collection of sales tax on the cross-border sale of digitized products. However, such an approach would represent a fundamental shift in the legal liabilities for tax collection, and also raises a number of important issues. For example, to apply Canadian sales tax structures, financial intermediaries would need to know, at the very least, the location of the supplier and the purchaser, the place of supply, whether tax had already been collected by the

---

[700]Dittmar & Selling, *How to control Internet Transactions? A contribution from the Point of View of German Tax Inspectors,* Intertax 88 (March 1998).

supplier, the tax status of the purchaser, and the nature of the product. (...)
The feasibility of solutions that involve enlisting financial or transaction intermediaries in collecting sales tax for governments will depend on how electronic commerce processes and information-gathering techniques and capacities expand.

Tax withholding may be a method of last resort, particularly if the trader registration of non-EC operators would turn out not to offer an effective basis of VAT accountability and collection.

5.2.2.7. *Practical business challenges of electronic commerce*

As electronic commerce will cause an acceleration of global trading, it gives rise to the attendant need to VAT register in multiple countries. In most countries the process is not standardized and it is both arcane and expensive. Tax representatives can be used, but because many countries require them to have joint and several liability, they are hard to come by. Some countries automatically invoke income tax registration with VAT registration. VAT rules and procedures thus raise a number of issues which are pertinent in practical ways to companies conducting electronic commerce. Companies need to internalize this and have a strategy for optimizing their VAT registrations, such as using multi-VAT registered entities as their e-commerce vehicles.

Because an invoice is the primary document for the collection and recovery of VAT, some tax authorities do not permit electronic invoicing and those that allow it have strict requirements. These requirements are country-specific and, as such, require multiple solutions. There is no legislation or standards covering the use of electronic invoicing on a cross-border basis. Simplification and international standards should be promoted. The same applies to electronic records retention.

On-line calculation of VAT in relation to transactions on a website that sells multiple products to multiple countries with multiple customers will be very complex. Any error will be almost impossible to correct subsequent to the completion of a transaction (unless an origin-system is applied).[701] These VAT issues present major business challenges and should be resolved.

---

[701] U.S.A. IFA Branch, *Comments on Electronic Commerce Report* (5 May 1998) (on file with the authors).

5.2.2.8. Consistent and neutral characterization of electronic transactions

The choice of the right rule for the categorization of electronic transactions is important, but gathering a consensus is equally important. The definition of basic telecommunications services found in the Community tax legislation is borrowed from the Melbourne Convention and has the advantage of being internationally accepted. This is not the case with the definitions and interpretations of other types of electronic services. To avoid VAT taxation that creates double taxation and restricts international trade, common definitions and rules of interpretation should be detailed in a general multilateral agreement among OECD Member countries or in bilateral agreements following some OECD, EC or other VAT Model Convention. Within the Community a more consistent and neutral VAT treatment should be achieved through the European Court of Justice and the VAT Committee or by reevaluating the Directives amending the Sixth Directive.

Electronic commerce blurs the traditional distinctions between goods and services as well as the traditional distinctions among types of services. In doing so, it gives rise to inconsistent tax treatment relating not only to applicable rates, but to place of supply and applicable tax procedures. The parties to transactions may apply those inconsistencies to minimize or avoid their VAT liability by purchasing digitizable goods as services, or vice versa, by purchasing data processing services as transmission services or by combining services as a single composite supply, or vice versa. A different categorization of electronic services and soft goods, especially in transactions between EC countries and non-EC countries or between non-EC countries, also poses the risk of giving rise to situations in which the same service or software is subject to double taxation.

The OECD-CFA document offers few guidelines as to how transactions should be evaluated when traditional distinctions — in particular the line between goods and services — become blurred as in the case of such digitizable goods as music, video, software, etc. The Committee on Fiscal Affairs concludes that the line between goods and services should not depend on the means of distribution (*e.g.,* the sale of standard software through a retail outlet versus the same sale via the internet) (para. 69). The Communication of the European Commission also deals with the issue of whether a supply (in particular from a non-EC supplier to a private person in the EC) should be treated as a good (subject to VAT) or as a service (not subject to VAT) when it is acquired by a private person via the electronic network: "It is the policy of the EU to consider products ordered and delivered on networks to be services. EU VAT legislation makes a basic distinction between the supply of goods and the supply of services. All types of electronic transmissions and all intangible products delivered by such means are deemed, for the purposes of EU VAT, to be services. This is in keeping with the position taken by the EU and its Member States at WTO. In the tax area, this also allows for a clear set of rules to be applied." In the United States, where sales taxes have the same issues as VAT regarding physical versus digital delivery, approximately 15 states tax the physical delivery of software, but consider software downloaded over the internet to be an exempt service.[702]

Not everybody shares this view. The German IFA Branch Comments (Prof. Strunk) challenge the conclusion that the VAT treatment of digitizable products should depend on the form chosen for their presentation and focuses on their intellectual content:

> It does not appear to be correct that qualifying digitizable products as a supply of goods or of services depend on whether the information was downloaded from the Internet or was supplied to the customer in a tangible form. The decisive criterion can only be the economic content of a contract governed by the law of obligations that forms the basis for the supply of goods of services. Thus the current qualification of books and music CD's as tangible assets and the transfer of title thereto as a supply of goods is an incorrect consequence as the buyer as a rule does not have an economic interest in the tangible medium but in the intellectual content and creative form.

This solution should be compared with the solution proposed by the other (Portner) Comments of the German IFA Branch:

> We would like to stress the principle of tax neutrality. Tax treatment of a transaction should be independent of the form of the order, delivery or technology used. Therefore, an electronic version of a book should be treated as a book.

The distinction among types of services should also be reevaluated in the light of the new digital environment. Should there be distinction in the

---

[702]*Id.*

era of the Internet and video conferencing? If it is concluded that differences should not be based on the (non-)taxable status of the recipient for the purpose of applying VAT according to his place of establishment, the issue becomes that of reevaluating the place of supply rules of Article 9, in particular the choice between the common criterion of the place of recipient's establishment (when he is a private consumer or non-taxable business) and that of the supplier's place of establishment. That issue of choice of place of supply was discussed in 5.2.2.3 (place of origin) and 5.2.2.4 (place of consumption). The latter option means that the supply of electronic services and soft goods — including those derived from suppliers outside the EC — is taxable in the same manner as telecommunications services under the derogatory regime.

5.2.2.9. International cooperation and consensus

Individual countries may find solutions for tackling domestic VAT issues, but when they tackle cross border situations from an individual perspective, they risk creating double or non-taxation, trade distortions and tax enforcement problems. International VAT issues have been explicitly dealt with by the 15 EC Member States. Accordingly, the harmonization of the EC's VAT system is well developed in the Sixth Directive. However, electronic commerce was not considered in the Directive. Its adaptation to the new phenomenon of international electronic commerce may necessitate Directive amendments. The Confédération Fiscale Européenne expressed to the European Commission the view that the EC VAT regime should be updated. To this effect, it reviewed a list of provisions to meet the challenges of the 21st century, taking the technology of the last 20 years into account.[703] If any new provisions are to work throughout the EC, the interpretation of critical VAT concepts and rules should be common. It is the responsibility of the European Court of Justice and the VAT Committee. The latter should become regulatory rather than advisory.

As the need to find an appropriate international framework for the taxation of electronic commerce is global and the risk of double taxation is, therefore, general, non-EC trading partners should participate in a com-

---

[703]Confédération Fiscale Européenne, *Modernization of VAT. An opinion statement submitted to the European Commission,* 1996/1997.

mon reevaluation of VAT rules, policies and administrative procedures. The appropriate international forum for such discussion is that provided by the OECD. A multilateral agreement may provide for the orderly interaction of the rules of supply, international procedures for settling conflicts, suitable ways to deal with audit trail difficulties and mutual administrative assistance. In this exercise, the OECD and its Special Section on Consumption Taxes should recognize the contributions of the European Commission over the last 30 years.

The problem of the territorial restrictions on jurisdiction with respect to cross border transactions is not new, but it is exacerbated in the case of cross border electronic trade. It requires a treaty-based obligation of mutual assistance. The framework for the exchange of information among the VAT authorities of EC Member States is set by the EC Directive of 6 December 1979 (79/1070/CEE). The Directive extended the scope of the existing Direct Tax Directive 77/799 to VAT. The Multilateral Council of Europe/OECD Convention of Mutual Assistance in Tax Matters, of 25 January 1988, which entered into effect in 1995 and applies to VAT and other general consumption taxes also provides a basis for information exchange. Because of those multilateral VAT undertakings, information received under bilateral income tax treaties may be given to VAT authorities in other Member States. However, the extent of the exchange of information relating to electronic commerce under those conventions is still largely determined by national regulations. National regulations may provide for a different regulatory framework concerning the reciprocal disclosure of information regarding taxation of electronic commerce: Is there legal ground for obtaining and using the information? How is the territorial limitation on the access to information regulated?

In July 1998, the European Commission presented a proposal for a Directive to ensure that taxpayers cannot evade tax claims established in one Member State by moving — themselves or their assets — to another Member State. The use of electronic commerce makes it difficult to locate them. The proposed Directive would update Directive 76/308/EEC on mutual assistance for the recovery of VAT claims. Furthermore, to ensure an effective concerted approach to non-payment of tax by Member States, a program of Community action was adopted to improve the indirect taxation systems of the internal market (Fiscalis program). The need for global measures justifies initiatives to widen the scope of EC information exchange and cooperation by involving WTO member countries.

5.2.2.10. VAT-moratorium

It may make sense to provide for a moratorium in an OECD or WTO context. During the next few years no new taxing concepts or rules would be introduced. The point of such a moratorium would be to see what experience emerges from the Community telecommunications rules of jurisdiction and collection, from the further study of the issue, the consultation with relevant industries, the interpretation of critical taxing concepts such as fixed establishment and place of effective use and enjoyment, and from the direction of an international consensus.

The appropriateness of a moratorium is raised in the Turku OECD document: "This evaluation of existing tax laws will be a complex and lengthy endeavor, especially at international level. To avoid a proliferating patchwork of tax laws that would stifle e-commerce while this review is being conducted, it has been suggested that a moratorium should be imposed on any new tax initiatives for the Internet. Such a moratorium would allow the authorities to participate actively in devising international consistent policy recommendations." The 1998 Communication of the Commission, *E-Commerce and Indirect Taxation* likewise concludes: "At this stage, where E-commerce is still developing and patterns of trade are as yet unclear, it is not necessary or possible to change the existing scheme of tax."

The "wait and see" option places more emphasis on the tactical approach than on substantive tax policy. However, it is essentially conservative. The risk of a moratorium approach is the difficulty or even practical impossibility of updating the rules, if such update would turn out to be necessary but no longer acceptable to states having a "vested" interest in maintaining the status quo.

5.2.2.11. VAT-free zone

The Advisory Group of the Dutch Underminister of Finance, in its 1998 Notice, submitted far-reaching proposals to zero-rate or lower the VAT rate with respect to electronic transactions on the basis of the following arguments. In the present stage of Community legislation, particularly concerning "place of supply," the export of electronic services by EC-based suppliers to foreign markets is handicapped by VAT burdens which are not imposed on EC competitors based in countries (*e.g.,* the United States) which do not apply VAT or a similar consumption tax. For that reason a

VAT exemption should be applied to Dutch — and other EC-based — suppliers by zero-rating all electronic transactions. This would be based on the legal fiction that they are entered into with customers in non-EC countries, thereby giving rise to the deduction of the full input VAT. The exemption would also apply to supplies of electronic services within the Netherlands (and other EC countries). Unlike supplies of tangible goods (taxable on the local market), such supplies have the merit of avoiding production costs and physical transport costs.

The VAT exemption would last as long as the competitive disadvantage lasts or at least for some specified period of time. During the initial period, EC-legislation causing the competitive disadvantage would be amended. Electronic commerce would thus be given the opportunity to expand in the EC. The harm to suppliers of physical goods and the loss of tax revenue would be limited because this trade segment is still not very significant.

The Advisory Group to the Dutch Underminister also proposes lowering VAT rates for digital information products. These would include CDs and soft goods downloaded onto consumers' PCs in the Netherlands (as well as consumers in other EC countries). The idea is to promote Dutch — and overseas — trade in these goods and eliminate the VAT disadvantage of Dutch suppliers. Non-EC suppliers often have the luxury of selling soft goods to Dutch consumers free of VAT. The low rate measure would be extended to on-line equipment and telecommunication charges so as to reduce the costs of using these media.

The starting point of the Dutch proposal is the neutrality principle and safeguarding the competitive position of Dutch (as well as other EC-based) suppliers of electronic products operating in foreign markets. To the extent their VAT handicap is caused by inadequacies in certain place of supply rules, a more appropriate remedy would be to correct those jurisdictional rules. The proposal becomes questionable where, using arguments of tax neutrality, it effectively favors the competitive position of Dutch suppliers in the global market place. The Dutch proposals are also questionable where they disregard the loss of the tax revenue involved in the measures.

However, it is noted that the proposed tax regime of zero-rating transactions would provide normal VAT obligations and audit trails unlike the system of the ordinary exemption which would bring a state of tax anonymity (no man's land). The Dutch idea is, therefore, different from action that would seek multilateral agreements through the WTO to establish that activity on the internet and interactive computer services is exempt worldwide from customs duties (in accordance with the 20 May 1998

Agreement among the 138 WTO members) and VAT or other sales taxes. The objections against a tax free superhighway would relate to the loss of tax revenue on this rapidly growing segment of trade and to the lack of neutrality between the taxation of electronic and traditional trade. The idea was rejected in the OECD-CFA discussion document (which does accept the idea of the internet as a duty-free zone for the delivery of goods and services): "There is no intention in this proposal (of tariff-free zone) to limit the application of VAT/GST to goods and services, as appropriate (when delivered electronically), by national tax administrations." (para. 85).

5.2.2.12. No new taxes

Based on the unique characteristics of electronic commerce and the difficult challenges regarding the traditional principles and systems of international taxation, alternative tax ideas have been proposed under such names as "bit" or "cyber taxes." Alternative taxes are tax formulae of last resort. They should be considered only if and when the general consumption and income tax system fails in realizing the aforementioned objectives. This is the view expressed in the OECD-CFA document: "In the physical world, collecting taxes is a challenge that, by and large, governments have met. They will probably be equally successful in the 'virtual' world insofar as countries interpret and apply existing rules in an internationally consistent fashion. If they succeed in this, they will not need to create new taxes specifically for electronic commerce." The 1998 European Commission, in *E-commerce and Indirect Taxation,* likewise concludes that "VAT, as opposed to any new form of tax, is appropriate to electronic commerce, just as it is to traditional ways of conducting business . . . In the field of indirect taxation all efforts should be concentrated on adapting existing taxes and more specifically VAT to the developments of e-commerce. No new or additional taxes are therefore to be considered."

5.3. ALTERNATIVE TAX FORMULATIONS

The following ideas of new tax regimes for replacing or supplementing existing VAT (and income) taxes have been proposed. A detailed critical evaluation of their merits, or lack thereof, is not part of this study, which focuses rather on the challenges of applying and adjusting existing general (income and VAT) regimes to the challenges of international electronic commerce.

5.3.1. Bit Tax

A first approach is radical or even revolutionary because it does not fit in the framework of income or consumption-based taxation. The bit tax would be levied on the number of computer bits transmitted over the internet and received by its user. The tax is presented by some as the new fiscal framework for distributing the productivity and added value of network interactivity. Proponents also tout it as a tax that can help reduce what they perceive as the threatening congestion on the Information Superhighway.[704]

Others question the merit of the bit tax. It is counterproductive in that it burdens electronic commerce and its productivity and discriminates against internet users and providers. It is also viewed as unfair as it taxes consumers regardless of the economic relevance of the message being transmitted (*i.e.*, a vital medical report would be treated in the same manner as unsolicited junk mail). Its flows can be transferred to ISP's in jurisdictions that do not apply a similar tax (however, the limited number of telecommunications companies should help in tax monitoring). Last but not least, bits and bytes are hardly an expression of economic value or wealth. Theoretical and practical experiences have demonstrated that, for decision-making in a business entity and for allocating resources in the community, mankind has no better tool than economic value.[705]

---

[704]Cordell, *Multi-Jurisdictional Taxation of Electronic Commerce;* Soete and Kamp, *The bit tax: taxing value in the emerging Information Society,* in 1997 Spring Symposium, Harvard, l.c. It is not clear why proponents believe that private market forces will not adequately deal with issues of supply and demand in this area as in other areas.

[705]The Comments of the Swedish IFA Branch question the merit of the use of bits and bytes for purposes of economic measurement as follows. "The number of eggs is a valid expression for exactly the number of eggs produced by the hen. It might also be representative for the health of the hen but you cannot take for certain that it also represents the value in economic terms. It might be important if the eggs are brown or white, small or big, round or egg-shaped. It might depend on season, packaging, transportation. Their value is that of the whole market package and not of number of eggs or of bits and bytes. The bit tax measures what it measures and nothing else. It puts aside all that we consider as market conditions." Swedish IFA Branch, *Comments on Electronic Commerce Report* (1998) (on file with the authors).

The bit tax idea is rejected by most official organizations and tax experts because it would not be in accordance with basic principles of international taxation. In its April 1997 Communication, the European Commission rejected the suggestion, in the January 1996 Reflections of its own High Level Group of Experts.[706] It did so in summary fashion, alluding to the tax neutrality principle: "While some commentators have suggested that there might be a need to look to alternative taxes such as bit tax, the Commission is of the opinion that this is not appropriate since VAT already applies to these transactions." The same conclusion and reasoning is found in the guidelines of the Commission's Communication (1998):

> VAT, as opposed to any new form of tax, is appropriate to electronic commerce, just as it is to more traditional ways of conducting business." The idea of bit tax is also dismissed, with a footnote, in the Discussion Paper of the US Treasury: "Treasury believes that these new technologies should not be used to justify new taxes. Accordingly, Treasury is not considering any type of value added tax (VAT), bit tax, or other new excise tax on electronic commerce."

The US IFA Branch, and most other IFA Branches, do not favor the enactment of new taxes. However, if it is proven that global commerce creates a more mobile tax base, the OECD may be uniquely qualified to propose global solutions, including a universal tax at a low rate subject to international coordination and cooperation. On the other hand, it can be argued that no tax system should impede the development of electronic commerce. It appears that we need a forum other than bilateral treaty negotiations to resolve these concerns.[707]

---

[706]Commission Report, *Building the European Information Society for Us All*, January 1996. The report is not a tax document but contains the controversial paragraph: "How will governments be able to continue to raise funds in an increasingly information-based world in which value is generated through clearly identifiable material production and exchange? The Expert Group would like the commission to undertake research to find out whether a bit tax might be a feasible tool." Soete (*The bit tax*, 1997 Spring Symposium Harvard, l.c.) defends the research option on the bit tax: "Let the traditional policy reader thus be warned: apart from a few papers by Cordell, there is virtually no literature on this subject. This is a 'no-man's research' land. For this reason only the EU experts' group request for further research seems to be more than justified."

[707]U.S.A. IFA Branch, *Comments on Electronic Commerce Report* (5 May 1998) (on file with the authors).

5.3.2.   Transaction Tax

A transaction tax would be levied on money flows on the internet and its on-line services. It would be automatically withheld by the banks involved in money transfers between accounts or in the issuance of electronic cash. Its proponents argue that a tax rate of 1%, for example, might suffice to replace all existing taxes, as the volume of payments is much greater than individual country's GDPs. The goal of a fairness could perhaps be accomplished through the transaction tax as a taxpayer's money flows increase with income and wealth. The transaction tax is applied to money flows because they can be tracked on the internet.

The tax would be collected in the country of the bank where the transfer is submitted. The risk that flows might end up in offshore banks may be minimized by cooperation between national authorities and EC Member States.[708] However, it seems likely that there will always be a market for tax havens and such nations might be unwilling to harmonize their tax rules. These nations depend on the harmonization of other nations' tax rules to provide a market for their more taxpayer-friendly tax provisions. The issue of whether CFC — or other — type anti-abuse legislation can be effectively used should be explored.

As long as there is no fixed relation between money flows and taxable income in the form of business profits, the tax seems questionable as it could have serious effects on the allocation of resources and the manner in which business is organized.

5.3.3.   Telecommunications and PC or other Internet hardware taxes

A telecommunications tax would be levied on basic telecommunications services as a percentage of the charge to users. The risks are that it could be avoided by displacement of telecommunications companies or by

---

[708]Vording, H., *Internet en de Transactiebelasting,*Weekblad Fiscaal Recht, 1997/6229, 23 January 1997, 100. The tax ideas were first developed by Tobin and Feige in the narrower contexts of taxation of speculative transactions at the stock exchange and of unofficial money.

the relocation of their businesses to countries without a telecommunications tax. These risks may be minimized by imposing the tax under EC-harmonized conditions and by international agreements which regulate other aspects of telecommunications services and their operators. However, tax competition would likely lead some nations to provide taxpayer-friendly treatment outside any general international agreement. The risk that the telecommunications tax could be avoided by the offshore establishment of a telecommunications company is reduced if it is collected at the points of connection in the country of the user. Technologically, that may not be possible. For example, policing mobile connections with overseas telecommunications operators may be problematic.

A tax on PCs would be imposed on PCs or other physical internet infrastructure located in the territory of the taxing state. A special tax would thus be levied on the registration of PCs or modems providing access to the internet. Another tax could be levied on automated teller machines (ATMs) and collected by their operators from customers using them for their financial transactions. It has been argued that this application to the fixed or tangible links of the infrastructure would make the collection of such taxes more effective from a territorial standpoint.

Specific taxes, as those applied to the amount of telecommunication charges or linked to hardware giving access to the internet in the territory of the taxing state, are less radical than bit or transaction taxes. However, being special consumption or excise taxes linked to the type of supply, they do not fit in the framework of a neutral and, therefore, general VAT. Several specific tax solutions for different branches or different types of supplies should be avoided because they could have the consequence of creating competitive disadvantages. They also have the negative consequence of being cumulative with the VAT or other general consumption tax.

5.4.   INSTITUTIONS

This report has demonstrated how international electronic commerce, by virtue of its essential characteristics (section 3), poses new challenges or amplifies existing challenges to present tax systems (section 4) and policies (section 5). The new business uses made of the new information and communication technologies, with the help of new intermediaries in the environment of cyberspace, create or exacerbate problems regarding jurisdiction, categorization of income or transactions and tax administration and enforcement.

There is a question as to whether institutions are available which can put forth the efforts necessary to meet those challenges. Institutions, in matters of domestic and international taxation, are mostly national. They will remain so as long as nations are sovereign and insist on the exercise of their sovereign rights when it comes to taxing power. Tax policies, tax legislation or interpretations and their adaptation to the challenges of electronic commerce will thus take place at the national level.

The Introduction to this report (section 1) notes that national governments rely on similar tax objectives and principles in dealing with the common challenges posed by electronic commerce. However, divergent national interests (*e.g.*, between net electronic commerce exporting and importing states) and different implementations of common but vague tax principles and objectives do not guarantee a uniform application of existing tax rules and concepts to the new phenomenon of electronic commerce. Individual approaches to the challenges of electronic commerce in the global marketplace have the potential of giving rise to a proliferation of divergent solutions that may exacerbate the international tax problems created by electronic commerce. The problems are well known: double taxation, no taxation, excessive tax competition, tax abuse, competitive disadvantage, ineffective tax administration and loss of tax revenue. Electronic commerce — more than traditional ways of doing business — helps to expose differences in national tax systems. A global and comprehensive tax framework may be needed to correct those differences.

Some believe in the spontaneous convergence of national tax systems and tax policies through independent action by taxing states. They rely on the interplay of market forces and on competition among national legislators, especially where the market place is as borderless, transparent and fluid as it is with electronic commerce. Others will point to the gigantic overstatement of the harmonious convergence potential of a process that is dictated by blind market forces. They fear that the process may, in fact, result in destructive fiscal competition, ruinous government financing and orientations dictated by market and global industry in a (tax) field which should remain the prerogative of targeted public policy. Their fear grows as electronic commerce plays a greater and greater role in international trade. It would be wonderful if the global market forces produce increasing convergence in the national tax regimes dealing with electronic commerce, but those forces may require shaping by a comprehensive global tax framework. The creation of a framework begins with a study of the challenges and methods of meeting them. The contribution of the relevant industries is important.

To succeed, a global framework requires international participation and cooperation. At the level of the EC, the institutional framework for tax coordination exists. However, the restrictive conditions for exercising Community powers and the political reluctance of Member States to harmonize their income tax laws are such that currently no attempt has been made or considered at the Community level to regulate — beyond OECD initiatives — income tax rules and concepts as they relate to electronic commerce. This is true notwithstanding the fact that national tax differences are particularly explicit and sensitive in the internal market and that their effects may run contrary to essential objectives. The prospects for Community harmonization are more tangible at the VAT level, as evidenced by the 1997 Council derogations and the Commission proposal to regulate, by means of a specific amendment of the Sixth Directive of the place of supply rules for basic telecommunications services. VAT rules may also have to be specifically harmonized with respect to electronic commerce, unless the European Court of Justice, in line with its practice of teleological and constructive interpretation, succeeds in adapting the concepts and rules of the Sixth Directive to the specific challenges of electronic commerce.

The challenges of electronic commerce are global. As such, the design of a global tax framework is a matter of concern to all nations. Where no super-national institutional framework is available, the appropriate legal instruments and fora may be those of multilateral agreements and international organizations. This is so even if their charters do not provide for the ambitious objectives of establishing a common market or economic and monetary union and for a transfer of national tax powers to a central regulatory institution. Some commentators have called for "a GATT for Taxes":

> The confluence of the problems identified above [to which the rapporteurs add: the taxation of electronic commerce] leads me to believe that the 21st century may — and should — see the first steps toward creation of what might be called 'a GATT (General Agreement on Tariffs and Trade) for taxes,' a multilateral agreement on the ground rules for taxation of international

flows of income from capital [the rapporteurs adding: and from electronic commerce] that make more sense than the largely ad hoc conventions that now guide policy in this area [the rapporteurs adding: and which are entirely missing in the specific tax field of electronic commerce].[709]

After dealing, in the March 1997 Information Technology Agreement, with the removal of customs duties on imports of almost all types of information technology products, WTO members might conceivably deal with the competitive tax conditions created by electronic trade. Untaxed virtual imports of international electronic business into tax haven countries is a concern that justifies global measures. The Cox-Wyden legislation in the United States — concerning a moratorium on new internet taxes — would include a declaration that the President should seek bilateral and multilateral agreements through the WTO, the OECD, the Asia Pacific Economic Cooperation Council, or other international fora. The United States proposes that activity on the internet and interactive computer services should be free from tariffs and new forms of taxation.[710] This specific tax initiative may be questionable as a policy approach, but it highlights the general need to marshal international cooperation on the international tax aspects of electronic commerce. The 1998 Communication by the European Commission, *E-Commerce and Indirect Taxation,* points to the Joint EC-US Statement on Electronic Commerce, of 5 December 1997, accepting that "taxes on electronic commerce should be clear, consistent, neutral and non-discriminatory." It also points to the 6 July 1997 Bonn Declaration, signed by 29 countries, stating that "tax issues of electronic commerce call for international co-operation and, where appropriate, coordination in order to avoid distortion of competition." The WTO decided to launch a comprehensive work program on electronic commerce and the European Commission plans to play an active part in considering the way in which indirect taxation should be applied to electronic transactions.

---

[709]McLure, *supra* note 36.

[710]The "Internet Tax Freedom Act" is working its way therough the U.S. Congress. The House of Representatives has passed H.R. 4105 in June of 1998. The Senate is considering S. 442, its version of the bill. It is likely that the legislation will be enacted into law, providing for a limited (between 2 and 6 years, depending on the final agreement) moritorium on newly introduced internet taxes. Existing broad-based taxes can be applied to internet transactions.

The primary forum for cooperation in the area of the international taxation of electronic commerce is the OECD. The OECD Committee on Fiscal Affairs, supported by the activities of its various Working Parties, is the central international organization for proposing, to its Member States, adaptations of their tax rules and concepts in dealing with the challenges of the internet and for reaching international consensus to this effect.

The global scope of electronic commerce and telecommunications services may suggest that the response, to be effective, should be formulated and organized within the framework of institutions with worldwide regulatory, administrative and even judicial tax powers. Conceivably having electronic commerce in mind, Mr. Tanzi, Head of Fiscal Affairs of the International Monetary Fund, sees the need for such an institution as follows: "There is no world institution with the responsibility to establish desirable rules for taxation and with enough clout to induce countries to follow these rules. Perhaps the time has come to establish one." Many will consider such an approach to be unrealistic or even inappropriate as long as the need for such an institution is not supported by the economic significance of electronic commerce in total world trade and by the inadequacy of the actions of national governments and the cooperation organized by existing international organizations. Possible guidelines for a global framework of VAT and income tax policies and legislation have been examined in this study within the parameters of the existing institutional framework.

Whatever solutions — within the parameters of an institutional framework — are devised for the tax problems described in this report, they must be devised with the new technological advances in mind. This will assure that the solutions are intellectually sound and, at the same time, administratively feasible. In the end, in evaluating any proposed changes to the current international tax principles, the question reformers must ask is: "compared to what?" Any tax system is going to have flaws. The issue that must be determined is whether, flaws and all, the system under consideration is better than other possibilities.

Précis

By Jean-Pierre le Gall (France)
Jeantet & Associés, Paris

The purpose of this précis is to compare the conclusions of the Rapporteurs, Richard Doernberg and Luc Hinnekens, and the comments National Branches of the IFA had the opportunity to make either in writing or through their representatives at the meeting held in London on May 9, 1998. Those conclusions and comments address the present situation and possible modifications.

I.   PRESENT SITUATION

One of the basic issues raised by electronic commerce is to determine whether the traditional concept of permanent establishment retains its relevance where business is carried out through the internet, i.e. without physical presence of the seller in the market territory (A). More generally the principal question arises as to whether taxation should take place in the source or residence country, or both. On those issues, National Branches have conflicting views among themselves and sometimes with the Rapporteurs.

A.   Permanent establishment concept

All countries, at least Treaty countries, use the concept of permanent establishment as a basic tool for taxation of business profits (1). This concept is still commonly used (be it not as a primary tool) by countries which apply a VAT regime (2).

1. Taxation of business profits

The **French** Branch of IFA considers that the concept of permanent establishment should be modified to adapt it to electronic commerce.

In this view, a rule should be adopted according to which the permanent establishment would be characterized by the fact that there is the possibility and /or effective use in a given territory, or negotiation, or contracts entered into or even payment by electronic means. However, such an adaptation of the permanent establishment concept seems difficult, if not impossible. To keep this rule would require such modifications that it might be just simpler to find another principle.

A "laissez faire" policy would be advantageous for commercial operators who sell goods abroad. It would lead to a loss of taxable revenues in some countries. This loss could be only temporary, but the question whether some countries with small connection potential would accept such a measure is doubtful.

For **Argentineans,** applying current permanent establishment principles to electronic commerce will unfairly distort the balance in favor of residence state taxation.

According to the **Japanese** Branch even if a permanent establishment has been formed, the amount of income attributable to that permanent establishment would not be large because its functions in the source country would be marginal. Also, the general and administrative expenses incurred by the head office must be allocated to the permanent establishment. Given the minimal presence likely to exist in the customer's country, it would cast doubt on the meaningfulness of arguing the permanent establishment issue if only a very small amount of income can be found to be attributable.

The **USA** Branch recommends that the permanent establishment concept should not be broadened because of electronic commerce. Accessibility of a web site from a particular country should in no case be considered as giving rise to a place of business in that country for tax purposes and the ownership, exclusive or shared use of equipment in a source country should not by itself give rise to a permanent establishment.

Germans consider that a web site, a server or telecommunications facilities located in the country of source should not constitute a permanent establishment. However, the paper of Dr. Strunk concludes that there must be legal amendments in order to assign to the source country a right to tax commercial services for which connecting factors with the domestic territory are missing.

If it is held that equipment such as a server creates an establishment for electronic commerce purposes, then that could have a far reaching effect for supplies of international telecommunications which, outside the USA, are currently taxed under the simple origin or destination principle. Apportionment in such circumstances would be impractical and undesirable.

2. VAT

For the **USA,** VAT registration processes are arcane, expensive and not standardized in many countries. Countries need to internationalize this and have a strategy for optimizing their VAT registrations.

There are no legislation or standards covering the use of electronic invoicing on a cross-border basis. Simplification and international standards should be promoted, as for electronic records retention. On line calculations of VAT on a web site will be very complex and errors almost impossible to correct. Attention should be paid to electronic invoicing and documented estimates of the relative size of the portion of the economy that can and is likely to be digitized and sent electronically as a percentage of total commerce as well as on line calculation of VAT.

Italians make some observations on the traditional VAT definition of sale of (tangible) goods, which appear to be obsolete in light of the rapid increase of direct electronic commerce, particularly assuming that the tangibility of the good is not a valid criterion: the sale of books will be replaced by the sale of telematic files containing the text of the book.

More emphasis should therefore be placed on the analysis of the rights which are transferred upon the sale. A tax system should treat similar income similarly, whether earned electronically or through non-electronic means. A reasonable way to achieve such neutrality is through the adaptation, to the extent possible, of existing tax principles and rules rather than the introduction of new tax regimes.

The Branch in **Chinese Taipei** believes that administrative difficulties may arise if VAT is levied at the place of the server, which is considered to be only a medium, not a place of business. Because VAT involves registered businesses, it may be administratively easier for the VAT to be levied according to the registered place of the entity.

Colombians believe that intending to circumscribe the services rendered through the internet to a particular territory is fictitious. The essence of the internet relies on the possibility of both inserting and accessing the information from any place in the world. The territorial bases are now no longer important. When the transactions follow through traditional means, using the internet as a mere promoter, it will still make sense to maintain the traditional tax concepts. But when the goods or services are obtained through the net, involving no territorial linkage, it would be awkward to try to impose those rules.

In **Argentina** it is thought that as far as VAT is concerned, the permanent establishment notion falls short of giving an adequate response to the objective of preserving the business income tax base of source countries. To preserve the primary right of source countries to tax new treaty law principles concerning the taxation of electronic commerce income need to be developed outside traditional permanent establishment principles.

B.   Conflict between residence and source country taxation

If the concept of permanent establishment keeps being used under its present definition, taxation :

- will almost exclusively take place in the countries of residence because there is no reason to locate the server in another country. If the web site is deemed to be a permanent establishment, the income attributable to this establishment will be very small because the marketing and sales costs incurred in the source country will be small.

Irrelevance of the permanent establishment concept opens a discussion as to the attribution of the right to tax profits generated by electronic commerce.

By and large most National Branches concur with the Rapporteurs to consider that conflict between residence and source country taxation may be solved in different ways.

In order to preserve the right of the source country to tax, the following principles could be applied :

- Adopt a rule similar to article 17 of OECD model convention : the income accrued by electronic commerce would only be taxable in the source country, even when there is no permanent establishment in this country.

- Abandon the concept of permanent establishment and adopt, non exclusively, the principle of taxation in the source country. The permanent establishment concept embodies the definition of a threshold of activity under which the company is taxed only in the country of residence: a threshold which could be abandoned in favour of a minimum turnover. The countries will have to agree on the way to determine where income is originated and on the practical difficulties of taxing a person who has no physical presence in the source country.
- Abandon the permanent establishment concept and adopt the principle of exclusive taxation in the source country. This solution could be developed in countries that are essentially consumption markets. It is the country where the activity takes place who has the right to tax the income derived from this activity.

In other order to preserve the right to tax in the residence country, other principles could be applied :

- Adopt a clause similar to article 8 of the OECD model Convention, so that the profits are taxed only in the country of residence of the company, whether the company only gives an access to the net or whether it has an activity through the net, or directly adopt the principle of exclusive taxation in the country of residence. Taxing all the income in the country of residence of the beneficiary would prevent many conflicts while being extremely negative for developing countries, which are not residence countries of companies engaged in such activities.
- Combine the taxation rules in articles 8 and 17: taxation in the residence country for companies giving access to the net and taxation in the source country for companies having a commercial activity on the net.

On top of that, determination of the residence of a company is extremely difficult if it is based on the concept of effective management, since it is always possible to manage a company by phone, which situation is enhanced by the net.

A new criterion could however be found which would take into consideration the country of residence of the managers or shareholders, in order to stop artificial domiciliations of companies. The country of residence can also be determined in a mathematical way: a formula taking into consideration the residence of the employees, the shareholders, or the managers could lead to a global international consensus. Finally, global integration would make the legal entity disappear on the tax point of view and would allow the direct taxation of shareholders like in a partnership.

It appears to the **Argentineans** that tax systems applying source based jurisdictional rules may give reasonable answers to the issue of allocating income from electronic commerce in an international context. The internationally recognized right to tax of source countries should not be altered even with the legitimate purpose of accommodating new forms of international commerce.

Adoption of non-exclusive source-based rules appears to be a reasonable approach to cope with the issue of allocating electronic commerce income in an international context, both for the internet service and content providers. Argentine internal tax law on non-residents has long been built on this basis and the system has proved to be workable in practice.

Applied to electronic commerce income, the system would permit the existing international tax equilibrium between residence and source countries to be maintained, while recognizing the primary right of the source country to tax. Although conflicting source rules between the source and residence countries may always lead to international double taxation, this is not a problem inherent to the application of the source principle to electronic commerce income but to the international allocation of income generally. Besides, conflicting source rule issues are usually solved by the application of bilateral tax treaties.

Building an international consensus on source principles applicable to electronic commerce income would be most desirable. Surveying existing source rules on income from intangibles, sales and service income might be a place to start.

The problem with corporate residence, as underlined by the **Japanese,** is that companies using a tax haven as a basis for worldwide electronic commerce in order to avoid taxation will present a serious concern to countries of residence. The relevant provision should be amended to make sure that the exemption provided by the existing Controlled Foreign Corporations (CFC) regulations will not be applicable to Internet operators in a tax haven.

II. MODIFICATIONS SUGGESTED

A. Recommended policies

The **German** position on this matter is simple. Tax neutrality is a principle that must be endorsed. Electronic commerce reflects a change in the facts and circumstances involved in these transactions which have to be taken into consideration in the application, interpretation, and modification of existing tax rules.

The development of electronic commerce is not a revolution and does not require introduction of a new tax regime. It only requires a legal framework which is flexible and utilizes self-regulating measures.

The tax principle of neutrality best is respected through adoption of existing tax principles and rules rather than specific rules regulating electronic commerce. New developments implicating a world-wide challenge requiring a complete reformulation of all traditional tax principles by redefining the territorial concept, the sourcing rules and income qualification should be clearly denied, even if some, changes are however necessary.

Tax treatment of a transaction should be independent of the form of order, delivery or technology used. Therefore an electronic version of a book should be treated as a good. Consistent with the principle of neutrality, no special taxes should be placed on electronic commerce.

However, for Dr. Strunk changes at least in the national law may be necessary to protect the right of the source country both in terms of connecting factor and allocation of the increased profit if the use of the internet results in a drop of cost of sales.

The **French** recommend going towards a simpler system with less categories of income or a uniform treatment of the various categories of income in order to avoid the constant search for tax optimization. CFC legislations which do not include "active" income generated by a subsidiary in a tax haven, will need to be modified because the net will give way to placing subsidiaries engaged in business activities in such places. The **Israeli** Branch does not express any view as to the alternative policies with respect to taxation of electronic commerce.

The **Colombian** Branch believes that the creation of legal fictions that will establish where internet services should be deemed rendered is a possibility. Traditional concepts will never render complete solutions. The international community should get involved in the creation of a general agreement on electronic commerce, similar to the intracommunitary system.

The **US** Branch recommends against the enactment of new taxes or licensing requirements aimed at the electronic commerce. It would be appropriate that electronic commerce be taxed similarly to other business activities whether carried out electronically or by physical means. The US Treasury White Paper appears to support the view that no tax system should impede the development of electronic commerce.

The ideal situation, according to the **Irish** Branch, would be to have a comprehensive overall solution which could be implemented immediately, but this is clearly not practical as the whole area of electronic commerce is constantly evolving.

Consequently, a more sensible approach would be to put in place some basic principles which would deal with the majority of transactions. These principles could then be developed and refined to deal with other specific and non routine transactions.

Koreans think that new substantive rules would have to be developed with global consensus on electronic commerce, which should not discourage trade flows.

All kinds of specific tax solutions for different branches or different types of supplies should be, as recommended by the **Swedish** Branch, avoided. In addition, separate taxes mostly have the negative consequence of cumulative taxation. Economic value has been theoretically and practically demonstrated as the best tool in taxation.

The type of issue that should be supported by the IFA, according to the **English,** is the development of Electronic Data Interchange (EDI) invoicing. For EDI to develop its full potential as a facilitator of electronic commerce, it is vital that EDI invoicing be accepted not just within countries but also cross-border. Within the EU there is still not an acceptance of EDI in all countries.

Taxing on the basis of an infrastructure is potentially distortive; a distinction needs to be drawn between the internet platform and the information/trading being conducted over it. Furthermore, trying to tax trading on the basis of infrastructure alone, such as a server, would lead to it being located in a tax haven.

Malaysia's overall concerns are those shared by developing countries generally. Electronic commerce will result in a substantial erosion of the country's tax base if the conventional principles of international taxation (source-based vs. residence-based) are applied.

This is why suggestions are made to modify the traditional principles in order to introduce new rules of taxation.

According to the **Japanese,** the desirable trend is toward an indirect tax which would be charged at a low rate. The tax rate applied should be rather small, such as 0.5 or 1%, in order not to create a harmful effect on electronic commerce. To deal with this within an income tax framework may require fundamental changes under both domestic tax laws and income tax treaties.

The **Italian** Branch believes that the increasing capacity to carry on international business activities from the country of residence is not a new phenomenon, but the continuation of an ongoing trend. It suggests keeping the permanent establishment definition (art. 5 of OECD model convention). Changes should be limited to essential ones, and the commentary of article 5 may be the place to include observations and recommendations. The trend of using corporations located in tax havens can be discouraged by jointly using the residence criteria (place of effective management and control, and place of effective business) and a CFC legislation which includes specific provisions on electronic commerce.

The solutions that will probably be reached by the countries of the EU will not be applied on the Colombian territory, it is stated by the **Colombian** Branch. Only a minority of the countries on the globe that have or will eventually have access to the internet belong to communities with common tax regulations. The Colombians underline the fact that solutions reached through intracommunitarian obligations will not permit, for the near future, the challenges posed by electronic commerce to be overcome outside the communities.

Therefore, the abandonment of income taxation in favor of transactional taxes is viewed as an interesting possibility. However, enforcement problems relating to income generated by electronic commerce may also arise in attempting to impose transactional taxes.

Colombian authorities believe that a General Agreement on Taxes is an excellent long-term idea but will take a long time to achieve.

B.   Introduction of new taxes

The **German** position on this matter is simple: in no way should alternative taxation methods such as bit tax or withholding or consumption tax be introduced. The **Italians** consider that these alternative tax ideas make sense.

1.   Bit tax

One of the most serious proposals is to set up a new tax called bit tax.

In **France,** it is thought that the tax on bits, if based on the number of bits received by the user, would be discriminatory for users of the net. Moreover, this blind tax does not take into consideration the value added to the information in the bit. The French note that this system was not accepted in the USA nor in Europe.

The **English** consider that any new tax such as bit tax should be opposed as it bears no relation to the value of information or services being provided. According to them, the present VAT system in the EU can be adapted to meet the needs of electronic commerce. Solutions such as formulary approach and transactions, telecommunications or bit taxes are rejected for well known reasons.

Colombian authorities consider the bit tax not such a good idea because it is not concordant with the principles of taxation. It would lead to a breach of the principle of neutrality. If no solution is reached, it could be a complementary measure, even though it constitutes an exception to the mentioned principle, in order to preserve the income of national Treasuries. Similar comments are made regarding the tax on PC's or other physical internet infrastructure located on the territory of the taxing country.

For **Italians,** the bit tax on information and messages being electronically transmitted and the tax on PC's are to be recommended.

2.   Transaction tax

A transaction tax is a tax the basis of which would be the flow of money processed by electronic commerce. Such a tax would be automatically collected from banks operating money transfers or organizing electronic payments.

As underlined by the **French** Branch of IFA, the risk is that transactions could be done by offshore banks who have no tax obligations.

For **Colombia,** the transaction tax and the telecommunications tax are also interesting possibilities. But the risk that the flow might end up in offshore banks is present. As well, the problem of enforcement is not resolved.

In **Italy,** alternative tax ideas make sense, like the transactions tax on money flows on the internet and its on-line services.

3. *Consumption tax*

This tax would be calculated on the basis of services offered to the clients by companies giving access to the net. Once again, according to the **French** Branch, the risk is the same as above: service companies located in offshore countries.

Telecommunications tax on basic telecommunications services as a percentage of the charge by their providers to their users is considered as a good idea by **Italians.**

4. *Withholding tax*

The **Germans** (Portner report) do not see a necessity to introduce a withholding tax in order to seek some revenue sharing between electronic commerce net exporting and importing countries.

Any move to clarify or indeed eliminate the need to characterize transactions in order to determine whether a tax should be withheld or not, according to the **English** Branch, would be very much welcome by the business community.

III. CONCLUDING REMARKS

Although this Précis does not pretend to consider all the comments, remarks or criticism of the IFA National Branches, it brings out several elements:

1. Electronic commerce is regarded as a tremendous perturbation of the rules and techniques traditionally implied in international taxation.

2. Conflicting views are expressed as to the relevancy and efficiency of existing rules and techniques.

3. Similarly conflicting views are expressed as to the modifications needed to those techniques, both on the principle itself of such modifications and on the purpose and nature of such modifications.

4. It is commonly agreed that the balance between developing and developed countries can be shifted as a consequence of the increasing use of electronic commerce.

5. It is also commonly acknowledged that no satisfactory arrangement could be worked out without a very broad consensus among the various countries involved in this new type of doing business. Although of a more limited scope, the Communication 98/374 of the EU Commission gives an interesting example of such arrangements. The Commission suggests that all transactions carried out through the internet (order and delivery) be characterized as services.